INDUSTRIAL REVOLUTION IN MEXICO

Industrial Revolution in Mexico

By SANFORD A. MOSK

NEW YORK / RUSSELL & RUSSELL

To
MARY

Preface

THE WORD REVOLUTION is a familiar one in Mexico. Ever since the revolt against Porfirio Díaz broke out at the end of 1910, Mexico has been undergoing a continuous revolution which is always referred to as "the Revolution," and always written with a capital R. The first ten years of the Revolution were years of civil warfare, in which little was accomplished in a positive way. During this period, however, a legal foundation was established for land reform and other measures designed to promote the welfare of the laboring class.

For about twenty years after the civil strife came to an end, agrarian reform and agrarian policy occupied the center of the stage in Mexico. The policy was not one of steady advance. Laws were changed from time to time, and enforcement was subjected to even greater fluctuations. Nevertheless, the main economic and social problem with which the government concerned itself, and the principal basis for economic and social improvement in Mexico, was that of getting land into the hands of the peasants. For two decades Mexico was bent upon carrying out an agrarian revolution.

But since 1940 the center of attention has shifted sharply from agriculture to industry. In a few years' time Mexico has made great headway in establishing a base for a full-scale industrial development, already an impressive achievement though the process is just in the beginning stages. The Mexican government has thrown its weight into the industrialization effort, it has acted in many ways to encourage and to support industrial expansion, and it has made industrialism the keynote of Mexico's economic and social future. Mexico, it is clear, has begun its industrial revolution. This is the new revolution in Mexico,—revolution indeed, but in a new sense of the term.

To analyze and evaluate this revolution in the Mexican economy is the aim of this work. Industrialism in Mexico represents a sharp break with the past, in social outlook as well as in industrial structure; that is why Part I deals with attitudes and points of view. Here we shall examine the basic attitudes upon which the drive to industrialize rests, and also the perspective from which leaders in business, in government, and in labor circles view the nature and the function of Mexico's industrial growth. In addition, the actual policies of the Mexican government directed toward encouraging and advancing industrial development are dealt with in detail in this part of the volume.

[vii]

Part II is concerned with the record of industrial growth in recent years, mainly since the beginning of the Second World War. Most of this section of the volume, after bringing out the place of manufacturing in the Mexican economy, is a survey of developments in the principal industrial fields. Several industries and special industrial projects are taken up individually. My aim in doing this is not to give a detail by detail account of what went on in one industry after another, but rather to explain and evaluate the most important lines of industrial development and to set out the factual evidence upon which the appraisal rests. In Part II is included also an analysis of Mexico's experience in subsidizing development in manufacturing by means of tax exemptions.

The problems with which Mexico is confronted as her economy is increasingly reshaped by industrialism form the subject of Part III. Economic problems are dealt with for the most part, but related problems of a social nature are not neglected. As the chapter titles indicate, the questions taken up in Part III relate to the size of Mexico's internal market, to the financing of industrial development, to the mobilization of Mexico's human resources for the industrial effort, to the inflationary effects of the industrialization process, and to the changes which industrialization is bringing about in the international economic position of Mexico. The bearing of these problems upon Mexican economic policy is the subject of the concluding chapter.

In writing this book I have had constantly in mind the larger theme of the nature and problems of industrialization in underdeveloped economies. This study on Mexico is a case study in a new aspect of economics to which relatively little attention has been given as yet, but one which requires much investigation if we are to understand what is going on in the countries where human, capital, and physical resources are being mustered for a new economic effort. This aspect of economics is of necessity institutional in character, for the fundamental problems arising in such countries are rooted in economic, social, and political institutions. My analysis of the changing Mexican economy is, therefore, based on my understanding of prevailing modes of thought and behavior with respect to key factors in the economic life of the nation.

Perhaps it should be pointed out that this book is addressed to the general reader as well as to a professional audience. For that reason, I have avoided, wherever possible, the technical vocabulary of economics.

It is a pleasure to acknowledge my gratitude to the John Simon Guggenheim Memorial Foundation for the fellowship which made it possible for me to spend a year in Mexico making firsthand observations and gathering material for this study. In my first contacts with Mexico a number of years ago I was concerned with research of a different character, mainly historical in nature. Nevertheless, the opportunity to live and travel in Mexico at that earlier time has contributed in a real sense to my understanding of the country and its problems. For that reason I should like to acknowledge as well earlier financial support for research in Mexico obtained from the University of California and from the Social Science Research Council.

My understanding of Mexico has been enriched, too, by many years of association with three colleagues in the University of California who know the country intimately, Carl O. Sauer, Lesley Byrd Simpson, and Paul S. Taylor. Professor Simpson graciously read the entire manuscript and has made many suggestions for its improvement. To another colleague, Melvin M. Knight, I owe a major intellectual debt for stimulating and sharpening my thinking about the colonial economies of the world, both from the perspective of history and from the standpoint of present-day problems. In making these acknowledgments to my colleagues I do not intend to imply that they are necessarily to be considered as in agreement with everything I have set down in this volume, but rather to express an appreciation of what it has meant for me to enjoy informal discussion with them.

My research in Mexico was facilitated by a number of persons who gave generously of their time to discuss the problems in which I was interested and to direct me to materials and sources which yielded further results. Víctor L. Urquidi and Gustavo Polit of the economic research division of the Bank of Mexico were always gracious and helpful in spite of the frequency with which I called upon them for assistance. To them and to their colleagues Francisco J. Pratt, Eliel Vargas, and Raúl Velasco, I am deeply indebted. In the industrial research division of the Bank of Mexico Manuel Bravo and Miguel Gleason Alvarez were extremely helpful. Josué Sáenz, then head of the Dirección General de Estadística, and Federico Bach, head of the Oficina de Barómetros Económicos, did much to lighten my labors in getting at statistical data and analyzing them. For clarifying numerous questions relating to the operations of Nacional Financiera, I am grateful to Raúl Ortiz Mena, head of the department of financial studies.

To Merwin L. Bohan, Counselor for Economic Affairs of the American Embassy, and to his staff, I should like to express my appreciation for the many ways in which they assisted me in getting information and in testing the tentative judgments I formed about Mexico's economic problems as I carried out my research. In particular, I should mention the names of the following members of the American Embassy staff: William F. Busser,

Lew B. Clark, Ana M. Gomez, Frederick R. Mangold, Mindee McLean, Albert E. Pappano, and Mildred Tomich.

I am indebted to the University of North Carolina Press for permission to quote at length from Eyler Simpson's *The Ejido,* and to Lesley B. Simpson for permission to quote from his book, *Many Mexicos.* Also, the Columbia University Press has allowed me to draw heavily upon the chapter I wrote for *Inter-American Affairs, 1945* (Arthur P. Whitaker, ed.). The chapter entitled "Capital and Credit" was published, in somewhat modified form, in the first number of *Inter-American Economic Affairs.* The editors of this journal have kindly allowed me to use my article as the nucleus of chapter xii in this volume.

In preparing the manuscript for publication, it was necessary to set December, 1948, as the terminal date for the material included. However, because of long delays in the publication of Mexican statistics, it was not possible to get figures for 1948 in all cases. This is true, for example, of the production figures in chapters vii, viii, and ix. In this connection, I should like to call the attention of the reader to the first part of chapter vii, where he will find a rather full discussion of the problems of using Mexican economic statistics.

SANFORD A. MOSK

Contents

PART III: PROBLEMS

Part I

ATTITUDES AND POINTS OF VIEW

CHAPTER I

The Urge to Industrialize
in Latin America

In THE ERA of great economic expansion between the middle
of the nineteenth century and the First World War, the countries of the
world tended to fall into one or the other of two broad economic groups.
The United States along with western and central Europe made up one
group, consisting of industrialized nations. In these two areas were concentrated the world's factories and industrial machinery, and here were evolved
the most productive methods of manufacture.

In the remainder of the world, economic effort was devoted to producing
foodstuffs and raw materials. Only a fringe of industrialism existed in these
regions. The manufactured goods they consumed were, for the most part,
imported from the industrialized nations. To pay for such imports, the
colonial economies, as they are called, exported to the manufacturing countries the products of their fields, forests, and mines. When these products
left the producing countries they were either in the raw state in which they
had been harvested, gathered, or dug from the earth, or at best they had
been slightly processed in order to reduce their bulk and shipping weight.

The products which the colonial economies shipped abroad were the
major part of what they produced.[1] They themselves were but small consumers of their own output. In fact, it can be said that, with few exceptions,
their own consumption was a negligible fraction of their commercial production. Their export markets, which they found in the industrialized
nations, were, therefore, of the utmost importance to them.

The world made enormous gains in economic productivity after the
middle of the nineteenth century, as a result of great technical developments in industry and in transport, and also as a result of the opening up
of large resources which hitherto had lain unused, or virtually so. These
factors constituted the technical and the physical basis for a rising curve of
productivity. In addition, an important part was played by developments
of an institutional character, such as those which enabled capital and people

---

[1] In some cases production of food for local use by self-sufficient farmers may have been
larger than production for export, but such production was an unknown quantity statistically,
and, in any event, it did not enter into commercial channels.

to move with comparative freedom from one part of the world to another. It would be difficult to imagine a process by which technical improvements and newly exploited resources could have been made to function associatively in the late nineteenth and early twentieth centuries, without the existence of a high degree of mobility of capital and an extraordinary mobility of people.

To analyze this process here would take us far afield from our main task.[2] The point to be stressed here is that the improvements in economic efficiency made on a world-wide scale after the middle of the nineteenth century created an unparalleled opportunity for the enjoyment of higher standards of living.

Higher standards of living were indeed realized. Popular consumption of goods and services increased both in amount and in range. But not everywhere. It was in the industrialized nations that human wants were satisfied more abundantly than ever before in history. The colonial economies were left far behind. Those who worked in producing raw materials and foodstuffs in the colonial economies made small gains, if any, in their living standards. The fruits of the world's economic progress were not shared equally between industrialized and nonindustrialized areas.

During the First World War industry made some progress in the countries with colonial economies, but with few exceptions they still maintained at the end of the war their fundamentally nonindustrialized character. In the postwar years the position of the colonial economies vis-à-vis the industrialized nations was even less favorable than it had been before 1914. The difference in living conditions, so far as it changed at all, became greater rather than smaller.

The experience of the colonial economies in world economic development since the middle of the nineteenth century has led to the conclusion that the key to higher standards of living is industrialization. This point of view is now dominant among people living in countries of colonial economies. Furthermore, it has been strongly reinforced by the principal operative factors in world economic and political affairs in recent years. Notable among these was the collapse of export markets during the deep depression of the 1930's. Important also were the stringencies experienced during the Second World War, when the flow of manufactures from overseas sources was cut off entirely or reduced to a mere trickle. On the political side, a strong wave of nationalism is impelling countries to establish themselves on an economically independent footing with a view to safeguarding their political independence.

Since the end of the Second World War the ambition of the colonial

---

[2] This question is discussed in my article, "Latin America and the World Economy, 1850–1914," in *Inter-American Economic Affairs*, vol. 2, no. 3 (Winter, 1948), pp. 53–82.

economies to reorganize themselves economically by industrializing has been expressed with renewed vigor and determination. From almost all quarters we hear of the same ambition—from China, from India, from the Middle East, from nonindustrialized countries in eastern Europe, and from Latin America.[3] It can hardly be doubted that we are in the beginning stages of a development that will go far in changing the shape of the economic world as we have known it. A new and important chapter is being added to the story of the industrial revolution of modern times. In our own day we are witnessing the end of the pre-1914 equilibrium between industrialized and nonindustrialized regions, and at the same time the inception of new basic economic relations among the countries of the world.

Economic Colonialism to Industrialism[4]

The twenty republics of Latin America have properly been classified as colonial economies. This has been true of all of them, although there are many important differences in economic structure, just as in social and political structure, from one country to another. Every Latin American country has shown the qualities of a colonial economy in significant degree, and in some countries these qualities have appeared in extreme form. "Few areas in the world," write Olson and Hickman in the first sentence of their book dealing with Latin America in relation to world economy,[5] "are as dependent upon foreign trade and investment as Latin America."

As in all economically colonial areas, a large fraction of the economic effort of the population, outside of subsistence farming, has been concentrated on the production and transportation of commodities that are scarcely consumed in any amount within the producing country itself. In some cases they are not consumed at all in the form in which they are produced. For some of the principal commodities with which we identify Latin America as a great producing region, it may be said that foreign markets are of overwhelming importance, for example, copper, tin, petroleum, coffee, bananas, and sugar.

Satisfactory statistics upon which to base estimates of the importance of exports in the economies of the Latin American republics are difficult to find. The few estimates which can be cited are, however, suggestive. For Chile, exports have been estimated at 25 to 30 per cent of national income.[6]

[3] See, for example, the chapters dealing with undeveloped countries in Mordecai Ezekiel (ed.), *Towards World Prosperity* (New York, 1947), and also Ezekiel's introductory chapters.
[4] In writing this section I have leaned considerably on my chapter on "Issues in Inter-American Economic Relations," in Arthur P. Whitaker (ed.), *Inter-American Affairs, 1945* (New York, 1946), pp. 100–120. For permission to do so, I am indebted to the Columbia University Press.
[5] Paul R. Olson and C. Addison Hickman, *Pan American Economics* (New York, 1943), p. 1.
[6] P. T. Ellsworth, "Chile," in Seymour E. Harris (ed.), *Economic Problems of Latin America* (New York, 1944), p. 305.

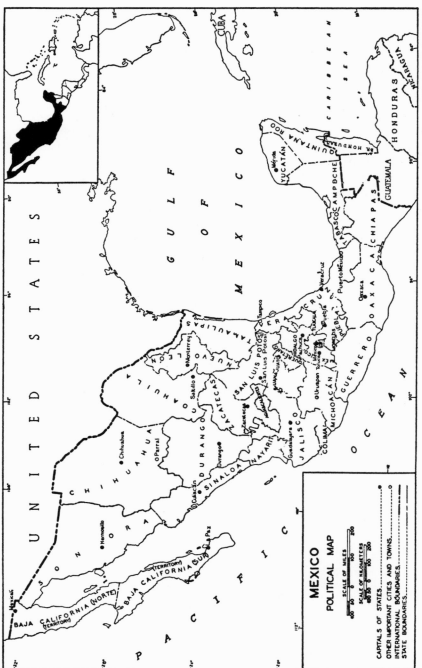

MEXICO
POLITICAL MAP

SCALE OF MILES
200   100   0   100   200

SCALE OF KILOMETERS
200 100 0   100   200

CAPITALS OF STATES..........
OTHER IMPORTANT CITIES AND TOWNS....
INTERNATIONAL BOUNDARIES.....
STATE BOUNDARIES........

Uruguay, it has been calculated, derived about 25 per cent of its prewar national income from exports.[7] Data available for Argentina for 1941 show that approximately 22 per cent of the national income was derived from exports and other foreign transactions; exports alone accounted for 15 per cent.[8] For the twenty Latin American republics as a group, Professor Harris has suggested that exports are 20 per cent or more of national income.[9] By way of contrast, in the United States the ratio of exports to national income has been about 6 per cent.

Because exports have been so large, decisions vitally affecting the economies of Latin America have in large measure been made abroad, in the industrialized countries where the markets for Latin American raw materials and foodstuffs have been found. The word "decisions" here refers to the results of informal market forces rather than to calculated action by governments or business groups, although such action has not been entirely lacking. Whenever changes in demand and price have occurred in the industrialized areas, the Latin American economy has proved most sensitive and vulnerable to these external economic fluctuations.

For most of the Latin American republics, changes in the demand for one or two products have been sufficient to cause serious disturbances, because of the dominant position of such commodities in the total export picture. In Cuba, for example, sugar alone accounted for more than 70 per cent of prewar (1938) exports. A comparable position was held by tin in Bolivia and by bananas in Panama. Even more striking was position of Venezuela, where petroleum accounted for 90 per cent of total exports, and that of El Salvador, with coffee at a similar percentage. In Chile, copper and nitrate exports combined were two-thirds of the total value of all commodities shipped out of the country.

In every country of Latin America before the war (1938) a single product accounted for 20 per cent or more of total exports.[10] In all countries but one the three principal exports combined to form at least 50 per cent of the total. Mexico was the exception. There the combined weight of the three main exports was 37 per cent of all exports.

An appreciable decline in exports, therefore, sometimes confined to a few products, has always created serious economic problems for the countries of Latin America. Whenever foreign markets have contracted, the volume of payments flowing out of the export industries in the form of wages and material purchases has been correspondingly reduced. Since

[7] Olson and Hickman, *op. cit.*, p. 3.
[8] "Monetary Developments in Latin America," *Federal Reserve Bulletin*, vol. 31. no. 6 (June, 1945), p. 524.
[9] Harris, *op. cit.*, p. 7.
[10] Olson and Hickman, *op. cit.*, p. 6.

these have been the most important income-producing industries, the whole economy has been thoroughly upset. Incomes have fallen, unemployment has spread, and contraction has affected the entire Latin American economy.

The reverse has, of course, been the case whenever there has been a substantial increase in exports. But this is hardly an adequate compensation for the depressive consequences of a decline in exports. The fatal facility with which their economies have shrunk as the total value of exports has fallen, is, naturally, a source of grave concern to the Latin American nations.

The second external influence which has had an important bearing on the Latin American economies has been foreign investment. The Latin American countries, like all economically colonial areas, have been large importers of capital. The inflow of capital to a Latin American country has frequently been a large item in the country's balance of payments. In such cases, fluctuations in the volume of new foreign investment, especially the downward trends, have had pronounced effects upon the whole economy.

Experience has shown that the movement of foreign capital to a Latin American country is likely to be erratic. It rises and falls abruptly, and has been known to cease entirely over a period of years. To some extent this movement has been based upon speculative calculations.[11] In any event, the decisions relating to the expansion and contraction of new foreign investment have been made chiefly abroad, rather than in the country which has imported the capital. The capital has come almost exclusively from the major industrialized areas of the world, that is, western Europe and the United States, and it is to be expected that investors in these areas are affected greatly by economic conditions at home when they contemplate increasing their investments abroad or undertaking new development in foreign lands. Thus the amount of new foreign investment in Latin America has tended to fluctuate with economic conditions in the advanced industrialized nations.

The volume of new foreign investment and the volume of exports for Latin America have thus depended upon the same factor, that is, the cyclical fluctuations of business in the industrialized countries. The two forces, investment and exports, have operated in the same direction, each reinforcing the other. Thus during depression periods the Latin American countries have felt a dual pressure radiating from the industrialized nations. Their markets and their main sources of new investment have dried up simultaneously.

The effects of this depressive reaction will be better appreciated if we

[11] Robert Triffin, "Central Banking and Monetary Management in Latin America," in Harris, *op. cit.*, p. 108.

take into account the monetary repercussions in a Latin American country resulting from a decline in exports and in new foreign investment. They diminish the inflow of foreign exchange and therefore tend to reduce the monetary reserves of the country. This, in turn, leads to a contraction of credit by the commercial banks. Actually, since the commercial banks maintain fractional reserves, the contraction in credit, and therefore in money supply, will be a multiple of the loss in foreign exchange reserves. Thus the original loss has a magnified effect upon the whole economy.

It is true that a decline in payments made abroad, principally in those due for imports, will take place at the same time. This acts as an offset to the loss of sources of foreign exchange. However, because of their social as well as their economic structure, the Latin-American countries have a high propensity to import. A reduction in the volume of imports necessary to offset a fall in either exports or in foreign investment may take place automatically, but a reduction of the size needed to offset a simultaneous fall in both is difficult to achieve—especially when they fall off rapidly. A shrinkage in imports, therefore, has tended to act only as a partial offset to the combined effect of a drop in exports and in the amount of new foreign investment.

The well-known Argentine economist, Raúl Prebisch, has expressed a similar conclusion in a brief but pointed analysis of the cyclical relations between the highly industrialized regions and the economically colonial areas. In the following quotation from Prebisch, the former (especially the United States) are referred to as the "cyclical center" and the latter are termed the "periphery."

During the phase of expansion in the principal cyclical center there is a tendency for money accumulated during the depression in the form of gold and foreign exchange to radiate to the periphery. This shift in money occurs because of an increase in imports provoked by the expansion of economic activity and because of foreign investment. The countries of the periphery receive the money thus discharged from the center, on the basis of which they develop their own expansionist phase. When the process of contraction sets in in the principal cyclical center the money tends naturally to return to the cyclical center; and the greater the preceding expansion of credit in the periphery, the greater the reverse flow of money. Thus if the contraction in the cyclical center is intense—as it was after 1929—the countries of the periphery are compelled to return not only the money they had previously received but also a part of the pre-existing stocks of gold in their monetary reserves.[12]

It is also true that central banks can take action to offset the monetary effects of a loss in sources of foreign exchange. But a number of circum-

[12] Raúl Prebisch, "Panorama general de los problemas de regulación monetaria y crediticia en el continente americano: América Latina," in *Memoria de la primera reunión de técnicos sobre problemas de banca central del continente americano* (Mexico, 1946), p. 26.

stances inherent in domestic investment habits, in traditional government fiscal practices, and in the financial structure at large have made it difficult for central banks in Latin American countries to take advantage of off-setting measures like those which have been employed in other nations under similar conditions.[13] Broadly, it may be said that legal limitations on the powers of central banks, combined with the lack of well-developed money markets, have made it impossible to carry out effective offsetting transactions. Although these handicaps have to some extent been removed in very recent years, they are not easy to eradicate because they are rooted in long-established customs and practices.

The preceding discussion has brought out the crucial significance for Latin America of fluctuations in export values and in the flow of foreign capital, operating through the inflow and outflow of foreign exchange. In Latin America these fluctuations play the same role that fluctuations in the level of domestic investment have played in the advanced industrialized economies. They are the dominant factors in determining the level of business activity. The savings-investment problem has not been the most critical one in Latin America. Failure to invest savings, of course, does tend to depress the level of economic activity. But the effect is a modest one in Latin America, compared to what happens in such countries as the United States and England, where a much higher percentage of national income is saved and where capital markets are highly developed.[14]

The dependence of Latin America upon foreign markets and foreign investment did not become generally recognized as a serious problem until the 1930's when the great depression set in. If we go back to the years before the First World War, few Latin Americans were aware of such a problem, or even of the basic problem inherent in the failure of standards of living to rise in Latin America as the world's economic productivity went up by leaps and bounds. Undoubtedly the tendency to ignore this basic question of standards of living is explained by the fact that the edu-cated people, who were but a handful in numbers, were not themselves faring badly. The large numbers of Latin Americans who lived in poverty and in permanent poor health were inarticulate.

Aside from this basic and important problem of low living standards, it may be said that the results of the close tie between Latin America and the industrialized economies of the world were favorable before 1914. The patterns of economic specialization in Latin America which directed com-mercially productive activity in the main toward industrial raw materials

---

[13] An excellent discussion of this whole question is given by Triffin, *op. cit.*, pp. 104–113.

[14] For a fuller discussion of this question, see Soule, Efron, and Ness, *Latin America in the Future World* (New York, 1945), pp. 105–110.

and foodstuffs, were fashioned in the fifty years or so before the First World War. On the whole they were satisfactory during that period because the world enjoyed a workable international economy in which products, capital, and people moved across international boundaries with relative freedom.

To illustrate this, we may appeal to the economic experience of Argentina, a topic I have dealt with elsewhere at greater length.[15] From about 1880 to 1915 Argentina made great strides in economic development on the basis of producing meat and grains for export. The markets were found in the industrialized countries of western Europe. Technical developments, such as the introduction of barbed wire and refrigerated shipping, played a large part in making it possible for Argentina to supply these markets. But other forces also made important contributions. Notable among these was the inflow of European capital (for example, for railroad construction) and immigration derived from European peoples. In short, the rapid economic advance of Argentina before 1915 was the product of a smoothly functioning international economic order.

This international economy was shaken loose from its foundations by the First World War, and it is well known that the strenuous efforts made subsequently to reconstruct it were without success. The atmosphere in which economic relations were conducted among nations in the 1920's was distinctly unhealthy. In addition, the prices of raw materials and foodstuffs declined, relatively, that is, to the prices of manufactured goods. Thus the Latin American countries, together with the other colonial economies around the world, suffered an added disadvantage in the international economic setting of the postwar period.

The full consequences of their dependence upon export markets and foreign capital were brought home to the Latin American republics during the economic depression of the 1930's. As world trade shrank to a fraction of its former volume after 1929 the Latin American countries suffered great losses in export markets. In some countries the drop in exports reached almost fantastic proportions. In Chile the recession from 1929 to 1932 amounted to 88 per cent. Her foreign trade suffered more in those years than that of any other country in the world.[16] Bolivia experienced an 80 per cent fall in exports between 1929 and 1932, while Cuba also had the doubtful honor of sharing the lead in this respect with a decline of 70 per cent. For the twenty Latin American republics as a group, the aggregate value of exports fell by approximately 65 per cent in the short span of three years.

At the same time the flow of capital to Latin America slowed down

[15] See above, p. 4, n. 2; and also Frank Tannenbaum "Argentina, the Recalcitrant American State," *Foreign Affairs*, vol. 23, no. 2 (January, 1945), pp. 271–283.
[16] P. T. Ellsworth, *Chile: An Economy in Transition* (New York, 1945), p. 7.

and in some cases it came entirely to a halt. In the absence of aggregate figures, this may be illustrated from the experience of Argentina and Chile.[17] In Argentina there was a net inflow of capital amounting to 500 million pesos in the period 1926–1928. In 1929, however, capital imports stopped entirely. For 1930 there was again a net movement of capital into the country, amounting to 500 million pesos, only to be followed by a net outflow in the years 1931–1932. Chile underwent a similar experience about the same time. Loans from abroad reached a total of 1,100 million gold pesos in the years 1929–1930. In the following two years, however, the total was only 75 million, and in 1933 no new foreign investments at all were made.

Thus in the depression period of the 1930's a decline in exports with a parallel decline in new foreign investment combined to exert a strong depressive influence on economic conditions in Latin America. However, many foreigners acquainted with Latin America are inclined to believe that, since widespread unemployment was not apparent, the depression was not severely felt there. Large numbers of farmers engaged in self-sufficient agriculture were, they point out, unaffected by what happened in foreign trade. Such farmers were not integrated into the market structure enough to react to demand and price changes.

It is true that there is a dichotomy in the economies of virtually all the Latin American countries, and that one of the two parts is subsistence farming. In many of the countries, especially where Indian populations or Indian mores prevail, this sector of the economy includes most of the population. In every one of the twenty republics, with the possible exceptions of Argentina and Uruguay, it embraces a substantial fraction of the inhabitants. In Mexico about 70 per cent of the population has lived wholly or largely outside the commercial framework, although Mexico actually has had a more diversified economy than most of the Latin American countries. Subsistence farmers in Latin America have produced mostly for their own consumption; they have had only minor contacts with commercial markets and their purchases have been limited to essentially local barter transactions. Since they practice primitive farming methods, their crop yields have been meager. Their standards of living have also been very low.

The other part of the typical Latin-American economy may be called, for want of a better term, "modern." It includes the producers of export commodities, and all the commercial, financial, and transport organizations that deal with exports and imports. Commercial production for domestic markets also fits into this sector of the economy. Finally, the governments

    [17] "Monetary Developments in Latin America," op. cit., p. 525.

of the Latin American republics obtain almost all their revenues from the "modern" parts of their economies.

The economic processes analyzed in the preceding pages have been related only to the "modern" sector. It is there that we find the institutions that are directly and readily influenced by international trade and international capital movements. But this does not mean that the subsistence sector is untouched by these influences. It, too, has a stake in the prosperity of the "modern" sector.

The two parts of the economy are connected by the movement of persons from one to the other. In times of prosperity, some people leave the rural communities and shift into the "modern" sector, where employment yields as a rule higher standards of living. In times of depression, the movement of people is reversed. This shift, which is both regional and occupational, explains why unemployment never reaches large proportions in a Latin American country. Instead of suffering absolute unemployment in time of depression, workers transfer themselves to much less productive occupations.

The subsistence economy thus serves as a shock absorber, because strong family ties make it possible for persons to return to their former places in rural life. Given the low productivity of the agricultural organization to which they return, they add very little if anything to farm output. And yet they consume. Thus the cost of depression adjustment is borne by the rural families and communities as a whole, in the form of reduced consumption and lowered standards of living. The impact of a depression may be less forceful and less striking in the subsistence sector than in the "modern" part of the economy, but it is nonetheless real.[18]

The depression of the 1930's in Latin America, therefore, penetrated the whole economic and social structure. Hardly anyone was sheltered from its impact. Unemployment figures were not large and bread lines were unknown, but these facts should not be allowed to obscure the reality of the depression experience.

From the Latin American point of view the great depression of the 1930's appeared as an import—an import received from the industrialized nations which had failed to keep up their purchases of Latin American export products and their flow of capital to Latin America. The validity of this viewpoint can hardly be doubted. The industrialized areas have been the centers of cyclical disturbances which have spread from them to the nonindustrialized parts of the world. The economically colonial areas

---

[18] The possibilities and opportunities for commercializing agricultural output in the subsistence sector, for raising its productivity, and for improving its standards of living also depend significantly upon the "modern" sector. For a discussion of this question I may refer to my chapter in Whitaker, *op. cit.*, pp. 105–106.

have played a passive role. Depressions have originated in the industrialized countries as a group out of forces peculiar to a highly industrialized society, and they have been transmitted to the remainder of the world principally through a fall in demand for raw materials and foodstuffs and through a slackening in foreign investment. Decline in demand for imported manufactured goods in the economically colonial areas has been of a secondary and cumulative nature, and not a primary force in generating a depression.

The impact of the depression of the 1930's in Latin America reacted strongly on the thinking of statesmen and others who were concerned with national problems. The Latin American countries, it was agreed, were far too vulnerable to external economic factors. Their economies were too specialized. Even a minor change in market conditions in the industrialized countries, such as a change in consuming habits or in a manufacturing process, could have serious effects on a country that depended upon exports of only one or two products as the mainstay of its economic life, and a general depression in the industrialized nations was sure to create havoc. Even the kinds of measures which in the industrialized countries proved partly effective to combat deflationary pressures from abroad were difficult to adopt in Latin America because of extreme economic specialization.

Thus in Latin America in the 1930's the costs of specialization came to be regarded as excessive. Obviously, the solution for this problem was to diversify their economies, to establish a broader foundation for economic activity, to develop along new lines so that they would no longer be economically "one-sided," and, of the various means by which economic diversification could be achieved, industrialization was considered the most promising.

This whole trend of thinking in favor of economic diversification was reinforced by the experience of the Latin American countries in trade negotiations in the 'thirties. The international economy, which had broken down badly in the 'twenties, collapsed utterly during the depression of the early 'thirties. Nation after nation adopted measures to promote recovery by expanding exports and by curtailing imports. In effect, countries were trying to pass the burden of the depression along to their neighbors, and to stage their own recovery at the expense of other nations. Tariffs were raised, import quotas and other restrictions were introduced, currencies were depreciated, and exchange controls were put into effect. Economic nationalism was dominant.

Although no basic change in international economic relations occurred following revival of business from the low point of the depression, new trading alignments were worked out by negotiation among countries. Some of these new arrangements were strictly of a bilateral nature whereas others followed a multilateral pattern, and they lasted for varying periods of time. In all cases, however, they involved bargaining between one country and another. It was in this connection that the Latin American republics felt keenly their lack of economic weight and their dependence upon the industrialized economies. In bargaining with the highly industrialized nations they were at a great disadvantage. This disadvantage, inherent in their economically colonial position, was magnified by the degree to which exports were concentrated in a few products, or in even a single product.

It is not surprising that a number of Latin American countries, like countries in southeastern Europe, fell victims to the bold and ruthless trade methods of the Nazis in the 1930's. A well-known illustration of how they fared is found in the Brazilian-German clearing agreements.[19] But even the reciprocal trade agreements which they made with the United States, in which this country refrained from making the most of its economic weight (because of the very nature of the reciprocal trade agreements program), found them at a considerable disadvantage. In many cases the United States was the largest market for their products, whereas they were only minor markets for American exports.

There is some significance in the fact that United States exports to Latin America increased more in the years 1938 to 1940 than United States imports from that area. The trade agreements cannot be held solely responsible for this outcome, since there were many other forces also playing across the lines of international commerce during the same period, but they must bear some responsibility. And in any event, Latin-Americans came to think of the United States trade agreements program as a device for increasing United States exports, and they have doubted that Latin American nations could ever benefit from the program until they have achieved a greater degree of economic independence.

International commercial negotiations as well as the depression, therefore, directed the Latin American countries toward economic diversification during the 1930's. The main expression of this diversification was found in the development of manufacturing, and government after government adopted policies to stimulate industrial expansion. Some of these policies actually operated through negative measures, especially through exchange control; foreign companies, unable to send all their profits abroad, were induced to invest in local manufacturing enterprises. On the whole, however, the positive measures, such as subsidies and protection from foreign competition, were more important.

The gains in industrial development were naturally distributed among the twenty republics of Latin America in a very uneven manner. The

[19] See Percy W. Bidwell, *Economic Defense of Latin America* (Boston, 1941), pp. 38–47.

greatest strides were made in Argentina, Brazil, Mexico, Chile, and Colombia. To illustrate the significance of the manufacturing development achieved by Argentina, we need only point out that the proportion of imports in its annual consumption dropped from 38 per cent in 1914–1918 to 26 per cent in 1936–1938.[20] The advances made by Mexico, where policies specifically designed to promote manufacturing development in the 'thirties were less actively pushed than in the other four countries named, are described in chapter iv of this volume.

Some time toward the end of the 'thirties decade two other explanations of the need to industrialize in Latin America came into prominence. Neither was new, but neither had been featured in the earlier part of the decade. One was the now familiar proposition that industrialization was the best means, or the only means, of attaining higher standards of living. The other was the thesis that the nation which is dependent economically upon other countries has a weak foundation for its political independence.

In view of all that has been heard about the first of these propositions in more recent years, it is curious that it did not emerge earlier as a major slogan with which to justify the promotion of industrialism. Nor is it clear why it came to the fore so strongly in the last years of the 'thirties. Possibly this development was associated with the growing strength of the labor movement in Latin America, and in particular with the formation in 1938 of the Confederación de Trabajadores de América Latina (CTAL), an international labor federation for Latin America.

The emergence of the second proposition may be ascribed to the wave of nationalism which has been sweeping through Latin America with growing force since the First World War. To build stronger national states has become a recognized objective in all the countries of Latin America, with full public support behind it. The Second World War has quite naturally strengthened the nationalistic point of view in Latin America, already on the upswing in 1939.

During the Second World War manufacturing development took a pronounced spurt in Latin America.[21] This was especially true in the five countries which were already leading the field, but it was experienced everywhere. Many of the manufactured goods formerly imported could not be obtained abroad at all during the war, or could be secured only in limited quantities. In the face of a reduced supply, the demand for such commodities was actually increased through the operation of strong inflationary forces. These conditions were ideal for the establishment of new

---

[20] Miron Burgin, "Argentina," in Harris, *op. cit.*, p. 229.

[21] For details, by countries, see George Wythe, *Industry in Latin America* (New York, 1945). Additional material, by industries, can be found in Lloyd Hughlett (ed.), *Industrialization of Latin America* (New York, 1946).

manufacturing plants and for the expansion of those already in existence, whenever the necessary equipment could be obtained.

Given the background circumstances which we have sketched above, the industrial expansion of the war period in Latin America is far from being regarded as a temporary development, to be written off now that more normal conditions are being restored. The industrial gains achieved since 1939 are looked upon as a base from which to score further and more important advances, and in almost every one of the twenty countries ambitious undertakings of an industrial nature have been started or planned since the end of the war.

Thus, prospects of industrialization are giving new vitality to economic life in Latin America, and the attitudes of businessmen and statesmen are being shaped accordingly. These attitudes are more sharply defined in some countries than in others, but they are sufficiently common to all alike to produce a uniform outlook on questions of international economic policy. The homogeneity and the tenacity of their viewpoint has shown itself especially in their opposition to the international economic program sponsored by the United States. This has been abundantly clear since early 1945, when the Inter-American Conference on Problems of War and Peace (Chapultepec conference) was held in Mexico City.

The economic issues taken up at the Chapultepec Conference gave rise to lively and vigorous debate—much more so than the military, political, and social questions on the agenda. The spirited discussion which took place on economic problems was centered on a group of proposed resolutions which the United States delegation submitted under the rather grandiose title of the "Economic Charter of the Americas." This document set forth basic objectives and guiding principles for economic development and economic policy in the Western Hemisphere. Although the United States delegates expected to have their proposal undergo a certain amount of modification in the conference, they were obviously surprised at the strength of the Latin American reaction to it, and they were clearly disappointed over the result. The Latin American delegates as a whole were opposed to important items in the proposal, they expressed their opposition strongly and with a frankness seldom manifested in international gatherings, and they put through significant changes in substance.[22]

One of the questions most vigorously debated at the conference related to the reduction of trade barriers. The United States asked for an unqualified commitment on lowering barriers to international trade, with discussions on ways and means to be scheduled for an early date. A number of pertinent general questions were raised by Latin-American delegates.

[22] Carlos Lleras Restrepo, "La política económica continental," *Revista de América*, vol. 2, no. 4 (April, 1945), p. 7.

Should not the larger trading nations, those which weighed heavily in world economy such as the United States and Great Britain, take the first steps? How far was the United States itself prepared to go in lowering tariffs? (At the time of the Mexico City conference, it should be recalled, the U. S. Congress had not yet taken even the modest step of extending the Reciprocal Trade Agreements Act). In so far as past experience could be relied upon as a guide, there was little to warrant the belief that the United States would actually welcome imports on any very large scale.

In addition, the Latin Americans wondered about the real meaning of Assistant Secretary of State Will Clayton's plea for reducing tariffs and other barriers to trade in order to bring about a substantial expansion in world economy. "Most of the *latinos*," reports one observer, "understood 'expanding economy' to mean increased exports to Latin America."[23] Clearly what they were most afraid of was the industrial power of the United States.

In harmony with their broad viewpoint, the Latin Americans at Chapultepec presented a united front on three other questions. (1) Protection for their new industries was justified on "infant industry" grounds. (2) Any program to reduce tariffs needed to take account of relative states of economic development—that is, the standards appropriate for economically advanced countries cannot be applied to nonindustrialized nations. (3) Endorsement of the Bretton Woods monetary plan made it necessary to institute a certain measure of control over imports. As one of the Colombian delegates expressed it: "We want to pay fully for all that we buy, and to guarantee complete freedom for transfers. But precisely for this reason we must reserve the right of refraining from buying unless we believe that we can pay without causing grave disturbances in our monetary economy."[24]

Thus the Latin Americans at Chapultepec held firmly to the position that import regulations, in one form or another, were necessary for two purposes, (1) to prevent economic dislocations in the postwar transition period, and (2) to attain suitable long-run national objectives in economic development, especially in industrialization. As a consequence, the resolution finally adopted on the question of trade barriers was softened and qualified so as to be free of any definite commitment whatever.

A further indication of the desire of Latin-American countries for greater economic independence came out in the discussion of foreign capital. The United States had proposed freedom of investment for foreign capital. This was accepted, but it was hedged in with one very important qualification sponsored by Latin American delegates, namely, "except when the invest-

---

[23] Luis Enriquez, "A Latin Looks at Chapultepec," *The Inter-American*, vol. 4, no. 4 (April, 1945), p. 16.
[24] Carlos Lleras Restrepo, *op. cit.*, p. 12.

ment of ... foreign capital would be contrary to the fundamental principles of public interest." In this way the governments of Latin America reserved the right to influence investment decisions which might vitally affect their economies. The requirements of national interest were definitely placed above those of freedom of action for foreign investors.

As a final illustration from the experience of the Mexico City conference, we may cite the proposed United States resolution entitled "Elimination of Economic Nationalism." The original text—which dealt with this point briefly and bluntly—would have committed the signatory nations to the following policy:

In order that international economic collaboration may be realistic and effective, to work for the elimination of economic nationalism in all its forms.

Thanks to the Latin Americans, the tone of the final version was very different. Entitled "Elimination of Excesses of Economic Nationalism," it read:

To cooperate for the general adoption of a policy of international economic collaboration to eliminate the excesses which may result from economic nationalism, including the excessive restriction of imports and the dumping of surpluses of national production in world markets.

The effect of using the words "excesses" and "excessive" is obvious. But attention should also be called to the fact that dumping was specifically named as an undesirable practice. This was aimed at the United States. Again it reflected the fear of Latin Americans that their new industries would be stifled by competition from this country.

Even this brief survey of the results of the Chapultepec conference shows that the Latin Americans, in effect, transformed the "Economic Charter of the Americas" into a "Declaration of Economic Independence for Latin America." In doing so, they expressed their deep-seated conviction that the Latin American nations must diversify themselves economically, and that this must be achieved mainly by means of industrial development.

1 his conviction is just as firmly entrenched in the minds of Latin Americans today as it was at the time of the Chapultepec meeting,—perhaps more so. Certainly the issues upon which the clash of viewpoints occurred at Chapultepec are now more immediate and more practical issues than they were at that time. Postwar readjustments have helped to make them so. But even more important is the attempt, sponsored chiefly by the government of the United States, to get an effective international agreement for reducing the barriers to trade in all parts of the world.

Shortly after V-J Day, the United States government advanced a plan for freer international trade in the form of a State Department publication entitled *"Proposals for Expansion of World Trade and Employment."* This document became the nucleus of a draft charter for an International Trade Organization (ITO), drawn up at Geneva in 1947 by a special committee of the Economic and Social Council of the United Nations. In November of the same year, the Council staged at Havana a World Conference on Trade and Employment for the purpose of putting the ITO charter in final form. It was expected that the conference would concern itself with finishing touches, and that it would do its work quickly and adjourn. The results, however, were quite different. The conference dragged on for about four months, major differences of viewpoint were expressed vigorously, and the tone of the ITO charter was much modified prior to approval.

What occurred at Havana was a clash between the industrialized nations and the countries with colonial economies. The latter, with Latin American nations taking the leadership, contended that the Geneva version of the ITO charter did not allow them the latitude they needed in commercial policy if they were to develop economically via the industrialization route. The arguments of the Latin Americans at Chapultepec were stated again, more fully and more vigorously if anything, because more was now at stake. They fought hard to strike out a clause requiring countries to eliminate quantitative restrictions on imports.[25] They were not successful in their effort to have the offending clause removed. Nevertheless, in a combined effort with other underdeveloped countries, they did succeed in introducing escape clauses which give ample scope for taking steps of a protective nature. Even the right to establish quantitative trade controls was recognized under certain conditions. As a general proposition, it was agreed that underdeveloped nations have the right to protect, not only those industries which got a start during the war years, but also industries which might be established in the future to achieve a fuller use of their primary resources. By such action the republics of Latin America made it clear at Havana that they will not easily put aside their ambitions to industrialize.

It was observed above that the attitudes of businessmen as well as statesmen are becoming sharply defined as the process of industrial development makes headway in Latin America. Not all business interests have the same enthusiasm for industrialization. To understand the nature and problems of industrialization in any one country, therefore, it is necessary to know something about the alignment of business groups, and especially to identify the groups which are most aggressive in urging government to promote manufacturing development on a broad front. This will be done as a preliminary to the study of Mexico's industrial revolution.

---

[25] The official Mexican attitude, which was representative of the Latin American point of view, is discussed in chapter xv.

CHAPTER II

Mexico's New Industrialists

THE ATTITUDES, hopes, and fears of Mexican industrialists today can be understood only if we mark out one set of industrialists from all the rest. For the most part those classifiable in this special group are newcomers. Ten years ago they were unknown, and many did not emerge as industrial entrepreneurs until well after the Second World War was under way. They have no special name for their informal group, although the leaders often refer to themselves as "industrialists of youthful outlook" or as "progressive industrialists." For the sake of convenience I will refer to them as the New Group. It should be emphasized, however, that it is not their newness per se which distinguishes them from other industrialists in Mexico; rather it is the common outlook which they have on questions of industrial and national economic policy that sets them apart.

As in all social groupings, the line of distinction between New Group and other industrialists is blurred in individual cases. Crosscurrents are to be found on both sides, although in the very nature of the case we would expect to find fewer in the New Group than in the other. Since the crosscurrents are much less significant than the basic differences between the two sides, I shall neglect them and concentrate attention upon the main issues on which the two broad groups divide. This will be done later in this chapter. First, however, it is necessary to examine the composition of each group.

THE NEW GROUP

The New Group is composed chiefly of owners of small manufacturing plants. Most of these plants, moreover, came into being during the Second World War to supply articles no longer available from foreign sources in sufficient quantities to satisfy the Mexican market. Thus the industries represented by the New Group are small and of recent origin. A third important characteristic is that they use Mexican capital. This sets them off from those new industries in which American capital is participating, whether in the form of investment or in supplying technical direction. And last but not least in this list of characteristics, the New Group industrialists do not have good relations with the principal financial institutions in Mexico.

As these characteristics suggest, the businessmen who form this group do not yet feel that they are firmly established in the economy of Mexico. Uncertain about their future, they are gravely concerned about competition from the advanced industrialized nations where production of prewar goods is being resumed on a growing scale. Above all, they fear competition from the United States. They want the Mexican market for their own, and they expect the Mexican government to see that they have it. Since they are individually small and insecure, they welcome group solidarity. Thus they advocate maximum protection for all industries, and they would like to have all Mexican industrialists throw their support behind a general program based on this principle. Their feeling of insecurity, too, has led them to seek alliances with other groups in the general economy, such as agriculture and labor. This, doubtless, also explains why they have taken such pains to elaborate a rounded program for the development of Mexico.

Another distinctive feature of the New Group is vigorous, active, and aggressive leadership. The leaders are few in number but they speak out boldly and often. They are quick to comment on any development that might affect the industries they represent. They take the initiative in attacking opponents. They write pamphlets. Whether consciously or not, they have mastered the art of propaganda, especially in making blunt, categorical statements and in employing repetition, and they have also shown that they know how to go about getting a favorable press in Mexico.

The organization which expresses the point of view of Mexico's New Group industrialists is the Cámara Nacional de la Industria de Transformación (National Chamber of Manufacturing Industries). This is a comparatively new organization. It dates only from April, 1942. In spite of its youth, it has played a significant role in the development of an "industrial consciousness" in Mexico, for as the New Group crystallized, they took over the leadership of this cámara and converted it into a very active and effective body. From the standpoint of the New Group this was a conquest of great importance, because the organization has official standing as the recognized spokesman for a wide range of manufacturing industries.

In Mexico every firm is required by law to be a member of the cámara relating to its particular type of business. Each chamber has to be approved by the Ministry of National Economy, and it is then recognized as the appropriate agency to be consulted by the government on all questions relating to the kind of business under its jurisdiction. As matter of fact, the Minister of National Economy has authority to appoint a representative for each cámara. This delegate automatically becomes a nonvoting member of the directive council of the chamber.

The actual structure of cámaras is a complex and largely haphazard product of historical development nor does it follow any single principle of organization. From its title it would seem that the Cámara Nacional de la Industria de Transformación should include all manufacturing firms, since the term *industria de transformación* is roughly the Mexican equivalent of "manufacturing" in the United States. Actually, however, the chamber is more limited in scope, because some of Mexico's older and more important manufacturing industries do not belong to it but have separate associations of their own instead. This is true of the highly important textile industry, and also of the shoe, soap, and paper industries.

Among the industries affiliated with the Cámara Nacional de la Industria de Transformación, the following are represented through firms of age and substance: basic iron and steel, beer, tobacco, food processing, cement. But these firms, although highly important in the Mexican economy as a whole, are a small fraction of the membership of the chamber.

The majority of the concerns belonging to the Cámara Nacional de la Industria de Transformación are new or small, or both. The firms that loomed large in Mexico's manufacturing picture in the 'twenties and 'thirties are either not in the organization at all or else, like those in the industries just mentioned, they are numerically unimportant. Thus, when the newer and smaller industrial firms began to appreciate the advantages of acting as a group to influence Mexican policy, a development which can be dated roughly in the early months of 1945, it was easy for them to make this cámara their vehicle. The publicity value of the organization has unquestionably been great.

It is apparent that some of the older firms in the cámara do not agree with the majority on important questions of policy, and it is also clear that they are uneasy and uncomfortable as members of the organization. There is no reason, however, to expect a reversal of the steady decline in their influence. The Cámara Nacional de la Industria de Transformación will undoubtedly continue to speak for Mexico's New Group of industrialists.

OTHER INDUSTRIALISTS

In contrast to the New Group, the other Mexican industrialists do not form a unified body with a positive program. It is true that they have begun to show some signs of solidarity, but it is their opposition to the New Group which is bringing them together, rather than agreement on what should be done in a positive sense. This was apparent, for example, at the Third National Congress of Industrialists held in Mexico City in January, 1946. But there is little likelihood that they will be able to develop anything resembling the program of the New Group so far as scope, detail, and public appeal are concerned.

Three broad classes of manufacturing industries can be distinguished in Mexico apart from those represented by the New Group. These are (1) industries that were important in the Mexican economy before the Second World War; (2) certain new large industrial ventures that have connections with American enterprises or American capital; (3) older small-scale and handicraft industries that produce commodities for local markets.

The last of these three classes, although numerically large, is of slight importance for the questions we are concerned with here and may therefore be dismissed with a brief comment. It includes such establishments as the tiny local and neighborhood "mills" where the typical Mexican corn meal is prepared for daily consumption in the form of *tortillas*. Also included in this category are the many homes in the rural areas and small towns where such things as crude earthenware, reed mats, toys, and baskets are made. It is true that a tourist-export business has developed for the finer grades of some of these products in recent years, but they are made mostly for local markets by semi-isolated producers. Obviously, such "industrialists" do not register opinions on questions of national economic policy, even in groups.

Before the Second World War the principal manufacturing firms of Mexico were found in the following industries: textiles, iron and steel, beer, shoes, paper, cement, tobacco, soap, sugar refining, and flour milling. Naturally, each of these industries had its own history and problems, and it is not easy to generalize about the group.

All, however, had grown up under tariff protection which assured them the domestic market to the extent of their capacity. In practically every case it can be safely said that the operators were satisfied with the size and nature of the market for their products, although the precise reasons for this attitude may have differed somewhat from industry to industry. Expansion and risk-taking have had little place in their cautious and conservative business outlook. Such attitudes, which are the industrial counterpart of those typically found among large landowners in Latin America, obviously do not change with ease. Even the stimulus of wartime conditions has failed to affect them materially.

Thus, even without a direct clash of business interests, it is understandable that Mexico's older industrialists would be troubled and uneasy about development and expansion of industry along new lines. In particular, the outlook and methods of the New Group industrialists are a threat to that stability which they prize so highly. It is naturally difficult for them to see any advantages in the rise of this new class of business men.

This last point may be illustrated by reference to the question of tariff protection. There is no disagreement between the two groups on the principle involved. Both favor protective tariffs for Mexican industries. But disagreement does arise over the scope of tariff protection and the tactics to be used in attaining it. The older industrialists see no reason for supporting the New Group's general campaign for higher and more comprehensive tariffs. Their industries are already well taken care of, and, judging from past experience, they can get additional tariff protection if they require it. Far from feeling that they need the support of the newer industries for this purpose, they fear that the publicity accompanying an all-industry tariff campaign might actually be a handicap to them.

The following is instructive as a sidelight. Two of Mexico's older industries, textiles and beer, are definitely interested in holding the export markets they developed during the war years. This gives them a special reason for being shy of a program to raise tariff barriers on a wide range of articles. The textile industry may well call for higher protection on its own products, but clearly it would prefer to do so in its own way. So far as the breweries are concerned, it is doubtful that imported beer could at the present moment compete with the Mexican product even if the duties were taken off entirely. For several years to come the beer industry is not likely to be interested in protective tariffs.

It is important to realize that the older manufacturing firms in Mexico are an integral part of a larger business community which includes the leading banking and commercial institutions of the country. To some extent they are tied to banks by means of interlocking directorates. But even without such formal ties, the banks regard the older manufacturing enterprises as favored clients, a rank which they share with the great commercial firms. Before the outbreak of the Mexican Revolution in 1910 it was the large landowner who held this position alongside the big merchandising concern as a preferred credit risk. The progressive liquidation of large landholdings under the agrarian program, however, made it possible for the well-established manufacturing concern to take the place of the landowner in the credit structure.[1]

The older industrialists, the leading bankers, and the principal merchants seem to operate in a common atmosphere of cordial business relations. Apart from their normal business connections, members of all three groups occasionally join in urban real estate and construction ventures. There is little question but what these three groups see eye to eye on developments in the Mexican economy and on issues in national economic policy. And thus the reaction of the older industrialists to the rise of the New Group is shared and fortified by important elements in the Mexican financial and commercial world.

[1] Eduardo Villaseñor, *Ensayos interamericanos* (Mexico, 1944), pp. 134–137.

The remaining class of manufacturing industries—new and relatively large industrial ventures that have connections with American enterprises or American capital—is still a little known quantity in the Mexican economy. American participation in these enterprises has taken place in one or more of three ways: (1) technical direction, usually combined with the right to use special processes or patents; (2) capital investment by private firms; (3) Export-Import Bank loans to cover the costs of buying equipment in the United States. Although some of these new plants are merely branches of American firms, in others the Mexican interests are in a genuine sense operating jointly with the American. These Mexican interests appear as investors and also as participants in management.

Some of these new large industrial projects have been dear to the heart of the Mexican government. This probably accounts for the Export-Import Bank loans. In a few cases, at least, the enterprises have a semiofficial complexion in that the Mexican government has provided some of their capital through the medium of Nacional Financiera.

Because of their size and their ties with American interests, the new large enterprises in industry have little in common with the firms represented by the New Group. Indeed, the latter are distinctly hostile to such projects.[2] If the issues in national economic policy become sharper in Mexico, as is likely to be the case, we may expect the directors of the new large industrial firms to line up with the older industrialists rather than with the New Group, even though the alliance is based upon purely negative considerations and not upon a positive program of economic action.

The New Group, as we have seen, has converted the Cámara Nacional de la Industria de Transformación into the spokesman for its point of view. There is no comparable organization of industrialists on the other side. The principal organ for expressing opposition to the New Group is actually the organ of the national chamber of commercial firms, namely, the *Carta Semanal* issued by the Confederación de Cámaras Nacionales de Comercio. This can be explained by a natural antipathy of traders to the extreme nationalism of the New Group and also by the friendly ties that exist between the old industrialists and the owners of the larger merchandising firms. Similarly, the national bankers' association (Asociación de Banqueros de México) reflects the uneasiness and irritation of Mexico's older industrialists over the growing influence of the New Group.

---

[2] "Those large industries which it is thought will be established here by miracle and which are intended to equal North American industries, will not prosper. Industry, like everything else, has to follow an evolutionary process; it must begin small. . . . Ours is an industrial effort adjusted to the level of Mexico. . . ." These are the words of one of the leaders of the New Group, José Domingo Lavín, in *Memoria del Segundo Congreso Mexicano de Ciencias Sociales* (Mexico, 1946), vol. 3, p. 396.

Issues

In the preceding pages I have examined the composition of each of two broad groups in the Mexican industrial structure. Since each group works and thinks in a distinct business atmosphere, we would expect them to show differences of opinion on many questions. The fundamental differences, however, revolve about three main questions, namely, (1) labor policy; (2) the role of government in the economic sphere; and (3) American business interests.

The first of these questions has been the most important of the three, and it is likely to continue to be so. In the main it is an issue over negotiating with organized labor. The New Group seeks the coöperation of organized labor in promoting the industrialization of Mexico, pointing out that labor will share the fruits of industrialism in higher standards of living. Labor and management are engaged in a joint undertaking of national economic and social betterment. It is maintained that this identity of interest between employers and workers in Mexican industry far overshadows any disagreement that might arise, and that for this reason labor disputes can be settled peacefully and quickly by frank discussion in labor-management conferences. The New Group, therefore, welcomes negotiation with trade unions.

As a corollary proposition, they believe that discussion between workers and industrialists will lead to the establishment of higher standards of labor discipline and therefore to greater productivity and lower unit costs of production. Under general agreements with employers, the trade unions can be counted upon to take the initiative in setting up such standards.

The older industrialists of Mexico, on the other hand, are distinctly hostile to trade unions, and it is hard for them to assume a different position. For many years they have considered themselves the victims of laws which give power and advantages to labor in industrial disputes, and of the abuse of that power by the leaders of organized labor. It is not necessary here to try to assess how much justice there may be in this position. What is important for our purpose is the fact that the opinion is widely and strongly held. Since 1929 it has been expressed again and again by an employers' association known as the Confederación Patronal de la República Mexicana.

The difference between the two points of view on labor policy has been brought out by the labor-management pact of April, 1945. This document presumably was an indirect result of the Chapultepec conference, when the Cámara Nacional de la Industria de Transformación publicly attacked the United States tariff reduction proposal on the ground that it would destroy Latin American industries. Mexico's principal labor federation, the CTM (Confederación de Trabajadores Mexicanos), came to the support of the cámara; later the two groups held discussions which ultimately led to the labor-management agreement.

The pact itself was a very general statement to the effect that workers and employers were united in a joint effort to bring about economic progress and economic independence for Mexico, leading to higher standards of living for the Mexican people. It contained no specific commitments with respect to industrial relations. It was not a "truce." It was not even a signed document. It was merely a declaration of adherence to the broad proposition that both industrialists and laborers were working toward the common objective of improving the material welfare of the Mexican people. There was certainly nothing in the text itself to which the more conservative industrialists could object. As a matter of fact, a number of representatives of such business interests were present at the banquet in Mexico City where general approval was given to the pact.

In subsequent months, however, the older business groups drew back. Whatever enthusiasm they might have had for the pact cooled off. The agreement was made the subject of strong and persistent attacks, the burden of which was to picture the pact as a sinister plot directed against business and industry by labor leaders of leftist sympathies. No less vigorous has been the defense of the pact by the New Group industrialists who initiated it. To the outsider, the innocuous text of the document itself would hardly justify the ardor with which it has been attacked and defended. We must conclude, therefore, that it has become a symbol of a new employer attitude in labor relations, which the older industrialists consider dangerously weak.

This new attitude is compounded out of the following features: (1) a conciliatory rather than a hostile tone toward organized labor; (2) a willingness to negotiate grievances with a view toward quick compromises that would prevent strikes; (3) a frank recognition of the stake of labor in an industrial enterprise, as evidenced by readiness to consult with trade unions on such matters as measures calculated to raise productivity. Not only have the older industrialists disliked to accept this attitude of the New Group, but they have been suspicious of it and of the possible developments in labor relations to which it could lead.

As a consequence of this split on the side of management, the Cámara Nacional de la Industria de Transformación alone proceded to work out a mediation plan with the CTM. If a strike is threatened, either party may take the dispute to a mediation board (Comisión de Avenencia) composed of three members from each group. The board has the power to delay a strike for as long as sixty days; during this time the case is studied with the assistance of experts engaged especially for this purpose. If a mutually satisfactory settlement cannot be effected in this manner, the case is then handed over to the government's arbitration machinery.

According to statements made by the leaders of the cámara, the results thus far have been excellent; only twice in about two hundred cases has the board failed to achieve a settlement. Obviously, it is impossible to estimate the significance of these figures without knowing something about the nature of the cases themselves, but the very fact that the New Group has sponsored a voluntary conciliation board, indicates that it has at least made a start in putting its labor relations program into practice.

The question of what role the Mexican government should play in the economic life of the nation brings out a second main distinctive feature of New Group outlook. To get a proper perspective on this question, we must realize first of all that the New Group industrialists are not partisans of government ownership in business, as they are often represented to be by their opponents. Like the other industrialists of Mexico they are staunch advocates of private enterprise. The government, they contend, should not compete with private business. It is true, however, that they would define the proper scope for public enterprise more broadly than most men in the older business circles of Mexico, where it is still fashionable to maintain that electrification and irrigation should be left to private initiative.

On a more important side of this question, the New Group believes that the industrialists and the government together (with a certain amount of coöperation from labor) should work out and implement a program of industrialization for Mexico. By this they mean more than the drawing up of general plans. What they have in mind is continuous and intimate contact between the various government agencies and industrial groups, in which the latter are consulted on questions that have come up for administrative decision as well as on those dealing with the broad lines of economic policy. The mechanism for such a program of mutual collaboration, they point out, already exists in the *cámaras de industria,* which are recognized by the government as the proper agencies to be consulted on problems relating to industry.

What the New Group advocates, therefore, is by no means state intervention in the ordinary sense of the term. They assign the government a prominent role, it is true, but they want the government to arrive at its decisions on the basis of information and advice supplied by the interested industrialist groups. What they propose is business intervention in government rather than government intervention in business.

The point of view of the New Group can probably best be summed up by saying that they consider the government to be a necessary ally for the growing industries of Mexico. They want to keep this ally in their service, and they believe that they can do so.

The older industrialist groups certainly do not object to all forms of government intervention. Tariff and other specific measures on behalf of their industries are welcomed with open arms. They do object, however, to broad, comprehensive economic action on the part of the government, even with industry participating. At bottom, they distrust and fear the government, an attitude which can be explained principally by three features of government policy since the outbreak of the Mexican Revolution, namely, labor legislation, agrarian laws, and the expropriation of foreign oil holdings.

Starting with this attitude, the older industrialists are reluctant to clothe the government with any generalized economic functions. They are afraid that if this were done, the scope of government authority would extend itself progressively at the expense of private business interests and that the bureaucracy would become the master rather than the servant of industry. For that reason they strongly oppose the kind of working alliance between government and industry that the New Group believes is basic to further industrial development in Mexico.

The third fundamental difference between New Group and other industrialists relates to American participation in Mexican industrialization. The New Group is plainly hostile to American industrial interests in Mexico. This applies to American firms that are operating jointly with Mexican capital as well as to outright branches of American manufacturing concerns. Such an attitude is obviously consistent with their basic nationalistic position. Moreover, they dislike the American and quasi-American enterprises on grounds of size. The New Group, as we have seen, are owners of small plants. The enterprises with American connections are relatively large in Mexico, no matter how small they may seem alongside their American parent companies. These firms, it is feared, will dominate the Mexican market at the expense of the Mexican concerns in the same industry. That is why the New Group sponsors measures designed to discourage American firms from entering the field and to handicap those which are already established.[3]

The Mexican industrialists who are operating jointly with American firms are obviously at odds with the New Group on this issue, although many of them are also newcomers in the manufacturing field. For most of the older industrialists who do not have American connections the issue

---

[3] In certain nonindustrial lines the New Group would welcome foreign capital because it would make more domestic capital available for investment in manufacturing. These fields include electric power, highway development, and irrigation.

is not a critical one, since they are not directly threatened. It is probable that many of them are also unfriendly to new American firms in Mexico, but in a more passive manner. At least, they are annoyed at the aggressive way in which the New Group attacks American interests. It is the New Group alone that is active in the campaign to limit and handicap American manufacturing firms in Mexico.

As the New Group has formulated a position on important questions of business and national policy and as the older industrialists have crystallized an opposing point of view, open clashes between the two groups have become fairly common. A struggle has been taking place between the two for control of the Confederación de Cámaras Industriales. This catchall organization is a federation of all chambers relating to manufacturing, mining, electricity, transportation, communication, and petroleum. The Cámara Nacional de la Industria de Transformación is but one unit in this larger federation, while some manufacturing industries, such as textiles, shoes, paper, soap, and rubber, are represented by their independent chambers. A combination of older industries and nonmanufacturing firms (such as those engaged in mining) has thus far been able to keep the New Group in check within the federation, but this situation may prove to be only an armed truce.

The New Group needs to dominate the Confederación de Cámaras Industriales in order to speak authoritatively for Mexican industry as a whole. One important step in this direction would be the elimination of the nonmanufacturing industries from the federation. The New Group is working to this end by means of pressure on the government, for the government has the power to compel a reorganization. Other maneuvers also are, doubtless, being employed. Since gaining control of the Confederación de Cámaras Industriales would be a great victory for the New Group, we can expect them to carry on the fight with energy and determination.

CHAPTER III

The New Group Program

THE NEW GROUP program for Mexico's economic development, with which this chapter is concerned, is not set forth in any single document. To understand even its major points it is necessary to put together material from numerous and varied sources. These include pamphlets written by recognized leaders, remarks made at conventions of organized business groups or meetings of professional societies, policy statements of the Cámara Nacional de la Industria de Transformación, and newspaper interviews with New Group leaders or articles about them. In the discussion that follows the reader will find only a few footnote references of a bibliographical nature. These appear for the most part where direct quotations have been used. As for the rest, it seems needless burden these pages with manifold citations to support what appears in the text.

Of necessity the task of presenting the New Group program in terms of real significance calls not only for sifting and classification of material but for interpretation as well. It is inevitable that there should be some inconsistencies in statements prepared by different persons, even though their basic points of view are identical. In such cases I have chosen the proposition which seemed to me to fit the program as a whole best. On some questions, too, I have had to proceed inferentially because full explanations have not been forthcoming from the New Group itself. Wherever such inferences appear, or wherever I have inserted judgments and opinions of my own, they will be clearly distinguished as such by the context. Elsewhere it may be taken for granted that the opinions set forth are those of the New Group.

Finally, I have avoided scoring points off some rather obvious errors which the New Group writers have committed in analysis or in interpretation. Given their basic postulates, the main body of their economic program would stand in spite of such errors. Theirs is a program of business men, not of economists, and it must be treated as such.

THE PROGRAM

The avowed objective of the New Group program is to raise the standard of living of the Mexican people. The principal means to this end, they argue, is industrialization. Other phases of the economy must be developed, it is true, but none of these can give a like impulse in raising productivity and in spreading purchasing power among the mass of the population.

It is useless to expect agriculture to be the mainstay of economic and social progress in Mexico because natural handicaps are too great. Climate and topography have set limits which man can push back but little. Industry, on the other hand, suffers from no such limitations.

From this point of view, the development of manufacturing is not a mere business question, not just a matter of investing capital to make a return, or of giving employment to labor, but it is the vital force which will make social and economic gains possible, and without which Mexico is doomed to remain permanently in a state of cultural depression. Mexico, therefore, must industrialize; it is the only hope.

It follows, of course, that what is good for Mexican industry is good for the Mexican nation. This identity of interest is complete as long as the industrialists are residents of Mexico with no allegiance to foreign business interests. The process of industrialization, however, is not a painless one. Every social gain has its cost, and the Mexican people must be prepared to make temporary sacrifices in order to attain greater material and cultural advantages in the long run. The cost may be great. It cannot be too great, however, if it makes industrialization worth while, for there is only one alternative, namely, to continue the economic pattern of the past without hope of raising the material and social levels of the Mexican people. There is no middle road.

Thus, in the eyes of the New Group, industrialization emerges as a national movement for the economic and social betterment of Mexico. It is a new and higher phase in the unfolding of the Mexican Revolution. To participate in the movement is a patriotic obligation. Industrialism is to be the means of building a strong and independent nation.

For practical purposes the intense nationalism of the New Group is chiefly expressed by an antiforeign outlook, in which, parenthetically, they also continue the tradition of the Mexican Revolution. More explicitly, they are anti-American. There is no doubt that they capitalize upon the ever-present Mexican distrust of the United States to give their program emotional appeal and to gain widespread popular support, and there is likewise no doubt that this tactic has been fruitful. As a matter of fact, the opportunity to express opposition to the American government's proposals at the Chapultepec conference early in 1945 was the means by which the group itself achieved solidarity and by which they gained their first real prestige in Mexico.

It will be recalled that the United States delegation at Chapultepec sponsored a resolution firmly committing the American republics to a policy of tariff reduction, and that the resolution was ultimately rejected by the Latin American delegations.[1] Certainly no one worked harder to secure this outcome than the New Group speaking through Mexico's Cámara Nacional de la Industria de Transformación, and they like to think of it as their own private victory. Probably no one else feels the same way about this, but it is clear that the events of the conference gave the New Group valuable publicity, prestige, and momentum.

One of the arguments which they advanced during the Chapultepec meeting, and which has formed an integral part of their propaganda since that time, is that certain American business interests are conspiring to crush Mexico's industries in order to sell their own products in the Mexican market. The United States government, they contend, has been made a party to this plot through the influence of powerful business men who occupied key official positions during the war, and thus the mistaken tariff reduction proposal was put forth at Chapultepec. In the New Group propaganda this proposal is always referred to as the Clayton Plan, a dubious compliment to Assistant Secretary of State Will Clayton who presented it and fought to have it adopted.

The policy recommended by the American delegates at Chapultepec—writes a New Group leader, Sr. Lavín—did not represent the policy of the American people but rather the policy of a group of business men who at the present time control the international trade between Mexico and the United States. For these business men our flimsy international commerce of two or three hundred million dollars a year is a matter of interest, and they know that when Mexico becomes industrialized they will lose this trade; logically our imports in the future will consist of different kinds of goods, in accordance with the progress of our industrialization. ...[2]

No opportunity has been lost to remind the Mexican people of the Clayton Plan and of its sinister intent. Thus, when Lavín was asked by a reporter for his reaction to a Washington statement that the American government would seek to improve economic relations in the hemisphere by means of lowering trade barriers and eliminating discriminatory practices he replied, characteristically, that the United States was still trying to carry through the Clayton Plan in spite of the fact that it had been rejected at Chapultepec.[3] Large sums of money were being spent anonymously in Mexico, he went on to say, to reinforce the arguments of the Clayton Plan.[4]

A certain amount of spice is added to the stories about the plot of Ameri-

---

[1] See above, chapter i.
[2] José Domingo Lavín, *Dos conferencias* (Mexico, 1946), p. 55.
[3] The United States plan for an International Trade Organization is regarded as a broader application of the Clayton Plan.
[4] *Tiempo*, vol. 7, no. 169 (July 27, 1945), p. 26.

can business interests against Mexican industry by the use of such terms as "monopolies," "trusts," and "international capital." Any large American firm apparently qualifies as a monopoly merely by offering goods which compete with Mexican industrial production. If an American concern seeks to open a branch plant in Mexico it becomes an operation of international capital. The label with a sinister implication as a means of discrediting an individual or a group is, of course, a widely used device. In this respect there is certainly nothing peculiar about Mexico or about the New Group. The point is that these particular labels carry great weight in Mexico because most Mexicans believe that their country has been exploited and virtually robbed of valuable natural resources by huge foreign mining and petroleum companies.

Mexican merchants who ask for freer trade are also taken care of in New Group propaganda, usually by reference to the American conspiracy against Mexican industry. They are pictured as willing partners in the plot because they handle foreign-made goods and have close connections with foreign producers. They are a front for foreign interests, they are unpatriotic, and therefore they cannot be listened to on questions of national policy. The attack on such commercial interests is always sharp and bitter, and calculated to imply that they are disloyal to their country.[5]

We may now examine the New Group program in detail, remembering that its avowed intention is to raise the standards of living of the Mexican people by means of industrialization, and that it has a strong undertone of nationalism and of antipathy toward the United States.

NATURE AND SCOPE OF INDUSTRIALIZATION

On this broad problem the New Group program lays down some definite propositions but leaves other questions to be answered by implication. In the long run, it seems, any manufactured article consumed in volume in Mexico should also be produced there. They do not say this in so many words, but a careful reading of their various publications fails to reveal any exceptions to the industries that one day Mexico will see in operation. The ultimate goal is an industrial framework analogous to that of the United States. How long it should take to reach this objective they do not say, but one gets the impression that they consider twenty-five to thirty years sufficient if government and industry will only follow their specifications.

For practical reasons the New Group believes that certain lines of industrial development should be emphasized at the moment and in the immediate future. These industries are the ones which they are most

[5] See, for example, the report of a talk by Lavín, in *Tiempo*, vol. 8, no. 191 (December 28, 1945), p. 27.

anxious to call to the attention of the Mexican government and the Mexican public.

Foremost among the industries which should be expanded at once are those that use raw materials produced by domestic agriculture. Included in this class are the following: processing of cereals; the preparation of edible oils from various seeds and nuts; the production of sugar and sugar by-products such as alcohol; the fabrication of articles made from fibers, such as cotton, silk, wool, henequen, ixtle, and lechuguilla; production of raw rubber from various plants which grow in Mexico. This list is not intended to be complete, but illustrative. Similarly, industries based upon natural resources of the forests and the sea should be given immediate attention.

The chemical industry also qualifies for the front rank. Like the industries mentioned above, chemical factories can find in Mexico sufficient raw materials to meet their needs. This industry, moreover, is of strategic importance to the whole economy. Chemicals are vital raw materials in many branches of manufacturing, and by producing them in Mexico the industrial structure of the nation will be greatly strengthened. Agriculture, too, will reap benefits from an expanded and improved chemical industry, notably because a larger supply of fertilizers and insecticides will make it possible to increase farm output.

A less well defined group of industries which the New Group would schedule for early development are those which make equipment for the high-priority industries, such equipment as pumps, filters, centrifugals, mixers, heat exchangers, and compressors. Among other things, this development would require the elaboration of a machine-tool industry.

It is worth noting the grounds upon which the New Group rests the case for setting up machine-making industries in Mexico. Short supply in the advanced manufacturing nations, as an aftermath of the war, is mentioned as one reason. But the principal reason given is that the great industrialized countries have always been reluctant to export producers' goods and that they will purposely restrict such exports to a minimum in the future. Here again we find the plot against Mexican industry—a plot which business interests abroad (and especially in the United States) are able to implement through government action. To combat the plot requires the joint efforts of Mexican industrialists, Mexican labor, and the Mexican government.

This line of thinking leads to the suggestion that "private initiative, strongly supported by the government, should immediately set about establishing at least three large centers of heavy industry in Mexico [City], Guadalajara, and Monterrey."[6] These are visualized as the industrial nuclei

⁶ Cámara Nacional de la Industria de Transformación, *Conclusiones sobre los puntos del temario del Tercer Congreso Nacional de Industriales* (Mexico, 1945), p. 26.

of the nation and the bases from which great industrial gains will be scored. They would be designed to meet the needs of Mexican industry for electric power, fuel, chemicals, iron and steel, machinery, and tools. Similarly, agriculture and transportation would satisfy their requirements from the goods and services flowing out of these industrial centers.

The three cities just mentioned have been selected for early treatment because of their existing industrial structures. They are to be followed by others. The full elaboration of even the three centers is regarded as a long-term development. However, the leaders of the New Group always speak optimistically about the speed with which they could be whipped into shape to meet the principal immediate needs of Mexican industry.

To secure industrial development according to some order of priority the New Group considers government action necessary—but government action in the sense in which it was discussed in the preceding chapter, not unilateral planning by government departments. Everywhere in their program the role of the government is that of a coöperative agent, never that of an independent economic factor. Planning, to the New Group means planning by industrialists—or rather by true Mexican industrialists—with the collaboration and support of public officials. Once decided upon, the plans are then to be implemented and enforced by the government.

Import policy.—To insure success for Mexican industrialization no measure is more important for the New Group than a vigilant and effective import policy. Mexican industry, they assert, cannot withstand foreign competition because costs of production in manufacturing are higher in Mexico than in the advanced industrialized nations.

This competitive disadvantage is explained by a number of reasons, among which the following can be singled out: high rates of interest; small domestic market, leading to factories of limited size which cannot enjoy the advantages of large-scale production; weak spots or gaps in the industrial structure as a whole; inefficiencies in technical and financial management and in manufacturing operations. Such handicaps will not be eradicated overnight. For a number of years Mexican industry cannot possibly be expected to compete on even terms with foreign production.

The principal means by which the New Group would protect the domestic manufacturer from ruinous foreign competition is the tariff, and thus great pains have been taken to work out standards for a suitable Mexican tariff policy. Foremost among these is the proposition that tariffs must be high enough to keep out competitive goods entirely. Halfway measures will not do. If a protective tariff does not actually exclude the competing foreign product the effect is to cause disturbances in the Mexican economy without providing the corresponding benefits in stimulating industrial development. The Mexican producer must have the whole of the Mexican market. Without it he cannot hope to set up a plant that in time will operate on a low-cost, efficient basis. "Protectionism," says Lavín,

is worthless if it is not complete. We have proof of this . . . in that Mexico has been a protectionist country and yet we are extraordinarily backward. Why? Because the protective system has been a half-way system, it has been a protective system based on compromises and on interference from abroad. What we need is protection on the model of the United States. . . .[7]

Obviously the consumer in Mexico must pay for this protection, and the New Group industrialists make no attempt to dodge this issue. Their answer is that the Mexican people must make sacrifices in order to overcome their economic backwardness. But the sacrifices are justified because they are made for a great national purpose, and the people should not be afraid to make them. "We need," writes José R. Colín, "a national ethos on which to base and support a program of industrialization. This ethos is discipline, determination to reach an objective, a spirit of sacrifice, a clear idea of fulfilling a duty, and a feeling of national enthusiasm in working for the interests of the country."[8]

Colín also shows how the spirit of sacrifice is fundamental to consumer education in Mexico. This, too, should be expressed in his own words:

All means of propaganda must be used . . . to induce the consumer to accept and to prefer domestic products. In this sense a true national viewpoint has to be created. This will help to convince the consumers that any immediate sacrifice caused by the purchase of domestic goods, even if they are of lower quality and higher price, will be compensated in the future by economic independence for the country and a substantial rise in the standard of living of the whole Mexican people.[9]

It is significant that the New Group propaganda says very little about lower prices once the new industries have established themselves. They imply that such a development will follow, but they certainly do not make a point over it. In fact, they are reluctant to make any promises at all on this score. In the short run the nonmaterial satisfaction of participating in a national movement to build a stronger and more independent Mexico compensates the consumer for his sacrifices. Beyond this, they prefer to appeal to the people as members of producers' groups, such as wage earners and farmers, rather than as consumers, and much stress is placed upon the higher incomes that will flow out of the industrialization process.

Economists will be tempted to raise questions about how it is all going

[7] *Memoria del Segundo Congreso Mexicano de Ciencias Sociales,* vol. 3, pp. 391–392.
[8] José R. Colín, *Requisitos fundamentales para la industrialización de México* (Mexico, 1945), p. 12.
[9] Colín, *op. cit.,* pp. 40–41.

to work out in real rather than in money terms. Such questions do not trouble Mexico's New Group industrialists any more than similar questions bother articulate business groups anywhere. They are interested in making a case for certain lines of policy, and not in reasoning precisely about economic problems. And of course it is true that no analysis couched in real terms can ever match in public appeal a few simple claims about higher money incomes.

A second plank in the tariff program of the New Group is to make protection the sole purpose of import duties. Mexico's tariff system was set up in the first place principally for revenue ends. It must now, they maintain, be completely overhauled to eliminate all merely revenue duties, except a few on luxury articles that are not produced at all in Mexico. A revenue duty alone on other goods means that the Mexican producer is not getting the full protection that he needs, since some foreign products do thus make their way in.

A flexible tariff system is also part of the New Group program. Individual duties must be susceptible of quick and easy adjustment, so as to offset any external developments that weaken their protective force. Thus it is argued that the Comisión de Aranceles (Tariff Commission) should be given the power to make changes in duties instead of acting merely as an advisory body. At present this agency has authority only to conduct investigations and to recommend changes in import and export duties. The rates themselves are fixed by act of Congress.

The Comisión de Aranceles has already been given a mandate to encourage domestic industries and to suggest measures for using customs duties to "protect the national economy."[10] The New Group would go beyond this and give the Commission a freer hand in putting this directive into practice. This would mean flexible tariff administration. The Commission would, of course, have authority to lower rates as well as to raise them, but no reduction could be made without a six-month advance notice, thus giving the industrialists affected sufficient time to present a protest.

It is no exaggeration to say that the New Group contemplates tariff changes in one direction only—upward. This follows from another of their tariff principles, namely, that tariff protection must be permanent. No matter how fully an industry develops, no matter how good its apparent international competitive position, the New Group program calls for continued protection. This, they argue, is necessary in order to guard the industry from changes that might occur abroad and from dumping by foreign producers. Moreover, if the government would give assurances that tariff

[10] United States Tariff Commission, *Economic Controls and Commercial Policy in Mexico* (Washington, 1946), p. 11.

protection is to be permanent, this in itself would stimulate investment in industry by helping to overcome the traditional timidity of Mexican capital.

As a further measure to give Mexico a more efficient and more flexible tariff system the New Group has urged a shift from specific to *ad valorem* duties. Until 1947 all Mexican duties were collected according to weight, volume, or number of articles, regardless of value. An *ad valorem* system has certain advantages from the protective standpoint. If, for example, the Mexican price level is going up relatively to the American, the previous degree of protection would be more nearly maintained by *ad valorem* duties than by specific ones. Also, under an *ad valorem* system it is easier to make the tariff changes needed to restore the amount of protection lost through relative price level changes.

It might be added that, for the protectionist, a further advantage of an *ad valorem* tariff arises out of the practical need to handle commodities in groups. When duties are specific it is exceedingly difficult to get the desired amount of protection on each article in a group. This problem, while it also exists under an *ad valorem* system, is easier to solve when duties are levied according to value.

It is often pointed out that an *ad valorem* system is both costly and difficult to administer in Mexico. Efficiency and honesty in the thousands of routine operations required in public administration are still to be realized. Therefore, it is argued, it would be easy to file false import declarations in which values would be understated, and thus the tariff schedules would become meaningless. In a somewhat amusing manner, Lavín of the New Group has taken advantage of this argument to make out a case for introducing the minimum valuation principle.[11] He concedes that the danger of understatement is a very real one. There is, however, a simple way of coping with it, namely, to fix a minimum value, for tariff purposes, for every item to be protected. This would render harmless the false declarations that might be filed, and still enable Mexico to enjoy the advantages of an *ad valorem* system. In thus meeting the argument against *ad valorem* rates, we should observe, Lavín has suggested a measure which would increase the protective strength of the Mexican tariff, since if prices abroad should start to fall, the minimum valuations would be a first line of defense for the domestic producers.[12]

In addition to the highly protective tariff program sketched above the New Group favors direct import controls for certain products which are classified as basic primary materials.[13] These are semiprocessed or interme-

---

[11] Lavín, *Dos conferencias*, pp. 48–49.

[12] It is significant that the tariff decree of November, 1947, also introduced the minimum valuation principle. See chapter v.

[13] The purpose of the import control decree of May, 1944 (see chapter v) differs from the objective sought by the New Group.

diate products which are used in the manufacture of a large number of (1) finished articles, or (2) articles which are fundamental to the development of other industries. The list of products falling into this classification would have to be drawn up by the government in consultation with industrialists, but the following items can be taken as illustrations: pig iron, steel ingots, tin plate, electrolytic copper, sulphuric acid, caustic soda, rayon fiber, paper, and cardboard.[14]

The purpose of controlling imports of such commodities would be to allow the Mexican producers to sell their whole output without foreign competition. This would be achieved by granting import permits only to the extent of the difference between domestic production and estimated annual consumption. Obviously, no protective tariffs would then be needed for the products classified as basic primary materials.

Export policy.—As a further means of encouraging the development of industry in Mexico the New Group recommends a change in the principle upon which export duties, as well as import duties, are collected. In the past such duties have been levied for revenue purposes.[15] This should be changed so that the exclusive purpose of export duties would be to insure the retention of an adequate supply of domestic raw material for Mexican industry. If necessary, the duties should be raised to prohibitive levels.[16]

There is, however, one specific export tax which the New Group would eliminate entirely, the *aforo*. This tax was introduced in 1938 when the exchange value of the peso dropped as a consequence of the oil expropriation incident. (At that time the aforo was in effect a special tax on mineral exports that were being paid for in dollars under predepreciation contracts. Subsequently, however, it came to be used as an additional source of government revenue, amounting virtually to another form of export tax). Industrialists are now deeply concerned about the aforo because it raises the foreign prices of the manufactured goods they export. They fear that unless it is abolished, they will lose out in postwar competition in markets they gained during the war.[17]

Whether the New Group industrialists are vitally interested in the aforo question so far as their own industries are concerned is doubtful. As we have seen, they are not counting on export markets in the foreseeable fu-

---

[14] Colín, *op. cit.*, p. 10.

[15] During the war period, emergency export control and export duty measures were also introduced for nonfiscal reasons.

[16] An alternative export control plan, suggested by other industrialists, has also received New Group approval. Commissions of industrialists would determine the amounts of raw materials and semimanufactures required by domestic industries, and the Mexican government would allow exports only to the extent that supplies exceeded such amounts. Under this plan all export duties would be abolished.

[17] In May, 1947, the cotton textile industry won concessions on the aforo from the government. See chapter viii.

ture. Their stand on the aforo, however, appeals to other industrialists and business men in Mexico who have ambitions to cultivate export markets, and this doubtless explains why the New Group leaders have taken so much trouble to deal at length with the aforo problem.

Subsidies for industry.—The effective beginnings of a government policy to subsidize industrial development in Mexico date from 1941. Since that year special laws have made it possible for the Mexican government to grant subsidies to "new and necessary industries" by exempting them from taxes and from the payment of import duties.[18] This subsidy policy meets with the approval of the New Group, and they want the government to continue it indefinitely. However, they would like to see the policy extended and strengthened in certain ways.

One change recommended by them, and actually adopted by the government in 1946, was to lengthen the period of tax exemption to as much as ten years for some industries, instead of restricting the privilege to the five years provided for in the earlier legislation.

Much more far-reaching is the suggestion that the industries making basic primary materials as defined above, should receive direct, outright subsidies from the Mexican government, instead of mere tax-exemption privileges. This would represent an entirely new departure in national economic policy. The proposal is certainly an important factor in the New Group program for Mexican industrializatoin, and yet nowhere in the New Group literature is the argument behind it given a satisfactory airing. A reasonable explanation, however, can be constructed by inference.

If subsidies were awarded to the industries producing basic primary materials, they could sell their output at much lower prices than would otherwise be the case. These prices could be kept in line with those charged in the more advanced manufacturing nations; this incidentally gives a clue on the method of determining the amount of a particular subsidy. Since the commodities produced by the basic industries enter into the manufacture of many other articles, the subsidies would help to hold down industrial prices as a group, thus acting as an offset to the protective duties on finished manufactured goods.

The explanation which suggests itself, therefore, is that the New Group industrialists have hit upon this subsidy proposal as a means of disguising the costs of industrialization for the ordinary consumer. The so-called basic industries would not be given tariff protection, which would raise the prices of their products, but they would be sheltered from foreign competition by direct import controls. Subsidies would then bring down these prices until they compared favorably with those prevailing in the more developed

---

[18] See chapter v.

industrial countries. Costs of production and prices on a wide range of manufactured goods would be reduced, thus helping to offset price-inflating measures such as high tariffs on finished products.

The effects on the Mexican economy of such a subsidy program would not be confined to the industries producing basic primary materials, and sound public policy would require an analysis of all the likely consequences before adopting it. The subsidy plan itself, for example, is quite likely to promote inflation. The New Group industrialists simply do not bother to come to grips with such questions. And it may very well be that those who ultimately determine the industrialization policy of the Mexican government will likewise not bother to meet this and other issues, because a subsidy program is apt to look like a convenient way of postponing awkward developments until, somehow, the future takes care of them.

Other government measures to promote industrialism.—A number of other New Group recommendations for government policies to promote industry need only be mentioned briefly. Inevitably, like all business groups, they ask for tax reform. The tax burden on all manufacturing establishments should be reduced to encourage further investment. The policy of exempting new industries from federal taxation should be strengthened in certain details, but no fundamental change is required. Similar privileges, however, should be extended to the production of raw materials. Local and state governments, they claim, should also refrain from taxing raw materials, and an effort should be made to coördinate their tax levies with those of the federal government. Tax administration should be simplified and the traditional *mordida* (petty graft) eradicated, because it is both costly and disturbing in business operations.

Improvements in railroad administration—practically all the railroads in Mexico are now owned by the government—are urgently needed. The lack of coöperation between labor and management in the railroad industry, resulting in frequent stoppages, inefficient operation, and irregular service, is a serious handicap to manufacturing development in Mexico. Railroad administration must be removed from politics, and representatives of the consuming public must be given a voice in the directorate.

Also, the railroad rate structure needs to be overhauled because it is a carry over from an earlier period when the economy of Mexico was "colonial." Presumably, two steps are called for to correct this situation: (1) traffic charges on mineral exports should be raised relatively to those on domestic manufactured goods; (2) Mexican manufactures should pay lower freight rates than similar foreign products. In broad terms, the New Group wants national railroad policy to be directed toward one primary end, the industrialization of Mexico.

Recommendations for the petroleum industry, which is also owned by the government (Petróleos Mexicanos), are much the same as those dealing with the railroads. Industrialization of Mexico should be the principal objective of Petróleos Mexicanos, administration must be made more efficient and less political, and the consumers must be given a voice in directing the enterprise.

In electrification likewise the needs of industry should be given first priority. Electrification, however, differs from most other lines of development in that foreign investment is considered desirable by the New Group—this because they believe that the amount of domestic capital that can be used for this purpose is inadequate to meet the urgent requirements of the day.

Finally, the government should set up a special agency to study industrial problems and to coördinate all the functions of the government in promoting industrial development. This agency would also define minimum objectives for a national industrialization policy, periodically revised to keep pace with changes in the economy. As might be expected, the New Group would not allow the government to operate independently even on this general level of planning, for the officials who direct this agency are to be chosen from the ranks of recognized industrialists and technicians.

Credit.—In the eyes of the New Group credit conditions in Mexico are entirely unsatisfactory for industrial development. It is clear that they consider this handicap serious, and that they believe reforms in this field to be of vital importance.

A principal defect that the New Group finds in the present credit structure is the reluctance of the banks to make loans to industrial concerns. This reluctance does not hold for the older well-established manufacturing firms, as we have seen, but the newer and smaller firms feel it very strongly. The difficulty of getting credit from the banks is not only a bar to plant expansion but it is also a severe handicap in ordinary industrial operations that require more working capital than the owners are able to supply. Unable to get loans direct from the banks, small industrialists often have to borrow from other business establishments, especially from the large commercial firms (such as department stores) that do have immediate access to bank credit. Naturally, this middle step raises the cost of borrowing.

Even when borrowing is direct, however, rates of interest in Mexico are too high for the industrial welfare of the country. According to Lavín, an industrialist in Mexico is forced to pay 12 per cent for the same kind of a loan that would cost only 2½ per cent in the countries which are already industrially well-organized.[19]

---

[19] Lavín, *Dos conferencias*, p. 46.

Although a solution of the credit problem is obviously regarded by the New Group as an important question, their public statements thus far have dealt more with the defects of the existing system than with remedies for correcting it. Only in very broad terms have they outlined a credit program for Mexico.

Thus they argue that loans for industry should be given preference over all other financial requirements, but they say nothing about the mechanics needed to bring this about. Similarly, they stress the need for reducing interest rates on industrial loans, without specifying the measures which would achieve this objective. They also talk about changes which should be made in the laws applying to institutions that finance industry. The burden of such changes would be "to organize [these] institutions on bases similar to those prevailing in the developed countries. . . ."[20] Just what this would mean in concrete terms is not explained.

For one reason or another the leaders of the New Group have preferred to treat the positive side of the credit question delicately, rather than in their customary blunt manner. What they say about measures of credit reform by no means matches their estimate of the importance of the problem or the force with which they have criticized the banks for failing to meet their requirements.

One inference that can safely be drawn, however, is that the reforms must be achieved by government action. It is hard to believe that they would put any faith in a voluntary change of heart by Mexico's bankers, or at least in the chance that such a change would occur soon enough to do any good.

Furthermore, it is plausible to infer that the New Group would favor a government institution to supply industrial credit by means of direct loans. Such an organization would have a number of advantages from their standpoint. It would enable them to outflank the existing financial institutions. It would bring down rates of interest. And finally, successful operation would probably, in time, induce the commercial banks and their investment-banking affiliates to enter the field of financing small industrial firms on better terms for the borrowers.

Protection for the consumer.—One of the best testimonials to New Group thoroughness is the care with which they have worked out a program to protect the Mexican consumer. They frankly ask the consumer to make sacrifices—sacrifices that have to be made now in order to revolutionize the national economy and to lay the foundation for ultimate advantages in the form of higher standards of living. A temporary burden inevitably and justifiably falls on the consumer. But it is not justifiable to

[20] Cámara Nacional de la Industria de Transformación, *op. cit.,* p. 22.

allow the consumer to be made the victim of abuses. It is the duty of the government and of the industrialists themselves to protect the consumer by measures designed to insure the lowest prices consistent with adequate protection against foreign products and also consistent with the returns necessary to stimulate industrial investment and production in Mexico.

A principal guarantee for the consumer is found in competition, that is, in competition among domestic producers, since foreign competition is ruled out. Thus the government must take action to combat monopolies; measures similar to those used in the United States and other countries must be adopted. Details here are wanting, but apparently something like the Sherman Anti-Trust Act is intended. A related step would be to reform the existing law of monopolies to prevent it from being used as a means of promoting private gain at the expense of the general public. Again details are lacking, but this suggestion would seem to require a revamping of the policy by which, since 1937, certain industries have been declared "saturated" and therefore closed to the entry of new firms.[21]

Where direct antimonopoly policies prove ineffective, the abuse of private economic power can be curbed by appropriate tax measures. This is a favorite theme in the New Group literature, but unfortunately it is never developed or illustrated. It appears only as a general statement.[22]

But the industrialists must not leave consumer protection entirely to the government. They must take action on their own initiative. In the main this action must be directed against the merchants, who always appear in the New Group literature as the enemies of the public interest, in contrast with the industrialists who are working for the national good. This, it should be observed, is an important element in New Group propaganda. As a group the industrialists can do no wrong, because the only hope for social and economic progress in Mexico lies in industrialism. An exception has to be made only when foreign companies are involved. On rare occasions a true Mexican industrialist may behave contrary to the national interest, but he can easily be brought into line by pressure from his colleagues or by government antimonopoly measures. The industrialist is by nature a producer, not a speculator.

The merchant, it is granted, performs a useful function as a distributor and he is entitled to a return for this service. But the commercial interests of Mexico have levied on the community a greater charge than their services are worth. This is explained principally by two circumstances. One is speculation by merchant groups who have been in a position to dominate

---

[21] See chapter v.

[22] As an example I quote Lavín: ". . . The tax system to eradicate speculation will punish the speculator directly, and we think that there already exists an important group of industrialists who understand the situation sufficiently to coöperate loyally with it. . . ." (Dos conferencias, p. 51.)

transactions in important commodities. The excessively high prices caused by such operations have restricted the size of the market in Mexico, thus prejudicing the manufacturer as well as the consumer. The other condition which makes domestic commerce parasitic on the Mexican economy is the needless duplication of commercial establishments. The retail distribution system of Mexico, characterized by hundreds of tiny neighborhood stores and shops with two or three attendants in each one, is dreadfully inefficient and costly. Again, the burden is borne both by the consumer and the manufacturer.

The first of these two conditions, middleman speculation, is the one that the New Group industrialists are most concerned to eradicate. In the long run they hope to set up their own distributive outlets. Under this plan chains of stores established by manufacturing firms would sell products direct to the public. The middleman would be eliminated or at least subordinated. The industrialists realize, however, that it will take a long time to put such a system into operation, and therefore they are giving more emphasis to a scheme that could be applied at once.

Under the alternative plan the Mexican government would give industrialists the right to fix retail selling prices, allowing a suitable margin of profit for the various distributors. This, in effect, would convert the merchant into a commission agent for the manufacturer. Resale prices for consumer goods would be attached or stamped on the package, while those for raw materials and semifabricated goods would be published by the producers. The role of government in this plan, once the necessary legislation had been enacted, would be to enforce the prices fixed by the manufacturers. The producer would have complete autonomy in fixing his resale prices. No official agency would participate or interfere in the making of such decisions.

While the adoption of the pricing system just outlined is being awaited, the New Group leaders urge industrialists to sponsor consumer coöperatives among their workers. This development would have the double effect of putting immediate pressure on the merchants and of making the worker's wage go further. Of course, if a collateral effect were to reduce pressure for higher wages the industrialists would certainly have no objection.

International economic relations.—It is hardly necessary to say much about the New Group attitude on international economic relations, after what has already been brought out in the preceding pages. Their position is completely nationalistic. Mexico's only hope is industrialization. Industry must be wholly protected from foreign competition. We have already observed how this basic proposition finds expression in a highly restrictive import policy. Then, too, if Mexico is to get the maximum benefit from its industries they must be owned (or at least controlled) by Mexican citizens, for otherwise they will be subservient to foreign business interests and will be directed toward alien rather than national ends.[23]

Two additional legislative suggestions made by the New Group are intended to prevent the national program of industrialization from being sacrificed to internationalism. One of these would require the government to include representatives of industry and labor among the technical advisers attached to the Mexican delegation at any international conference where economic questions are discussed. As a further safeguard, the industry members would be selected by the national federation of industrial chambers (Confederación de Cámaras Industriales) rather than by the government.

The second measure would tie the hands of the government even more in making international economic commitments. It relates to commercial treaties. Mexico, like any other underdeveloped country, is reminded that it is not on an equal footing with the great manufacturing nations of the world and that it must take account of this fundamental fact in all international trade negotiations. The method suggested is simple, as the following quotation shows:

> In all commercial treaties Mexico must reserve the right to establish partial or complete restrictions on any importation that might injure its national economy under either normal or abnormal conditions.[24]

This obviously means more than the kind of flexibility allowed in the Mexican-American trade agreement,[25] since the agreement had been in force almost three years when the above words were written. If such a policy should be adopted, it would be virtually impossible for Mexico to participate in international agreements for lowering trade barriers, or even to negotiate commercial treaties with individual countries. Such a result would not displease the New Group. Indeed, it is fair to suggest that it is precisely the goal they are aiming at. From their standpoint any trade agreement is a weak link in the chain of protectionism with which they would encircle Mexican industry.[26]

---

[23] The New Group leaders approve the decree of July 7, 1944, which laid down the principle that any foreign interest in a Mexican business enterprise should be restricted to less than 50 per cent. (See chapter v.) They point out, however, that this principle has been violated in practice, and that both the law and its administration need to be made more rigid.

[24] Cámara Nacional de la Industria de Transformación, *op. cit.*, p. 29.

[25] *Reciprocal Trade Agreement Between the United States of America and Mexico* (Washington, 1943), Arts. X and XI.

[26] In October, 1946, it was announced that the Cámara Nacional de la Industria de Transformación would ask the Mexican government to terminate the trade agreement with the United States. Subsequently the Cámara conducted an active campaign, activated by paid advertisements in the press, to attain this objective. They won a partial victory in the decision of the Mexican government to open negotiations for a revision of the trade agreement. (See chapter v.)

Technical and vocational training.—Counting on a substantial and continuous industrial development in the future, the New Group industrialists properly concern themselves with technical training. It is obvious, they point out, that Mexico must equip itself with a technical personnel qualified to plan and direct industrial operations. One means of doing so would be to bring foreign technicians from abroad. To some extent this must be done. The practice, however, should be restricted to cases where highly specialized knowledge is called for in order to solve specific problems. It should not be the general rule.

The main effort in this field should go into providing scientific and engineering training for young Mexicans. Institutes specializing in such studies already exist in Mexico; more should be established. In all cases these should be financed by groups of industrialists and operated as private schools, although both government and labor should be represented on their directing boards. The government, on the other hand, should concentrate on vocational education of a much less advanced type, by setting up a large number of schools to teach industrial skills. From these schools industry will be able to recruit factory foremen as well as skilled workers.

The New Group believes in sending qualified young Mexicans abroad to learn the industrial methods used elsewhere. Apparently this, too, should be a government program. The students selected should, however, be imbued with a strong sense of patriotism and with the ideal of working to improve the well-being of the Mexican people, and they should be taught that they have a duty to fulfill when they return to Mexico. Just what this duty is supposed to be is not made clear in the New Group literature. Probably they mean that a young engineer, for example, should actually practice his profession when he gets back to Mexico instead of taking an easier and more lucrative position which requires no special technical knowledge, as has frequently happened. He must be guided by a spirit of self-sacrifice, and he must discipline himself accordingly.

Agriculture.—The leaders of the New Group are not the only industrialists in Mexico who talk about the need to stimulate agricultural production and to improve the lot of the farmer. They are unique, however, in that they are willing and even anxious to sit down with the leaders of agrarian groups to work out an agricultural program. In doing so, their principal concern is to find practical measures to increase farm output and farm buying power, necessary developments parallel to industrial expansion. It is doubtful whether they have any real interest in Mexico's agrarian problem per se, because from their viewpoint this problem will be solved in the long run by the economic and social progress resulting from industrialization. There are grounds for believing, too, that what the New Group leaders say on agricultural questions is opportunistically shaped toward gaining support from organized farm groups. Consequently, they may shift their ground from time to time, and they are even more likely to shift their emphasis on particular measures of a short-run character.

On the basis of the most recent statements available from New Group sources, the following are the principal measures they would have the Mexican government adopt in the agricultural field:

1). Continue the distribution of land in the form of *ejidos*.
2). Increase the size of holdings, both on irrigated and nonirrigated lands.
3). Open new lands to cultivation through irrigation, and also by means of drainage and health programs in the coastal areas.
4). Encourage the production and use of fertilizers and of farm machinery.
5). Assure adequate credit for farmers.
6). Fix minimum prices for farm products in advance of the crop season.

Absence of a detailed discussion such as they have given to industrial policy makes it difficult to know just what specific action they would recommend under each of these headings. Most of the proposals are phrased broadly. The two most specific commitments are the first and the last points, in which they favor further land distribution to ejidos and a government program to put a floor under farm prices. It is likely, however, that they will get down to cases on some of the other topics also, especially if their influence on national economic policy proves to be a growing one.

POPULAR APPEAL OF THE PROGRAM

The New Group program certainly has a number of elements which give it great popular appeal. It is more comprehensive and it is more specific than anything offered by any other business group. An outsider, it is true, might find the program vague or weak at critical places. It is the contrast with what others offer, however, that counts in Mexico, and on grounds of scope and detail the program of the New Group leads the field. It leads also in two other respects. It is a positive program rather than a negative one, and it has an up-to-date sound. The program rests (or, at least, appears to rest) upon an understanding of institutions as they exist in Mexico and in the world at large, and not, as is so often the case in Mexico, upon a desire to revive the prerevolutionary past. It is phrased in realistic terms. Moreover, it must be admitted that the antiforeign (especially anti-American) tone of the program is a good means of gaining public support in Mexico. In every way the program is a skilful work of propaganda.

The full propaganda value of the New Group program, however, is probably yet to be realized. There are good reasons for believing, as we shall see, that Mexico's rush to industrialize will give rise in turn to serious economic problems and social tensions. As the problems pile up and popular dissatisfaction mounts, the program of the New Group should gain headway because of its nationalistic character. It will be easy for the New Group to maintain that unfavorable developments in the economy, such as high prices, are caused by (1) conditions abroad, especially in the United States; (2) the activities of foreign companies; (3) speculative operations by Mexican merchants, who, by implication, are aligned with foreign interests. As a corollary, the solution will seem to lie in promoting the interests of Mexican firms, run by Mexican industrialists and using Mexican capital, that is, precisely the kind of firms represented by the New Group.

If it should be necessary to meet any direct criticisms of their industries for failing to supply consumer needs at satisfactory prices, the New Group can always fall back on the theme-song that the Mexican people must make temporary sacrifices in order to overcome their one hundred years of industrial backwardness and to attain ultimately standards of living like those found in the advanced manufacturing nations. In a period of economic distress, this theme of sacrifice for a great national purpose might help greatly in keeping public sentiment in line with their program.

Growing Influence of the New Group

Within the short space of a few years the New Group industrialists have made a place for themselves in Mexico and they have left their mark on national economic policy. Their influence has grown to the point where they must be reckoned with whenever the Mexican government is contemplating action which might affect domestic industry. But the leaders of the New Group do not always wait for the government to take the initiative. They have ideas, they mold them into practical suggestions, they put them before the appropriate government authorities and the public, and they work energetically to have them adopted. This aggressiveness will help them to extend their influence on Mexican policy.

The elements of popular appeal in the New Group program, brought out in the preceding section, give additional reasons for believing that the power of this group will become stronger rather than weaker in the years that lie ahead. The program makes it clear who is working for the interest of Mexico and who is working against it, in terms that the public feel they can understand. It caters to the deep-seated Mexican prejudice against foreigners (Americans). It caters to the distrust which a farming population inevitably feels toward merchants. And somewhere in the program is to be found a proposition that can be revamped to meet any situation likely to develop. No other business group in Mexico could possibly match the New Group on these grounds.

Finally, a source of growing strength for the New Group is found in the strategic alliances which they have made with labor and farm organizations. In each case the Cámara Nacional de la Industria de Transformación has established cordial relations with the principal organization in the field—the CTM for labor, and the Confederación Nacional de Campesinos for farmers. The three bodies occasionally hold round-table discussions on Mexican economic problems. When they touch the broader aspects of industrialism, the conclusions reached are obviously by-products of New Group thinking, as was true of the famous labor-management pact of April, 1945. To have the numerical weight of Mexico's leading labor and farm federations behind their program is politically a great advantage for the New Group.

It may strike the reader that the New Group program is too ambitious in scope and that many of its recommendations for Mexican economic policy are both extreme and unwise. While agreeing with this line of criticism, I should at the same time like to emphasize my belief, that the New Group is in the ascendancy and that the leaders will exercise a growing influence on the economic policies of the Mexican government.

In the leadership of the New Group idealism and practical abilities are combined in a way that usually gets results. They have an obvious self-interest in the industrial expansion of Mexico, but they also sincerely believe that industrialism is the only "way out" for Mexico and that their efforts will surely lead to higher standards of living for all the Mexican people. Critics are inclined to underestimate this sincerity, and in consequence they underestimate the power of these men to recruit and to hold a following. But the New Group leaders have missionary zeal, and they have the energy, determination, and skill necessary to make that zeal count. Actually, they are eager to fight a battle for any member of their group, no matter how small the issues may be, for they make capital out of the fight itself. Then, too, they invariably magnify the specific issue into a general case, thus scoring points for their program as a whole.

That the New Group leaders do not yield easily is evident to anyone who has followed recent events in Mexico with even a casual interest. Doubtless they will suffer setbacks and they will be forced to accept compromises. On balance, however, they can be counted upon to make gains, and it is probable that Mexican economic policy will move substantially in the direction they advocate.

CHAPTER IV

Government Economic Policy

INDUSTRIALIZATION was made the central feature of economic policy in Mexico by President Manuel Avila Camacho, after he took office in December, 1940, and the tendency to emphasize manufacturing development became defined with increasing clarity during the six years of his administration. At the present time the government of President Miguel Alemán is carrying forward the same policy with great vigor. President Alemán has, if anything, stronger convictions than his predecessor about the need for industrialization in Mexico.

CÁRDENAS ADMINISTRATION

In pinning their hopes for Mexico's future on industrialization, Manuel Avila Camacho and Miguel Alemán have departed from the thinking which dominated the Cárdenas administration of the period 1935–1940. To Lázaro Cárdenas, the solution for Mexico's economic, social, and political problems lay in carrying out the agrarian reform program that came out of the Mexican Revolution, that is, in getting land distributed to the peasants, in putting the ejidos (agricultural communities reëstablished or newly established under the agrarian laws) on a permanent basis, in strengthening the ejidos through coöperative practices, and in providing financial and technical assistance to the farmers who operated in the ejido system. Other developments were not neglected, and certainly important things happened elsewhere in the economy, as the oil expropriation incident of 1938 testifies, but agricultural policy was the main preoccupation.

The rate at which Cárdenas speeded up the application of Mexico's agrarian laws can be seen quickly in the figures on the amount of land distributed. When Cárdenas came to the presidency at the end of 1934 the agrarian program had been in operation for twenty years. In this twenty-year period about 8.3 million hectares of land had been parceled out to peasants. In the six years of his term (1935 through 1940 figures) Cárdenas distributed 18.6 million hectares, or more than twice as much as the amount of land made available to peasants in the twenty years preceding. Actually, when Cárdenas left office, he had accounted for 70 per cent of the total land distribution program up to his time. This achievement took up much of the time and energy of the whole Cárdenas administration.

Apart from making agricultural land available to rural communities, Cárdenas did much to incorporate the ejido into the economic and social structure of Mexico. He viewed the ejido, with collective ownership of lands, as a permanent institution and not as a transition stage to individual ownership of holdings. So strong were his convictions on this question, and so clear-cut his policies, that he gave a definite orientation to Mexican agrarian policy where wavering and uncertainty had prevailed before.

The basic measure that initiated the agrarian program in Mexico was a decree issued in January, 1915. For the first eight years of the program virtually no attention was paid to the economic and social organization of the ejido. Then, in 1922, it was decided that ejidos should be organized along coöperative and communal lines, and for three years thereafter an attempt was made to enforce a program which has been appropriately described as "simple collectivism."[1] This policy was abandoned, however, in 1925 when the Law of Ejido Patrimony was enacted, categorically providing that individual ownership would ultimately prevail for crop lands in the ejido. This amounted to making the ejido a method of redistributing land from large to small holders. The ejido was not to be an end in itself.

In practice, few tangible results came out of the Law of Ejido Patrimony. Perhaps its main achievement was to open a lively discussion of all issues relating to goals and methods of Mexican agrarian policy, including the question of the permanence of the ejido. While opposing points of view became more sharply defined, however, administration of the agrarian laws was haphazard and uncertain. No main course was being followed when Cárdenas was elected president.

To Cárdenas the ejido was the essence of the traditional social life of the Mexican Indian. His policy, therefore, was clearly defined; the ejido must be permanent. It followed, of course, that ejido lands must remain perpetually in community ownership. Also, it followed that steps must be taken to enable those who lived in the ejidos to improve their productivity and their material welfare. It was the concept of permanence of the ejido that gave shape and consistency, as well as force and vitality, to the Cárdenas agricultural program.

Financial and technical assistance figured prominently among the Cárdenas measures designed to improve the position of the ejido farmers. A new public bank, the Banco Nacional de Crédito Ejidal, was created to take over the job of supplying credit to such farmers. In splitting off this credit function from other agricultural credit, with which it had been merged under the previous setup, it was the intention of Cárdenas to make more funds available for this special purpose—that is, to increase the total

---

[1] Eyler Simpson, *The Ejido* (Chapel Hill, 1937), p. 321.

amount and also to increase the ratio of ejido credit to other kinds of agricultural credit. The Banco Nacional de Crédito Ejidal was organized in 1935 with a capitalization of 120 million pesos. This was larger than the capital of the existing farmers' bank, which had been handling all kinds of credit.

The Cárdenas program of technical assistance to ejidos included expert advice on all phases of farming operations. Specialists, often associated with the Banco Nacional de Crédito Ejidal, were sent to the ejidos to give counsel on crop planning, seed selection, methods of tillage, and marketing. Guidance of this kind had been provided before, but only on a very small scale. It was now made a major undertaking of the government. An effort was also made to provide farm machinery by setting up government-operated centrals from each of which a number of ejidos could draw equipment.

One of the outstanding features of the Cárdenas agrarian program was the development of the collectivized ejido, in which the lands belonging to the village were not only owned in common but were also cultivated in common by the peasants. This type of ejido was designed to meet special circumstances where the ordinary ejido, with individual cultivation of allotted parcels, would have meant a great sacrifice in advantages obtainable under large-scale production. These advantages sometimes had been realized by previous owners of the land, but sometimes they were of a purely potential nature. Each case presented unique features. In every one, however, large-scale operations were indicated because of the nature of the crops raised, methods of production, processing requirements, or irrigation conditions, or a combination of such factors.

The best-known and most significant experiment in collective operation of ejidos has taken place in the Laguna region, Mexico's oldest and most important cotton-producing area. This cotton belt lies in a large arid basin in north-central Mexico (in the vicinity of the city of Torreón) where cultivation has been made possible by irrigation development.

Until 1936 the Laguna region was untouched by agrarian reform. Large landholdings deriving from Spanish colonial titles had continued to dominate in the area, although by this time they were owned mostly by foreigners rather than Mexicans. On the whole, modern methods of agriculture were employed on these large-scale farms. However, the men who worked the land, whether renters, sharecroppers, or wage earners, were essentially peons in the pre-Revolutionary sense. Agitation for land reform had not been lacking, as is shown by numerous petitions to the federal government in the late 1920's, but no headway had been made in applying the agrarian code to the Laguna region.

The main result of this pressure for land reform was to induce the big landowners to make up a purse of 2,500,000 pesos for buying tracts of land on the outskirts of the region, for distribution among the landless inhabitants of the Laguna district. The land so purchased was turned over to the Mexican government to make the actual distribution. This attempt to stave off more far-reaching measures, however, took care of but a small fraction of the peasants, and basic conditions in the region were left unchanged.

In 1935 a new factor appeared in the form of labor organization, and soon the majority of the peasants of the Laguna were incorporated into unions. As they gained in group strength they became more militant about demands that the plantation owners pay higher wages, supply better housing, and provide some medical services. A number of strikes took place. The settlements arrived at were of short duration, and tension mounted progressively. Finally, in the late summer of 1936, a general strike of cotton pickers precipitated a conflict so acute that open violence became the order of the day in the Laguna area.

When this state of affairs was reached Cárdenas moved with the same boldness and dispatch that he showed subsequently in the oil expropriation affair. With one blanket decree he expropriated all the large landholdings in the Laguna region. This made about 60 per cent of the irrigated land of the area, and 10 per cent of the nonirrigated land, available for distribution to the rural inhabitants. Then, gathering a corps of government specialists about him, Cárdenas went to the Laguna region and spent more than a month there working out plans for collectivized ejidos.

The Laguna land reform episode was one of the spectacular events of the Cárdenas regime which tended to frighten private capital, both Mexican and foreign. The reaction in the Laguna case was strong. For one thing, a large and highly productive area was involved. Also, the expropriation occurred unexpectedly and dramatically. It involved lands owned by foreigners. And, finally, it led to a major experiment in collectivized agriculture, in that most of the lands in the area were to be cultivated coöperatively and not individually as in the typical ejido.

In the Laguna case, the decision to organize collective ejidos was based on three conditions. One was the erratic nature of the irrigation supply, with great variations from year to year in the amount of water available. If individual holdings had been established it would have been difficult, if not impossible, to guarantee each year an equitable, and at the same time effective, distribution of irrigation water. A second condition was the existence of a network of canals available for large units. To break these units into small holdings would have entailed heavy outlays for a new network of minor canals to bring water to each new unit. Finally, economies through using modern farm equipment, already developed in the area, would have been sacrificed to a significant extent by individual operation of small holdings.

Other experiments in collectivized agriculture, similar in nature to that of the Laguna although less spectacular, were undertaken by Cárdenas in areas devoted to the production of rice, coffee, henequen, and sugar.

In connection with sugar, Cárdenas took steps to revive, reorganize, and stimulate the refining end of the industry as well as the growing of sugar cane. One of his most important projects was in the valley of Morelos, where a flourishing prerevolutionary sugar industry had been utterly ruined by bitter and bloody fighting during the ten years of strife following the overthrow of Porfirio Díaz. Every sugar mill in this area had been wrecked. Wild native vegetation had invaded the cane fields and taken them over. Where cultivated fields were found they were mostly used for raising corn to yield a meager subsistence for peasants who had acquired small holdings under the agrarian laws. Sugar production in Morelos had been reduced to negligible amounts. Mexico had come to depend for its sugar supply on new areas in Sinaloa and Tamaulipas.

To rehabilitate the economy of Morelos the Cárdenas administration decided to build a large, completely modern sugar refinery at Zacatepec in the Morelos Valley. This mill, completed in 1938, was made a coöperative venture in which both refinery workers and peasants participated. The element of coöperation ran through the whole project. The peasants who raised the sugar cane were organized into a number of coöperatives. Then, as a group they participated in the management of the mill, coöperatively with the refinery employees.

The Zacatepec sugar project illustrates the Cárdenas point of view on industrial development in Mexico. Essentially the only kind of manufacturing he was interested in promoting was rural industry organized along coöperative lines. His basic philosophy led him to tie industry to agriculture. Thus the processing of farm products by rural industry appealed to him. Also, he wanted to encourage that type of industrial development which would permit the inhabitants of the small villages to dovetail industry with the cultivation of their fields. Such a development was to be made possible by coöperation plus an appropriate technology (e.g., the electric motor).

There was little place in the Cárdenas philosophy, therefore, for the building of large-scale industrial plants or for the growth of urban industrial centers. Industry was to be brought to the rural people in their small villages. The rural people were not to be forced into industrial cities. In

this way he hoped to obtain for the Mexican population the material advantages which industry could provide, without engendering the evils of
urban industrialism. No better expression of his ideal can be asked for
than the following quotation from an address by one of the officials of
his administration, delivered at the Institute of Public Affairs at the University of Virginia in July, 1935.

Some of us in Mexico have visualized differently the future of agricultural economy. We believe that Mexico finds herself in a privileged position to determine her
destiny. By being in a pre-capitalistic state with some of her people even in a pre-
pecuniary economy and at the same time by observing the effects of the last crisis
of the capitalistic world, we think that we should be able to use the advantages of
the industrial era without having to suffer from its well-known shortcomings. We
think that we should attempt to industrialize Mexico consciously, intelligently
avoiding the avoidable evils of industrialism, such as urbanism, exploitation of man
by man, production for sale instead of production for the satisfaction of human
needs, economic insecurity, waste, shabby goods and the mechanization of the
workmen. This is not an impossible dream. We are convinced that the evils of
capitalism are not to be found in the application of machinery to the productive
process, but rather are due to a merely legal question: who is the owner of the machinery. We want the land and its necessary equipment to be at the disposal of
those who till it, rather than be the means of exploiting these men. Some of us
believe, furthermore, that profit making is not the only incentive of human en-
deavour, but rather a motive that happens to have been chosen and over-developed
in the capitalistic regime.

There is nothing fatal in the mistakes of the system, or at least so we hope. We
have dreamt of a Mexico of "Ejidos" and small industrial communities, electrified,
with sanitation, in which goods will be produced for the purpose of satisfying the
needs of the people; in which machinery will be employed to relieve man from
heavy toil, and not for so-called over-production. In these communities machine-
made goods may still be beautiful for they will be made by the same people whose
artistic sense is now expressed by the work of their hands, and there is no reason
to believe that the changing tools will *per se* make them different. What mechanizes
men is not the use of machinery, it is the pressure brought to bear upon them to
produce at the highest speed the largest amount possible.[2]

Ironically, these words were spoken by the same man who now occupies
the post of Minister of Finance in the Alemán cabinet, Ramón Beteta. In
his present capacity he is active in trying to build large-scale, urban industrialism in Mexico, with the participation of foreign capital. There is little
in common between his outlook in 1935 and his outlook in 1947. In shifting
from the one to the other, he typifies the change that has taken place in
official economic philosophy since Cárdenas left office.

There has, therefore, been no continuity in government industrial policy

[2] Ramón Beteta, "Economic Aspects of the Six-Year Plan," in *Economic and Social Program
of Mexico* (Mexico, 1935), pp. 44 ff.

between the Cárdenas administration and those which have followed. Nevertheless, what went on in Mexico during the time of Cárdenas has had an indirect effect on the subsequent industrial development. Two main influences can be distinguished.

One of these relates to government spending for public works. Such expenditures were enlarged greatly after Lázaro Cárdenas assumed office, as the government embarked upon a big program of constructing irrigation projects, roads, water supply and sewage systems, schools, and other public buildings. These outlays gave a strong direct stimulus to the construction industries that were supplying materials for the public works, and through them the stimulus was passed on to other industries. The total of wage payments was expanded. Added purchasing power in the hands of wage earners expressed itself in a growing demand for consumer goods, including processed foods. A noticeable lift was given to all branches of industry by the public works program of the Cárdenas administration. In 1938, according to one study, real output in manufacturing was 25 per cent higher than it had been in 1933.[8] This increase, however, resulted from larger output in existing industries by a more intensive use of existing equipment, rather than from the establishment of new industries or plant expansion in the older ones.

To make the public works program possible, the Mexican government indulged in deficit financing, in which borrowing from the central bank played an important part. The supply of money, therefore, was expanded by the expenditures for public works, and an inflationary process was set in motion. By 1938 the rise in prices, especially sharp in the preceding year, was a cause of concern to the government. However, the dislocation caused by expropriation of the foreign oil companies in 1938 led to yet further measures of an inflationary character, with the result that the Mexican price level was rising at a rapid pace when the Second World War broke out.

I must reserve until later a full discussion of the inflationary situation in Mexico. For the moment I am dealing with the period of the Cárdenas administration, almost all of which lay in the prewar years. Although it must be granted that inflation was tending to erode away the stimulus to industry given by the public works program, it is probable that the benefits of the public works expenditures to the economy as a whole were greater than the damages suffered through inflation prior to the outbreak of the Second World War. Furthermore, an impulse was given to manufacturing development which facilitated subsequent expansion during the war years and served as a base for it.

[8] Raúl F. Cárdenas, "Política ocupacional," *Investigación Económica*, vol. 5, no. 2 (2d quarter, 1945), p. 155.

The reactions of the business community to the Cárdenas administration form the second main line of influence on Mexico's current industrialization development. The accelerated pace of social reform, especially in the agrarian program, an official tendency to favor labor in industrial disputes, and the expropriation of the foreign oil companies, all contributed to produce an atmosphere of uncertainty in Mexican commercial, industrial, and financial circles. This atmosphere was not newly created during the Cárdenas administration. It existed already as an outcome of the upheaval which started in 1911. No country can go through ten years of such internal warfare as Mexico experienced between 1911 and 1920 without business and investment psychology being profoundly affected for many years thereafter. Then, too, social experimentation and a certain amount of political instability during the 1920's helped to keep business men in an uneasy frame of mind. When Cárdenas came to the presidency in 1934, reluctance to make long-term investment (except in real property) was already a well-established attitude in Mexico.

However justifiable they may have been on other grounds of an economic nature, and on a social and political basis, it must be admitted that government policies during the Cárdenas administration made potential investors even more timid than usual. Hoarding increased. It was already customary for persons with means to hold substantial balances and investments abroad, particularly in the United States. After the oil expropriation incident in March, 1938, the flight of capital from Mexico assumed large proportions. Some of the additional funds that went abroad or into hoards would probably have gone into long-term investment in industry if it had not been for the Cárdenas policies.

This exaggerated reluctance to make long-term industrial investment was probably not considered a serious obstacle to economic development by the Cárdenas administration. But the heritage of this fear to invest has carried over into the period in which manufacturing has become the mainstay of the government's program for economic advance. In this way the reactions of business men to the Cárdenas program have had a retarding influence on the industrialization program of the Avila Camacho and Alemán administrations.

Avila Camacho Administration

Before Manuel Avila Camacho took office as president at the end of 1940 he had not formulated an economic program directed toward the industrialization of Mexico. Indeed, it is doubtful whether he held any firm convictions of a positive nature about the course of Mexican economic development. His strongest convictions seem to have been on the negative side, in the direction of slowing up the rate of social change which had been maintained for six years under Lázaro Cárdenas. From this point of view, it was especially necessary to slow up the land distribution and other agrarian programs. It is not unlikely, therefore, that Avila Camacho and his advisers came to a pro-industrialization program as a substitute for the agricultural program of Cárdenas. War conditions were in any event beginning to favor manufacturing development. Might this not offer a new and more orderly approach to the solution of Mexico's economic problems? Did not industrialization rather than the ejido point to the best "way out" for Mexico?

By the end of the first year of the Avila Camacho administration one major step had been taken in favor of industrialization, the enactment of the law of manufacturing industries.[4] Furthermore, the opinion had already crystallized within administration circles that manufacturing development should be pushed with full vigor. "Upon beginning the second year of its labors," said Eduardo Suárez, Minister of Finance,

the Administration proposes to work actively for the industrialization of the Mexican Republic, until this is attained. The State does not want to take the role of enterpriser, but rather to help private enterprise to take charge of transforming [the economy of] the country. The plan is to make ample credit at reduced rates of interest available to business men who wish to assume responsibility for expanding production, and who are also prepared to invest some capital in industries which the State is anxious to see developed.

Mexico will manufacture a good portion of the articles which she now imports, in order to reduce, in time, her outlays abroad. It is proposed to produce [in Mexico] all the steel consumed . . . , cellulose and derivatives, parafine and lubricants, vegetable oils, chemical products, and cement. . . .[5]

This statement suggested other lines of policy designed to promote industrial development, especially in providing attractive credit conditions. Details about what was actually done will be found below.[6] Here it is only necessary to point out that the pro-industrialization program of the Avila Camacho administration was progressively broadened and intensified during the remainder of its period. By the end of 1946 industrialization was clearly the heart of the government's economic policy.

ALEMÁN ADMINISTRATION

The economic outlook of Miguel Alemán, who succeeded to the presidency in December, 1946, is a logical extension of the viewpoint of Avila Camacho. In campaigning for election, Alemán made "industrialization" one of his

---

[4] This subsidy measure is discussed in chapter v.
[5] Press interview, quoted in an information bulletin of the Ministry of Foreign Relations, *Noticias de México*, año 1, no. 25, December 10, 1941, p. 5.
[6] On credit policy, see chapter xii.

three slogans, the only slogan relating to economic questions, since the remaining two dealt with other issues. His first Minister of National Economy was a prominent industrialist and an aggressive advocate of Mexican industrialization. Far from deviating from the path marked out by his predecessor, President Alemán is anxious to speed up the industrialization process, an impulse which can be explained partly by ambition to advance the material welfare of his nation during his term in office and partly by the need for greater output to combat inflationary pressures.

The methods used by Alemán to encourage industrial development are the same as those of the Avila Camacho administration, with one main difference of degree. Chiefly because of his desire to accelerate the rate of industrialization, he has gone much further than Avila Camacho in inviting foreign capital to participate in the economic development of Mexico. The Avila Camacho administration was cordial to American capital but was cautious about making this apparent to the Mexican public, in view of the strong reaction of the Mexican people to the events leading to the oil expropriation incident of 1938.

Alemán has taken a bolder approach. He and leading members of his cabinet, notably Ramón Beteta, Minister of Finance, have openly announced that they want American capital to participate in Mexico's economic development. Details about what they have said and done in this respect will be given below. Here it is sufficient to point out that there is a substantial difference between the Avila Camacho and the Alemán administrations in degree of receptiveness towards the inflow of capital from the United States. Under Alemán the door is being opened wider and a strong effort is being made to convince the Mexican public of the national advantages to be gained from this change in attitude.

In this chapter we have brought out the pronounced shift in the economic policy of the Mexican government after Manuel Avila Camacho replaced Lázaro Cárdenas as president. Since the early days of the Avila Camacho administration, the Mexican government has acted to promote industrialization. This policy has been carried forward with ever-increasing vigor. Industrialization has been made the great national goal, and the Mexican people are told, by every means of communication through which they can be reached, that the promise of a better life for them and for future generations is to be found in the transformation of Mexico from an agricultural to a manufacturing nation. Under Alemán, it is clear that the government is committed to a strong proindustrialization policy.

Some of the specific government measures to promote industry have been mentioned in this chapter, principally by way of illustration. These measures, and others, will now be examined in detail.

CHAPTER V

Government and Industry

IN THIS CHAPTER I shall examine the proindustrialization policies of the Mexican government in detail. These policies have been grouped under several headings of a convenient nature. Little will be said of interconnections among the various types of policies, for such interconnections as have prevailed have been of a minor order. Indeed, the policies can be said to form a whole only in the loose sense that they are directed toward the same broad end of stimulating industrial development. It is entirely appropriate to consider each arm of government policy as an independent line of action.

TAX EXEMPTION

One of the mainstays of Mexico's proindustrialization policy is tax exemption, a familiar device which has been employed in many countries as a means of inducing people to set up new manufacturing plants. Tax exemption, of course, is a subsidy measure. Inasmuch as the state gives up a part, or all, of its tax claim against an enterprise, the revenues thus sacrificed must be made up by extra levies upon other sources of government revenue. There is no need to discuss here the question, mainly of theoretical interest, of the way this subsidy burden may ultimately be distributed throughout the economy. For practical purposes, it can be said that the nation as a whole bears the cost of the subsidy. The people as a group pay for the subsidy in order to get the benefits, to be realized subsequently, of the industrial development which is being promoted in this form.

The principle of encouraging industrial development by means of tax exemption found its way into postrevolutionary Mexican policy some years before the current industrialization drive was launched. It started with a government decree in .1926. Only a restricted number of firms, however, could qualify for tax exemptions under this decree. Its benefits were confined to firms with a capital of less than 5,000 pesos. Nothing but a very small establishment, therefore, could enjoy the privileges available under the 1926 decree. In 1932 the restriction on capital was loosened somewhat, but still only a small number of firms could qualify for tax-exemption concessions.

It was not until 1939 that a new decree removed the capital limitation clause, thus opening the privileged field to any new firm of whatever size.

This step can be considered the real, legal beginning of the policy of subsidizing industrial expansion by means of tax concessions. However, since the Cárdenas administration was not interested in promoting manufacturing development on a broad front, the greater opportunities provided by the 1939 decree were not cultivated actively.

In 1941, with a new administration in office, an administration, as we have observed, holding a different economic outlook from that which preceded it, and with war conditions abroad beginning to make themselves felt in reduced exports of manufactured goods to Mexico, a more formal measure was enacted to encourage manufacturing expansion by tax concessions. This took the form of a law of manufacturing industries (Ley de Industrias de Transformación).

The act of 1941 authorized the Minister of National Economy to make concessions on taxes for five years (1) to new industries, and (2) to industries deemed necessary for the development of manufacturing in Mexico. To qualify for the privileges created by this law, therefore, a firm did not have to represent a new industry in a literal sense. If the position of an older firm in the whole industrial structure was considered strategic, in the sense that when the firm expanded its scale and output, this would make possible other lines of industrial expansion, it, too, could receive full benefits under the law. No age limitation was specified for a firm that qualified in other ways. It was left entirely to the discretion of the Minister of National Economy to decide whether a concern applying for tax concessions should receive such privileges. Likewise, the Minister of National Economy was to determine the degree of tax concession in each particular case.

The kinds of taxes which the Minister of National Economy was allowed to waive under the law of manufacturing industries included all the principal taxes collected by the federal government of Mexico, namely, income, excess profits, stamp, and industrial taxes. Any one of these was likely to represent a significant item to an industrial firm. If all were waived, the subsidy would be very substantial in amount.

In addition to releasing a firm from the payment of taxes, the Minister of National Economy was authorized by the same law to make concessions on customs duties. He could grant to such a firm the right to import free of duty all the materials and equipment which it had to purchase abroad. Similarly, he could waive the export duties on products which it shipped to foreign markets. This concession on export duties included the special aforo tax as well as the duties in the regular schedules.

To safeguard the national interest, the Minister of National Economy was required by the law of manufacturing industries to make a biennial check of the firms benefiting from the act. Also, he was enjoined to set up and enforce minimum standards of quality for the articles produced by such firms. These provisions of the act, it may now be observed, have not been taken very seriously.

The subsidy policy set in motion by the law of 1941 was given a new impulse by a law enacted in February, 1946, the law of manufacturing development (Ley de Fomento de Industrias de Transformación). This measure was enacted in order to expand, strengthen, and refine the policy already in operation, rather than to make a new departure in the tax-exemption program. It is the law which is now in force; no new developments have taken place since it was enacted.

The law of manufacturing development provides a threefold classification for firms which are deemed worthy of tax concessions. The first group includes firms that are "fundamental for the industrial development of the country." These, the most important concerns, are to receive tax exemptions for a period of ten years. In the second class are placed firms "of economic importance," and they are to enjoy the benefits of the law for seven years. The last group, into which all other firms fall, remain under the five-year rule established by the earlier law.

The principal change effected by the law of 1946 is the lengthening of the tax-free period. For firms falling into the first group the period has been doubled. The law itself says nothing about which industries are worthy of the designation "fundamental for the industrial development of the country." This is a question to be decided by the Minister of National Economy. A list of such industries, and also a similar list for the seven-year group, is supposed to be prepared and published in the *reglamento* (administrative regulations) of the law. As late as December, 1947, the reglamento had not yet been issued, however, and the Minister of National Economy was fixing classifications for each individual case.

Although five-year tax exemptions were retained for the third group, the broad designation used for group two suggests an intention to raise the effective minimum to seven years. The unqualified term, "of economic importance," certainly allows great latitude in the definition of this class.

The law of 1946 grants the privilege of ten- and seven-year tax exemptions to properly qualified firms which had received their concessions under the act of 1941. They do not have to wait for their five-year exemptions to run out, but may apply for the extended concessions at any time.

In one sense, the 1946 law is less generous than its predecessor. It does not permit the waiving of export duties or of the aforo tax on exports. This change, reducing the incentive to export articles produced by privileged firms, was made because of the tight supply situation which prevailed for many manufactured goods.

Two other clauses of the law of manufacturing development deserve to be mentioned, although at the moment it is not clear just what use the government will make of them. When the reglamento for the law is issued this question may be clarified, but there is no way of knowing when this action will take place. Meanwhile, these two provisions are potentially important arms of government proindustrialization policy because they give broad powers to the executive branch of the government.

One of the clauses authorizes the president to prescribe tariff changes which he considers essential for the development of the new and necessary industries receiving privileges under the law of manufacturing development. This means authority to make changes in tariff rates without recourse to Congress, changes for which no limit has been set. The power conferred by this clause is certainly a broad one, inasmuch as the industries coming under the law produce a wide range of manufactured articles. For this purpose it is the range of goods produced, and not their volume of production, which is important. Unless limited by the reglamento, therefore, the president now has authority to make tariff changes at will on most of the manufactured articles that Mexico produces.

The other clause provides that any firm exporting domestic raw materials must first satisfy the raw-material needs of the new and necessary industries at the lowest export prices. Here again the implications are broad, although less significant than in the preceding case. Strictly interpreted, this clause would require permanent export control (licensing) for virtually every raw material produced in Mexico, including minerals as well as agricultural, pastoral, and forest products. From the standpoint of the whole Mexican economy, the delays and obstructions attendant upon export licensing of raw materials could easily offset any advantages accruing to the manufacturing industries. This provision of the law of manufacturing development, therefore, may never be made effective, or it may be used only in isolated, extreme cases.

A number of state governments in Mexico have also adopted a policy of subsidizing "new and necessary" industries by means of tax exemptions. Such concessions are additional to those given by the federal government. Details about the state laws and their operation are now hard to get. The best information available on this question is the material being assembled by the industrial research staff of the Bank of Mexico. Much remains to be done, however, before all relevant material is gathered, classified, and evaluated.

The state laws do not as a group promise to be significant because the level of industrial development in most states is low and likely to remain so indefinitely. Mexican industry is concentrated in four or five principal areas. Outside of Mexico City and the Federal District in which it lies, new manufacturing plants have been springing up mainly in the states of Mexico, Nuevo León, and Jalisco. All of these have tax-exemption laws.

The state of Mexico, which borders the Federal District on three sides, is especially generous in concessions to industries that locate in designated "industrial zones." Most of these zones are adjacent to the northern limit of the Federal District, where they are still within easy reach of the heart of Mexico City. There is no doubt that the very attractive privileges offered by the state of Mexico have been successful in drawing factories across the state line. Such privileges can be enjoyed for periods ranging from eight to twenty years, with the larger firms getting the longer tax exemptions.

The state of Nuevo León, which includes the active, basically industrial center of Monterrey, requires new industrial firms to pay only 25 per cent of their tax bills for periods running from five to twenty years. Tax concessions are also made to induce established concerns to expand their plant capacity.

The Federal District, consisting of Mexico City and environs, is analogous to the District of Columbia in that it is under the jurisdiction of the federal government. A presidential decree issued in the latter part of 1944 permits "new and necessary" industries in the Federal District to enjoy very substantial savings on local taxes for periods ranging from two to ten years. In addition, the same decree requires the government of the Federal District to assist new industrial firms to get land at low prices, and to provide at its own expense means of access (roads) to the new plants. All concessions granted by the Federal District, it should be observed, are additional to any that might be made by the federal government under the law of manufacturing development.

TARIFF POLICY

Mexican import duties in the past, as the New Group points out, have been levied chiefly for revenue purposes. A protectionist element, however, has been present in the tariff structure from the very early years of the national period.[1] This element has by no means been negligible. The hope, if not the effort, to become an industrialized country is a long-standing one in Mexico, and protective tariffs have been accepted as a principal means to this end by successive governments. Since actual industrial achievements have fallen far short of expectations over the life span of the nation, the burden thrown upon the Mexican public by protective tariffs on articles

[1] See Daniel Cosío Villegas, *La cuestión arancelaria en México: historia de la política aduanal* (Mexico, 1932); also the brief summary of Mexican tariff policy by Antonio Manero, "El fomento industrial de México," *Memoria del Segundo Congreso Mexicano de Ciencias Sociales* (Mexico, 1946), vol. 2, pp. 223–225.

of primary consumption has been excessive. Many, perhaps most, of the benefits which the consumer was to receive one day in compensation for his sacrifices are yet to be realized.[2]

If Mexico's tariff policy is viewed as a whole, the following stand out as main features.[3] First, the highest duties are generally found on agricultural products and foodstuffs that compete with domestic production, although individual items in other classes may be subjected to more extreme duties. Second, relatively high rates apply to manufactured articles that can be produced in Mexico, and to luxury items. Third, moderate revenue duties are collected on raw materials, machinery and equipment not produced in Mexico but which are needed by domestic manufacturing plants. Fourth, free entry has frequently applied for commodities of prime necessity, mining materials and equipment, supplies for ship construction and repair, and materials used by the federal and state governments.

The basic tariff law now in force in Mexico dates from the year 1930, although a number of modifications have been made in the intervening years. According to an analysis made by the Oficina de Estudios Especiales del Comité de Aforos y Subsidios al Comercio Exterior,[4] when the act of 1930 first took effect the commodity group bearing the heaviest duties was that of textiles and textile products. All Mexican duties have been specific, but *ad valorem* equivalents have been readily ascertainable. Thus, the levies on textiles and textile products in 1930 ranged from 40 to 100 per cent of their values. Also in the high-duty category were numerous food products, such as canned meats, eggs, lard, corn, wheat, and sugar.

Other commodities given substantial protection in the tariff law of 1930 include the following items, all of which were subject to duties on which the *ad valorem* equivalent amounted to 25 per cent or more: wool; leather; cotton; cotton seed; copra; essential oils; lubricating oils; paraffin; crude rubber; furniture; iron and steel manufactures; caustic soda; potassium and sodium chlorate; paints and varnishes; tanning extracts; alcoholic beverages; motion pictures; paper; felt hats; keys; valves.

Finally, such items as the following were subjected to purely revenue duties in the tariff of 1930: construction lumber; scrap iron; refractory brick; large-diameter pipe; copper; hides; Kraft paper; books; numerous chemical and medicinal products.

During the 1930's the general level of the Mexican tariff moved upwards. Many of the changes were designed to bolster the revenues which

---

[2] Oficina de Estudios Especiales del Comité de Aforos y Subsidios al Comercio Exterior, "Problemas del comercio exterior," *Memoria del Segundo Congreso Mexicano de Ciencias Sociales*, vol. 3, p. 240.

[3] Based on United States Tariff Commission, *Economic Controls and Commercial Policy in Mexico*, p. 9.

[4] *Op. cit.*, vol. 3, pp. 241–242.

the government was getting from customs duties. Others were made in order to restore the protection lost when foreign prices fell in relation to Mexican prices. The revision of January, 1938, which covered about one-third of the items subject to duties, for example, has been justified as such an offsetting measure.[5]

One effect of the changes, although perhaps incidental, was to extend and strengthen protection for domestic industries. Thus, the modifications made in January, 1937, raised the duties on many items, including a number of manufactured articles competitive with the output of Mexican industries.[6] Then, a further revision in January, 1938, brought increases ranging from 25 to 400 per cent. These duties were in many cases prohibitive.[7]

The peak duties of this measure lasted less than a year. By the time they were reduced, however, the exchange value of the Mexican peso had fallen considerably as a consequence of the petroleum expropriation incident. Whereas in March, 1938, the peso was valued at 3.60 to the dollar, by the end of the year it had slumped to around 5.00 per dollar. For the year 1939, the average rate was 5.18. Mexican industry, therefore, gained a substantial amount of protection in the form of currency depreciation. Thus, tariff rates could be lowered in the latter part of 1938 while industry continued to enjoy about the same degree of protection that the peak rates had afforded.

Since 1941 tariff protection has been on the ascendancy in Mexico, both in thought and in action. Mexico has harvested a crop of "war baby" plants established to make goods that foreign producers could not supply in adequate amounts under wartime conditions. Inevitably, new vested interests in tariff protection were created after 1939, and especially after 1941. The Mexican public began to hear much talk about infant industries and the need for tariff protection to give these infants a chance to grow up. To make these new industries comfortable, and to encourage long-term investment, it was further argued that tariff changes should be made during the war years even though the full weight of foreign competition would not be felt until the postwar period. The Second World War has made Mexico infant-industry conscious.

In addition, the economic philosophy of the Avila Camacho administration, in making industrialism the key to Mexico's future, gave added support to protectionist sentiment. Increasingly, protectionism was accepted as a corollary of the national goal of industrialization. True, President Avila Camacho always tempered his approval of protective tariffs with

[5] Oficina de Estudios Especiales del Comité de Aforos y Subsidios al Comercio Exterior, *op. cit.*, vol. 3, p. 243.
[6] United States Tariff Commission, *op. cit.*, p. 10.
[7] *Ibid.*

warnings about the danger of going too far, but his warnings seemed to allow plenty of scope for tariff action. Thus, early in December, 1944, he expressed concern about a measure than pending in Congress to raise duties, adding that "Mexico should not raise tariff barriers that would cut her off from the rest of the world."[8] This was obviously a generous formula. Indeed, about two weeks later it enabled Avila Camacho to sign an executive decree giving a substantial boost to tariff rates (see below).

During the six years of the Avila Camacho administration the most powerful adviser on questions of economic policy was Eduardo Suárez, Minister of Finance. Close observers of Mexican affairs credit Suárez with staunch protectionist leanings, a belief which is supported by his occasional references to protection in public addresses or statements. To judge from a newspaper interview with Suárez early in 1946, he favored protection for practically every new industry that had grown up in Mexico during the war years.[9] In large measure this was the policy of the Avila Camacho administration.

The growth of protectionist strength in Mexico can be seen in tariff moves made during the war when imports of manufactured goods could scarcely be called abundant. The steps taken strongly suggest that the Mexican government was then preparing for postwar readjustments.

In November, 1943, an executive decree provided for substantial increases on a wide range of duties. Nearly 600 items were included in the list of commodities affected. Most of the increases ranged from 10 to 50 per cent, although some went as high as 100 per cent. Officially it was announced that the changes were being made for revenue purposes, but a study of the items affected shows that the protectionist element was actually very important.[10]

This tariff decree of November, 1943, was never put into force. Within a few months time the decree was canceled because of an energetic protest from the United States government, which presumably contended that the tariff increases violated the spirit, if not the letter, of the Mexican-American trade agreement. Details about the protest and the response of the Mexican government have never been made public. The most plausible explanation for the willingness of the Mexican officials to cancel the decree is that they were then very anxious to get scarce equipment and machinery from the United States for several large power, irrigation, and industrial projects. They did not dare risk the consequences of insisting on higher tariff rates at that time. If it had not been for this factor, the decree of November, 1943, would probably not have been rescinded.

---

[8] Quoted in *Tiempo*, vol. 6, no. 136 (December 8, 1944), p. 3.
[9] *Excelsior*, January 11, 1946.
[10] This is the conclusion reached by the United States Tariff Commission, *op. cit.*, p. 25.

About a year later, however, substantial duty increases were ordered for a number of items. The measure (December, 1944) was much less comprehensive than the one previously planned, but it showed that the Mexican government was anxious to increase the protective strength of the tariff structure. Items subjected to higher rates included chemical products and iron and steel manufactures. In addition, a number of commodities formerly on the free list were made dutiable, such as stoves, locks, certain chemical products, and leather items.

Late in 1945 and early in 1946, the Avila Camacho administration took two further steps to raise duties on imports. Revenue ends were important in these measures because a number of luxury and semiluxury articles were affected, but protectionist features were also strengthened. A number of old industries were given added protection, and protective tariffs were established for some of the new industries. Among the new industries so favored, we may cite the manufacture of electrical apparatus and of rayon cloth.

The protectionist leanings of the Avila Camacho administration are clearly stated in the official account of its stewardship, *Seis años de actividad nacional*. In this volume, in the chapter prepared by Agustín Cue Canovas dealing with economic developments, we find the observation that "steps were taken to make a systematic revision of the Mexican tariff policy, so that duties on foreign trade should serve as an aid to the development of new industries. . . ."[11]

Mexico's tariff policy during the war years has been criticized by a number of Mexican economists for its lack of discrimination.[12] Not that they think that tariff making in other countries is done in a wholly scientific manner. Their knowledge of economic history would certainly not lead them to the conclusion that Mexico is unique in its methods of framing tariff laws and making tariff changes. However, it is plausible for them to argue that the recent Mexican brand of tariff making is extremely unscientific in character, when account is taken of the resources, possibilities, and structure of the Mexican economy.

It is a fact that protection in Mexico has been applied or increased without any study of the industries involved. Especially lacking have been estimates of the volume of production that the protected industries would be able to supply, in relation to anticipated consumption. The Comisión de Aranceles (Tariff Commission) has made no such studies, although presumably it was created for this very purpose. According to one outspoken and shrewd (if verbose) writer on Mexican economic problems, the commission's studies "are confined to mere considerations of the amount of

[11] Secretaría de Gobernación, *Seis años de actividad nacional* (Mexico, 1946), p. 311.
[12] *Revista de Economía*, vol. 7, no. 9–10 (October 31, 1944), p. 5.

imports and the desirability of ceasing to import the product which is to be manufactured [domestically]."[13]

Many of the producers benefiting from recent tariff protection are still able to supply only a small fraction of the Mexican market in spite of the encouragement the government has given them in this and in other ways. This suggests that an unduly heavy burden has been thrown on the consumer. Also, capital has been encouraged to go into industries the development of which could have been postponed indefinitely. Inasmuch as Mexico does not possess abundant capital resources, it cannot afford the diversion of capital into such fields at the expense of investment in other developments which would have brought much greater benefits to the national economy.

In December, 1942, Mexico and the United States signed a reciprocal trade agreement in which more than 120 Mexican duties were bound against increase. This agreement unquestionably acted as an influence on the Mexican government restraining it from making subsequent increases in protective tariff barriers. Among the items on which Mexico obligated itself to make no tariff increases during the life of the agreement were a number of manufactured goods. Items of a similar character, not covered in the treaty, were subjected to higher duties in the measures reviewed above. It is reasonable to conclude, therefore, that if no trade agreement had been negotiated with the United States the list of tariff increases in the years 1944–1946 would have been appreciably longer.

In Mexico it is fashionable for government officials, as well as for business men, to argue that the degree of protection afforded by Mexican tariffs has fallen steadily in recent years.[14] Sometimes the proposition is put in relative terms, namely, that protective levels have fallen in relation to those of other countries.[15] Such arguments are always based on the crude proposition that Mexican tariff rates are specific and that the rates have remained more or less constant while prices have risen substantially. If the rates had been *ad valorem*, it is pointed out, the previous degree of protection would have been more nearly maintained. Invariably, raising tariff rates is justified as a defensive move by which Mexico is simply catching up with other countries.

So far, however, no one has actually made a careful analysis of the changes in the protective strength of the Mexican tariff. Obviously this is a complex problem, especially if relative shifts in the Mexican and other

[13] Moisés T. de la Peña, "La industrialización de México y la política arancelaria," *El Trimestre Económico*, vol. 12, no. 2 (July–September, 1945), p. 201.

[14] See *Memoria del Segundo Congreso Mexicano de Ciencias Sociales*, vol. 3, p. 288.

[15] See Antonio Manero, "La hacienda pública mexicana durante el gobierno del Presidente Avila Camacho, 1944–1946" *Revista de Economía Continental*, vol. 1, no. 1 (August, 1946), p. 21.

price levels have to be taken into account. It will not be easy to give a clear-cut answer to such a question. But it should be investigated as scientifically as possible. In view of all the propaganda that has been built around this point, an objective study is urgently needed. Meanwhile, I feel that it is perfectly proper to question the easy generalization so frequently heard in Mexico that the degree of tariff protection there has declined at the same time as tariff strength has been gaining in other countries. Apart from the analytical difficulty just suggested, this generalization does not square with the facts, since Mexican tariff rates on a number of important protected items have not remained even roughly constant, but have been increased by substantial amounts in several past years.

Although it is not possible to give a quantitative answer to the question of whether the effective protectionism in Mexico's tariff structure has been rising or falling, it is clear that the philosophy of protectionism has been making great headway. No voice of political importance nowadays is heard questioning the need for a stiff protective tariff policy to encourage industrial development. Moreover, a subtle but nonetheless real shift in attitude has occurred; protective tariffs are so far taken for granted that no one feels called upon to apologize for a stand in favor of extending or raising duties. The burden of proof rests wholly with the person who argues for a reduction in tariffs. The dogma that Mexican industry requires protection is rarely questioned.

It is true that almost everyone pays lip service to the point of view that protection should be applied with discrimination, that it should be extended only to industries which are "economically justified." No public agency, however, shows any inclination to determine which industries should or should not be given favorable treatment. It is difficult to imagine any public official in Mexico suggesting the withdrawal of tariff protection from anything but the shakiest of the small industries established during the war years. Protectionism is more thoroughly entrenched in Mexico now than at any time in the past.

When Miguel Alemán became president there was a tendency in official circles to play down tariff protection as an instrument of national policy, and to talk more about other questions and policies relating to the economic development of Mexico. This was interpreted in some quarters as a forerunner of a significant shift in government policy, which would lead to a moderation of Mexico's protective tariff barriers. This interpretation was hardly justified at the time, and it certainly has not been borne out by the trend of events since.

President Alemán, it should be remembered, is irrevocably committed to a program of industrializing Mexico, of making industry the core of

Mexico's economic structure. As a candidate for office he made "industrialization" his economic slogan. Furthermore, if we examine his campaign program in detail, we find the additional proposition that Mexico should produce "the machines and tools which up to now have been imported and which are essential for increasing our production, both agricultural and industrial."[16] Development of basic industries in the degree suggested by this quotation implies substantial and continuous tariff protection. Such industries in Mexico are the ones likely to be most vulnerable to foreign competition.

Also in his campaign program, Alemán stated that the experience of all industrialized nations shows that manufacturing development without protection is difficult to achieve. This led him to the conclusion that the appropriate commercial policy for Mexico was to permit the greatest freedom in foreign trade consistent with the necessity of industrializing the country. Industrialization of Mexico, it will be observed, was given clear-cut priority over international action to expand world trade. This position he restated in his inaugural address as President, although his remarks on the tariff question at that time were very brief.

In the first year of his administration President Alemán took steps to tighten protection for Mexican industry. It may well be that he acted with reluctance, as the tone of official statements suggested. He could well enough have had misgivings about carrying forward the trend toward extreme protectionism at this particular time. In part, his protective measures can be considered a result of the logic of a whole set of related developments, policies, and problems, set in motion by his predecessor in office, among which the following are principal factors: the attempt to attain rapid industrialization for Mexico; industrialization on a broad front; credit policy, especially in failing to curb lending for speculative and urban construction purposes; a large volume of public investment; inflation. However, even if these and other background circumstances had been less aggravated, some new action to regulate imports would have been a likely result of the readjustments in world economy following the end of the war.

The most important protective measure of the Alemán administration was announced dramatically in July, 1947, when two decrees relating to imports were issued simultaneously. One decree provided for an extension of direct controls over imports; this will be discussed in the next section. The other provided for increases in a number of duties. The official justification for both measures was the need to protect Mexico's monetary reserves against the heavy drain imposed upon them by a great excess of

[16] "Síntesis del programa de gobierno que sustenta el candidato a la presidencia de la república, Señor Lic. Miguel Alemán," El Economista, no. 149 (October 1945), p. 41.

imports over exports. As larger amounts of goods became available for export from the United States following the end of the war, Mexico's trade balance tipped increasingly toward the import side and her gold and dollar exchange holdings started to decline. From about 350 million dollars on V-J Day they fell to approximately 200 million in July, 1947, a drop of about 40 per cent in less than two years. This rapid rate of decline was considered alarming enough to warrant the new trade-control measures.

The intention of the measures was to reduce the importation of luxury goods and other nonessential articles and thus conserve Mexico's foreign exchange assets for necessary consumer goods and for capital equipment vital to the economic development of the nation. It appears, however, that both measures went beyond this. They have brought added protection into Mexican commercial policy.

The selection of items for tariff increases suggests a protectionist impulse. Most items included in the list can hardly be classified as luxuries or nonessentials, except in the sense that there are domestic sources of supply. (But this is obviously not what "nonessential" is intended to mean in the official statements justifying the action.) The duty on canned fish was raised by more than 100 per cent. Among the other commodities affected were artificial fibers, aluminum products (mainly cooking utensils), locks, calcium carbide, buttons, cigarette paper, felt hats, machetes, and a variety of metal articles. Although not many commodities were subjected to tariff changes, the increases were substantial in amount. In most cases the rates were doubled; on some articles they were even tripled.

The tariff decree of July 1947, therefore, brought an added element of protection into the Mexican tariff structure. The higher rates were inspired by a balance of payments emergency, but the previous schedules are not likely to be restored when pressure on the balance of payments is no longer a delicate issue. This opinion is suggested not only by world-wide economic experience, but also by subsequent action of the Mexican government. Before six months had elapsed, tariff rates were raised again. The new revision, which was announced in November, was far-reaching, in that it affected almost all import duties except those bound against increase in the Mexican-American reciprocal trade agreement.[17]

The tariff change of November, 1947, was significant for other reasons besides the raising of rates. The method of levying duties was changed from specific to compound—that is, a combination of specific and *ad*

---

[17] A month later, in December, 1947, similar changes were made in the duties bound by the Mexican-American trade agreement. This action was intended to restore the degree of protection that prevailed in 1942 when the agreement was signed, but additional protection was given to some items, such as paints and varnishes. The United States government consented to all these changes.

valorem methods. This step, it was explained officially, was taken in order to restore the prewar degree of protection. While this explanation has merit, it must also be recognized that the new system gives greater flexibility for increasing protection. Also, an intention to raise protective levels was suggested by two other features of the tariff decree of November, 1947. The Ministry of Finance was authorized to establish official prices for the purpose of collecting *ad valorem* duties, such prices to take precedence over invoice prices whenever invoice prices were lower. This move, of course, introduces the principle of minimum valuation advocated by the New Group. The other feature to which attention needs to be called is the statement that one of the principal aims of the tariff decree was to establish an adequate margin of protection for Mexican industry and agriculture.[18] It is true that this statement could be understood to mean nothing more than adjusting tariff rates to higher price levels, but the United States Department of Commerce has interpreted it as an intention to strengthen and extend tariff protection for Mexican industry.[19]

Another step which the Alemán administration has taken toward increasing protection for Mexican industry is to open negotiations for a revision of the Mexican-American reciprocal trade agreement. In this connection President Alemán has yielded in part to growing pressure from Mexican industrialists, especially from those whom we have called the New Group, whose spokesman is the Cámara Nacional de la Industria de Transformación. Ever since V-J Day these industrial interests have been urging the Mexican government to abrogate the 1942 commercial agreement with the United States. By every means of publicity available, the Cámara has tried to convince the Mexican people and its government that the American trade agreement is the death warrant of Mexican industry. In 1946 and 1947 hundreds of press items developing this theme appeared in the Mexico City dailies in the form of paid advertisements and otherwise.

When Alemán took office he seemed to be cool toward suggestions to do something about the Mexican-American trade agreement. Doubtless his judgment was influenced by a number of circumstances, not the least important of which was his desire to obtain new loans for Mexico from the Export-Import Bank. Associated with this objective was his desire to get American support for Mexican loan applications pending at the World Bank. At this very time the United States government was preparing to take the leadership in drawing up a charter for lowering barriers to international commerce, and was ready to negotiate a number of new reciprocal trade agreements as a means of giving the charter a favorable setting in

---

[18] *Foreign Commerce Weekly*, November 22, 1947, p. 16.
[19] George Kalmanoff, "Economic Pressure Spurs Mexico to Important New Steps," *Foreign Commerce Weekly*, September 11, 1948, p. 4.

which to start operating. This was certainly not an opportune time for the Mexican government to talk about abrogating its trade agreement with the United States.

The balance of payments crisis which led to the import control and tariff decrees of July, 1947, added to the pressure from New Group industrialists, apparently induced Alemán to change his policy on this question. It is possible, too, that he was disappointed over the amount of new Export-Import Bank loans which Mexico was able to get (50 million dollars), and over the indifferent reception which the World Bank had accorded to Mexico's application for loans. In October, 1947, it was officially announced that the Ministry of Foreign Relations, at an unspecified earlier date, had notified the American State Department of its desire to open conversations as soon as possible on revision of the trade agreement.[20]

In asking for a revision, Alemán has refrained from going as far as the Cámara Nacional de la Industria de Transformación would like. The position of the Cámara is that the agreement should be terminated, not revised. However, even the request for a revision is significant, for it shows the determination of the Alemán administration to intensify and extend tariff protection for Mexican industry. The restraining influence of the 1942 commercial treaty is to be in part removed and the Mexican government given a freer hand in the protectionist sphere.

In harmony with the steps taken to tighten Mexico's protective system has been a tendency which administration leaders have developed to talk more frequently and more firmly about the need of countries with underdeveloped economies, such as Mexico, to defend themselves against ruinous foreign competition. Not that they are saying anything especially new in this connection, nor anything which they did not believe when the administration took office. The point is that now they talk about this question, and speak with vigor and with passion, whereas earlier they were silent. This development is most interesting in relation to the international aspects of Mexican industrialization, and therefore it will be discussed in the appropriate chapter in Part III, where the implications can be fully explored.

DIRECT IMPORT CONTROL

In 1944 the Mexican government took a step of great potential significance when it introduced a system of direct import controls. At the time this action took place the Mexican government was exercising control over imports only in a limited sense, namely, through the machinery which had been set up in coöperation with the American government to regu-

[20] *El Nacional*, October 3, 1947. Negotiations were started in May 1948, but no new agreement had been written by the end of the year.

late exports from the United States to Mexico. The decree of 1944, authorizing the Minister of Finance to draw up lists of commodities for which import licenses would be required, set up an entirely new and independent import-licensing system. It represented unilateral action by the Mexican government to regulate the flow of imports in its own way and for purposes about which it would be the sole judge.

The import-control decree of 1944 was issued under an emergency war powers act. However, it later became clear that the Mexican government was inclined to keep import controls as a more permanent feature of its commercial policy. When the war powers act expired shortly after V-J Day, President Avila Camacho asked Congress for legislation extending indefinitely a number of the emergency powers he had exercised during the war. Included among these was the authority to control imports. The law was passed, and thus the President of Mexico was given unlimited power to control imports for an indefinite period.

The official justification for the import-control decree of 1944 cannot be found in the decree itself. Unlike most decrees issued in Mexico, this one does not have a preamble in which the reasons for taking the action are set forth. From various collateral statements of an official nature, however, two reasons stand out as justification for the decree of 1944 and for its continuation in more permanent legislative form at the end of the war. These are: (1) fear of dumping (i.e., selling a product abroad for a lower price than that charged in the domestic market); and (2) effective use of accumulated foreign exchange reserves.

There has been much clamor in Mexico in recent years about dumping. In the 1930's, of course, all countries were sensitive about dumping, and probably all over the world a heritage of suspicion about what other countries might do, continued throughout the war years. Certainly this has been true in Mexico. It is especially significant that persons important in Mexican government and business circles believed that goods were dumped into the Mexican market in substantial volume even during the war period, particularly in the last year or so of the war. The strength of this attitude comes as a surprise to the outside observer, who naturally wonders about the amount of dumping that was likely to have taken place during the period of wartime stringencies.

There can be no question, however, about the opinions of persons in leading official and business positions in Mexico on this question. These opinions, too, have been transmitted to the public at large, and the Mexican people have become convinced that (1) American firms were dumping goods into Mexico during the war, and (2) that defensive measures are essential to prevent similar and more extensive dumping in the future.

One of Mexico's leading economists, then a high official in the Ministry of Finance, wrote the following in December, 1944:

. . . it is certain that in recent months . . . an invasion of American goods has been observed in some Latin American countries—surplus war goods, for which an attempt has been made to find easy markets. The evil of this is that these exports frequently constitute true acts of dumping, with serious harm for the weak economies of the countries south of the Rio Grande.[21]

Given the suspicion about American dumping during the war, it was a certainty that the resumption of more normal conditions after V-J Day would bring out a strong reaction in Mexico. In 1946 the cry "dumping" was heard on all sides, as the volume of United States exports began to assume larger proportions. As typical of the reaction, I cite a news item in the Mexico City daily *El Nacional* (February 27, 1946) referring to imports of glassware. American glassware, it was pointed out, "has begun to invade the national market," thus causing serious difficulties for the domestic glass industry. The prices of glass products had been dropping. From these facts it was felt to be the simple conclusion that the American producers were dumping into the Mexican market. This illustration could be multiplied many times over by items taken from the news columns of the Mexican press since the end of the war.

It is probably true that isolated cases of real dumping have taken place in Mexico in the past few years. Persons closely in touch with business and economic conditions in Mexico with whom I discussed this question believe that there have been such incidents, but that they have been few in number. Mostly the cry of dumping has been raised when a foreign article has appeared in the Mexican market at a lower price than that which the domestic producers have been charging. Unquestionably this was the case in the glassware illustration cited above.

In truth, both government and industry in Mexico have found dumping to be a wonderfully convenient term to apply to any foreign shipment that can be sold in the Mexican market for less than the prevailing price of a similar Mexican article. It does not matter whether the shipment is a true case of dumping. As in all social affairs, everywhere, it is easier, more convenient, and more effective to hurl an epithet than it is to make an analysis of the facts.

The indiscriminate use and misuse of the term dumping in Mexico have been sharply criticized by a number of economists in the country. One of these, Víctor L. Urquidi, has written the following words, in connection with a discussion of the attitudes and problems that are coming

[21] Jesús Silva Herzog, "La conferencia económica interamericana," *Revista de Economía,* vol. 7, no. 11–12 (December 31, 1944), p. 25.

to the fore as Mexico carries forward its industrialization program in the postwar world.

Suddenly things change. Foreign industries resume shipments to the national market, with their former products—of better quality and cheaper. Meanwhile, domestic monetary expansion continues to raise costs. Then another magic word emerges: dumping. The industrialists and the politicians rapidly scan textbooks on economics, they find out that there is something called dumping and they demand . . . the protection of the State to defend their "important" domestic industries, . . . Emotions are excited, and anyone who sells at a lower price [than the domestic producer] is accused of dumping.[22]

As supply conditions ease further in the advanced manufacturing nations, especially in the United States, we may be confident that the accusations of dumping in the Mexican market will be heard again and again. The government will feel continuous pressure to use import restrictions as a defensive measure against dumping.

The second reason given for the introduction of direct import control in 1944 was the need of insuring wise use of the foreign exchange reserves accumulated by Mexico during the war years. Mexico, it will be recalled, does not have exchange control. Import controls can be a substitute. Requiring permits for certain kinds of imports can be made a means of preventing the dissipation of foreign exchange balances in the importation of luxuries and semiluxuries. Imports of such articles can be restricted to small quantities, and a preference thus given to goods which contribute most to national economic development.

Similarly, the import-control system can be used to channel investment into industries which the government has decided to emphasize.[23] This is done by allowing such industries to bring in all the machinery and equipment they need while the same privilege is denied to other industries.

Before the summer of 1947, one general list and several minor lists had been issued by the Mexican government to designate the commodities for which import permits were to be required. After examining these lists one can hardly reach the conclusion that they were drawn up with a view to conserving foreign exchange reserves by discouraging luxury imports. Indeed, one is led rather to the conclusion that this objective could not have played a very important role in composing the lists. They contain only a few items that can properly be classified as luxuries, even when we remember that this term must cover a wider range of products in Mexico than in the United States. High-priced automobiles are an example. Although such cars were appearing in ever-increasing numbers on the fashionable streets and boulevards of Mexico City, at the cost of a substantial drain on foreign exchange resources, no attempt was made to place them under import control.

On the other hand, many of the commodities for which import licenses were required were semimanufactures or finished products that were competing with the output of Mexican industries, especially of those industries which expanded their productive capacity during the war period. This was true for a number of iron and steel products, including metal furniture, for chemicals, for paints and varnishes, and for glass products, and it may also have been true for other articles. Import licensing for such items suggests that there was a strong protective quality in the new import regulations.

This inference is supported by a statement of Minister of Finance Eduardo Suárez made almost simultaneously with the publication of the general list of commodities requiring import licenses, in December, 1945. After asserting that the government had formulated a plan of protection for Mexican industry, Suárez went on to name five branches of manufacturing which the government was particularly anxious to encourage. These were steel furniture, sheet steel, paints and varnishes, chemicals, and toys. Most of the plants turning out such products were "war babies," but Suárez made it clear that the government considered them to be permanent and essential developments in the economy, and not temporary substitutes set up to meet a wartime situation.

The point of view maintained here that the import controls instituted under the decree of 1944 were substantially directed toward protectionist ends finds additional and unexpected support in an interesting statement in the United States Tariff Commission's study on *Economic Controls and Commercial Policy in Mexico* (1946). Obviously, as an official agency of the United States government, this commission must be cautious in passing judgment publicly on the economic policies of other nations. In spite of this, however, the commission was willing to go so far as to say: "... it is conceivable that the intention may have been, or the actual outcome may be, that the new import controls will be employed to extend further protection to Mexican industries."[24] Allowing for a necessary degree of understatement, this observation has a significant ring.

In July, 1947, in response to the balance of payments crisis which we have discussed in the preceding section, a new and much more important step was taken in regulating imports for the purpose of conserving foreign exchange. The importation of over 120 articles was forbidden for an indefi-

---

[24] *Op. cit.,* p. 26.

nite period. As long as this drastic measure is continued it will have a substantial influence on Mexico's balance of payments, inasmuch as the commodities affected made up about 20 per cent of total imports at the time the ban was put into effect.

It must be granted that luxury items occupied a prominent place in the list of goods the importation of which was not to be allowed. Probably a large majority of the articles would have to be classified as luxuries. In the context of the Mexican social and economic structure, there should be little hesitation about pinning a luxury label on the following, all of which were included in the list: furs, furniture (specified kinds), perfumes, alcoholic beverages, antiques, radios, phonographs, washing machines, pianos, fresh fruits, jewelry, diamonds, crystal ware, and automobiles. In addition, there were a number of articles sufficiently close to the luxury category that it would be difficult to quarrel about including them also.

In a few cases, however, a suspicion of protectionism is warranted. All kinds of wearing apparel, for example, were banned from importation. Kraft paper was listed, although there seemed to be a severe shortage of this type of paper in Mexico at the time. Carpets and velvet were questionable items, as were metal furniture and refrigerators. Although the action was directed chiefly against luxury products, therefore, it is fair to suggest that a protectionist element was not lacking.

The import prohibitions decreed in July, 1947, are intended to be temporary in nature, and they were so designated in the decree itself. From official statements made subsequently, it appears that they are supposed to be temporary in two ways, (1) they are to be maintained during the period when the disequilibrium in Mexico's balance of payments is being corrected; (2) import prohibitions are to be replaced by import quotas, commodity by commodity. It has been implied that such quotas are also to be temporary in the sense of the first of these two propositions.

The tone of official explanations and comments, however, indicates that the new restrictions, in the form of absolute prohibitions or quotas, are here to stay for some time. It is reasonable to suppose that they will not be dropped quickly. Shortly after the decree was issued, Josué Sáenz, head of one of the principal departments in the Ministry of Finance, stated that it would take probably one to two years to redress Mexico's balance of payments and that the import prohibitions would therefore last at least that length of time.[25] In view of the excitement, amounting almost to a panic, which swept through Mexican business circles at the time the new import-control decree was issued, this estimate can be considered a conservative one.

---

[25] *El Nacional*, July 18, 1947.

The import-quota or import-ban policy is likely to remain in force for several years, during the period in which Mexico is attempting to realize its ambitions in industrialization and in other fields of economic development. From this standpoint, the balance of payments emergency is not a short, sharp crisis but a continuing circumstance. Dr. Sáenz's estimate, which I deem cautious, of one to two years is significant in this connection. Furthermore, a means has been provided for converting the import bans into import quotas, which suggests a more permanent policy than a highly temporary crisis would warrant. Although the decree of July, 1947, may have been drawn up hastily, in order to enable the government to cope with an immediate situation, it looks as though it had been done with an eye to the future. The principle of maintaining selective import controls has rooted itself more strongly in Mexican commercial policy. The Mexican public is being educated to appreciate such controls at this stage in Mexico's economic development.

It is possible, of course, that Mexico may be deflected from this import-control policy by developments on the international economic front, such as those which might take place through the International Trade Organization recently set up at Havana. This question will be taken up in the latter part of the volume, but I would like to state here my conviction that Mexico's import-restriction policy will not be given up lightly. Very large Export-Import Bank or World Bank loans, if they should materialize, may be effective in inducing a shift in Mexican policy, but the chances for such loans seem dim at the present writing.

We must also remember the factor of protection, strong in the earlier import-control measures and also found in the emergency decree of July, 1947. Vested interests in import controls have been created. Import quotas are regarded as an effective complement to tariff protection. Apart from public policy considerations, therefore, the Mexican government will feel pressure from domestic industrial interests for the continuation of import regulations in a substantial and significant form. This will help to make more elastic the concept of the "temporary period" during which such restrictions are considered necessary.

GOVERNMENT POLICY ON FOREIGN INVESTMENT

During the Cárdenas administration foreign capital became wary about investing in Mexico, and the Mexican government in turn became hostile to foreign capital. Open conflict occurred in 1938 when the foreign oil companies and the Mexican government were unable to adjust their differences, and the result of this conflict was the well-known oil expropriation incident. Already nervous over social and economic trends under Cárdenas, such as the rapid pace of agrarian reform, advanced labor legislation and its administration, and railway nationalization, foreign capital became exceedingly timid about further investment in Mexico when the government took such drastic action against the British and American oil companies. The outlook for foreign investment was toward retrenchment, not expansion.

After Avila Camacho succeeded Cárdenas in the presidency the policy of the Mexican government toward foreign capital began to shift in the opposite direction. Steps were taken to arrange a final settlement of the foreign oil companies' claims, a question on which little progress had been made in the years immediately following expropriation. In November, 1941, an agreement was reached with the United States government whereby each government designated an expert to estimate the amount of indemnity which should be paid, with the understanding that if these two experts should come to an agreement it was to be binding so far as the two governments were concerned.

Such an agreement was actually reached in April, 1942, by Morris L. Cooke, the American expert, and Manuel J. Zevada, the Mexican commissioner, calling for a payment of 24 million dollars for the American petroleum claims not previously settled. This sum was very much less than the amount claimed by the oil companies, inasmuch as the American expert accepted the legal position of the Mexican government that uncaptured subsoil assets were the property of the Mexican nation. However, it represented a substantial increase over earlier estimates made by the Mexican government of indemnities owing to the expropriated concerns.

The Cooke-Zevada agreement itself was not binding on the American oil companies, but they afterwards accepted the terms agreed upon by the two experts. In this way the oil question was finally settled.[26]

Negotiations to settle the British oil claims proved to be more difficult. Nevertheless, Avila Camacho was able to establish a preliminary basis for settlement in February, 1946, when an exchange of notes between the Mexican and British governments set forth formal procedures for negotiation. These negotiations had their ups and downs. They bore fruit, however, in a settlement announced by President Alemán in September, 1947, whereby the former British owners of oil properties were guaranteed an indemnity of 81 million dollars for the holdings expropriated in 1938. "This settlement," commented the London *Economist,* "has been warmly welcomed by the [British] Government and by the City."[27]

Avila Camacho also succeeded in making settlements to clear up Mexico's old external debts which had been in default for many years. The

[26] The last installment of the $24,000,000 indemnity was paid in September, 1947.
[27] September 6, 1947, p. 417.

defaults dated back to 1914, when the chaotic conditions attaching to the Revolution made it impossible for the government to meet its obligations. A basic agreement on these debts was reached in 1922 by the Mexican government and the International Committee of Bankers on Mexico, but Mexico was unable to make the payments as they fell due in the following years. Further negotiations occurred at sporadic intervals, without satisfactory result. When Avila Camacho became president he was determined to strengthen public credit as a means of attracting capital from abroad to speed up the economic development of the nation.[28] Two years after he took office a settlement was made on practically all the externally held bond issues, with the exception of railway bonds. Then, in February, 1946, the protracted negotiations on the railway debt were concluded by a similar agreement. For practical purposes, this action completed the task of making settlements with the foreign holders of Mexico's defaulted bond issues.

Under Avila Camacho, the Mexican government probably offered to foreign creditors substantially better terms than those which earlier administrations had been willing or able to offer. That such was true is suggested by his concurrent anxiety to encourage a flow of American capital to Mexico for developmental purposes, and also by his appreciation of the improved dollar-exchange position of Mexico as a consequence of its wartime excess of exports over imports. It is suggested, too, by the following quotation from an address given in 1945 by James Drumm, executive vice-president of the National City Bank of New York. In discussing the handicaps to the movement of capital from the United States to Latin America, Mr. Drumm makes these observations:

... Unfortunately, the dollar external indebtedness of most of the countries on this continent has not been settled to the satisfaction of the American bondholder. This, of course, has dampened the enthusiasm of the private investor of this country to invest in Latin American securities of any type. Fortunately, some of the countries have already reversed their more aggressive trends and policies during the past few years. It is interesting to note that, in addition to United States government financing in Mexico, a certain amount of private American capital has been invested during recent years. Though the amount is not large, the trend is in the right direction and will undoubtedly increase. Constructive measures were taken by our Mexican friends in attracting foreign capital to Mexico, and it is hoped that some of the other countries on the continent will follow the Mexican pattern.[29]

While Avila Camacho was in office a number of loans were negotiated with the Export-Import Bank. Broadly speaking, most of these credits were provided for projects relating to Mexico's war effort or to the maintenance

---

[28] *Seis años de actividad nacional*, p. 349.
[29] James Drumm, "Financing New Industry on the International Front," in *Proceedings of the Mexican-American Conference on Industrial Research, September 30–October 6, 1945.* (Chicago, Armour Research Foundation, 1945), pp. 143–4.

of her economy during the war years, but in seeking the loans the Mexican government also had in mind their contribution to the long-run industrial development of the country. Notable among the loans authorized were the following: (1) $8,000,000 for steel mill equipment to be used for the new Altos Hornos plant; (2) $15,000,000 for railroad equipment; (3) $20,000,000 for equipment, materials, and supplies to be used in the electrification program; (4) $10,000,000 for gasoline refinery equipment.

This last credit, authorized in January, 1944, was used in adding a plant to produce high-octane aviation gasoline to the Atzcapotzalco refinery near Mexico City. Such a loan would not have been possible if Avila Camacho had not been successful in negotiating a final settlement with the expropriated American oil companies.[30]

On foreign investment, as on most questions relating to Mexican economic development, the policy of the Alemán administration is an extension and amplification of the Avila Camacho policy. Alemán has brought the question of foreign investment much more into the open. He has been more candid than his predecessor about telling the Mexican people that their government wants to encourage an inflow of foreign capital (with safeguards, of course), and he has also been more energetic about trying to educate his nation to appreciate the benefits to be realized from regulated foreign investment. Similarly, he has been more open about letting potential investors in the United States know that foreign capital is welcome in Mexico.

The attitude of the Alemán administration toward foreign capital was made clear a month after it took office. Early in January, 1947, the *New York Herald Tribune* published a special supplement on Mexico, in which it was pointed out that President Alemán was counting on American capital, private as well as public, to help put over an ambitious program for economic development. As one of the *Herald Tribune's* writers put it, "the welcome sign [has been] hung out to foreign investors."[31]

The *New York Herald Tribune* also caught the rumor, frequently heard in Mexico at that time, that foreign capital would reënter the petroleum industry. Thus one story in the special supplement was headlined: "Expropriated Oil Men Hope for Change in Mexican Policy on Natural Resources." This was followed by the captions: "Chance is Seen of Going

---

[30] In this connection, it is significant that the Committee on Interstate and Foreign Commerce of the U. S. House of Representatives in the fall of 1948, following a visit to Mexico, urged that "the State Department and appropriate lending agencies . . . give consideration to the matter of a loan for the expansion and construction of Mexican petroleum facilities, including such items as an oil line across the isthmus, gas lines into consuming centers both in Mexico and the United States, a refinery on the west coast, and other aspects of the program which the committee has not examined in detail." House Report No. 2470, 80th Congress, 2d Sess., *Fuel Investigation—Mexican Petroleum* (Washington, 1949), p. 16.

[31] *New York Herald Tribune,* January 4, 1947.

Back to Rich Fields; Outside Interests Believe Better Times Are Ahead Under New Regime."

Such rumors continued to circulate, in spite of officially inspired statements that they were without foundation. It became increasingly clear that President Alemán was not satisfied with the performance of PEMEX, the government oil monopoly, and that he was especially concerned about the inability of PEMEX to finance exploratory drilling operations. The solution he has hit upon for this problem is to hire foreign companies to work petroleum resources for the Mexican government, paying them for their services in oil rather than in cash. This policy began to take shape in 1947, for in October of that year a correspondent of the London *Economist* reported as follows from Mexico:

Talks with American interests have been started with a view to securing "substantial new investments" in the oil industry, in which no appreciable capital has been sunk since its expropriation. The terms offered are that the Government should retain subsoil rights and pay operators a royalty on each barrel—a broad reversal of the old system.[32]

In April, 1948, it was announced that a contract of this type had been concluded with the Cities Service Co. This transaction, however, was a special case because Cities Service Co., through a Mexican subsidiary, still had control of some land in northeastern Mexico, which had not been subjected to expropriation in 1938. Agreements with other American oil companies were much more difficult to arrive at. In June it was reported that fifteen American companies had turned down contracts on the ground that the terms offered by PEMEX involved too much risk. The company which did the drilling, it was pointed out, would have to bear the entire loss if no oil were struck.[33] No further arrangements had been concluded by the end of 1948,[34] but negotiations were going on all the time, and occasional statements made on both sides of the border suggested that bargaining was bringing PEMEX and American oil companies closer together. As the year 1948 drew to a close, therefore, additional contracts for drilling appeared probable.[35]

In the months following the inauguration of the Alemán administration invitations to American capital to participate in Mexico's industrialization were repeated with great frequency. Thus, in April Minister of

---

[32] *The Economist*, October 4, 1947, p. 569.

[33] *Mexican-American Review*, June 1948, p. 53.

[34] A contract signed by the Texas Co. and PEMEX attracted attention, but it was an entirely different kind of transaction. The Texas Co. contracted to buy 250,000 barrels of Mexican crude oil per monh for a period of five years, and to pay a certain amount of the purchase price in advance of shipment.

[35] See, for example, the report referred to above, *Mexican Petroleum*, by the House Committee on Interstate and Foreign Commerce, No. 2470, 80th Congress, 2d Sess., pp. 12–14.

Finance Ramón Beteta told the Texas Section of the Investment Bankers Association of America that foreign capital had nothing to fear in Mexico as long as it complied with the laws of the country, and that there was no danger of discrimination against foreign investments. He also urged the investment bankers to seek to interest small American investors in securities of Mexican industrial concerns and in bonds of the Mexican government. Comparatively high rates of return could be obtained on such investments, he argued, without corresponding risks.

President Alemán visited the United States shortly after his Minister of Finance made these statements. During this visit it was announced that new Export-Import Bank loans were to be granted to Mexico and that the agreement for the stabilization of the peso had been renewed. To get additional credits of $50,000,000 from the Export-Import Bank at that time represented a substantial achievement for Alemán, inasmuch as the bank was near the limit of its lending capacity, and many other nations were pressing for loans. Then, with the national spotlight fixed on him, in an address to the Pan-American Society of New York, Alemán made an appeal to private American capital to seek investments in Mexico. The drift of these remarks on foreign investment was well summed up by the official organ of the Mexican government, *El Nacional*,[36] under the caption, "Welcome All Investment of Foreign Capital That Promotes Our Progress." In addition to making it clear that Mexico did welcome foreign capital which genuinely stimulated the economic development of the nation, Alemán took pains to point out that many Americans were already enjoying happy and prosperous times in Mexico and that much American capital was comfortably and profitably invested there.

In my country thousands of Americans have found favorable conditions for the development of their talents and for the establishment of their homes. They live happily there. Similarly, much American capital has been invested in Mexico in accordance with our laws; some has joined with Mexican capital. The enterprises thus created operate in my country without obstacles and they make substantial profits.

No opportunity has been lost to reiterate the desire of the Mexican government to set in motion a flow of American capital to Mexico. Thus at the Inter-American Conference in Rio in August, 1947, the Mexican Minister of Foreign Relations, Jaime Torres Bodet, held a press interview for the purpose of highlighting this attitude.[37] Although he added nothing to what President Alemán and Minister of Finance Beteta had already said, the significant thing is that he used publicity afforded by the Inter-American Defense Conference to emphasize their pronouncements.

[36] May 3, 1947.   [37] *El Nacional*, August 18, 1947.

In addition to official statements concerning foreign capital, Alemán took some tentative steps in the first year of his administration to strengthen the confidence of foreigners in Mexican investments. One of these moves is directed toward a closer definition of the "rules of the game" for joint investment of Mexican and foreign capital.

In July, 1944, during the term of Avila Camacho, an emergency measure was enacted authorizing the Minister of Foreign Relations to require Mexican ownership to the extent of at least 51 per cent in any company in which foreign interests were involved; when the measure expired at the end of the war, new legislation was passed to carry forward the same principle. This legislation has been the source of much confusion, both to the Mexican public and to foreign investors. To the Mexican people it has appeared that the law laid down an absolute requirement that Mexican citizens control all firms organized subsequent to its enactment. Foreign investors, on the other hand, have been led to believe that the law sets up a general requirement of 51 per cent Mexican ownership but that the Mexican government is willing to make exceptions with a liberal hand. In fact, such exceptions have been numerous. Also, in many other cases compliance with the 51 per cent rule has been more nominal than real. It has been an open secret that American concerns contemplating the construction of new factories in Mexico need not worry about a strict application of the rule.

While Avila Camacho was in office no information was released to the public regarding the administration of the foreign investment law. Alemán, with an openly acknowledged policy of encouraging foreign capital, has already acted to clarify the thinking of the Mexican people on this question and, by the same token, to make foreign concerns more comfortable about potential investments in Mexico. Soon after assuming the presidency he appointed an Inter-Departmental Committee on Investment of Foreign Capital for the purpose of drafting a new series of regulations. Although this committee has not yet completed its study of the whole question, a public statement issued by the head of the committee suggests that an official effort may be anticipated to prepare the Mexican public for a mild rather than a vigorous application of the principle of requiring majority Mexican ownership.

"There is no law," the chairman of the committee stated, "which limits the investment of foreign capital to 49 per cent of the total invested in the firm, for all kinds of businesses and industries, and which would consequently require that 51 per cent [of the ownership] be in the hands of Mexicans, as a general rule without exceptions."[88]

---

[88] Statement of Miguel Angel Ceniceros, October 30, 1947, quoted in *El Mercado de Valores*, November 10, 1947, p. 2.

The statement then goes on to stress the proposition that what the law does is to give discretionary power to the Minister of Foreign Relations to determine the lines of business in which 51 per cent or more of Mexican capital is to be required. This way of putting it suggests that the 51 per cent requirement is to be treated as the exceptional case, and not the other way around, as the Mexican public had earlier been led to believe. This is certainly a significant shift in emphasis.

Equally revealing is the following list, released at the same time, of the kinds of firms for which the Minister of Foreign Relations had stipulated majority Mexican ownership: radio broadcasting; production, distribution, and exhibition of motion pictures; air transport operating entirely within Mexican territory; urban and interurban transportation; fishing; production and marketing of carbonated beverages; publishing. The brevity of this list shows clearly that the Mexican government has made no attempt to apply a 51 per cent requirement to the wide range of new industrial establishments that have been formed by the joint investment of American and Mexican capital.

Finally, the statement of the chairman of the interdepartmental committee is interesting in that it shows no immediate concern about extending the list. Instead, the main preoccupation of the commission was a technical question relating to proof of ownership, and the tone of the statement implied that this issue would continue to be the center of attention for some time to come.

For practical purposes, the Inter-Departmental Committee on Investment of Foreign Capital has served notice on the Mexican people that they need not expect majority Mexican ownership in the larger industrial corporations where foreign capital is involved.

In concluding this section on foreign investment, it is interesting to note some of the observations of the National Advisory Council on International Monetary and Financial Problems relating to recent Mexican policy toward foreign investment. This body, made up of representatives of various agencies of the United States government, made the following statements in a report prepared for the Senate Committee on Finance in December, 1947.[39]

... In certain fields, such as petroleum, the [Mexican] Government exercises a monopoly and competition by private firms is an impossibility. But even in this politically controversial field, economic considerations seem to be initiating a trend toward renewed limited participation by technically superior private interests, as evidenced by recent moves to award contracts for exploration and development to private United States firms. In most other fields, Government participation appears

[39] Senate Committee on Finance, 80:1, *Foreign Assets and Liabilities of the United States and Its Balance of International Transactions* (Washington, 1948), pp. 108–109.

to be limited to lending assistance to new private enterprises that might otherwise not be initiated, and competition with Government-owned companies does not seem to be a matter of concern at present.

... Judging from postwar United States private interest in Mexico as a market for investment, particularly in manufacturing, numerous well-known United States firms are apparently convinced that the expropriatory nationalization activities of the Cardenas period are not a matter of concern in the present or foreseeable future. The attitude of the present regime, as indicated both in official pronouncements and in concrete acts, seems to be very friendly toward the investment of foreign capital that will participate in its program of industrialization and economic improvement, although it quite definitely reserves the right to regulate such investments.

MEXICAN-AMERICAN COMMISSION FOR ECONOMIC COÖPERATION

One of the triumphs of President Avila Camacho on the industrial front was the organization of a joint Mexican-American Commission for Economic Cooperation during the war period. This proved to be a significant achievement, possibly more so than was realized at the time the commission was set up. A joint committee appointed by the two governments, it was a by-product of conversations held in the border area in 1943 by presidents Roosevelt and Avila Camacho.

The broad objective of the commission was to help solve the acute economic problems of Mexico arising out of wartime conditions, and in this way to keep up the flow of Mexican strategic materials for the war effort. The most pressing problem was inflation, caused by the disparity between aggregate money incomes and the supply of goods. Since the first of these two factors was a question for action by the Mexican government alone, the joint commission fixed its attention upon the second, the supply of goods. To increase production in Mexico, therefore, became its principal goal. This led the commission to concern itself with ways and means of increasing the exportation of machinery and equipment from the United States to Mexico, in order to make it possible for Mexican industries to expand their output of consumer goods.

To appreciate the advantage to Mexico of organizing such a commission, it will be recalled that the United States government already had in operation an elaborate machinery for determining the requirements of foreign countries for goods in short supply, and also for apportioning the export quota among them. Details about the system are not important here. It did not work perfectly, but it worked reasonably well. In any event, there is no doubt that Mexico had been getting at least its proper share of what was available for export. If there had been a discrepancy in the Mexican case it had been on the high side, not on the low, because overland transport made it possible to send goods to Mexico when shipping shortages and the submarine menace seriously interfered with exports to other Latin American nations. This advantage in transportation continued throughout the war, although on a diminishing scale.

The Mexican-American joint commission was a unique institution. No parallel organization was set up for dealing with any other country. Mexico enjoyed a privileged position. Officially this was justified by the degree to which Mexico had diverted its economy to producing strategic materials for the war effort. It was presumed, therefore, that the extent of this diversion had not been properly measured in the ordinary export-control machinery. Other reasons of a political or military nature may also have played a part in the American decision to set up such a commission.

Whatever the motives, the existence of the commission was of enormous importance to Mexico during the critical war years because the American members of the commission were able to exert pressure in Washington to get equipment and materials for all the projects they had approved. Thus, when the commission submitted its final report in January, 1945, it could boast that arrangements had been completed for supplying all the equipment needed from the United States for the so-called Minimum 1944 Program. This program involved twenty projects with an aggregate cost of about 24 million dollars. Included among these were developments in the steel, textile, cement, paper, and chemical industries. Most of the projects were already under construction when the report was written.[40] It is virtually certain that nothing approaching this result could have been achieved without the intervention of the commission.

In addition, about thirty long-range projects recommended by a subcommittee on industrial development were approved. These included irrigation and power projects, as well as a number in the manufacturing field. Here, again, the influence of the commission brought results. It was announced in the final report that the greater part of the equipment required for these projects either had already been delivered from the United States or was in process of manufacture.

Finally, apart from special projects, the commission was able to increase the export of all scarce goods from the United States to Mexico. The words of the report on this point are worth quoting, for they show that Mexico was getting special treatment.

. . . the Commission has also reviewed the general requirements (i.e., requirements not related to specific projects) of Mexico for commodities in short supply and has urged revisions in allocations from the United States, on the basis of changed conditions in Mexico, or on the basis of data heretofore not available. This additional

[40] "Report of Mexican-American Commission for Economic Cooperation," *Foreign Commerce Weekly*, February 10, 1945, p. 10.

information on Mexico's requirements has been most useful to the war agencies and, in view of such information, certain allocations have been increased or established for additional products.[41]

Surely if a similar joint commission had been set up between the United States and any other Latin American country during the war, a similar result would have followed; as compared to the regular export-control process, changed conditions would have been evaluated more precisely and data previously not available would have been brought out. As a matter of fact, the rather abrupt way in which the Mexican-American commission voted itself out of existence suggests that the American government was afraid that the pressure from other Latin American republics for comparable treatment would have been irresistible. Such a development would have wrecked the whole system of export controls.

Thanks to the Mexican-American Commission for Economic Cooperation, therefore, Mexico did handsomely during the war years in getting machinery, equipment, and other scarce goods needed by her for industrial development. Naturally, industrialists who were expanding their plants wanted more than they were able to get, and they did not hesitate to criticize the United States export-control system. Compared to their colleagues in the other Latin American republics, however, they fared very well. The work of the joint commission was clearly a boon to industrial development in Mexico during the war years.

TECHNICAL RESEARCH AND EDUCATION

As the industrialization process gained headway after 1940 the Mexican government became increasingly concerned about promoting scientific and technical research, and also about providing more facilities for vocational education. The economic past of Mexico, like that of other nonindustrialized countries, had supplied few developments along these lines. It was realized that much had to be done in all branches of the general field of technical-scientific training.

The Instituto Politécnico Nacional (National Polytechnic Institute), which had been founded by Lázaro Cárdenas in 1936, was strengthened and extended in a number of ways under Avila Camacho. New curricula were introduced for scientific training at the professional level, notably in industrial chemistry, and additions were made to the laboratories and other physical facilities of the institute. On the nonprofessional level, a program designed to give training in industrial skills was expanded. This program was drawn up by the government in collaboration with labor groups and interested industrialists. It appears, however, that not much progress was

---

[41] *Ibid.*, p. 11.

made in this field until 1947. In that year much publicity was given to the nonprofessional work of the Instituto Politécnico Nacional.

The Avila Camacho administration also embarked upon an ambitious plan to construct what is known as the Laboratorios Nacionales de Fomento Industrial (National Laboratories for Industrial Development). These laboratories are being built on the outskirts of Mexico City. The first unit, which houses the government's bureau of standards, was inaugurated in November, 1946. The project when completed will include fourteen other laboratories, each concerned with technical research relating to a particular branch of industry. Apparently all sorts of technical and scientific problems are to be investigated. Studies are to be made of industrial processes and methods, of by-product utilization, of the relative merits of domestic and foreign raw materials, and the like. Finished products are to be tested for suitability.

Among the products or industrial branches to be covered by these government research institutions are rubber, petroleum derivatives, hard fibers, fats and oils, woods, textiles, tanning, and electricity. The precise basis on which these laboratories will coöperate with private industry has not been made public. In some degree at least, they appear to be substitutes for private industrial research laboratories. It will take some years before the extent of their contribution to Mexico's industrialization can be known, but it is immediately clear that they can be highly useful.

The obvious need to raise the levels of technical and scientific performance in Mexico as the country continues to industrialize at a rapid rate, suggests that what the government has done thus far in this field is just a beginning. At the moment, President Alemán seems to be carrying forward the Avila Camacho program. Before he leaves office he probably will have expanded it considerably.

Two Short-Lived Measures

During Avila Camacho's administration two related measures to promote industrialization were initiated without being carried far enough to get a real trial. Both steps, one rather more than the other, were intended to give a certain amount of coördination and direction to industrial development. The failure to make a genuine effort in either case shows the absence of a program or plan of industrialization. If the administration had been determined to introduce even the modest amount of planning contained in these measures, at least one of them would have been made promptly effective.

The first, enacted at the end of 1941, provided for setting up a fund to promote industrial advance in Mexico. Three main objectives were prescribed for the fund: (1) to assist new industries whose economic viability was assured (economic viability to be determined by criteria set forth in the law); (2) to help existing firms in expanding or rationalizing their plants; (3) to make a survey of the industrial resources and possibilities of Mexico.

In order to carry out these functions the directors of the fund were authorized to buy the bonds or preferred stock of any qualified industrial firm. They were also allowed to guarantee a minimum rate of interest on the bonds of such companies, or a minimum dividend on preferred stock. Certain kinds of firms were to have priority in getting financial aid from the fund, namely, those which were critically needed for subsequent economic development, those which used domestic raw materials, and those which would free the country from burdensome imports. The last is a significant reminder of the protectionist thinking in Mexican government circles.

The commission directing the fund consisted mostly of officials of Mexico's central bank, the Bank of Mexico, and technical administration of the fund was also entrusted to the bank. Everything was neatly provided for—except the money for the fund. On this critical question the law simply said that the Bank of Mexico would receive from the Ministry of Finance the money or credits to constitute the fund.

Details are lacking about what steps were actually taken to set up this fund and to operate it. The annual reports of the Bank of Mexico are silent on this question. It is known, however, that practically nothing was accomplished by the measure, this on the authority of one of the Mexican public officials who has been most concerned about government action to assist industrial firms in getting funds.[42]

In the summer of 1944, with much fanfare, a Federal Commission for Industrial Development (Comisión Federal de Fomento Industrial) was created. This was done at the suggestion of the Mexican-American Commission for Economic Cooperation. A clause in the law authorizing the Federal Commission for Industrial Development nullified the act of 1941 which had set up the fund discussed above. The new body was to take over any money that had been allocated to the fund.

The Federal Commission for Industrial Development was given rather broad powers because it was intended to be a functioning as well as a planning organization. Its principal task was to promote industries which private investors had not been willing to undertake but which were deemed essential to a rounded and rational industrial development of Mexico. Such industries were to be planned, financed, and organized by the commission,

[42] Antonio Manero, "El fomento industrial de México," *Memoria del Segundo Congreso Mexicano de Ciencias Sociales,* vol. 2, p. 227.

and they were to be operated by it until private entrepreneurs were willing to take them over. Public ownership and operation were to be temporary only. Nevertheless, the need for public investment as an initiating force was recognized. Then, too, authority to select and establish new industries of vital importance to the economy made the commission a powerful planning agency. Drawing up a basic program of industrialization, with attention to priorities and chronology, was fundamental to its work.

Many persons in Mexico had high hopes for the Federal Commission for Industrial Development. At last, they believed, industrialization in Mexico would become less of a haphazard process and take on a certain amount of order. Manufacturing would be developed in accordance with natural resources, with technical conditions, and with the requirements of the economy as a whole. Gaps in the industrial structure would be filled, and needless duplication of plant facilities discouraged. Through initial public action private investment would be tempted into underdeveloped but important fields.

The provision of the law of 1944 which allowed government ownership and operation of industries proved to be a source of deep concern to business circles in Mexico. American firms with plants in Mexico, or those planning to set them up, were especially alarmed. It was feared that the Mexican government was going in for a broad program of public industrial development and that the scope for private industry would be substantially reduced. So strong was this reaction that government authorities found it necessary to deny any such intention and to stress the temporary nature of whatever public investment the commission might make.[43] No time was lost in issuing such statements. This incident shows how anxiously the Avila Camacho administration was trying to placate private investors.

Far from exercising a profound influence on the Mexican economy, the Federal Commission for Industrial Development has not even left a recognizable mark. Even if the three members of the commission had wanted to take effective action they were precluded from doing so by two fundamental deficiencies, lack of staff and uncertainty of funds. To carry out its functions properly it is obvious that the commission would have required a large staff of investigators trained in technical fields as well as in economics. Gathering the basic data needed for the commissioners' decisions would have called for much time-consuming research, for even economic data of a reasonably reliable sort are hard to come by in Mexico. On the question of staff and research the law was at best vague.

The budget put at the disposal of the commission was, as Manero has said, problematical. Apart from the balance, if any, remaining in the previ-

---

[43] See, for example, *Mexican-American Review*, vol. 12, no. 7 (July, 1944), p. 42.

ous (1941) fund for industrial development, money was to be derived from two sources: (1) 50 per cent of the profits obtained by the federal government from the operation of the various national credit institutions, such as the Bank of Mexico, the Banco Nacional de Crédito Agrícola, and others; (2) allocations that might be made in the federal budget. According to Manero, all three sources combined fell far short of the fund of several hundred thousand pesos which he estimates as the amount required to do the job for which the commission had been created."

The Federal Commission for Industrial Development, therefore, like its predecessor, has come to naught. If it managed to achieve anything tangible at all, the Mexican public certainly has not been informed about it.

LAW OF INDUSTRY SATURATION

The Mexican government has at its disposal a powerful weapon to influence industrial development in a law which authorizes the government to close any industry against the entry of new firms. So far the law has been applied only in five cases, but it offers interesting possibilities for the future. It may well play an important role in future national economic policy.

The legal basis for such action is found in Article 28 of the Mexican Constitution and in the Law of Monopolies enacted in 1934 to implement this constitutional provision. The law of 1934 allows for an exception to the prohibition on monopolies, in the case of an industry which is suffering from ruinous competition or threatened with it. In 1936 Congress gave the president power to apply this law whenever he considers that an industry has reached such a state of development that further expansion would be harmful to management and labor, or to the public. He is authorized to declare the industry saturated. The fundamental premise for such a step is that the state must intervene to maintain an equitable relation among profits, wages, and prices.

By declaring an industry saturated the president automatically halts expansion in the industry whether by way of the entry of new firms or by additions to the equipment of existing plants. This moratorium is intended to be temporary in the sense that it is to last only until an emergency situation is over. However, only one of the five industries so far classified as saturated has been released from control by the government. The five industries which have come under this form of control, with the years when they were termed saturated, are: silk and rayon, 1937; matches, 1941; flour milling, 1943; rubber, 1943; cigarettes, 1944.

In the rubber industry conservation of a scarce raw material was undoubtedly the motive for putting a halt to expansion. This is the industry

" *Op. cit.*, vol. 2, p. 229.

in which control was eliminated in November, 1946, when the supply situation eased. Raw material shortage also accounts for the continuation of control in silk and rayon production after the outbreak of the Second World War, although it would not explain the beginning of control in 1937. The other three cases are no doubt to be explained simply by pressure from the interested producer groups. There is absolutely no evidence that the government made careful studies of the structure of any of these industries before acting to close them against new firms. To open the door again will not be easy because the established concerns will fight hard to maintain their privileged position.

Whatever the motives for applying this law in the past, it is obvious that it could be used to serve other ends, notably to help in channeling investment into lines that the government wants to see developed. It is true that this could be done only in a negative fashion under the saturation law, by closing certain industries against new investment. Applied on a substantial scale, however, this could be effective. Capital would be forced to look for outlets in a restricted area of the economy. Obviously, this negative measure would not compel capital to move into the fields selected by the government, but it would reinforce the effects of other policies of a more direct nature, such as those relating to credit and tariffs.

A further possibility is that the law of saturation will be used to discourage foreign investment in industries in which the Mexican government prefers the employment of domestic capital. This would call for flexible application. Although this is not likely to occur in many cases, those selected might be important ones.

INDUSTRIAL FINANCING

Highly important in Mexican government policy to encourage and promote industrial development have been measures of a financial character, in connection with both long-term investment and short-term credit. Such measures have been applied and administered mainly through two agencies, Nacional Financiera, the official investment bank which is often referred to as Mexico's RFC, and the Bank of Mexico, the central bank.

It is difficult to analyze what has been done by Nacional Financiera and the Bank of Mexico in financing industrial development without at the same time discussing the functioning of private banking and financial institutions. In this field the public institutions have been geared to the operations of private financial interests, in the sense of backing them and filling the gaps they have left in the investment and credit structure. The work of public and private organizations can only be understood in relation to each other.

To introduce here a discussion of the whole question of financing industrial development would carry us far afield from the main theme of government policy on industrialization. It is advisable, therefore, to defer our analysis of the role of Nacional Financiera and the Bank of Mexico in industrial financing until the problem can be treated fully.[45] This procedure, based on convenience of exposition, should not be allowed to obscure the importance of the financial arm in the proindustrialization policy of the Mexican government. It has been of the utmost importance in the effort to make that policy effective.

---

[45] See chapter xii.

CHAPTER VI

Organized Labor
and Industrialization

THE BROAD PRINCIPLE that Mexico should become an industrialized nation is fully supported by organized labor in Mexico. All working-class groups have a stake in this question, and thus numerous groups have expressed opinions on the methods and policies which should govern Mexican industrialization. To analyze the differences among such points of view would carry us too far afield. For our purpose we may take as representative of the labor viewpoint the position of the largest federation of Mexican trade unions, the Confederación de Trabajadores de México (CTM).

Since the founding of the CTM in 1936, membership figures have tended to be erratic because factional disputes have often led to temporary withdrawals of component unions. Sizable fluctuations have occurred with little warning. Also, at any one time the status of some of the member unions is apt to be unclear, and the claims of the CTM regarding affiliations may conflict with statements coming from other sources, including leaders of the unions in question. Unity in the Mexican labor movement is far from being a reality. However, it cannot be doubted that the CTM embraces the majority of the organized workers of Mexico, and thus it is reasonable to accept the official position of the CTM as the point of view of Mexican labor as a whole.

Parenthetically, it may be noted that broad, general propositions in the CTM platform on industrialization are identical with those to which important trade-unions in other Latin American countries have subscribed, through the agency of the Confederación de Trabajadores de América Latina (CTAL). This identity can be verified by comparing the resolutions adopted at the CTAL congress of 1944 with the platforms approved at various CTM conventions or with the speeches of CTM leaders.[1] Sources of all three kinds have been used in preparing the discussion which follows.[2]

[1] Compare, for example, *Segundo Congreso General de la Confederación de Trabajadores de la América Latina, Cali, Colombia, Diciembre 1944* (n.p., n.d.), with Vicente Lombardo Toledano, *El nuevo programa del sector revolucionario de México* (Mexico, 1944).

[2] Vicente Lombaro Toledano, although no longer an official (or even a member) of the CTM, was the leading figure in setting up the organization and in shaping its policies during its formative years. He, more than any other person, has influenced the thinking of the CTM

Like the government administration and the New Group industrialists, the CTM leaders define two basic objectives to be attained by industrialization in Mexico, namely, higher standards of living for the people, and economic independence for the nation. It is probably not fair to say that they emphasize the second at the expense of the first, but even a casual survey of what they have been saying and writing will show that they develop the second proposition at greater length and with more ardor. Mexico, it is argued, cannot consider itself an autonomous nation, even politically, as long as it is "dependent on the great international monopolies, . . . a zone of investment for foreign capital, . . . a region producing raw materials to supply the great factories of the industrial powers, and . . . a market for goods manufactured abroad."[3]

This proposition leads at once to a number of specific proposals regarding foreign investment, of which only the principal ones need be summarized here. (1) Foreign capital is required in Mexico because domestic savings are inadequate to meet the needs of a comprehensive developmental program, but it should be allowed to enter the country only on terms laid down by the Mexican nation. (2) The industries considered fundamental to the national economy must not be allowed to pass into the hands of foreign interests. (3) Foreign investment should take place in conjunction with domestic capital, and it should be channeled into fields where it will satisfy the most urgent economic needs of the country. (4) The foreign company should be restricted in taking profits out of Mexico; it should be required by law to reinvest most of its net earnings in productive activities in Mexico.

With the national interest guaranteed by regulations concerning foreign investment and by the active participation of Mexican capital, the CTM leaders hold that industry is the key to Mexico's future development. Thus, Lombardo Toledano has often referred to industrialism as the new objective and the coming phase of the Mexican Revolution. In the earlier phases of the Revolution, he argues, labor gained its basic rights and the bulk of the rural population received land through agrarian reform measures. But now the agrarian program has been in large part completed. Moreover, Mexico can never depend on agriculture to be the mainstay of its economic structure because natural handicaps are too great. Industry, on the other hand, does not suffer from such handicaps. Mexico has the raw materials and physical resources necessary to become an important industrialized nation. There are no insurmountable obstacles to impede this process. "Now the industrial revolution must take place."[4]

---

on economic questions. His point of view, therefore, can be taken to represent the CTM point of view on the issues discussed here.

[3] Lombardo Toledano, *El nuevo programa del sector revolucionario de México*, p. 21.

[4] Quoted from an address by Lombardo Toledano, reported in *El Universal*, April 7, 1945.

When Lombardo Toledano and his fellow trade-union leaders speak of the industrialization of Mexico they mean the development of heavy industries as well as consumer-goods manufacturing. Basic industries within the country itself are regarded as necessary for low-cost production of consumer goods, and the existence of appropriate raw materials makes it possible to establish them. Included in the list of basic industries, according to a statement of Lombardo Toledano,[5] are coal, petroleum, electric power, iron and steel, industrial chemicals, railroads, and machine production. Mexico, he contends, has all the natural resources required for the establishment of each of these industries, and the technical capacity to develop them. Special stress is placed on building up industries to manufacture machines. Mexican industry will never be able to stand on its own feet as long as there is need to import the basic machines used in manufacturing, together with replacement parts.

Although they emphasize the basic fitness of Mexico for well-rounded industrial development, the CTM leaders point out that obstacles to industrialization are not wanting. One such obstacle is the lack of confidence on the part of Mexicans that the country is capable of becoming an industrial nation. This attitude must be corrected. A change in national psychology must take place. On the material side, an important handicap to industrial development is found in inadequate financial support. This must be overcome by a firm credit policy which would direct private as well as public capital into productive activities and prevent the use of funds for speculative transactions.

The foreign economic policy of the United States is also regarded as an impediment to the industrialization of Mexico. Ever since the Chapultepec conference of 1945 the CTM leaders have been highly critical of the official position of the United States government on the reduction of barriers to international trade. This policy, they argue, is designed to promote American trading interests at the expense of internal economic development or reconstruction in other countries. It would be disastrous for other nations, including Mexico, to go along with such a policy. Any tendency in Mexico to do so must be fought as a policy antagonistic to the national interest.

It follows that the CTM accepts protective tariffs as a desirable as well as an effective method of stimulating industrial development in Mexico. Protectionism must be the guiding principle for Mexico's international commercial policy. However, since labor has an important consumer interest as well as producer interest in this question, the support of protection given by the CTM leaders is necessarily hedged in with certain qualifications. They are willing to make concessions on the short-run consumer

---

[5] *Tiempo*, March 28, 1947, p. 43.

interest of labor in order to attain the long-run advantages of industrialization, as long as the protected industries make advances in efficiency. As an illustration of what should *not* happen, they invariably cite the Mexican textile industry, for they agree with those who contend that this industry has remained technically backward because it has been sheltered by a high protective tariff.

On the positive side, in contrast to the negative side of the tariff question, they are less specific—necessarily so, in the nature of the case. The following quotation from an address by Lombardo Toledano is about as positive as any CTM statement on the tariff question.

The CTM will fight alongside the industrialists and merchants in a solid and true national front for tariff protection for our industries—but on the condition that this does not lead to backwardness in industry, nor to permanently expensive products, nor to raising the cost of living.[6]

There would be little point in dwelling on the apparent elements of inconsistency in this statement. The most interesting thing about it is the implication that the CTM leaders are willing to go along with a comprehensive high-tariff program right now, but that they are reserving the right to protest against protection on particular industries later on.

The extension of American interests in Mexican industry is considered by the CTM as an obstacle to wholesome industrial development. Branch plants of great American "octopuses" are not regarded as true Mexican enterprises, although they might be welcome in a restricted number of industries which Mexican capital has not yet entered. Antipathy to American capital rests, of course, on a broader base than that of handicapping industrial development. The CTM leaders always make much ado over the dangers of American imperialist penetration. American investment is considered a vital threat to Mexico's national sovereignty. They admit that Mexico could make rapid progress industrially by giving free rein to foreign capital, but the cost of such action in sacrificing national sovereignty would be too high. Foreign capital should be allowed to participate in the work of modernizing the Mexican economy, but only under conditions carefully prescribed by the Mexican nation.

To some extent the recent outbursts of CTM leaders against American capital are related to the attempt of the Mexican government, discussed in the preceding chapter, to get American oil companies to carry out exploratory drilling for PEMEX. The reaction of Mexican labor was not slow in expressing itself when the rumors of this new policy began to be heard early in the Alemán administration. On March 18, 1947, the ninth

---

[6] *Ibid.*, p. 44.

anniversary of the oil expropriation decree, Lombardo Toledano delivered
an address in which he took special pains to answer all the arguments for
inviting foreign capital to reënter the petroleum field in any form whatso-
ever, and at the same time he warned the Mexican government that organized labor would staunchly oppose such a step.[7] The CTM has set itself
solidly against any development which would weaken national ownership
and operation in the petroleum industry.

In fighting against foreign intervention in Mexican oil production, it is
possible that the CTM leaders have been overstating their opposition to
American capital in other industries as well. That they are hostile to American capital in principle cannot be doubted. On practical grounds, however,
their opposition to some industries is less than that shown to others.

In the main, the CTM leadership sees eye to eye with the New Group
industrialists on questions relating to Mexico's industrialization. We have
already observed how the two groups joined forces at the time of the
Chapultepec conference in 1945 and how this alliance led to a labor-
management pact in April of the same year. As an outgrowth of this pact,
a joint committee of the CTM and Mexican industrialists submitted to
President Avila Camacho an eight-point program for industrialization.
This read very much like a New Group tract.[8]

The wide area of agreement between the CTM and the New Group
industrialists, however, should not be allowed to obscure certain basic differences in viewpoint, especially in relation to long-run issues. The leaders
of the CTM are Socialist in ideology. They do not make an issue over So-
cialism here and now because they believe that in the present stage of
Mexican development private property and private enterprise must prevail
as a general rule.[9] So far as nationalization is concerned, they strongly oppose any moves to backtrack in the two main industries already nationalized in Mexico, petroleum and railroads, but they speak only in vague
terms about further nationalization in basic industries, such as iron and
chemicals.

Aside from the very long-run question of nationalization, the labor
leaders differ significantly from the New Group industrialists on government intervention. They regard the government as an independent entity,
whereas the industrialists tend to look upon the government as an agent
of industry—or, at least, this is what their position amounts to in practical
terms. When the CTM leaders talk about giving the government authority
to regulate the whole economy, they mean something quite different from

---

[7] The text of his address is found in *Tiempo*, March 28, 1947, pp. 41–46.
[8] The text of this statement appeared in *El Nacional*, August 27, 1945.
[9] See, for example, the text of an address by Vicente Lombardo Toledano, in *Cámara Nacional de la Industria de Transformación, Pacto-obrero industrial* (Mexico, 1946), pp. 15–28.

what the New Group industrialists have in mind when they refer to the need for government intervention. To labor, the government represents a public interest quite distinct from the profit-seeking interest of the industrial owner. In regulating the economy, therefore, the government must have a head of its own, although it should invite the coöperation of industry.

Under the present working alliance between the CTM and the New Group industrialists this difference in viewpoint on government intervention has been relegated to the background. However, changing circumstances may one day bring it out as a major issue between the two groups.

Part II

INDUSTRIAL PROGRESS

CHAPTER VII

Industry in the Mexican Economy

THIS CHAPTER is a survey of Mexican industrial development in quantitative terms, in which are used the best figures available for the purpose. Such a survey must be understood in terms of the limitations of Mexican official statistics. This question will be treated below. But it is also important to remind the reader that a statistical picture, no matter how comprehensive and precise the figures may be, cannot be a complete one.

The statistical approach neglects qualitative changes. No figures can bring out the qualitative importance of the transition in the economic and social structure of a nation following upon pronounced growth in one branch of the economy, such as manufacturing. Furthermore, a development of this nature, especially when it takes place at a rapid rate, transcends the immediate quantitative changes involved, such as those relating to the number of persons employed or the value of output, because quantitative effects are not fully realized at the time. Several years are necessary in some cases before the fruits of a particular development can be gathered. There is no need to labor the point. It is clear that an understanding of economic growth, no matter how broad or how narrow the growth may be in scope, requires judgment of a qualitative character as well as the use of statistical data. Indeed, if forced to choose, I would say that the qualitative judgments are the more important of the two.

The lack of accurate statistics in a study of economic and social questions in Mexico makes qualitative judgments all the more important. It is no exaggeration to say that everything relating to statistics in Mexico—gathering, compilation, and publication—is in a deplorable state. This can be said without criticizing the persons who have been in charge of statistical work in Mexican government agencies. Indeed, many of these have been quite as critical in private conversation, and almost as much so in public statements. Improvements have been made over the years, but in spite of the best efforts of many sincere, hard-working, and capable persons in responsible positions within the government, the statistical picture in Mexico still remains badly confused. It often happens, for example, that two or three different departments of the government will publish as many different sets of "official" figures for the same thing. Anyone who has worked with Mexican statistics will bear witness to this and to the long hours that must be spent in trying to hit upon and put together the most reliable figures for what would seem on the surface to be a well-established statistical series.

The handicap of poor and inadequate statistics is felt not only by the student of Mexican economic conditions but also by officials of the Mexican government. Now that the pace of economic change in the country has been speeded up, the need for accurate and timely figures has become more pressing than ever. Such figures are especially needed as a guide to short-run policies required to cope with immediate problems, such as policies designed to offset or to curb unhealthy developments in the economy. In a period of rapidly changing conditions, both inside a country and in the world at large, the government which does not have reasonably accurate and up-to-date figures on what is going on within its borders, is terribly handicapped. The long delays in getting out basic economic statistics in Mexico may, and probably do, prevent the government from taking action at the most effective time. It is highly important, therefore, for the Mexican government to make a major effort to improve its statistical work. Fortunately this point of view prevails in places in government circles, where the nature and magnitude of the problem are well understood.

A number of reasons can be suggested for the poor quality of Mexican economic statistics. The more important of these may be mentioned briefly. The gathering of figures on business operations does not have a long history in Mexico, and many business firms are unable to provide information of even an elementary character. This is especially true for small establishments, but it occurs also, surprisingly often, among the larger ones. Even when the figures are available, business firms are frequently unwilling to submit them—at least without a certain amount of tampering. The fear that any returns supplied to the government will be used for tax purposes causes firms to omit figures and to understate their operations and valuations. This tendency emerges very clearly whenever a commercial or industrial census is taken. Gaps and inconsistencies abound in the returns. As a consequence, not only do the returns have to be checked carefully, but much time and effort have to be spent in lengthy correspondence before the information can be brought to a usable stage. The antistatistical bias found in Mexican business circles rests also upon the fear that business information will be divulged to competitors by government clerks. In view of the low salaries paid in the civil service, and the long tradition of petty graft, this fear is justified whenever confidential business information is involved. Further, among the very small business units, especially in agriculture, lack of education and even of literacy play their part in lowering the quality of Mexican statistics. In the principal fields of industry, however, this is, of course, not a source of defective figures.

Finally, it must be pointed out that government departments have been known to "manufacture" figures, at least in the sense of publishing rough estimates as though they were precise, final figures. Corrected figures sometimes fail to make their way into print. The temptation to make a good public showing for the program which a government department administers has all too often taken the ascendancy over strict accuracy. This bureaucratic peculiarity explains many of the discrepancies among different sets of official figures. In other cases, the attempt to reconcile the figures prepared by different agencies has held up for years the publication of important statistical compilations, of which the disputed figures were only a part.

The attitudes and circumstances just reviewed will suffice to explain why Mexican statistics are so frequently inadequate, inconsistent, questionable, or delayed in publication. At the same time they suggest that the problem of improving the statistical situation in Mexico is actually very difficult. It will be many years before the investigator will be able to accept any set of official figures at their face value. Still, it is encouraging, as we have observed, that high officials in the Mexican government are aware of the problem and that they are trying to do something about it. Until their efforts bear fruit, however, it is essential to try to verify every series of figures that comes to hand, to find out how the data were arrived at, and to use them with much greater caution and restraint than we are accustomed to employ in using, say, comparable American figures.

With the above observations as an introduction, we may now examine the trends shown by such figures and estimates as inspire confidence. The first question which immediately comes to mind is the changing relation between manufacturing and the other branches of the Mexican economy, such as agriculture, commerce, transportation, and the like. In this connection, the years since 1940 form the most critical period. But full comparative data to show what went on during these years will not be available until the next decennial census is taken in 1950 and the results published. Meanwhile, we must rely on a few estimates that throw light on the question.

Before turning to such estimates, however, we should indicate the place of manufacturing in the Mexican economy in 1940, just before the drive to industrialize got under way. According to the census for that year, about 640,000 persons were employed in manufacturing, out of an economically active population of some 5,860,000 persons (excluding domestic servants).[1] This was far less than the number engaged in agriculture, 3,830,000, but it exceeded the number in any other single occupational group shown in

[1] Dirección General de Estadística, *Compendio estadístico* (Mexico, 1947), p. 48.

the census. Commerce, for example, employed approximately 550,000, while only 150,000 were occupied in communications and transportation, and 107,000 in mining and petroleum production.

If we look at contributions to national income, manufacturing appears even more significant. Here we can appeal to the calculations of Dr. Josué Sáenz, former head of the census bureau, whose estimates of Mexican national income for 1929 to 1945 are shown in table 9 (pp. 314–315).[2] He places Mexico's national income for 1940 at 6.8 billion pesos, out of which manufacturing accounted for 1.6 billion pesos. Manufacturing, therefore, contributed 24 per cent of the national income in that year, which was the largest single contribution. Mining and metallurgy, industries with which foreigners have typically associated the name of Mexico, contributed 860 million pesos.

The item for agriculture in Dr. Sáenz's table refers only to crop-raising. If we combine this with the item for livestock production, we find that the total contribution of agriculture to Mexico's national income in 1940 was 890 million pesos. Therefore, although the majority of the Mexican people were occupied on the land, agriculture accounted for only 13 per cent of the national income.

Ten years earlier, on the other hand, agriculture outranked manufacturing in contribution to Mexico's national income. According to Dr. Sáenz's figures, in 1930 agriculture accounted for 325 million pesos, as against 315 million for manufacturing. Commerce and finance held the lead in that year, with 503 million pesos. Somewhere during the years 1930–1940, actually in 1937, if we go by Dr. Sáenz's annual estimates, manufacturing became the principal branch of the Mexican economy from the standpoint of contributions to national income. This had already taken place before the current drive to industrialize Mexico was initiated.

Dr. Sáenz's table for the years following 1940 show little relative gain for manufacturing between 1940 and 1945. Out of about 12 billion pesos national income in 1945, the contribution of manufacturing was 3 billion, or 25 per cent. In 1940, it will be recalled, the percentage was 24. Although the 1945 figures are not calculated (those for the years 1941–1944 apparently are), Dr. Sáenz has not given a detailed account of the method by which he arrived at them. He considers them to be highly tentative. Unless they prove to be very far off, however, they indicate that manufacturing made only a slight relative gain as a contributor to national income in the period from 1940 to 1945, inclusive.

In employment, manufacturing appears to have made greater compara-

[2] Josué Sáenz, "El ingreso nacional neto de México," *Revista de Economía*, vol. 9, no. 2 (February 28, 1946), pp. 27–32.

tive gains since 1940. The Bank of Mexico has estimated that the number of persons engaged in manufacturing rose about 20 per cent during the years 1939–1945.[3] Then, in 1946 the bank reported an additional increase (1945 to 1946) of 2.8 per cent in industrial employment.[4] On the basis of these two estimates, we may place the average *annual* rate of increase in numbers of persons engaged in manufacturing at roughly 3 per cent.[5]

This estimate can be compared with the estimated rate of growth in the whole of Mexico's economically active population during the same period. The census of 1940, as we have noted, reported that approximately 5,860,000 persons were economically active in that year. In 1946, Dr. Josué Sáenz calculated that the economically active population of Mexico had reached a total of 6,200,000.[6] This shows an increase of approximately 6 per cent for the whole period 1940–1946, or an average annual rate of increase of about 1 per cent.

Thus the yearly rate of increase in the number of manufacturing employees has been about three times as great as that in the economically active population as a whole. By far the larger part of this gain was scored at the expense of agriculture. Dr. Sáenz calculates that the number of persons engaged in agriculture rose from 3,830,000 in 1940 to 3,850,000 in 1946, an increase of only 0.5 per cent for the whole period, or less than 0.1 per cent for the yearly average.

Estimates on numbers of persons occupied in other sectors of the economy, such as transportation and commerce, are lacking for the year 1946. It is not possible, therefore, to know whether manufacturing has also been gaining in relation to these activities.

I shall now examine the performance of industry itself, apart from the relation of manufacturing to the other branches of the Mexican economy. For this purpose the results of the industrial census of 1945 would be of the greatest value. Unfortunately, the work of analyzing the returns and tabulating the results of this census has not yet been completed. Apparently so much remains to be done that no one connected with the job will even hazard a guess as to when the census will be published. Parenthetically, it might be pointed out that the final figures for the preceding industrial census, that of 1940, have not yet been published either. Preliminary figures were released in October, 1941, but the

[3] Banco de México, *Vigésimacuarta asamblea general ordinaria de accionistas* (Mexico, 1946), p. 56.
[4] Banco de México, *Vigésimaquinta asamblea general ordinaria de accionistas* (Mexico, 1947), p. 61.
[5] It may be pointed out here that the average annual increase in physical volume of manufacturing output during the same period was greater (5 per cent).
[6] This estimate appeared in an address given by Dr. Sáenz in August 1946, a summary of which appeared in *El Universal*, August 24, 1946.

final figures, although available in the census bureau, have not yet appeared in print. Apparently an interagency dispute is responsible for the delay.

What was said above about the difficulties of collecting reasonably accurate figures from business firms in Mexico obviously applies with special force to an industrial census. It is probable, too, that the Dirección General de Estadística, the agency in charge of the work, has operated with a very limited budget. Nevertheless it is disappointing to all who attempt to analyze current economic trends in Mexico, including officials in the government, the public investment bank, and the central bank, that so little progress has been made in getting the 1945 industrial census material in shape for publication.

The only figures released thus far on the industrial census of 1945 are data of an exceedingly tentative character which cannot even be called true preliminary figures. In the annual report of the Ministry of National Economy for 1946,[7] some figures were published for leading industries as well as aggregate figures for manufacturing as a whole. All of these figures, however, were based on results obtained in the *padrón* rather than in the census itself. The padrón consists of a brief questionnaire sent out to industrial firms before the returns actually used in the census itself are drawn up. According to the results obtained in the padrón the census bureau makes decisions regarding the nature of the return to be employed in the real census, e.g., classification of industries, minimum size of firm to be covered, precise questions to be asked.

Thus the padrón is part of the machinery for setting up the census, rather than a means of making preliminary estimates. The nature of the questionnaire does not allow much scope for checking on internal consistency, so that the results obtained by the actual census may vary considerably from those obtained in the padrón, especially in individual industries. No one in the census bureau will even make a rough guess on how large any such discrepancy is likely to be.

Furthermore, the results of the 1945 padrón are not comparable with the census figures for 1935 and 1940. Neither the industrial census of 1935 nor that of 1940 included firms with an annual output valued at 10,000 pesos or less. The very small firms were thus eliminated. The 1945 padrón, however, covers all firms, regardless of value of annual production. In some industries this discrepancy may be unimportant, but in others it could be, and doubtless is, substantial. There is no way of estimating what the discrepancy will amount to in particular industries, much less in the aggregate figures for all industries. Presumably when the actual census figures for

---

[7] *Memoria de la Secretaría de la Economía Nacional, Septiembre de 1945–Agosto de 1946* (Mexico, 1946), pp. 96–103.

1945 are published they will be comparable with those for 1935 and 1940. Meanwhile there seems to be little point in trying to use the results of the 1945 padrón. For those who might be interested to know what they are, I have included them in table 10 (p. 316).

The best statistics now available on industrial production in Mexico since 1939 are the indexes compiled by the Oficina de Barómetros Económicos, a branch of the Ministry of National Economy. Indexes showing volume and value of output are prepared monthly for nineteen individual industries,[8] on the basis of sample firms for each industry. Over a period of years much has been done to improve record keeping and reporting by the coöperating firms, among which are included the most important enterprises in each industry. The trends shown by the figures for these firms, therefore, can be taken to represent the trends in their respective industries.

Also, the nineteen industries as a group include most of the significant branches of manufacturing in Mexico, as the following list indicates: (1) cotton textiles; (2) woolen textiles; (3) rayon; (4) clothing; (5) flour milling; (6) beer; (7) canning and preserving of foods; (8) vegetable oils; (9) sugar; (10) iron and steel; (11) cement; (12) glass; (13) shoes; (14) soap; (15) cigars and cigarettes; (16) matches; (17) rubber; (18) paper; (19) alcohol.[9] From the nineteen separate industry indexes, the Oficina de Barómetros Económicos calculates a composite production index. This is the best single index for showing trends in manufacturing output in Mexico.

The indexes for individual industries for the years 1939–1947 are presented in tables 11 and 12 (pp. 317 and 318). Some of them will also be found in the next chapter, in connection with the analysis of developments in particular industries, although in a few cases other available figures have been used in preference to those of the Oficina de Barómetros Económicos.

The composite index for manufacturing, showing value as well as physical volume of production, will be found on p. 116.

The index of physical volume claims attention first. The figures in above table show that from 1939 to 1946 the physical output of manufacturing in Mexico increased 40 per cent. On the average, therefore, each year saw an increase of about 5 per cent in industrial production. The upward trend was continuous in the sense that there were no setbacks until 1947. Each year's output exceeded that of the preceding year up till the recession of 1947.

It will be noted, however, that the greater gains were scored in the first half of the eight-year period, and especially in 1941 and 1942. From 103.0

[8] Actually, twenty different series are compiled because flat glass production is treated separately from that of other glass.
[9] Steps are now being taken to include the chemical industry, the most important single industry not yet incorporated in the group.

in 1940 the physical volume index rose to 112.0 in 1941, a gain of almost 9 per cent. In the following year the greatest single rise in the series occurred. For 1942 the index stood at 124.6, an increase of about 10 per cent over the 1941 figure. This was just about equal to the increase scored during the whole four-year period which followed, for from 1943 to 1946 the rise measured only 11 per cent.

Especially noteworthy are the very small increase which took place in physical volume of manufacturing in 1946 and the actual drop in 1947. From 138.9 in 1945 the index rose to only 139.6 in 1946. Then, in 1947,

INDEX OF MANUFACTURING PRODUCTION
(1939 = 100)

Year	Volume	Value
1939	100.0	100.0
1940	103.0	109.5
1941	112.0	125.6
1942	124.6	153.9
1943	125.9	192.9
1944	132.2	216.7
1945	138.9	250.7
1946	139.6	309.9
1947	136.0	331.1

Source: Secretaría de la Economía Nacional, Oficina de Barómetros Económicos, *Trimestre de Barómetros Económicos*, no. 5, June, 1947, tables 3 and 4; no. 8, March, 1948, tables 7 and 11.

volume fell to 136.0, a lower level than that attained two years earlier. This performance was obviously a disappointment to public officials, who had anticipated substantial gains. To account for this unsatisfactory trend in volume of national production, the Minister of National Economy offers the following explanation: (1) businessmen were made cautious through expecting a great reduction in exports and intense foreign competition in the domestic market; (2) the consuming public anticipated that prices would fall in the wake of an increase in the supply of goods; (3) shortages of raw materials.[10] These factors are stated, however, without much amplification or analysis.

To support the point about raw-material shortages, the Minister of National Economy cites the names of a few industries: clothing, flour milling, vegetable oils, and paper. However, he says nothing about the degrees to which such industries experienced shortages, although some

[10] Secretaría de la Economía Nacional, *Trimestre de Barómetros Económicos*, no. 5, June 1947, pp. 18–19.

evidence was presumably available to him. The fact of gaps in raw material supplies, from domestic as well as from foreign sources, cannot be denied, but it is a question whether they were as significant a handicap to 1946 production as the Minister of National Economy, and others in Mexico, contend.

The point about a "buyers' strike" stands on less firm ground. It is a very doubtful one, in view of the substantial price increases which occurred in most lines of manufacturing production in 1946 and 1947. As the table above shows, the insignificant increase in physical volume in 1946 was associated with an increase of 24 per cent in value of output (from 250.7 in 1945 to 309.9 in 1946). Even more revealing was the continued upward trend in value of output in 1947, when the index reached 333.1, in the face of a decline in volume of production. On the average, the prices of manufactured goods produced in Mexico rose 36 per cent from 1945 to 1947.

Probably the most important of the three factors has been the cautious behavior of Mexico's industrialists. Once the war came to an end, uncertainty about the future became a strong influence on business decisions. Especially in the older industries, such as textiles, clothing, and shoe manufacture, hopes of further expansion were replaced by fears of retrenchment. Such a pattern of thinking was consistent with the knowledge that industrial output and plant expansion after 1940 had been greatly stimulated by wartime conditions. It was also consistent with the nonventuresome outlook which has generally prevailed in Mexican industrial circles in the past.[11] As a guide to business decisions, stability has been held more important than change.

The annual report of the Bank of Mexico for 1946 also examines the circumstances relating to the failure of Mexican industrial production to maintain its rate of expansion.[12] The discussion, although brief, is pointed, and it adds a good deal to an understanding of the problem. In two particulars the report of the Bank of Mexico agrees with the explanation offered by the Minister of National Economy, namely, uncertainty regarding the future of Mexican industry, and raw material shortages. However, the following additional factors are brought out: (1) credit intended for productive purposes was directed to commercial operations; (2) deficiencies in the distribution of fuel, mainly petroleum; (3) shortages in the supply of electric power; (4) inadequate railroad service; (5) labor-management conflicts in basic industries.

In thus fixing attention on the slackening of industrial output in 1946 and 1947, I may tend to understate what has been achieved in the indus-

---

[11] See, for example, the section of chapter viii relating to the cotton textile industry.
[12] Banco de México, *Vigésimaquinta asamblea general ordinaria de accionistas*, pp. 21–23.

trialization process as a whole. Obviously, many developments do not show up immediately in production figures. The index of production could not take account of the potential importance of plants that were being constructed during the war years but which were either not completed by 1947 or were not yet operating at full capacity. The aggregate contribution to manufacturing production of such plants is likely to reach substantial levels in future years.

It is also true that a number of the new plants in Mexico are filling gaps in the industrial structure. Thus their importance in the whole process of industrialization is out of proportion to their actual output. Developments in the chemical industry, for example, are apt to be of this character.

Nor can the index of production give adequate weight to the advantages that result from an agglomeration of industries. These advantages do not express themselves in increases in output. To some extent this must already have happened in Mexico, but it will take some years before its influence is fully realized. For a country like Mexico, without a long tradition of industrialization, one of the most important consequences of industrial diversification is the elaboration of skills. New industries are making a contribution to the common pool of industrial skills, from which the older industries also will draw substantial benefits.

To this extent, therefore, I must qualify the impression of manufacturing development in Mexico which is obtained from looking at the movement in the index of production. The index necessarily neglects factors of a qualitative nature, and thus it tends to give a minimum picture of what has been going on. In making this point, however, I do not wish to minimize the impression given earlier in this discussion that government officials in Mexico were seriously disappointed by the trend of industrial output in 1946 and 1947. The disappointment was real, and it had a real basis in the facts of the Mexican economy. It certainly deserved to be, as it was, a source of concern in official circles.

Also disturbing to the government was the discrepancy between the rise in physical output and the rise in value of output. From 1939 to the peak in 1946 the physical volume of production in manufacturing rose about 40 per cent. This was completely overshadowed by an increase of more than 200 per cent in the value of output during the same period. If reference is made to the table presented above, it will be seen that the value of industrial production rose to 309.9 in 1946 whereas the volume index reached only 139.6 (in both cases 1939 = 100).

This discrepancy measures the degree of inflation in the prices of manufactured goods produced in Mexico. The figures just cited show that an index of such prices would register about 220 in 1946 compared with 100 in 1939. This is not out of line with the increase in the general price level in Mexico in the same period. Actually, the wholesale-price index of the Bank of Mexico, also with 1939 as base, stood somewhat higher in 1946, at 228.

However, if 1946 is taken by itself, the upward trend was more marked in the prices of manufactured goods than in the price level as a whole. The average rise in price for manufactures in 1946 amounted to 23 per cent, whereas the increase in the general price level was only 15 per cent. Taken in combination with the exceedingly slender increase in manufacturing output in 1946, this price deviation was properly a cause of uneasiness. It suggested that an unhealthy situation might be developing in the Mexican economy, and, therefore, that the government might have to take action of a drastic nature to keep the economy on a reasonably even keel.

The implications of the production and price trends of 1946 were reinforced by Mexico's industrial experience in 1947. Manufacturing output in 1947 was more than 2 per cent below the level of 1946, while the value of production was about 8 per cent higher. The prices of Mexican manufactured goods rose by an average of 10 per cent during the year 1947. It is true that this rise was considerably less than the 23 per cent increase of 1946. Nevertheless, it was large in relation to the rise in the price level as a whole, for in 1947 the general level of prices advanced only 6 per cent. Thus 1947 saw a continuation of the earlier tendency of industrial prices to advance more rapidly than prices in general.

In concluding this analysis of statistical trends, it will be useful to place the period under scrutiny, 1939–1947, in the perspective of trends over a longer period of time. This may be done by reference to the figures in table 1 (p. 120) showing Mexico's index of manufacturing production for the years 1899–1946. This is the same series which we have already examined for the period 1939–1946, except that the base year is 1929 instead of 1939. For the earlier years of the series, the Oficina de Barómetros Económicos has made changes in composition and weighting to correspond with the industrial structure of that period. It is, therefore, a representative series. The only drawback in using the figures relates to the civil war years of the Mexican Revolution, roughly 1911–1920. The chaotic conditions existing in Mexico during those years make it advisable to neglect them in analyzing industrial trends.

It was pointed out above that the physical volume of manufacturing output in Mexico increased on the average 5 per cent per year during the period 1939–1946. This is considerably greater than the average annual rate of expansion in the early years of the century. From 1900 to 1910, for example, the rate amounted to about 1.5 per cent per year. What is more significant, however, is the fact that the 5 per cent figure was matched by the rate of output expansion in the years preceding 1939. For the 1920's I use the figures covering the years 1922–1929, since those for 1920 and 1921 obviously reflected civil war conditions. The yearly increase for the period 1922–1929 averaged about 5 per cent. And for the years 1930 through 1938

TABLE 1

INDEX OF MANUFACTURING PRODUCTION

(1929 = 100)

Year	Volume	Value	Year	Volume	Value
1899................	35.5	11.3	1924..............	85.6	91.1
1900................	58.7	19.6	1925..............	87.6	89.0
1901................	47.1	17.1	1926..............	99.4	97.4
1902................	49.7	21.5	1927..............	90.1	84.3
1903................	54.1	24.1	1928..............	94.4	85.5
1904................	56.4	30.4	1929..............	100.0	100.0
1905................	50.5	29.1	1930..............	105.3	87.5
1906................	68.1	38.1	1931..............	125.2	75.9
1907................	68.3	40.4	1932..............	90.8	66.6
1908................	67.7	39.2	1933..............	84.1	59.2
1909................	72.7	42.3	1934..............	125.4	118.1
1910................	69.1	43.5	1935..............	122.0	108.6
1911................	65.3	42.7	1936..............	140.5	128.9
1912................	53.0	33.2	1937..............	147.2	150.3
1913................	61.4	39.9	1938..............	151.5	165.9
1914................	45.8	34.0	1939..............	160.5	184.9
1915................	54.9	44.0	1940..............	165.3	202.5
1916................	50.5	42.4	1941..............	179.8	232.2
1917................	46.0	40.7	1942..............	200.0	284.5
1918................	43.7	64.8	1943..............	202.0	356.6
1919................	55.3	66.4	1944..............	212.2	400.6
1920................	53.6	63.4	1945..............	222.9	463.6
1921................	52.7	53.5	1946..............	224.1	573.0
1922................	71.8	57.9	1947..............	218.3	610.2
1923................	81.5	76.7			

Source: Secretaría de la Economía Nacional, Oficina de Barómetros Económicos, *El desarrollo de la economía nacional bajo la influencia de la guerra, 1939–1946* (Mexico, 1946), p. 57. The figures for 1946 and 1947 are calculated from the index of manufacturing production based on 1939.

the rate was again 5 per cent. Thus the rate of increase in physical volume of manufacturing production in Mexico since 1939 has not jumped to new levels, but has remained in line with the previous pace of development.

This stability in rate of output expansion does not take account of the qualitative changes which have occurred in connection with industrial development since 1939, such as those discussed earlier in this chapter. Nevertheless it is an important fact in its own right. It suggests that Mexico, in its current industrialization drive, has been engaged more in building industrial plants than in producing goods. We have already noted how disappointed the Mexican government was over the meager industrial performance in 1946 and 1947. This disappointment takes on deeper meaning when it is considered in the light of the failure of industry to speed up its rate of output over the whole period since 1939, in spite of the investment of large sums of money in new plant and equipment. It is small comfort to know that one day the flow of industrial output will rise to higher and higher levels as a consequence of what has been taking place, when pressing problems are arising at this very hour out of the industrialization process. But this opens avenues of speculation which I must defer following until the last part of the volume, where the problems can be considered in a rounded way.

CHAPTER VIII

Manufacturing Development

THIS CHAPTER, and the one which follows, will bring out the main developments that have been taking place in manufacturing in Mexico in recent years. In this chapter, the principal industries will be treated. In the next chapter I shall deal with more specialized developments. In some cases the latter do not fall conveniently into a category of industrial classification, while others are sufficiently unique to stand out as special features in the process of Mexican industrialization. They are for that reason best treated separately.

In surveying the whole range of new and expanding industrial undertakings in Mexico, I have selected for discussion those which seem to me to have particular importance in the changing industrial and economic structure of the country. Not all of Mexico's industries will be considered in the following pages.[1] The selection of industries and projects to be included has been determined by one or more of the following criteria: (1) striking expansion in the period since 1939; (2) strategic importance in the industrial structure; (3) potential importance for other branches of the economy, such as agriculture; (4) joint participation of private and public capital, or of Mexican and American capital; (5) strong encouragement by the government; (6) sources of current and future problems.

TEXTILE INDUSTRY

COTTON MANUFACTURE

Textile production in Mexico, as elsewhere, has been a leader in industrial development. Encouraged by government subsidies, the industry took hold in the 1830's, and by 1843, 57 cotton mills, as well as a number of woolen and silk mills, were in operation.[2] It was not until the last years of the nineteenth century, however, that rapid expansion began. Most of the firms important in cotton and woolen manufacturing today were established around the turn of the century.

In this new phase of development of the textile industry European enterprise and capital played a large part; French and Spanish immigrants were

---

[1] A brief but very useful survey of the whole Mexican industrial structure, principally as it existed in 1940, will be found in the U. S. Tariff Commission, *Mining and Manufacturing Industries in Mexico*, pp. 55–95.

[2] Wythe, *Industry in Latin America*, p. 299.

responsible for the principal new plants of that period. Some of these immigrants started in the retail business, dealing in imported fabrics. Then they branched out into manufacturing by setting up mills to supply their own stores with the light-weight cotton goods for which there was such a large popular demand in Mexico.[3] As a matter of fact, this linkage between distribution and manufacturing has continued to the present day. All the larger department and dry goods stores in Mexico City also own and operate cotton mills. The industry is thoroughly integrated along vertical lines.[4]

The textile industry has all along been of first-rate importance in Mexican manufacturing. According to the census of 1940 the industry employed 84,000 persons, or about 30 per cent of the total number employed in all manufacturing industries. This employment figure put the textile industry in first place. The industry also ranked first in total amount of wages and salaries paid out, again with about 30 per cent of the total. In two other important categories, value of production and capital investment, textile manufacturing was exceeded only by the food-processing industry. Although all these data are from the 1940 census, figures for earlier years could be cited to show that the textile industry has consistently occupied the same relative position. It shares with the food-processing industry the distinction of being the most important branch of manufacturing in Mexico, when judged by standards of statistical performance.

Cotton manufacturing is the principal branch of the textile industry in Mexico. The majority of the workers employed in the textile industry are engaged in making cotton products. Value of production is also greater in this branch of the industry than in others.

In contrast to the woolen, silk, and rayon mills, the cotton mills of Mexico have been able to get their principal raw material from domestic sources. This has been true for several years. The raw cotton for Mexico's textile plants today is obtained almost entirely within the country. Imports, consisting of long staple cotton which is scarcely raised in Mexico, have averaged for several years less than one per cent of domestic production. Mixed with native cottons, the imports have been used chiefly in the manufacture of high-grade yarns. Before the war most of the long staple cotton was brought to Mexico from Peru and Egypt.

Mexico's cotton is raised principally in the north. Foremost among the producing areas is the Laguna region around Torreón, an area in which one of the most interesting, important, and controversial chapters of the Mexican agrarian program is being written. More than 50 per cent of

[3] A. M. Romero and George F. Zealand, "The Textile Industry," in Lloyd J. Hughlett (ed.), *Industrialization of Latin America*, p. 422.

[4] Gonzalo Robles, "La industrialización en Iberoamérica," Colegio de México, *Jornadas*, no. 17, p. 51.

Mexico's cotton crop is raised in the Laguna district. The Mexicali area in the northwest produces about one-fourth of the annual crop. Two other areas of importance are the Matamoros district in the northeastern corner of the country and the Juárez district near El Paso. In addition to these four main regions, cotton is also raised in a number of small areas.

The principal manufacturing centers for cotton fabrics are far removed from the raw-material producing districts. Orizaba, with ready access to water power, has long been such a center. Puebla, too, has been a leader

OUTPUT OF COTTON MANUFACTURE
(1939 = 100)

Year	Volume	Value
1939	100.0	100.0
1940	101.8	108.5
1941	122.7	128.6
1942	131.4	148.0
1943	148.0	221.5
1944	151.1	258.1
1945	163.8	291.8
1946	164.9	338.3
1947	145.6	332.9

Source: Secretaría de la Economía Nacional, Oficina de Barómetros Económicos, *Trimestre de Barómetros Económicos*, no. 5, June, 1947, tables 3 and 4; no. 8, March, 1948, tables 7 and 10.

in the industry since the middle of the nineteenth century. In recent years Mexico City and its environs have made especially large gains in cotton manufacturing. Guadalajara and Monterrey, followed by San Luis Potosí, have also assumed importance in the cotton industry.

Cotton manufacturing in Mexico expanded remarkably under the stimulus of wartime conditions, when imports fell and internal demand increased, as the figures in the above table show.

Thus in the eight-year period 1939–1946 the industry expanded its output by 65 per cent. Even more striking than this increase in volume, however, was the increase in value of production, which by 1946 had climbed to a point 238 per cent above the 1939 level.[5] Examination of the above table shows that the steepest rise in value occurred from 1942 to 1943, when the index jumped from 148.0 to 221.5. This represented an increase of about 50 per cent in one year's time. During the same year, it will be observed, the physical volume of output increased only 13 per cent. Al-

[5] Special attention should be directed to the discrepancy between the increase in volume and that in value from 1945 to 1946.

though the general inflationary trend in Mexico would account for some of this discrepancy, the difference is so great that special forces must have been at work.

The explanation for this sudden jump in value figures, and for the discrepancy between the increase in value and the increase in volume, is to be found in exportation. Before the Second World War Mexican exports of cotton textiles were negligible. They remained small until 1942. When the United States was forced to reduce its exports after Pearl Harbor, however, Mexican mills began to fill orders from importers in other Latin American countries, especially in Central America and the West Indies. In 1941 Mexico exported only 670 tons of manufactured cotton goods. In 1942 such exports increased more than ten-fold to 7,200 tons, and in 1943 they rose further to 9,000 tons. In 1944 they declined somewhat, but they rose to new heights in 1945 and 1946. For 1946 such exports amounted to 15,800 tons.[6] It has been estimated that in the years 1942–1945 from 15 to 20 per cent of Mexico's annual output of cotton textiles was sent abroad.

The increase in supply of cotton goods available in Mexico during the war years, therefore, was substantially less than the increase in Mexican production. Exportation naturally helped to boost the prices of cotton products in Mexico. Reflecting the new levels of exports as well as an enlarged domestic demand, cotton manufactures rose about 33 per cent in price from 1942 to 1943. During the same period wholesale prices in general rose only 20 per cent. Although subsequent increases in other prices averaged somewhat more than the increases in textiles, the substantial shipments of cotton products to foreign markets continued to exert price pressure through 1946.

The expansion noted in cotton textile output after 1940 was achieved mainly by lengthening the working period. Some new mills were set up and additional equipment was installed in old plants. However, such developments were so handicapped by shortages of machinery that their effect on output was much less than that achieved by a more intensive use of the facilities which existed at the outbreak of the war. Before the war, plants typically operated one eight-hour shift. During the war they went on a three-shift basis where they had enough power available, and where the machinery would stand up under constant use. Some of these plants even gave up their routine maintenance shut-downs. Those plants that could not sustain twenty-four hour operation worked two shifts daily.

This wartime experience of stepping up production showed clearly the antiquated nature of Mexico's cotton textile industry. Technically the

---

[6] Secretaría de Agricultura y Ganadería, *Boletín Mensual de la Dirección de Economía Rural,* no. 257 (October, 1947), p. 870.

industry has remained in a backward condition. Breakdowns were common during the war years because much of the machinery in use was old and in poor repair. This was especially true in weaving. In 1942 the Dirección General de Estadística made a study of the age and condition of equipment used in the textile industry, and, although a limited sampling was used, the results are believed to be representative. It was found that about three-fourths of the looms in use in 1942 had been installed between 1898 and 1910; these machines were at least thirty-two years old when the survey was made, and they may have been as old as forty-four years. For other kinds of machinery 85 to 88 per cent of the installations had occurred in the period 1898–1910. This evidence supports the generalization often heard in Mexico that the cotton textile industry is forty years out-of-date.

The causes for this backwardness in textile production have been discussed widely in Mexico in recent years. One factor in particular has become the subject of heated debate, namely, trade-union policy. Owners of textile mills contend that they would have introduced improved machinery long ago were it not for the fact that the unions, fearing unemployment, insist on severely limiting the number of machines that a single operator is allowed to handle. The unions, apart from defending the restrictions, have argued that other factors are more important, and that the owners themselves have been reluctant to assume the costs of introducing new machinery.

There is no doubt that trade-union resistance to technical change has been a real problem for the industry. In weaving, for example, collective bargaining contracts have usually set the ratio of looms to operatives at four to one, whereas in the United States the normal ratio is about thirty to one. Such restrictions have been greatest in weaving, where modern equipment would cause a substantial displacement of workers. In other branches of the industry the rate of displacement would be lower. One student of the problem in Mexico has estimated that introducing modern laborsaving equipment in the whole industry would displace about 25 per cent of the working force.[7]

During and since the war the textile unions have shown a willingness to relax the restrictions previously enforced and to allow an increase in number of machines per worker. They have come around to accepting the point of view that a certain amount of displacement is inevitable and that they will have to take on the burden of readjustment as a group. They realize that it would be worse for all in the long run if they should try to retard technical improvement in the industry.[8] It is now argued by textile

[7] Ricardo Torres Gaitán, "El futuro de la industria de hilados y tejidos de México," *Revista de Economía*, vol. 7, no. 9–10 (October 31, 1944), p. 14.

[8] Ana Mekler de Martínez, "Industria textil," *Revista de Economía*, vol. 9, no. 4–5 (May 31, 1946), p. 16.

union leaders that the opportunity to introduce the most advanced labor-saving machinery will induce enterprises to establish new plants, thus absorbing some of the displaced personnel. Also, because of greater productivity, the improved older plants as well as the new ones will be able to pay higher wages and provide better working conditions for those who continue to work in the industry. This trend of thinking in trade-union circles has distinctly weakened the workers' resistance to the use of up-to-date, laborsaving machinery.

Tariff protection over many years is also held responsible for technical backwardness in cotton manufacturing. From its early days to the present time the industry has been strongly protected, and for much of their output the producers have had a virtual monopoly of the domestic market. Cost-reducing pressure from foreign competition has been a negligible factor in the industry.

Although this point is generally admitted in Mexico, there is a tendency among Mexican observers to minimize its significance. It is frequently argued that foreign textiles do not compete with all Mexican products, especially with the grades of cotton cloth most commonly consumed in Mexico. For example:

No foreign product competes with the plain white cotton cloth ("manta") consumed by a very large proportion of Mexican peasants; neither is any foreign competition present in the manufacture of the coarse blue cotton cloth ("mezclilla") from which workers' overalls and clothing are made; nor is there much competition either in low quality cotton goods consumed by the lower middle classes in the cities.[9]

Certain doubts occur immediately about the statement just quoted. For one thing, cheap cotton cloth of the kind consumed by the Mexican lower middle class has long been produced in the major industrialized countries and exported around the world to available markets. It certainly would seem that foreign competition would bear heavily upon these products were it not for customs duties. The same could be said of the coarse blue cotton cloth referred to in the quotation. The crude *manta* is a peculiarly Mexican product. But similar fabrics have been used elsewhere. Even in the less developed countries their use has for the most part been abandoned in favor of other low-priced cloths. This experience certainly suggests that the low-income Mexican population would also have accepted substitutes for the traditional manta if such substitutes had not been excluded by the tariff. It is hardly correct to contend that there are no foreign competitive products for the cheaper cotton textiles consumed in Mexico and it is safe to say that in all ranges of its production Mexico's cotton textile indus-

[9] *Reports Presented to the Conference of Commissions of Inter-American Development by the Mexican Commission of Inter-American Development* (Washington, 1945), p. 29.

try has enjoyed substantial protection. Since costs are admittedly high, very little of the industry could have survived foreign competition without such protection. The tariff must be counted as an important factor in weakening the incentive to achieve lower costs by introducing the most advanced equipment available.

During the war, under the stimulus of an active foreign demand as well as the domestic, a certain amount of improved machinery was introduced in cotton manufacturing. This development would probably have been carried further if it had not been for the difficulty of getting such equipment from the producing countries. Very little machinery could be found. Moreover, much of the equipment which Mexican mills were able to purchase was secondhand rather than new, so that the so-called improvements rarely resulted in the introduction of the most up-to-date methods used elsewhere.

If the industry achieved some technical improvement during the war, it also suffered a setback in deterioration of machinery because of constant usage. As seen, two or three shifts became the rule during the war period, and maintenance operations were reduced to a bare minimum. Some machinery had to be scrapped because it was impossible to get parts for repairs. Mexico's cotton textile industry as a whole was in all likelihood worse off technically at the end of the war than it was at the beginning.

Since V-J Day there has been much talk about bringing the industry up to modern levels of performance, but thus far not very much has been accomplished. A few new plants with first-class equipment have been established. So far as can be determined, all these new mills are located outside of the principal textile centers, a development which can be explained partly as an escape from trade-union restrictions and partly as a shift toward areas where the market has been expanding rapidly. Some of the older mills have renewed part of their equipment since 1945, but the difficulty of getting machinery has continued to be a handicap. Some additional secondhand machinery has been purchased in the United States and installed in Mexican plants.

Apart from the problem of getting first-rate machinery, a question may properly be raised about the willingness of the millowners to undertake the investment necessary to rehabilitate the industry. Once the war reached its end, their outlook on the future became clouded. During the war they had become accustomed to very high rates of profit, and now they had to look forward to much lower returns. In the markets to which they had sent exports during the war years they could now expect to meet competition from producers in the great industrialized nations. Thus, reduction had to be anticipated in exports, possibly to the point of their absolute extinction. There was a possibility, too, that foreign competition would be felt in the Mexican market. But even if this did not materialize, postwar readjustments in the whole economy were bound to create uncertainties in the internal market.

When we remember that the entrepreneurs in Mexico's cotton textile industry have always been cautious and conservative in their business outlook rather than venturesome,[10] it can readily be understood that such postwar considerations as those just mentioned would affect them profoundly. It is the economist and the government official in Mexico who talk enthusiastically about putting the textile industry on an efficient, low-cost basis which will enable it to compete in foreign markets and to satisfy the domestic market more effectively than it did in prewar days. This enthusiasm has not been shared by the textile manufacturer.

Early in 1947 the strains of postwar readjustment began to be felt. Exports of cotton fabrics declined substantially; precisely how much cannot be ascertained from the official figures published thus far, because the figures are not adequately broken down. Unofficial estimates put the decline at 60 to 70 per cent.

Quickly, the industry returned to a one-shift basis. Output was reduced (see table). Spokesmen for the textile industry began to speak of a "crisis" and of the need to shut down plants. In addition to losing its export markets, they contended, the Mexican market was being flooded by imports of low-priced cotton fabrics from the United States. It was strongly hinted that the government would have to take action to protect the industry and to stimulate exports if widespread unemployment in the industry was to be prevented.

This pressure from the textile industry achieved prompt results in one direction. In May, 1947, the aforo, an export tax, was abolished on all cotton textiles except *manta* and the coarse blue fabric known as *mezclilla*. These exceptions were made in order to protect the low-income consumers of cheap cottons.

The official statement accompanying the suspension of the aforo on cotton manufactures, issued by the Ministry of Finance, is sufficiently curious to warrant a brief summary.[11] It started out by saying that domestic consumption of textiles had been declining in the past five years because exports profitable to the producers had reduced the domestic supply. The interests of the Mexican consumer had been sacrificed by such exports. The prices of cotton manufactures had gone up more than the price level in general. Also, cotton textile prices had gained substantially on costs,

---

[10] I could go even further and say, as many do, that the business tradition of the cotton manufacturing industry in Mexico is one of extremely shortsighted business policies.

[11] The text of this statement can be found in *El Nacional*, May 29, 1947.

thus creating greater profit margins. Estimates showed that cotton manufacturing costs had just about doubled from 1941 to 1946, while prices had tripled. These facts led to the conclusion that prices of cotton manufactures should now fall into line with other prices and with costs. In this way the Mexican market would be able to absorb all that the industry could produce and at the same time the producers would make a reasonable profit.

In view of this line of reasoning, it is surprising that the government decided to suspend the aforo on cotton manufactures, thus stimulating exports and complicating the problem of bringing about the desired fall in prices. The step was justified on the ground that the government was interested in having the Mexican producers keep the markets they had gained during the war. This must be considered a significant indication of the kind of economic policy likely to be followed during President Alemán's administration. The textile industry is criticized for making unduly large profits at the expense of the Mexican public. A policy of forcing a drop in textile prices is announced, and it is explicitly stated that there is no need to fear a crisis in the industry or widespread unemployment among textile workers if such a price decline occurs. And yet the aforo on a wide range of cotton textiles is abolished, with the effect of helping to keep up exports and to retard the price decline.

It must be concluded that the cotton industry has strong supporters in Mexican political circles. In return for the concession on aforo the industry was asked only to promise not to exceed certain prices (unspecified) for the two kinds of coarse cloth on which the aforos were maintained. The mildness of the government's requirement, and the inconsistency between the stated policy of causing textile prices to fall and the simultaneous action taken to encourage exports, suggest that the industry will be able to call upon further government support if necessary. Thus it is probable that in the years to come additional tariff protection will be given to cotton textiles, and that the Mexican market will be preserved for the domestic producers over the broad range of fabrics.

In view of the industry's claim that it has already been hit by a postwar crisis, we may well be skeptical about the eagerness of the industrialists to modernize their plants. The likely outcome now is that there will be no wholesale modernization, such as was promised a few years ago for the postwar period, and that the rehabilitation of the industry will proceed more or less in accordance with necessities forced upon it by the physical obsolescence of the old equipment.

It is possible, of course, that new firms will come into the industry, using the most up-to-date machinery, and that this will force the older firms to make like improvements. I do not believe, however, that the entrance of new firms will be a significant factor, because the principal existing firms are too well integrated into the powerful "old industry-financial-commercial" business community to allow this to happen on a disturbing scale. Their weight in government circles, too, makes it unlikely that the government would give the same kind of encouragement to new firms in cotton manufacturing that it provides for new firms in other industries, for example, tax exemptions, and financial assistance through Nacional Financiera. In private banking circles, a prospective new firm would probably get a cool reception, if it intended to compete with the existing firms in the industry.

WOOL MANUFACTURE

Manufacture of woolen textiles is the second most important branch of the textile industry in Mexico. As in cotton manufactures, the demand for Mexican woolens was stimulated by wartime conditions, but the production of woolen cloth increased in a much lower ratio. Tabulated (p. 132) are the indexes for volume and value of woolen products, 1939–1946.

It will be observed that physical output declined after the war broke out and that the subsequent increases failed to bring about a material expansion in production. In 1946 output was only 17 per cent higher than it was in 1939, and roughly 25 per cent above the low point of 1940. In 1947 there was a sharp drop in output; production in that year was but little more than that of 1939. Since plant capacity was not enlarged, the increase in production of the period 1942–1946 was attained by working extra shifts in the mills.

The problem of expanding woolen manufacturing during the war years was complicated by the dependence of the Mexican industry on foreign sources of raw materials. Mexico produces wool but not in sufficient volume to satisfy her needs. In the prewar period only about one-third of the raw wool consumed in Mexico was raised domestically. The remainder was imported from Australia, the United Kingdom, Argentina, and the United States. In the latter part of the war period Argentina was by far the principal supplier of raw wool. On the whole, imports of foreign wool during the war compared favorably with prewar imports, but the internal demand for woolen textiles had increased, creating in turn a larger need for the raw product. Also, shipments to Mexico became so irregular that the mills were sometimes short of the imported raw material. So far as possible they overcame this handicap by introducing larger amounts of domestic wool in the manufacture of fabrics, but this practice caused a substantial deterioration in quality of product.

The sheep-raising industry of Mexico has been notoriously deficient in a qualitative as well as a quantitative sense. About half of Mexico's wool crop is produced on small holdings, that is, on small farms and ejidos. Although the ejidal holdings vary in size, they, as well as the small farms, are mostly less than 10 acres in extent. In each case raising sheep is an incidental operation. Even where sheep are raised on larger holdings in Mexico, it is doubtful that selective breeding for good wool is practiced except in isolated instances.

The handling of raw wool, such as in cleaning and in carding operations, is rarely done with care. The burs, insects, and dirt particles that abound

OUTPUT OF WOOLEN MANUFACTURE
(1939 = 100)

Year	Volume	Value
1939	100.0	100.0
1940	94.3	111.7
1941	96.4	123.6
1942	100.5	139.2
1943	100.6	167.8
1944	110.5	190.4
1945	112.4	217.8
1946	116.9	261.7
1947	102.6	270.9

Source: Secretaría de la Economía Nacional, Oficina de Barómetros Económicos, *Trimestre de Barómetros Económicos*, no. 5, June, 1947, tables 3 and 4; no. 8, March, 1948, tables 7 and 10.

in the native wool naturally affect the quality of the yarns and fabrics made from it. Thus the Mexican mills have typically avoided the exclusive use of domestic wool except in the manufacture of low-grade products. For the most part they have used it only in combination with imported wool, employing two or three times as much foreign wool as domestic. Handicraft weavers in the small towns have been the users of Mexican wool.

The larger use of Mexican wool during the war years has created a vested interest which may force the mills to continue using more than the prewar percentage of the native material. Thus, when Australian wool began to reach the Mexican market in larger volume after the end of the war, the woolraisers appealed to the government for additional protection. Their appeal was successful, and the duty on raw wool was raised. At the same time a subsidy of 1.50 pesos was granted to the woolen mills for each kilogram of native wool used in the manufacture of textiles.[12] This action suggests that the Mexican government is anxious to stimulate woolgrowing, even at the expense of some sacrifice in the quality of woolen manufactures.

[12] *Foreign Commerce Weekly*, May 4, 1946, p. 28.

As in cotton manufacturing, the difficulty of getting new equipment and replacement parts was another major difficulty to be faced by the woolen industry during the war period. The use of antiquated machinery, however, is less of a handicap in woolen manufacturing than in cotton, and the woolen industry does not require modernization in anything like the degree needed by cotton manufacturing. On the other hand, woolen production suffered from a lack of technically trained operatives during the war. This condition will have to be remedied if the industry is to expand its output further.

Mexico's woolen industry, like cotton manufacturing, enjoyed a boom in Latin American markets during the war. In absolute terms exports did not reach large figures but notable increases were scored in percentages. In 1939 Mexico exported only 11 tons of woolen manufactures. The big jump occurred in 1942 when 254 tons were sent abroad. In 1943, the peak year, exports amounted to 372 tons, or more than thirty times the 1939 figure.

A change occurred, too, in the composition of Mexico's woolen exports. Before the war woolen cloth was unimportant in the export picture, compared with felt and felt manufactures. During the war cloth became by far the greatest woolen export item.

The future of the woolen industry in Mexico, however, depends on the domestic market. There is little chance that the Mexican woolen mills will be able to hold their wartime gains in Latin American markets. Exports will probably return to their prewar character. On the other hand, the industry will undoubtedly be fully protected in the domestic market. Should the pinch of foreign competition be felt at home the government can be counted upon to extend additional protection. From the standpoint of the government, wool manufacturing is a valuable industry not only in its own right but also because it provides a market for the woolgrowers. Expansion of sheep production is considered important to the agricultural development of Mexico. Thus the step already taken in raising the tariff on raw wool and giving a subsidy to the mills for using Mexican wool is a significant one. It is not just a temporary measure, but on the contrary it suggests a decision to adopt a long-range policy for promoting both wool production and woolen manufacturing in Mexico.

RAYON MANUFACTURE

Rayon manufacturing in Mexico was in its first stage of growth when the Second World War broke out. In the early 1930's rayon-weaving plants began to multiply rapidly. Many of these establishments, however, consisted of nothing more than a few machines located in back patios of urban houses, where cheap fabrics were produced for consumers in the low-income

brackets. Because of complaints that such firms were often operating sur-
reptitiously and evading taxes and labor regulations, the government in
1937 declared the industry "saturated."[13] As in all such cases, this step gave
the government the right to forbid the entry of new firms into the industry.
In addition, an agency was set up to regulate the importation of rayon yarn
and machinery. Import licenses were to be granted only to the firms that
showed compliance with tax and labor laws.

Although many of the household shops were driven out of business by
the controls instituted in 1937, a large number of small firms continued in
existence. In 1943 about two-thirds of the rayon-weaving plants employed
fewer than 30 looms each, and most of these had fewer than 10 looms. Of
the larger mills, only four operated as many as 150 looms.[14] As earlier, the
bulk of the firms in the industry were producing cheap rayons.

During the war the experience of the rayon-weaving industry in Mexico
was very different from that of the cotton industry and even the woolen
industry, because rayon manufacturing was extremely dependent upon
foreign sources of raw materials. No rayon yarn was produced in Mexico
before the war.

Mexico's principal supplier of rayon yarn in 1939 was Italy. A trade
agreement, amounting virtually to a barter agreement, was then in force
between the two countries, whereby Mexican petroleum was exchanged
for Italian rayon yarn. Japan was the second supplier, and additional
amounts were received from the United Kingdom and other European
countries. Shipment from Europe naturally declined after the war broke
out in 1939, and the Japanese supply was cut off after Pearl Harbor. The
United States, which in prewar times was an unimportant supplier, became
practically the only source of rayon yarn. American production, however,
could satisfy only a modest fraction of the demands made upon it. The
Mexican mills were unable to maintain their prewar imports of rayon yarn,
much less to get all the raw material they would have liked to buy in order
to satisfy an expanded internal market.

Thus the rayon-weaving industry was forced to retrench. Plants curtailed their operations by reducing the number of working hours per day.
Some of the smaller establishments shifted to producing other kinds of
cloth, while others went out of business entirely. The number of rayon
weaving firms was reduced from about 250 in 1943 to 140 at the end of
1945, a decrease of almost 45 per cent.

The effect of shortages of raw material on output of the rayon industry
can be clearly seen in the table on p. 135.

---

[13] For a discussion of the "saturation law" see chapter v.
[14] U. S. Tariff Commission, *Mining and Manufacturing Industries in Mexico,* p. 70.

The sharp and continuous decline in output from 1939 to 1943 brought the volume of production down by approximately 50 per cent. In 1944 output began to rise, and in 1945 it reached 75 per cent of the 1939 figure. The upward trend, however, was not sustained in 1946, when production fell by about 3 per cent, nor in 1947, when an additional drop of 16 per cent took place.

Because of the pressure of demand, the prices of rayon textiles rose greatly during the war years. They even surpassed the rise in cotton textile

OUTPUT OF RAYON MANUFACTURE
(1939 = 100)

Year	Volume	Value
1939	100.0	100.0
1940	88.2	97.0
1941	86.0	99.2
1942	66.3	87.7
1943	51.5	87.1
1944	64.0	113.6
1945	75.0	134.0
1946	72.5	155.0
1947	60.8	150.7

Source: Secretaría de la Economía Nacional, Oficina de Barómetros Económicos, *Trimestre de Barómetros Económicos*, no. 5, June, 1947, tables 3 and 4; no. 8, March, 1948, tables 7 and 10.

prices between 1939 and 1945, although the difference was not large. The price rise for rayon manufactures can be appreciated by comparing the value index in the above table with the volume figures. While physical output was falling by almost 50 per cent, the value of output fell only 13 per cent. Both indexes reached their low point in 1943. Even after output began to increase, the value of production continued to rise relatively. Thus, by 1945 output had risen 45 per cent over the 1943 figure while value had climbed 54 per cent. Then, in 1946 when physical output fell off, the value index rose again by 16 per cent. In 1947 both indexes dropped, but while the volume of production fell 16 per cent, the value of output declined only 3 per cent.

According to one economist, Ana Mekler de Martínez, black-market transactions in imported rayon were partly responsible for the heavy increases in the price of rayon manufactures.[15] The distribution of imported rayon yarn among the weaving mills was under the control of an official agency, and the mills bought the yarn at prices fixed by the government.

[15] Ana Mekler de Martínez, "Industria textil," *Revista de Economía*, vol. 9, no. 4–5 (May 31, 1946), p. 19.

Actually the mills were forced to pay higher prices in order to get the yarn, for the personal benefit of the government officials in charge of distribution. Because getting yarn was a life-and-death matter to the mills, such transactions must have had a substantial effect on the prices of finished rayon articles. Indeed Mrs. Mekler de Martínez goes so far as to say that they were responsible for a three- to four-fold increase in the costs of rayon manufacturing.

In 1942 a small beginning was made in the production of rayon yarn in Mexico. Secondhand equipment for the production of viscose rayon yarn was purchased in the United States by a Mexican firm and installed in a plant near Mexico City. Rayon yarn was supplied to the weaving mills at the rate of approximately 1.5 millions pounds per year. The quality of the yarn produced was reported to be low and costs of production were high, but the mill had no difficulty disposing of its output during the war years. It was then the only firm in Mexico producing rayon yarn. Toward the end of the war this firm was bought out by the Celanese Corporation of America and reorganized under the name Artisela Mexicana. New equipment has been introduced, plant capacity has been expanded, and steps have been taken to improve the quality of product.

Of much greater importance for the future of the Mexican rayon industry was the organization in 1944 of a new 20 million peso firm known as Celanese Mexicana. This is a joint Mexican-American venture, in which the American interest is represented by the Celanese Corporation of America. It is reported that the American company owns 51 per cent of the stock in the Mexican concern.[16] Most of the remainder of the stock is held by private investors in Mexico, including banks. However, the public investment bank, Nacional Financiera, holds about 12.5 per cent of the capital stock. Apparently Nacional Financiera's holding was not acquired until 1946, since Nacional Financiera did not report it in earlier years. In addition, the Mexican government, via Nacional Financiera, has made a loan of 15 million pesos to Celanese Mexicana; this loan may be repaid by 1950, or the corporation may at that time elect to convert the loan into a 6 per cent bond isue which would not have to be paid off completely until 1960.

Although construction of the Celanese Mexicana plant was begun during the war, it was not completed until April, 1947. Construction took place under the supervision of the American participating company. The plant, about fifty miles from Guadalajara, the second largest city in Mexico, is equipped to produce acetate rayon. At the time the plant was opened it was scheduled to produce 3 million pounds of rayon yarn per year, but its

16 "Report on Mexico's Chemical Industry," *Chemical and Metallurgical Engineering*, June 1946, p. 122.

production rate was subsequently raised to nine million. Late in 1948 it was announced that further plant extensions were being undertaken.[17] It is calculated that full-capacity operation will require the employment of more than 500 workers.

Celanese Corporation of America is also interested in another rayon plant, in the state of Michoacán, which started operating early in 1949. This enterprise, the Viscosa Mexicana, has a capitalization of 35 million pesos. Nacional Financiera, the government's investment bank, holds 20 per cent of the stock, and in addition has pledged itself to take the whole of a 12 million peso bond issue of Viscosa Mexicana. When finished, it is estimated that the plant will be able to produce 6 million pounds annually of viscose rayon yarn.

Mexico's capacity for producing rayon yarn, once the new plants are fully in operation, will be substantially in excess of her average yearly consumption in the prewar period. Estimates of future consumption, however, are very optimistic. It is widely believed in Mexican business circles that the use of rayon fabrics will undergo an expansion analogous to that which took place in the United States some years ago. Trade sources talk about a consumption of 20 to 25 million pounds of rayon yarn annually at the end of the first postwar decade. In spite of the shift that is likely to occur from the use of other fabrics to that of rayon, such estimates are probably far too optimistic. For the years that lie immediately ahead, it can be taken for granted that Mexico's capacity for producing rayon yarn will be adequate to satisfy domestic requirements.

It can also be taken for granted that the domestic market will be reserved for the domestic producers. The Mexican government has not only been anxious to have the rayon industry establish itself in Mexico but it has also taken a big financial step to encourage this development in lending 15 million pesos to Celanese Mexicana. In addition, we have the financial support which Nacional Financiera has given to the industry. It cannot be doubted, therefore, that protection against foreign competition will be forthcoming in the form of tariffs or otherwise, should the industry call for it.

The situation in rayon yarn manufacturing is an interesting illustration of what has been happening in the Mexican economy in recent years. In the first place, American interests are dominant. Indeed, since all three firms producing rayon yarn are tied to the Celanese Corporation of America, it can be said that the Mexican industry is practically a branch of this American concern. A second feature is the joint-investment structure, whereby Mexican and American capital are joined in the same enterprise. Finally,

---

[17] *Foreign Commerce Weekly*, October 30, 1948, p. 37.

there is the mingling of public and private investment in the two big rayon yarn corporations, Celanese Mexicana and Viscosa Mexicana. The Mexican government itself appears as a lender to Celanese Mexicana. In addition, the official investment bank of the Mexican government, Nacional Financiera, is both a shareholder and a bondholder in these two concerns.

Thus, a large American corporation, private Mexican capital, and the Mexican government are intertwined in this industry. Whatever the advantages of such an arrangement, it must frankly be recognized that many Mexicans are troubled by such close association between their government and large American firms. The inflow of American capital into Mexican manufacturing in recent years has fostered the belief that the nation is allowing itself to be kept in a semicolonial economic status rather than freeing itself from the remaining ties which have kept it dependent upon the United States. This point has been stressed by numerous Mexican industrialists and trade-union leaders in raising their voices in protest against the penetration of American influence. The Mexican public at large has very likely lent a receptive ear to what they have said.

Mexicans are indeed beginning to wonder whether they are returning to the days of Porfirio Díaz, when the foreigner was better treated by the Mexican government than the Mexican. The memory of the oil expropriation of 1938 is fresh in the popular mind. The average Mexican regarded the oil incident as a decisive blow against foreign corporate interests which had a stranglehold upon a vital industry. Now they find their government welcoming large American corporations in new and promising industries, and even going so far as to put public funds into joint-investment ventures. Will not these powerful foreign companies consider themselves to be above the law in Mexico as the oil companies did in an earlier period, and will it not be necessary some time to curb them by similar action? This is the question which is troubling the people, in spite of repeated assurances by the government that the interests of the Mexican nation are being adequately safeguarded in the new wave of American investment.

The optimistic estimates for rayon consumption in Mexico in the next several years were noted above. Even if such estimates should be realized only in part, as seems likely, there will be a substantial expansion in the weaving branch of the rayon industry. It is doubtful, however, whether many new mills will be built, since the "saturation law" has been applied to the industry for more than a decade. The industry could be opened again to new firms, of course, but the existing firms will probably be able to convince the government of the desirability of keeping it closed indefinitely. A greater demand for rayon products will be met by expansion of the larger plants now in operation.

It may be anticipated, too, that the rayon-weaving industry will seek tariff protection against foreign rayon fabrics. Their argument for such protection has been strengthened by quality improvements achieved during the war years. Such improvements were substantial, and the industry is now in much better position than it was before the war to satisfy the demand for the various kinds of rayon cloth consumed in Mexico. Not everyone would consider this a justification for higher protection but it is a factor that will carry weight when publicized by a favorably disposed government.

IRON AND STEEL INDUSTRY

Mexico's iron and steel industry received an enormous stimulus to expand production through the economic conditions prevailing in the country during the war period. Before the war, about half of Mexico's requirements for iron and steel products were satisfied by imports.[18] Total prewar consumption was estimated at 400,000 tons per year. Shipments from Europe naturally fell off greatly after 1939, but imports from the United States took up the slack in 1940 and 1941. In 1942, however, there was a sharp drop in United States exports to Mexico; only 80,000 tons of iron and steel products could be obtained in that year, compared to 113,000 in 1941.

In the following years the tonnage of United States iron and steel shipments increased greatly, rising to levels much higher than those of the prewar period. It must be remembered, however, that these exports were deficient in a qualitative sense. Many of the semifinished and finished iron and steel products which Mexican firms wanted to import could not be obtained at all or could be had only in restricted quantities. To a large extent steel exports from the United States to Mexico were confined to uses which contributed directly to the American war effort, such as the production and transportation of metals and other strategic materials. Thus an attempt was made to produce domestically some of the types of iron and steel manufactures that were formerly imported.

At the same time the demand for iron and steel products expanded to proportions that were far out of line with prewar requirements. The construction industry was extraordinarily active; much steel was needed for apartment houses, office buildings, and factories. Expansion of industry naturally created many other needs for steel articles. Finally, an especially important requirement came from a railroad rehabilitation program which the Mexican government undertook with the financial and technical assistance of the American government. This program alone called for several thousand tons of rails from the Mexican steel industry in the years after 1942.

---

[18] U. S. Tariff Commission, *Mining and Manufacturing Industries in Mexico*, p. 80.

Although many demands had to go unsatisfied, Mexico's iron and steel industry did achieve a material expansion in output during the war years. Unfortunately, it is impossible to get a statistical picture of this expansion from the official figures published by the Mexican government because the basis for computing such figures has obviously been changed from time to time during the period. Even the indexes of the Oficina de Barómetros Económicos, the production indexes of which have been used to gauge output changes in other industries, are regarded as unsatisfactory for the iron and steel industry because of the absence of good basic data.

Persons familiar with conditions in the Mexican industry estimate that the production of pig iron in 1945 was about double that of 1939. In finished iron and steel products, no satisfactory estimate can be made for 1939 or 1940, but it is calculated that output in 1941 amounted to 165,000 metric tons. By 1945 finished iron and steel products were being produced in Mexico at the rate of approximately 300,000 tons per year. This represented an increase of about 80 per cent over the 1941 figure.[19] These estimates of output expansion, although considerably greater than those registered by official figures, are believed to be conservative.

Beginning in 1942 the Mexican iron and steel industry made substantial additions to plant capacity in all branches of production. Among the most important additions are those achieved by the Cia. Fundidora de Fierro y Acero de Monterrey. This firm has been in operation since soon after 1900, when it established the first modern steelworks in Latin America. It has also been, until recently, the largest single producer of iron and steel products in Latin America; only in the past few years has it been surpassed by developments in Brazil. Fundidora is principally a Mexican-owned enterprise. At the time the company was originally organized, foreign holdings of shares were substantial, but large blocks of these holdings have been acquired by Mexicans. About three-fourths of the stock is now Mexican held.[20]

Before the war, Fundidora operated one blast furnace, for which it supplied iron ore from its own mines. The capacity of this furnace was about 400 tons per day. In 1943 an additional, larger blast furnace was installed, with an increase of approximately 500 tons in daily output. Since 1942 changes have also been made in the steel-making equipment of Fundidora, leading to increases in quality as well as in quantity of output. Writing in 1945, George Wythe reported that in addition to the two blast furnaces already mentioned, Fundidora operated five open-hearth furnaces capable of making 200,000 tons of steel annually, one 40-inch blooming mill, one

[19] "War Spurs Mexico's Steel Industry Growth," *Steel*, vol. 116, no. 19 (May 7, 1945), p. 80.
[20] George Wythe, *Industry in Latin Amercia*, p. 303.

reducing mill, one rail and heavy section mill, and three merchant bar mills.[21] In 1945 two more open-hearth furnaces were added. The principal products of Fundidora's plants are structural shapes, rails, bars, and wire rods, but a variety of other articles are produced, including railway-car wheels and castings. Altogether, Fundidora has accounted for about 75 per cent of the total annual Mexican output of semifinished and finished iron and steel products.

The other major additions to Mexico's capacity for iron and steel production have occurred in connection with the Altos Hornos plant at Monclova. This firm has had a brief but rather checkered career. Launched in 1942 with much fanfare, it was hailed as the solution to Mexico's wartime steel shortage problem, as a development of first-rate importance for the long-run future of the Mexican economy, and as an example of the joint Mexican-American enterprises which the Mexican government was anxious to have established. The concern was organized by private Mexican interests, with the participation of the international affiliate of the American Rolling Mill Co. of Middletown, Ohio.

The contribution of this American firm is made through technical direction, patent rights, and management. For supervising the construction of the plant and permitting its patents to be used, American Rolling Mill has received 4,122,500 pesos of common stock and 1,212,500 pesos of preferred shares in Altos Hornos, making a total share-holding of 5,335,000 pesos.[22] In addition, the American concern will receive as a management fee one dollar for each metric ton of product shipped from the plant for fifteen years. These arrangements between the American Rolling Mill Co. and Altos Hornos follow the pattern which has become common in joint Mexican-American enterprises, namely, that the investment of the American firm consists of technical supervision and patent rights rather than cash.

The original capital of Altos Hornos was fixed at 22,310,000 pesos, but this was soon raised to 40,000,000. In addition, a bond issue, also amounting to 40,000,000 pesos, was authorized in 1942. The first issue of stock, apart from shares allocated to the American Rolling Mill Co., amounting to more than 17,000,000 pesos, was taken up by a syndicate of financial institutions organized by the Banco de Descuento.[23]

Indirectly the Mexican government has played a prominent part in financing the Altos Hornos steel plant. This has been done through Nacional Financiera, the official investment bank, which has invested heavily in Altos Hornos securities. According to the latest figures available, Nacional Financiera owned almost 60 per cent of the capital stock on De-

[21] *Ibid.*, p. 303.
[22] "Altos Hornos de México, S. A.," *Revista de Economía,* vol. 5, no. 8 (August 20, 1942), p. 8.
[23] *Excelsior,* March 9, 1944.

cember 31, 1947. On the same date Nacional Financiera owned the entire issue of Altos Hornos bonds. The size of these Nacional Financiera holdings can be taken as a measure of the great importance which the Mexican government has attached to the project.

The United States government has also given financial support to Altos Hornos by means of an Export-Import Bank loan arranged at the time the company was founded in 1942. The amount of the loan was originally $8,000,000. It was granted principally to cover costs of purchasing equipment in the United States, and the difficulty of getting such equipment may explain why the credit was not used until about the middle of 1946. The whole of the credit, which had been reduced from $8,000,000 to $7,500,000, was disbursed during the last six months of 1946.[24]

The Altos Hornos plant is equipped with a blast furnace formerly used in the United States; the furnace was dismantled and shipped to Monclova for installation. This operation was carried out much more slowly than was originally anticipated, so that the furnace did not begin to function until the summer of 1944. It has a daily capacity of 350 tons.

The most important feature of the Altos Hornos plant consists of facilities for making sheets and plate. It is supposed to be Mexico's largest producer of such products, with a projected annual output of 66,000 tons of plate, 16,500 tons of cold-rolled sheets and strip, and 22,000 tons of tin plate.[25]

Although the production of sheet steel was begun shortly after the blast furnace was inaugurated in 1944, the installation of all the fabricating facilities planned for Altos Hornos proceeded slowly and with many interruptions. Some delays were caused by the difficulty of getting equipment from the United States during the war. Inefficiencies within the Altos Hornos organization may also have played a part; at least one hears a good deal about them from informed persons in Mexico. In the annual report of Nacional Financiera covering the year 1945 it was stated that the factory was complete except for the strip mill, but no figures on output were given. Only estimates on productive capacity were cited. The same report, too, contains the following interesting observation on Altos Hornos:

It is hoped that within a short time the enterprise will be operating normally at a rate which will permit it to reduce its costs and make a profit.[26]

By the end of 1946 all of the planned installations had been made and the statistical picture of operations had improved. Nacional Financiera re-

[24] Export-Import Bank of Washington, *Third Semiannual Report to Congress for the Period July–December, 1946* (Washington, 1947), p. 35.
[25] Wythe, *op. cit.*, p. 304.
[26] Nacional Financiera, *Duodécima asamblea general ordinaria de accionistas* (Mexico, 1946), p. 35.

ported that the total output of iron and steel products of Altos Hornos in 1947 amounted to approximately 85,000 tons.[27] This figure, it will be observed, is about 80 per cent of the projected aggregate yearly output as reported by Wythe. In spite of the improved statistical picture, however, one continued to hear the rumor in Mexico that Altos Hornos was operating inefficiently and that the whole project had been erected on an unsound base.

The prices charged for Altos Hornos products have caused at least one outburst of complaint in Mexico. This was voiced by José R. Colín,[28] a leader of that sector of Mexican industrialists to whom I have referred elsewhere as the New Group; these have pointed out that plate produced in the United States was being delivered in Mexico, after paying freight and duties, at one-third to one-half of Altos Hornos prices. Obviously such a comparison is vulnerable to the objection that large differentials exist between American and Mexican prices on many manufactured articles. Also, it is well known that Colín and the New Group industrialists are hostile to enterprises like Altos Hornos because they are large firms and are connected with American interests. This criticism of Altos Hornos can thus be partly discounted, and yet it is significant that no defense of Altos Hornos was made publicly. In view of the fact that such attacks ordinarily give rise in Mexico to vigorous rejoinders in the form of newspaper advertisements, it seems that the case for Altos Hornos was weak.

Stock exchange quotations for Altos Hornos shares show that investors are skeptical about the firm. The par value of both the common and the preferred stock is 500 pesos. In examining the record of transactions on the Mexico City stock exchange for the period June, 1946, through June, 1947, I found that only one sale had actually been completed, involving a block of 50 shares of common stock. These shares were sold at 450 pesos. Apart from this transaction, the highest bid for Altos Hornos common was 425. Preferred stock was bid for only once during the whole period, at 350.

Another suggestion that all is not well with Altos Hornos is the fact that its shares have been removed from the list of eligible securities on the Mexico City stock exchange. When the Comisión Nacional de Valores (National Board of Securities) took this action in May, 1947, the president of this board explained that it was done because of a technical violation of the rules, namely, that the Altos Hornos company had failed to file with the board the required statements showing its financial condition.[29] No

[27] Nacional Financiera, *Décimacuarta asamblea general ordinaria de accionistas* (Mexico, 1948), p. 35.
[28] *El Universal*, December 23, 1946.
[29] *El Mercado de Valores*, June 2, 1947, p. 2.

satisfactory answer was given to the interesting and significant question of why the company failed to provide the statement when due. Also significant is the fact that as late as January, 1949, more than a year and a half after the suspension order, the listing of Altos Hornos stock had not been resumed.

The facts and opinions available about Altos Hornos, therefore, show that the organization has made little contribution to the Mexican economy. Far from measuring up to the high hopes that prevailed in official circles when the firm was established in 1942, the Altos Hornos steel plant has become a source of embarrassment to the government and especially to the public investment bank, Nacional Financiera, which has such a great stake in the enterprise. It is entirely possible that Nacional Financiera will take a substantial loss on its holdings if the government elects to take steps of a face-saving character and put Altos Hornos on an apparently paying basis by scaling down the firm's bonded indebtedness.

A third important plant in Mexico's iron and steel industry is La Consolidada. This rather unusual concern dates from about 1907.[30] La Consolidada operates two open-hearth furnaces at Piedras Negras, across the Rio Grande from Eagle Pass, Texas. This plant has depended chiefly on Texas sources for iron and steel scrap, and it has also been supplied with natural gas from Texas. Two small electric furnaces supplement the open-hearth furnaces in the Piedras Negras mill.

From Piedras Negras, La Consolidada ships steel ingots to its Mexico City mill for further processing. The principal rolling-mill products are structural shapes, concrete reinforcement and other steel bars, and wire rods. At its Mexico City plant La Consolidada also carries out many other operations. It has facilities for electroplating and for manufacturing automobile springs of alloy steel, and wire, bolts, and nuts. Steel castings of various sizes and types are produced, and sideline products include hydrogen, brass, and lead.

Although La Consolidada operated at top speed during the war years in an effort to keep up with the Mexican demand for steel products, no major plant expansion was undertaken. Only in relatively minor degree did this firm add to its productive capacity.

Since the end of the war, La Consolidada has ramified and expanded its operations, principally by building a new mill to make structural steel at Lechería, a short distance north of Mexico City. The Lechería plant is operated by Lamidora de Acero, a wholly-owned subsidiary of La Consolidada. To assist La Consolidada in financing this extension, a loan of 1.5

---

[30] For a popular account of La Consolidada, see "Mexican Steel," *Fortune,* October 1940, pp. 81 ff.

million dollars was granted by the Export-Import Bank in September, 1948. This loan, which is guaranteed by the Mexican government and administered by Nacional Financiera, is to be amortized over a period of five years.[31]

Mexico's capacity for iron and steel production has also been increased since 1940 by scattered additions to smaller prewar plants and by the establishment of several new plants. Most of the latter are also small mills. One, however, deserves special mention because of its projected size. This is the plant of Aceros Nacionales in the new industrial district which is springing up at Tlalnepantla, just north of Mexico City. Plans call for an electric furnace and a rolling mill with an annual capacity of about 60,000 tons of sheet bars, wire rods, structural shapes, and reinforcing bars.[32]

The phase of expansion that got under way in Mexico's iron and steel industry in 1942 seems to be nearing an end. When all the new projects reach full-capacity operation, it is doubtful whether other developments of a substantial nature will be undertaken for some years thereafter. In pig iron production, it is estimated that Mexico's capacity is larger than her domestic consumption at the present time.[33] A margin already exists in this branch of the industry for meeting greater requirements with the existing facilities.

In semifinished and finished iron and steel manufactures, the picture is less clear because of the absence of satisfactory prewar statistics, but it seems that Mexico is reaching a capacity for such products roughly equal to her prewar consumption. Even if consumption had not risen, however, this would not satisfy all of Mexico's requirements. Many specialized products will continue to be imported because it would be much too uneconomical to install equipment to produce them in small amounts. Although each item of this kind may account for only a minor fraction of Mexico's total iron and steel consumption, as a whole they will form a notable quantity.

The remainder, actually the larger share, of Mexico's requirements for iron and steel manufactures can now be produced by domestic plants. Her needs are now greater than they were before the war, and they will remain permanently on higher levels than those of the prewar period. However, it is likely that by making comparatively small additions to existing plants Mexico's iron and steel industry will be able to satisfy the domestic market for nonspecialized products for many years to come.[34]

[31] International Monetary Fund, *International Financial News Survey*, vol. 1, no. 15 (October 7, 1948), p. 123. The circumstances leading to the application for the loan are discussed briefly in *El Mercado de Valores*, October 4, 1948, p. 2.

[32] *Foreign Commerce Weekly*, November 2, 1946, p. 25.

[33] U. S. Tariff Commission, *Mining and Manufacturing Industries in Mexico*, p. 81.

[34] Presumably Wythe holds the same opinion, when he says, "With the completion of the new plants, Mexico will be able to produce most of its normal requirements in basic items." (*Op. cit.*, p. 304.)

Neither in the basic branch nor in the fabricating branch of the iron and steel industry, therefore, is further expansion to be looked for, except on a minor scale.

CHEMICAL PRODUCTION

Mexico's chemical industry is truly a new industry in view of the degree to which plants have expanded and production has been diversified since 1940. The chemical plants are "war babies." Not only has the industry undergone a rapid expansion since the Second World War began but the men who own the chemical plants are strongly imbued with the outlook and attitudes typically associated with "war baby" industries. It is significant that the leaders of the industrialist group which is most actively fighting for tariff protection in Mexico, are representatives of the chemical industry. More will be said about this matter in the pages which follow.

The diversified nature of chemical production makes it extremely difficult to get a picture of the development of the industry as a whole. According to official Mexican figures made available to the United States Department of Commerce, the value of output in the chemical industry rose from 30 million pesos in 1940 to 170 million in 1944, an increase of about 450 per cent. In the same period the number of persons employed in chemical production increased more than 200 per cent, from 3,000 to 10,000.[35] The precise number of new establishments appearing in the industry cannot be ascertained until the 1945 industrial census data are released, but an estimate of a 20 per cent increase could be called conservative.

Reference to the data on tax exemptions for industrial firms, analyzed more fully in chapter x, suggests that the new establishments are organized on a larger scale than the prewar concerns. Of the total number of firms receiving tax exemption privileges from 1940 through the middle of 1946, 83 can be identified as belonging to the chemical industry. Although some older firms are included in this figure, most of them are new ones. The remainder are plants which made additions in order to increase their output. The average capitalization for the 83 concerns was 450,000 pesos, whereas in 1940 the average firm in Mexico's chemical industry had a capital of only 170,000 pesos (see table 5, p. 193). Even if account is made of the increase in the Mexican price level after 1940, the average capitalization of the tax-exempt firms remains substantially greater than that of the firms covered in the 1940 census. As shown in table 5, the 83 firms had an average capitalization of 231,000 pesos in terms of pesos with 1940 purchasing power.

In number of employees, too, the tax-exempt chemical establishments are larger than those recorded in the 1940 census, namely, an average of

---

[35] *Foreign Commerce Weekly*, April 6, 1946, p. 32.

46 as against 32. By this measure the average plant in this group was almost 50 per cent larger than that of the census group.

In spite of certain limitations inherent in the nature of these data on tax-exempt firms, it is clear that the average chemical plant set up in Mexico after 1940 was significantly larger than the average prewar establishment in the industry.

The performance of Mexico's chemical industry during the war years was uneven and erratic. Such production figures as are available show ups and downs more often than continuous increases, in spite of the enlarged demand for chemicals of domestic manufacture. Caustic soda may be taken as an example. In 1940 total output was 685 tons, but in the following year it jumped to 2,640 tons. In 1942, however, production of caustic fell to 1,490 tons, and this was followed in 1943 by another substantial decline to 980 tons. A sizable increase was reported for 1944, when output reached 1,700 tons, but estimates for 1945 showed another drop to about 1,200.[36]

Erratic output for chemicals is explained by a number of circumstances. In the first place, the Mexican chemical industry is dependent upon imports for many raw materials. Before the war approximately one-half of the raw material used by the industry was brought into the country from foreign sources. Just how much this percentage was changed by wartime conditions cannot be determined, but it is known that acute shortages occurred from time to time in the supply of imported materials. Domestic sources of raw materials also failed to meet requirements at times, insofar as the materials were by-products of metallurgical operations or of petroleum refining. Variations in the output of such materials depended upon circumstances wholly unrelated to the chemical industry.

Another factor which must be emphasized in explaining the uneven output in industrial chemicals during the war period is the high mortality rate of chemical firms. A substantial number of firms lasted only one to two years each. Contributing to such failures were the difficulties of getting all the equipment needed to make a plant a profitable unit. Also it was difficult to find a sufficient number of well-trained technicians to lay out a chemical plant and to operate it economically. Some of the establishments, too, were started with insufficient capital. Yet, in spite of numerous failures, expectations for success continued to be good enough during the war years to induce new firms to try where others had given up. The succession of new attempts naturally tended to make output figures jerky.

Bottlenecks in the supply of new equipment also affected the older firms in the chemical industry, in that they often found it impossible to replace

[36] "Report on Mexico's Chemical Industry," *Chemical and Metallurgical Engineering*, June 1946, p. 125.

worn-out machinery and apparatus. This difficulty, for example, is said to explain a decline in output of carbon bisulphide during the war.

In spite of handicaps and irregularities in output, Mexico's chemical industry made headway toward satisfying national requirements in the war period. Even a small export business to other Latin American markets was developed for certain chemicals, such as calcium carbide. According to a survey made in March 1946 by the managing editor of *Chemical and Metallurgical Engineering,* Mexico was well on the road to satisfying her needs for a number of basic chemicals and was actually self-sufficient in six or seven products.[37]

This trend toward self-sufficiency will undoubtedly continue. Within the next few years a number of plant additions and new plants will go into operation; some of these were partly completed during the war but were held up by shortages of equipment. One of the most important of this group is Sosa Texcoco, which is producing soda ash, caustic, table salt, and potassium-salts on the margins of Lake Texcoco near Mexico City. Both the dry bed and the remaining waters of the lake are being exploited. The firm has been given the right to use a huge solar evaporator constructed in 1939 by the Mexican government, which was used by another company until 1943 when operations were suspended.

At full operation it is calculated that Sosa Texcoco will produce 100 tons daily of soda ash, of which 30 tons will be converted into caustic. This plant alone will, on the basis of recent consumption figures, supply about 30 per cent of Mexico's requirements for caustic soda, thus providing a much larger Mexican source of this raw material for various industries than formerly. The soap industry will supply the main market, inasmuch as about two-thirds of the caustic used in Mexico has been consumed in soap production. Petroleum refining, textile manufacturing, and production of vegetable oils have taken most of the remainder in about equal amounts.

When the projects now being completed are added to the plant expansion accomplished since 1939, Mexico will have a well-rounded chemical industry in the opinion of those who have followed chemical developments there closely. During the war the industry suffered from gaps, in the sense that chemicals needed as raw materials in the industry itself were often lacking. Such gaps are now being filled. Similarly, the industry will be better able to supply the requirements of other industries, such as the manufacture of paints and varnishes, soap, pharmaceuticals, printing ink, matches, industrial oils and waxes, glues, plastics, etc. Chemicals are critical raw materials for a long list of Mexican industries, and the demand admits of no abatement.

[37] "Report on Mexico's Chemical Industry," *op. cit.,* p. 123 (see table).

For the raw materials used by the chemical industry itself, Mexico has many sources of supply within its own borders. Sulphur deposits are found in a number of areas, principally in the state of San Luis Potosí. Salt is obtained in large quantities not only in the coastal regions but also in the interior. Close to the industrial area of Mexico City, Lake Texcoco is an important source of salts. Both petroleum and coal are available as raw materials. Mexico is a notable producer of two other minerals especially important in chemical production, namely, arsenic and mercury. From agriculture come two major contributions, sugar cane for the production of alcohol, and limes for making citric acid and lime oil. This list of raw materials, is, of course, by no means intended to be complete; it is simply illustrative. In addition to the resources already exploited for chemical production in Mexico, it is known that there are potential sources to be tapped when needed.

With respect to technically trained personnel for the chemical industry, Mexico is only moderately well supplied because of deficient technical education. The deficiencies are discussed at length elsewhere, for Mexican industry in general, and certain lines of improvement in recent years are noted.[38] The chemical industry, probably more than any other industry in Mexico, has benefited from the immigration of Spanish refugees. A number of chemical firms, especially the new ones, have taken advantage of the opportunity to hire scientifically trained Spaniards, now exiled from their native land. Although these men do not always appear in the principal technical jobs in Mexico's chemical industry, they are clearly contributing notably in raising the levels of technical performance in chemical production.

The importance of chemical training for Mexican industry is recognized in a fellowship program which the central bank, the Bank of Mexico, started in 1944. Fellowships are awarded by the bank to qualified young Mexicans to cover the expenses of studying technical subjects abroad for one to two years. The largest group of these students is found in the field of chemistry. Fellowships in this field accounted for about one-third of the total number awarded in the first two years.

It has been pointed out that the chemical industry is a stronghold of protectionist sentiment in Mexico. The position of the industry makes this wholly understandable. It is an industry of "war babies," the products of most of which have little chance of competing with chemicals produced in the advanced manufacturing nations. Unlike the older industries in Mexico, they have no assurance that the government will provide them with tariff protection. Unlike some of the other new industries, most of the

---

[38] See chapter xiii.

chemical firms do not have connections with large American concerns. Where such connections exist in other industries, the American firms are a source of business strength and of influence in international commercial negotiations. As a matter of fact, the chemical firms fear that the Mexican government will sacrifice their interests in the course of trade negotiations with the United States, in order to get financial support for projects which the government is anxious to promote in other industries and in public works.

Even as a group the industrialists in chemical manufacturing feel weak and insecure. It is not surprising, therefore, that they call upon all Mexican industrialists to join in a broad campaign to insure maximum tariff protection for every Mexican industry. They need support for this purpose, and also for persuading the Mexican government to abandon its reciprocal trade agreement with the United States. Through the Cámara Nacional de la Industria de Transformación they have succeeded in whipping up sentiment for both aims.

It must be recognized that the case for tariff protection in chemicals, specifically, rests upon strong grounds, as long as the Mexican government is determined to advance industrialization by such means as tariffs. In a broad way the case rests on the well-known infant-industry argument. In addition, the chemical industry can get most of its raw materials from Mexico itself. From the standpoint of national economic policy this is an important factor because it makes the development of the chemical industry a stimulus to other productive branches in the economy. It also means that the balance of payments will not be strained by importing basic materials for chemical manufacturing, and that uncertainties of supply, such as those caused by war conditions, will not hold up production. Thus the many other industries that consume chemicals in Mexico will be able to count on domestic sources for the supply of important basic materials. Obviously, such reasoning could apply to many industries in Mexico. The point is that it applies with special force to the chemical industry. Given the demand for chemicals growing out of the industrial development already achieved, the chemical industry establishes itself as a deserving candidate for government encouragement.

One branch of the chemical industry must be singled out for particular attention because of its potential importance to Mexican agriculture, namely, fertilizer production. The use of artificial fertilizers has been little known in Mexico. In the hacienda system as it existed before the Revolution there was little incentive to improve farming methods in any way, inasmuch as the basic conditions of production were given by cheap labor and large amounts of land. On the small holdings which have progressively

replaced the hacienda as the agrarian program has moved forward, the introduction of better techniques has been retarded by a number of bottlenecks,
such as the weight of tradition, excessively small holdings, inadequate
credit, and insufficient allocation of government funds for experimentation.
Differing viewpoints on the agrarian program lead students of the question to stress different factors, including a number not mentioned in this
list, but the fact of technical backwardness in Mexican agriculture is not
doubted in any quarter.

Before the war Mexico imported from about 12,000 to 15,000 tons of
fertilizer annually, principally nitrates from Chile. Most of these imports
were used for a handful of specialty crops, such as cotton, sugar, and winter
vegetables, which were raised by comparatively large scale methods of
production. In the remainder of Mexican agriculture, only manure and
bat guano were used. Most of the land cultivated in any one crop year
received no fertilization. As late as 1946 it was estimated that the total
consumption of all types of fertilizers in Mexico amounted to less than
30,000 metric tons per year.

Anxious to expand agricultural output, the Mexican government has
tried by various means to stimulate the use of artificial fertilizers. Special
agricultural stations have been set up to experiment with fertilizers, and
steps have been taken to educate small farmers about the advantages of
using improved methods. Moreover, since 1942 the government has subsidized the use of fertilizers by sharing with some ejidos the costs of buying
the fertilizers they need. In the five-year period 1942–1946 over 3,000 tons
of fertilizer were purchased under this program, at a total cost of 846,000
pesos.[39] About 45 per cent of the cost was borne by the government, the
remainder by the farmers.

This subsidy program, in which only small amounts were involved before 1947, is considered just a modest beginning, and will, it is expected,
be continued on an expanding scale in the future. In addition to what the
federal government does in this respect, state governments are counted
upon for similar subsidies.

The government has also taken steps to increase the production, as well
as the consumption, of fertilizers in Mexico. For this purpose Nacional
Financiera, the official investment bank, set up a special corporation in 1943,
known as Guanos y Fertilizantes, capitalized at 10 million pesos. The capitalization was subsequently increased to 30 million pesos. Fifty-one per
cent of the stock is held by the Mexican government, via Nacional Financiera. Guanos y Fertilizantes, a publicly-owned concern, is destined to be
the main arm in the government's attack on the problem of extending the
use of fertilizers in Mexico.

---

[39] *Seis años de actividad nacional*, p. 196.

Guanos y Fertilizantes has constructed three plants, the first of which went into operation in December, 1946. This plant, near Mexico City, is the smallest of the three units; its productive capacity is around 5,000 tons per year. At San Luis Potosí, Guanos y Fertilizantes is operating a plant capable of producing normal superphosphate at the rate of 30,000 tons annually; this plant is also equipped to supply guano mixtures. The principal guano mixing plant of the enterprise is at Guadalajara, where a unit capitalized at about one million pesos went into operation in 1947.

According to estimates of Nacional Financiera, full operation of the three plants of Guanos y Fertilizantes means an output of approximately 70,000 tons of fertilizers per year.[40] At the present time there are two other plants in Mexico, not connected with Guanos y Fertilizantes, manufacturing about 8,000 tons of superphosphate annually. If we assume that full production in the new plants has been attained, Mexico now has capacity for producing roughly 80,000 tons of fertilizers per year, almost one-half of which consists of superphosphates. Although this total figure is more than double the estimated prewar consumption, it promises to be small in relation to the amounts needed for effective agricultural development in Mexico.

Guanos y Fertilizantes has received from the Mexican government the exclusive right to exploit the guano resources of Mexico. These consist of large deposits of bat guano in Jalisco and Chihuahua, and of marine guano along the Pacific Coast from Lower California to Acapulco. Total guano production was calculated at 2,100 tons in 1945 and 3,500 tons in 1946, but the new processing facilities opened in 1947 are expected to induce a tenfold, or even greater, expansion in output.[41]

Like so many of Mexico's wartime industrialization projects, Guanos y Fertilizantes has failed to match the performance expected of it when it was founded. Not only was plant construction delayed but there has been difficulty about getting a supply of suitable phosphate rock for the manufacture of superphosphates. Mexican phosphate rock is apparently low in phosphate content. It is reported that Guanos y Fertilizantes has found it necessary to import phosphate rock from the United States. Continuation of this practice may weaken the base of the fertilizer industry in Mexico, if it keeps costs of production in Mexico considerably above those in the United States. The use of fertilizers will have to be subsidized for some years to come because most farmers cannot afford them, even when they realize the advantages to be gained by their use. Thus, the question of the price of the Mexican product is extremely important, because a high

[40] Nacional Financiera, *Décimatercera asamblea general ordinaria de accionistas*, p. 39.
[41] *Revista Industrial*, vol. 1, no. 3 (December, 1946), p. 91.

price will react unfavorably upon Mexico's program for expanding agricultural output, a program which is critical for the whole economy. The facts on Mexican costs of producing fertilizers are not yet known, but at least one close student of agricultural problems, Marco Antonio Durán, doubts that Guanos y Fertilizantes will be able to approximate American costs for chemical fertilizers.[42]

The same writer also criticizes Guanos y Fertilizantes for failing to provide guano in larger amounts and at more reasonable prices than those charged thus far. He finds the performance of Guanos y Fertilizantes to be disappointing in every way. After more than two years of operation, Durán contends, Guanos y Fertilizantes has had no perceptible influence on Mexican agriculture, and he concludes that through Guanos y Fertilizantes "the government is spending large sums of money to little advantage."[43]

We shall probably never know whether Durán's appraisal of the early work of Guanos y Fertilizantes is correct. The fact is that the project is dear to the heart of the Mexican government, and the government has a large financial stake in it as well as a prestige investment. Guanos y Fertilizantes will be strengthened, not abandoned.

This was made clear in May, 1947, when Mexico received a new loan of 50 million dollars from the Export-Import Bank. At that time it was announced that a part of the credit would be used for the construction of a large, new fertilizer plant.[44] Also, a spokesman for Nacional Financiera indicated that it was futile to try to estimate Mexican requirements for fertilizers, since the potential demand was enormous. As an illustration, he calculated that there was already an effective demand for more than 50,000 tons of fertilizers annually in sugar cane cultivation. With statements such as these coming from official and semiofficial sources, there can be no doubt that the Mexican government is determined to expand fertilizer production. Additional measures beyond those already projected, will be taken to promote the fertilizer industry.

CEMENT INDUSTRY

The cement industry of Mexico started its recent course of expansion a few years before the outbreak of the Second World War. The impulse for expansion, following several years of comparatively little change, came from the government's program of public works during the Cárdenas administration. Large outlays were made for dams, water and sewage projects, schools, hospitals, and other public construction; an active demand for

[42] Marco Antonio Durán, "Del agrarismo a la revolución agrícola," *Problemas Económico-Agrícolas de México,* no. 2 (October–December, 1946), p. 74.
[43] *Ibid.*
[44] *El Nacional,* May 28, 1947.

cement was thus created. Between the two industrial census dates of 1935 and 1940 the volume of cement output in Mexico increased by approximately 55 per cent.

During the war the demand for cement in Mexico reached new high levels. Again public construction played its part with irrigation, power, highway, defense, public health, building, and urban improvement projects. Official figures show that public investment in Mexico during the six-year period 1941–1946 amounted to about 2.5 billion pesos.[45] A review of the individual items making up this total suggests that not less than 2.35 billion pesos were spent for projects that involved construction. This figure includes only outlays of the federal government. In addition, state and local governments spent sizable sums on construction projects.

The war years also witnessed a great boom in private construction in Mexico. Even before 1939 the cities were attracting large numbers of persons from the small towns and farms. During the war the rate of urban development was speeded up substantially. This is especially true of Mexico City, where it is estimated that the population increased approximately 40 per cent in the seven-year period 1940–1946. Although no other important city in Mexico matched this pace of population growth, large increases have occurred in Guadalajara, Monterrey, Puebla, and other urban areas.

In all cases the cities of Mexico have been going through a phase of modernization as well as of expansion. Again, this development is most striking in Mexico City where hundreds of old buildings in the heart of the city have been torn down to make way for new structures. Hundreds of office buildings, commercial establishments, and apartment houses have been constructed, and a number of new hotels have been put up. Huge amounts of cement have been used in such buildings.

Residential construction has experienced a similar, if not greater, expansion. This is especially noteworthy in the construction of homes for persons in the high and middle income brackets. The former group fared exceedingly well in the inflationary process of the war years, and the latter group enjoyed some of the fruits of inflation. Both groups were anxious, as well as able, to spend for home construction. In building huge luxury dwellings for the high-income group, large quantities of cement have been employed, and even the more modest homes built in recent years in Mexico have required substantial amounts of this material. For many uses cement has replaced the traditional sun-baked clay.

It is estimated that about 1.3 billion pesos were invested in private construction in Mexico during the six-year period 1940–1945.[46] In addition, a

---

[45] *Seis años de actividad nacional,* p. 367.
[46] *Ibid.,* p. 368.

sum, conservatively estimated at 50 million pesos, was spent for industrial construction. The building of new factories and the expansion of old ones, has also been a significant factor in boosting the recent demand for cement in Mexico.

The need for cement, created by expansion of public works and private building, proved to be greater than the industry could meet. Imports increased greatly in percentage terms, especially after 1943, but the aggregate amount imported was small in relation to Mexico's demands. All through the war period and to the end of the year 1946, Mexico was plagued by such a shortage of cement that it was necessary to delay and even to postpone indefinitely a number of construction projects.

The Mexican government tried to cope with the cement shortage in a number of ways, such as by (1) encouraging the establishment of new plants and the expansion of old ones through tax exemptions; (2) planning the location of new cement-producing facilities in order to minimize costly shipments about the country; (3) enlisting the support of the Mexican-American Commission for Economic Cooperation as a means of getting machinery from the United States for the cement industry; (4) suspending import duties on cement in 1944; (5) setting up a system of priorities for the distribution of available cement, with 50 per cent reserved for public projects and the other 50 per cent allocated among private users according to essentiality; (6) introducing price controls.

The increase in actual output of cement in Mexico during the war period is shown in the tabulation on p. 156. Following an increase of 44 per cent from 1939 to 1942, the volume of production actually fell for the next two years. This decline has been explained as the result of a combination of factors, fuel shortages, transportation difficulties, and labor disputes. In 1945, however, output was notably increased, by 23 per cent as above 1944. A slight drop occurred in 1946, but 1947 saw a new high, a little above the preceding peak of 1945.

The typical wartime discrepancy between the increase in physical output and the increase in value appears in the cement data. During the period as a whole, while output rose only about 65 per cent, the value of cement produced increased 335 per cent. Actually this comparison understates the price rise in cement, for the value figures cited are based on officially fixed ceiling prices. Much of the cement, however, was sold in the black market at a heavy premium above the legal price.

Much more impressive than the actual increase in cement output attained in Mexico during the war period was the groundwork laid for future expansion. In 1939 there were seven plants in operation and one under construction. By the middle of 1946 fourteen cement plants were in production, and four more were being built. The inevitable wartime shortages made it very difficult to equip the new plants with machinery. New equipment was almost entirely out of the question, and even secondhand machinery was hard to come by. Some used machines, however, were found in abandoned or remodeled plants in the United States and shipped to Mexico for installation, for example, in the plants of Cementos Veracruz at Orizaba and Cementos Portland del Bajío at León. The problem of finding such machinery and of securing permission to export it was greatly simplified

OUTPUT OF CEMENT
(1939 = 100)

Year	Volume	Value
1939...................	100.0	100.0
1940...................	118.4	140.5
1941...................	131.3	175.8
1942...................	143.7	208.1
1943...................	141.3	236.5
1944...................	132.3	237.1
1945...................	162.3	322.2
1946...................	161.2	364.8
1947...................	163.3	435.2

Source: Secretaría de la Economía Nacional, Oficina de Barómetros Económicos, *Trimestre de Barómetros Económicos*, no. 5, June, 1947, tables 3 and 4; no. 8, March, 1948, tables 8 and 11.

by the intervention of the Mexican-American Commission for Economic Cooperation. To a lesser extent, similar equipment was purchased in Canada. Because of the results obtained in the face of the lack of first-class equipment the new Mexican cement mills have been known as "miracles of improvisation."

A number of old plants also found it possible to make enlargements during the war years, with substantial additions to productive capacity. For example, one of the larger plants, Cementos Mexicanos at Monterrey, increased its capacity by 80 per cent when it purchased a kiln from a dismantled plant in Michigan. A smaller plant, the Apasco concern in the state of Hildalgo, was able to double its capacity in 1943. Most of the other additions were less effective in percentage terms, but improvements were achieved in practically all plants.[47]

Thus, in spite of wartime handicaps, the number of cement plants in Mexico was doubled, and plants already established before the war were

[47] Details can be found in Oliver Bowles and A. Taeves, *Cement in Latin America,* U. S. Bureau of Mines, Information Circular 7360 [mimeo.] (1946), pp. 4–13.

able to add to their capacity. These developments are not yet complete, for additional equipment is needed for full utilization. Also, some of the secondhand machinery will probably need to be scrapped. But when all the returns are in, Mexico will have recorded a notable expansion in cement capacity during the years 1939 to 1947. In 1939 Mexico's production of cement was about 410,000 metric tons. This figure can be taken as a measure of the industry's productive capacity in that year, since construction was then very active. In the summer of 1946 it was estimated that existing plants, plus new installations then taking place, would yield a capacity of 1,700,000 tons per year. In round figures, therefore, Mexico achieved a fourfold increase in capacity for cement production during the Second World War.

The wartime expansion of Mexico's cement industry is important in still another way; the government made an attempt to insure the location of the new plants in places where they would most benefit the national economy as a whole. As a matter of fact, the cement industry is the only one in which a plan of development was worked out by the government. In spite of much talk about a "plan of industrialization" in Mexico, so far no general program of industrial development has been drawn up. The only thing that could be considered a part of such a plan in Mexico is the government's program for the cement industry.

Under this plan the country was divided into six zones, in each of which it was considered feasible and economical to build up cement-producing capacity to meet long-run needs. In delimiting these districts, account was taken of sources of raw materials and of availability and costs of transportation. It is expected that the movement of cement between zones will be small.

To implement its program for the cement industry, the government has had at its disposal three powerful weapons. One of these was the system of wartime import controls. As with all goods in short supply, the Mexican government worked closely with the United States government in selecting the firms which could import the limited amount of cement-making equipment available. In addition, the Mexican government exerted its influence in the Mexican-American Commission for Economic Cooperation in favor of the projects that fitted its regional plan of development in cement production.

The second weapon was found in the law of manufacturing industries, by which subsidies are granted to firms in "new and necessary industries." Such subsidies, as we have seen, take the form of exemptions from federal taxes and from the payment of import duties on raw materials and equipment. Here again the government could make a selection among firms by encouraging the establishment of new plants in zones where they were needed according to the plan, and also by granting subsidies to existing firms for expansion according to zonal requirements.

The third method of carrying out the government's zoning program in the cement industry was provided by Nacional Financiera, the official investment bank. This agency has taken an active part in promoting and financing plant expansion in cement. Thus, Nacional Financiera was the prime mover in setting up Cementos Oaxaca, the only plant in the southern part of the country. The most recent figures available show that on December 31, 1947, Nacional Financiera held 50 per cent of the shares and about 70 per cent of the bonds issued by this enterprise. Two other cement firms in which Nacional Financiera has played a prominent part are Cementos Portland del Bajío and Cementos Portland Moctezuma. At the end of 1946 Nacional Financiera's holdings in the Bajío company amounted to about 12 per cent of the capital stock and 45 per cent of the bond issue; in the Moctezuma firm Nacional Financiera held almost one-fourth of the shares and the entire issue of bonds.

It is, of course, too soon to attempt an appraisal of the zoning program for the cement industry. To judge from official statements and from the brief official account given in the 1946 annual report of the Ministry of National Economy,[48] the plan has been drawn up with special reference to anticipated needs for seven or eight years immediately ahead, and it is on the basis of experience in this period that it will have to be evaluated. Apart from whatever advantages it will prove to have for cement production, the plan should benefit the Mexican economy as a whole by reducing the strain on transport facilities. This in itself will be a significant achievement during the period when Mexico is rehabilitating and improving its transportation system.

So far as can be ascertained, Mexican rather than foreign capital has taken the lead in setting up new firms in the cement industry. However, the two largest plants, Cementos de Mixcoac and La Tolteca, have been owned by a single British interest known as Associated Portland Cement Manufacturers, Ltd.; apparently neither of these British holdings was liquidated during the war. American capital is involved in at least three plants, including a large one in Puebla.

One very interesting feature of Mexico's cement industry is coöperative ownership and operation. In three plants experiments have been undertaken in coöperation. Two of these date from the early 1930's, when the previous owners, finding it unprofitable to continue operating the plants,

[48] Memoria de la Secretaría de la Economía Nacional . . . Septiembre de 1945–Agosto de 1946, pp. 75–83.

proposed to shut them down. Both were old plants; Cementos Hidalgo, near Monterrey, had been built in 1903, and La Cruz Azul, at Jasso in the state of Hidalgo, dated from 1910. In both plants the Mexican government advanced the funds with which the workers, organized into coöperative societies, purchased the plants. The third coöperative is a branch of La Cruz Azul, far to the south of the parent firm, in Lagunas, Oaxaca. This comparatively small plant went into operation in 1944.

Given the economic philosophy of the present administration in Mexico, that of Miguel Alemán, such coöperative ventures are not likely to be encouraged. If extended at all, new coöperative projects will undoubtedly be confined to small plants, and, short of a major setback in construction, none of the older plants is likely to be sold to its workers.

The outlook for Mexico's cement industry is a promising one, in spite of the fact that the peak of the private building boom was passed in the latter part of 1946. Construction of apartment houses and office buildings will taper off and possibly fall to low levels for some years. Residential construction under private auspices can be expected to follow a similar course. On the other hand, if industrialization projects are carried forward as planned, factory building will continue to act as a stimulus to cement production. Demand for this purpose will offset some of the contraction in other kinds of private construction.

It is in public construction that the cement industry can expect to find a large and active demand for its product in the immediate future. During the administration of President Miguel Alemán it is expected that the government will spend much more on public works than was spent during the administration of his predecessor. Much of this expenditure will necessarily go into the purchase of cement. In addition, sizable outlays will be made in the same period for construction projects of the state and local governments.

If private construction should fall off substantially during the next few years, there is every likelihood that the Mexican government will step up its public works program in order to keep the construction industry fully employed. Perhaps the additional element would consist of building workers' colonies in the larger cities, to fill a real need for decent, low-cost housing among the wage-earning class. Whatever form it takes, expansion of public works will be the Mexican government's first and principal line of defense against economic depression. The cement industry, therefore, need not fear a recession or even a short depression in Mexico. Only a long depression would have an appreciable effect.

If contraction is not to be expected in the cement industry, expansion is likewise not to be anticipated on a material scale. Technical improvement will probably take place as new machinery becomes available, and productive capacity will be expanded accordingly, but it is doubtful that many new plants will be built in the immediate future. This can be inferred from the tone of statements of prominent government officials, and also from official estimates of Mexico's future capacity for cement production.

When the annual report of the Ministry of National Economy was drawn up for the period September, 1945, to August, 1946, it was estimated that by 1952 cement-making capacity in Mexico would reach 2,100,000 tons annually.[49] About one year later, however, the new Minister of National Economy announced that the government's plan of development would bring the cement industry in 1952 to an annual capacity of only 1,800,000 tons.[50] This change shows a substantial lowering of sights in official circles. Furthermore, since construction under way in the summer of 1946 was already carrying the industry to an annual productive level of 1,700,000 tons, the revised figure for 1952 suggests that the period of big expansion in Mexico's cement industry is over. Apparently the federal administration, as well as the industry, is satisfied with the progress already made, and is not likely to encourage new firms to establish themselves in cement production.

Other circumstances lend support to this conclusion. Under the government's program for zoning the expansion of cement-producing facilities during the war period, a territorial division of markets has been achieved in Mexico. As a general rule, the firms in each zone are supposed to sell only in that zone. Thus the government and the producers have already combined to harden the structure of the industry. Of some significance, too, is the fact that the producers and the government worked together during the war in controlling the distribution of domestically produced cement. The committee in charge of allocations consisted of representatives of the Ministry of National Economy, the Ministry of Finance, and the National Cement Producers' Association.

During the Second World War, therefore, the groundwork was laid for a system of quasi-public, quasi-private control in the cement industry. This might well lead to closing the industry to the entry of new firms under the "saturation law."

PAPER INDUSTRY

The consumption of paper in Mexico has naturally followed the rising curves of industrialization and of business transactions in recent years, but a number of other developments have also influenced the demand for paper products. An expanded public effort in education, including literacy cam-

[49] *Ibid.*, p. 80.
[50] *El Mercado de Valores*, June 23, 1947, p. 2.

paigns, has called for large numbers of new textbooks. The market for other kinds of books benefited from the gains which the urban middle class was able to make in the early stages of the wartime inflationary process. Wrapping paper of various kinds has come into increased use as public authorities have set up minimum packaging standards and as private concerns have come to imitate American methods of packaging foods (e.g., bread). Improved sanitary customs have played their part, as in the use of paper drinking cups and paper straws. Then, too, paper was often more readily available than other packaging materials during the war, so that it tended to be substituted in some uses for cloth, metal, and wood.

A few figures will illustrate these tendencies. The consumption of writing paper in Mexico is estimated to have increased 45 per cent between 1939 and 1946. In 1945 the United States Department of Commerce reported that in the five preceding years increases of around 100 per cent had occurred in Mexican consumption of book paper and lithographic products.[51] According to the same source, the use of some paper products expanded as much as 400 per cent during the same period.

Consumption of all kinds of paper was held down during the war by shortages of imports, for a substantial fraction of Mexico's prewar requirements was satisfied by foreign manufacturers. The entire supply of one important item, newsprint, was obtained by importation; the one mill which had formerly manufactured newsprint had discontinued this item in 1935. When the shortage in newsprint became severe in 1943, the government was forced to designate a special board to allocate imports among the different users. This same board rationed certain other kinds of paper in addition to newsprint.

The extent to which the Mexican paper industry increased its output of all classes of paper products is best shown by the indexes from the Oficina de Barómetros Económicos appearing on p. 162.

It is unnecessary to stress the widening discrepancy between value and physical volume increases after 1939, for this dislocation existed throughout the whole Mexican economy. However, it appears that paper production was one of the leaders in this respect.

The increase of 31 per cent volume of output from 1939 to 1945, although substantial, is less than that achieved in a number of other important industries in Mexico, such as cotton textiles, iron and steel, cement, and food products. It will be noted that the upward trend in paper production of the years 1940 and 1941 was interrupted in 1942; not until 1944 did output rise above the 1941 figure. Note too the decline in 1946 and 1947.

[51] "Pulp and Paper—Foreign Economic Developments in Mexico," U. S. Department of Commerce, Industrial Reference Service, vol. 3, pt. 6, no. 5 (September, 1945).

Raw material shortages are held responsible for the failure of output to increase steadily through the whole period since 1939. Before the war, from 75 to 80 per cent of the raw materials used by the Mexican paper industry were imported, the principal material being pulp. Supplies of pulp were obtained from Sweden, Norway, Germany, Canada, and the United States. During the war only Canada and the United States were able to ship to the Mexican market, and then only in reduced amounts. However, partially offsetting increases in the domestic production of pulp were attained by

OUTPUT OF PAPER
(1939 = 100)

Year	Volume	Value
1939	100.0	100.0
1940	104.8	128.7
1941	121.1	151.7
1942	112.3	182.7
1943	119.7	191.0
1944	127.0	218.1
1945	130.7	244.4
1946	123.4	251.4
1947	121.6	282.9

Source: Secretaría de la Economía Nacional, Oficina de Barómetros Económicos, *Trimestre de Barómetros Económicos*, no. 5, June, 1947, tables 5 and 6; no. 8, March, 1948, tables 9 and 12

Mexico's two leading producers of pulp and paper. On the basis of scattered figures, it is estimated that these plants increased their output of pulp, principally the mechanical type, by roughly 150 per cent between 1939 and 1943.

The increase in output of paper during the war years was achieved without any significant additions to plant capacity, either by way of extensions to old plants or by the opening of new ones. Three or four of the prewar firms continued to account for the bulk of production. Outstanding among these was the Cia. de las Fábricas de Papel de San Rafael y Anexas, a concern which dates from the 1890's. This company has been manufacturing about one-half of all the paper and paperboard produced in Mexico,[52] and it has also been the largest producer of pulp in the country. Second position, in pulp as well as in paper production, has been held by Fábricas de Papel de Peña Pobre. The plants of these two leading firms are situated near Mexico City, as is that of Fábrica de Papel de Coyoacán, the company that has ranked third in the paper branch. These concerns, and others of smaller

[52] Wythe, *op. cit.*, p. 305.

output, operated on a three-shift basis during the latter part of the war period, thus making it possible to expand production with existing facilities.

Early in 1945 construction was begun on a new pulp and paper plant which forms one of the most striking industrialization projects undertaken in Mexico in recent years. This project is known as the Atenquique. It is a project which the Mexican government has been most anxious to encourage, and to which it has given financial support as well as powerful assistance in getting scarce equipment.

The Cia. Industrial de Atenquique was organized in the latter part of 1941 with a capitalization of 6 million pesos. Like so many of the enterprises started during the war, the company found it necessary to raise its capital in order to fulfill its plans. This was done in a series of steps until 15 million pesos in capital stock were issued. Nacional Financiera, the official investment bank, has purchased 1 million pesos of preferred stock for the account of the Mexican government. This is an investment of the government, in which Nacional Financiera has acted merely as an agent. In its own name, however, Nacional Financiera has bought the whole of the Atenquique bond issue amounting to 10 million pesos.

In addition, Nacional Financiera, again acting as agent for the Mexican government, has granted the Atenquique company a twenty-year, interest-free loan of 10 million pesos for road construction. About 200 miles of secondary roads will be built with these funds. This network is considered necessary to connect the plant with the whole of the forest area from which it draws its raw materials. By decree the government has created a forest reserve of roughly 250,000 acres for the supply of Atenquique. Owners of timber in this reserve are required to sell to the Atenquique mill, but the Minister of Agriculture is supposed to protect them by setting minimum prices for the Atenquique company to pay.

Construction on the plant was begun in 1944. It was possible to start at that time only because of the Mexican-American Commission for Economic Cooperation. This commission presented the Atenquique case so strongly before the United States War Production Board that priorities were finally granted for the export of equipment needed to put the plant into operation. In pushing the Atenquique project, the Mexican-American Commission for Economic Cooperation was necessarily influenced by the Mexican government, which gave a priority to this project over other claimants for comparable amounts of scarce materials. In this way. as well as by the financial measures already mentioned, the Mexican government has shown itself to be a thoroughgoing supporter of Atenquique.

Late in 1945 the first units of the Atenquique plant were put into operation. At that time it was announced that its capacity for producing pulp would range from 35,000 to 40,000 tons per year, and that about three-fourths of this would be processed at the mill into Kraft paper and card-board; the remainder would be sold to other paper factories.[53] The plant was so designed as to allow room for expansion in both the pulp and the paper departments; equipment can be installed which would bring the annual capacity of both to 60,000 tons without constructing new buildings.

Plans for the future also call for installations to produce chlorine and caustic soda. These will be used to make white pulp, in order to manu-facture paper of fine quality. The two chemicals will be made by electrolytic processes. Low-cost electric power for this purpose is not now available, but it is expected that it will be supplied by a hydroelectric project planned for a near-by site. The necessity for awaiting this development suggests that it will be some time before the chemical units can be added. Both chlorine and caustic will be manufactured in excess of the amounts required by the Atenquique pulp mill; the surpluses will be sold to other users in Mexico.

The Atenquique project has a social as well as a business side. Although the plant is on the railroad line between Guadalajara and Manzanillo, there was no settlement near the site selected for the project. The company is, therefore, building a town to house its workers, at an estimated cost of 5 million pesos. When completed, the settlement will include a market, a school, and a hotel, in addition to dwellings, and it will be completely sup-plied with potable water, a sewage system, and electric power. The last three items are still newsworthy for small Mexican towns. At the time the plant began to operate, more than 200 workers were employed in the mill and about 50 persons were occupied in administrative jobs. No increases are expected in personnel until the plant is enlarged.

The Atenquique company now occupies second place in Mexico's paper industry. In physical volume of output it is surpassed only by the San Rafael concern mentioned above. At the outset, however, and probably for some time, Atenquique will not produce so wide a variety of paper products as any of the other large producers. Its effect on volume of production will be confined to Kraft paper and cardboard, but in these two lines the addi-tion to Mexican output will be very substantial.

When the plant was inaugurated, Aarón Sáenz, president of the board of directors, stated that costs of production at Atenquique would compare favorably with those of paper mills in the southern part of the United States.[54] The chemicals used as raw materials, he granted, would be more expensive, but labor would be cheaper, and eventually the wood used as raw material would also be obtained at a lower cost. In supplying the Mexi-

[53] El Universal, November 9, 1946.
[54] El Universal, November 9, 1946.

can market, too, Atenquique would enjoy an advantage in freight costs as compared with paper mills in the United States. In spite of these advantages, however, Sáenz indicated that "a reasonable protection" would be necessary on Kraft paper once the period of extreme scarcity was over. Also, the fact that he spoke about "the fundamental need for organizing production so that our costs will be as low as possible" suggests that he doubted that Atenquique would approach a competitive basis with American firms for some time to come. In effect, he was preparing the Mexican public for a request to boost the tariff on Kraft paper.

According to one avowed opponent of all large industrial projects in Mexico, José Colín of the Cámara Nacional de la Industria de Transformación, the Atenquique company at the time its plant was opened had already suggested an increase in the duty on Kraft paper from 20 pesos per ton to 300 pesos.[55] This contention cannot be verified. The only increase reported thus far took place in the general tariff revision of November, 1947, and this change was considered a restoration of the 1942 level of protection. However, it may be significant that Kraft paper was included among the commodities the importation of which was forbidden by the decree of July 9, 1947, intended to ease the strain on Mexico's monetary reserves by curtailing importation of luxuries and relatively nonessential goods.[56] Since Kraft paper was very scarce at that time, it is difficult to understand why it was classed as a nonessential import item. It is certainly not a luxury.

The Atenquique project, like that at Altos Hornos, will continue to command the support of the Mexican government, and for similar reasons. The government's prestige investment, as well as its financial stake in Atenquique, is too great to allow an obvious failure, and the project will go on. It will be given whatever protection it seems to require from foreign competition. These observations are not intended to suggest that Atenquique will not pay its way in the Mexican economy. It may very well do so. Economic history shows the dangers of calling such projects "unsound" merely because they cannot match foreign competitors at the outset, or because they are supported by public investment.

There is, however, still another possible defect in the Atenquique project from the standpoint of the Mexican nation, namely, that a part of its precious remaining forest cover will be destroyed. To operate the plant economically may require a greater rate of timber cutting in the reserve area than a sustained-yield program would allow. Mexico has progressive conservation laws on its books, but enforcement has, typically, been lax. It is possible,

[55] *El Universal*, December 23, 1946.
[56] See chapter v.

even probable, that the local people who supply the timber for Atenquique will cut indiscriminately and excessively and that it will be difficult for the authorities to control them. Forest destruction will then increase soil erosion and the destruction of cultivated fields. Many persons in Mexico who are familiar with the Atenquique area are convinced that setting up the paper mill is the beginning of a cycle which will permanently impair the economic worth of the whole region. How much thought the Mexican government has given to this long-run aspect of the Atenquique project is not known.

Atenquique is the only new large development in the pulp and paper industry to reach the stage of production. There are a number of others, however, in various stages of planning. One of substantial importance will be established in Monterrey, where a Mexican company has bought all the equipment of a plant in New York State, and hired American technicians to install it in a newly-constructed mill. This concern will make mechanical pulp at first, and later Kraft paper.

At Zacatepec in the state of Morelos a plant nearing completion will manufacture high-grade paper from sugar-cane waste (bagasse), using a process developed by a Spanish refugee chemist. The process is reported to be commercially feasible, although some of the experiments made elsewhere with bagasse for paper production have been unsuccessful. About 5 million pesos are invested in the Zacatepec project. The promoter and owner of the enterprise is a prominent Mexican capitalist who has shown a more venturesome spirit than most of his colleagues. He has been actively associated with a variety of business ventures in Mexico and in other Latin American countries.

Shortly after President Miguel Alemán took office at the end of 1946 he announced that during his six-year administration a large paper mill would be built to manufacture newsprint.[57] This plant, he stated, would be big enough to satisfy a substantial proportion of Mexico's requirements for newsprint. Technicians were already studying the project, which would probably be established in Chihuahua or Durango, where the forest reserves could best stand exploitation for this purpose.

Owing to the Atenquique and other developments under way or planned, Mexico's capacity for paper production is undergoing a substantial expansion. In the short-run future, output is likely to increase without encountering obstacles, and in many lines of paper products Mexico will probably be self-sufficient. In the long run, however, the need to conserve the remaining resources of fir, spruce, and pine seems bound to place restrictions on the development of the industry.

[57] *El Universal*, January 9, 1947.

Because of this possibility, there is a growing interest in Mexico in the use of tropical woods for the manufacture of paper. Other potential sources of raw materials are also being studied, including ixtle de palma and zacatón. Mexico has a fairly extensive source of esparto in the state of Veracruz. This could be used for making fine writing paper, as in Europe. Depending upon technical developments as well as upon economic factors, Mexico's paper industry may be able to achieve a stable fundation, in spite of the extent to which the most appropriate resources have been depleted.

FOOD INDUSTRIES

The industries which process foodstuffs and beverages, as a group, rank high in Mexico's industrial structure. According to the manufacturing census of 1940, this group was first in value of output and in value of capital invested, and it was surpassed only by the textile industry in number of persons employed and in total wages paid. Such industries, of course, are important in all countries, but they are especially prominent in relatively nonindustrialized nations like Mexico.

For our purpose it is not necessary to analyze production trends in the various food industries. Figures showing such trends will be found in tables 11 and 12 (pp. 317 and 318). From the standpoint of new industrial development, however, two food industries merit special attention. These are canning and sugar processing.

CANNING

In food canning, the outstanding development has taken place in fish. In 1945, the production of canned fish, in physical volume, was more than 40 per cent higher than prewar (1937) output.[58] The main expansion in this industry has occurred on the west coast of Mexico, in Sinaloa, Sonora, and Baja California, where ex-President Abelardo Rodríguez has taken an active part in setting up and operating fish canneries. It is Mexican rather than foreign capital which is making this development possible.

A number of new canneries have been established in western Mexico since 1939. Some of these are equipped to process vegetables as well as fish and shellfish. The Pesquera de Topolobampo, for example, has been set up to can oysters and mackerel, and, in addition, tomatoes.

These wartime developments in fish canning bear the stamp of permanency. Mexico certainly needs to expand its production of foodstuffs, and thus far it has made little use of the fish resources which lie off its

[58] Calculated from figures in Frank Jellinek, "Mexico Enters the Can Age," *Mexican-American Review*, January, 1947, p. 18. The output of canned shellfish increased 45 per cent in the same period.

coasts. The consumption of fresh fish in the interior, where the bulk of the population is concentrated, has always been severely restricted by high prices. Such prices, in turn, have been caused largely by the lack of transport and refrigeration facilities. Until material improvements can be made in these fields, and in the whole organization required to handle fresh fish, canning promises to be the best answer to the problem of expanding fish consumption in Mexico. It seems unfortunate in this respect that the firms in the industry seem to be looking to export rather than to the domestic market as their principal outlet.

Strides were also made during the war years in the canning of vegetables and fruits. Among the vegetables the most important development has been in processing tomatoes; pineapples have stood first among the fruits. In the Loma Bonita region, where the best Mexican pineapple is raised, three new canneries were constructed. Further expansion in pineapple canning seems assured. The well-known American firm of Libby, McNeill, and Libby has acquired an interest in a packing plant in eastern Mexico where pineapple is canned, and increased production can be expected from this plant as well as others. The output of this industry will probably go to export markets, and in future years canned pineapple is likely to become a valuable item in Mexico's balance of payments.

An unexpected development is now taking place in the canning of meat. Hitherto virtually nothing has been done in this field in Mexico. The sudden stimulus to this industrial development has resulted from the hoof-and-mouth plague which hit Mexico in December, 1946, with disastrous effects on cattle and other livestock. As soon as the disease was identified, the United States closed its border to shipments of Mexican cattle in an effort to keep the dreaded disease from spreading to livestock on this side of the line. This ban was a severe blow to ranchers in northern Mexico, who were mainly engaged in raising cattle for export to the United States. It is estimated that about 500,000 head of cattle had been sent annually from northern Mexico to the United States, where they were range-fed for a year before being shipped to mid-western feedlots. This business, estimated to be worth 25 million dollars a year, came to an abrupt end when transborder shipments were stopped.

In the months following the outbreak of the epidemic, many observers came to believe that the hoof-and-mouth disease would become endemic in Mexico, as it is in many other parts of the world. Even those who believed that it could be stamped out, were agreed that the problem was a difficult one, and that it would require a considerable period of time as well as the most stringent methods of control. The livestock interests of northern Mexico clearly had to make a readjustment. One way out was to build packing plants. Consequently some of the cattle raisers went into the meat-packing business, and a number of new plants were quickly planned for the northern part of the country.

In August, 1947, less than a year after the hoof-and-mouth plague hit Mexico, it was announced that organized cattle interests were engaged in promoting five meat-packing plants. One of these, at Tampico, was almost ready to begin operating. A much larger establishment was being constructed at Hermosillo in the state of Sonora at a cost of 12 million pesos. Two of the others, also under construction, were to be somewhat smaller than the Tampico plant. The fifth one was still in the blueprint stage.[59]

The Mexican government gave immediate aid to the cattle raisers in their packing plant program. President Alemán ordered the public credit agencies to provide financial support to the associations of livestock producers engaged in putting up and operating the new plants. Also, out of the 50 million dollar credit granted to Mexico by the Export-Import Bank in May, 1947, the Mexican government allocated one million dollars for the purchase of materials and equipment needed by these plants.[60] About the same time it became known that the United States was interested in buying a "significant amount" of Mexican canned meat for shipment to other countries.[61]

Government encouragement and the promise of a ready market persuaded the cattlemen's associations, and other interests as well, to set up a number of packing plants in addition to those mentioned above. By September, 1948, ten plants were in operation and six others were under construction.[62] These sixteen plants, which were expected to be able to process 900,000 head of livestock annually, represented an investment of more than 50 million pesos. The rapid development of this industry owes much to assistance from the United States government. In addition to the loan already noted, the United States government has helped the new plants to get equipment and machinery from American sources, and has sent technicians to advise on questions of efficiency of operation and quality of product.

The great stimulus from the American side, however, has been the market. Virtually the entire output of Mexico's meat-packing industry has been purchased by the United States government, for shipment to Europe under the European Recovery Program (Marshall Plan). This is a market of uncertain duration. Nevertheless, it has clearly oriented the new industry

[59] *El Nacional,* August 8, 1947.
[60] *Ibid.,* December 9, 1947.
[61] *El Mercado de Valores,* December 15, 1947, p. 2.
[62] E. Garrett, "U. S. Backs Meat Bonanza," *Mexican-American Review,* September, 1948, p. 17.

toward export markets rather than toward domestic consumption. Already there has been much talk in industry circles about exploring other markets to take up the slack when American purchases are terminated. Barter deals have been suggested as a means of cultivating such markets. Unfortunately, the industry has shown only a slight interest in the problem of raising the domestic consumption of meat.

This orientation toward export markets may not, of course, last beyond the time when European agriculture is rehabilitated. If so, the Mexican consumer may then find the price of meat more favorable, and he may be able to raise his consumption. Per capita meat consumption in Mexico, low at best, declined during the Second World War. In 1934 the average amount of meat consumed per head in Mexico was estimated at 17.5 pounds per year. In 1942 this average stood at 12 pounds, and in 1943 at 10.8. Expansion of the meat-packing industry for domestic consumption seems to be a sound development, socially as well as economically. Expansion for export purposes, except in a very temporary sense, would seem to be of questionable value, in spite of the effect which such a development would have on the Mexican balance of payments.

SUGAR INDUSTRY

The sugar-processing industry in Mexico merits individual attention because it has an importance transcending its productive function in the Mexican economy. It has substantial monopoly privileges under the sponsorship of the government. In their present form these privileges date from 1931 when active cutthroat price competition brought the principal producers together to prevent the further development of what they regarded as a ruinous situation. At the end of 1931 about half of the sugar mills in Mexico were either going through suits in bankruptcy or were being liquidated by the owners themselves.[63] In the following year such firms had a new lease on life thanks to the new producers' association they had formed with the consent and assistance of the Mexican government.

The National Union of Sugar Producers (Unión Nacional de Productores de Azúcar), as it is now called, has the power to regulate production by assigning quotas to individual sugar mills. This is its principal function. In addition, it performs collateral functions in distributing and marketing the output of the whole industry, in regulating imports or exports of sugar, and in extending credit to its members. At the outset, the association was faced with a heavy loss on sugar which it "dumped" abroad in order to get rid of accumulated surpluses. This problem was solved when the govern-

---

[63] Estimated from data in Julio Blumenkron, "Problemas actuales de la industria azucarera en México," *Revista de Economía*, vol. 8, no. 7 (July 1, 1945), p. 33.

ment asked the central bank to make a loan to the association. Ultimately the loss by "dumping" was spread over several years' operations.[64]

During the remainder of the 1930's, restrictions on output and withholding of stocks in certain years yielded prices which were satisfactory to the members of the association. Only a small amount of sugar had to be exported as an additional price-support measure.

In the years following 1940 there occurred in Mexico a substantial increase in the demand for sugar. Per capita consumption of refined sugar (excluding *piloncillo,* the unrefined brown loaf sugar) is estimated to have risen from about 17 kilograms annually in 1939 to 21 kilograms in 1944.[65] This increase in domestic consumption, although important, does not wholly explain the growth in demand, since large amounts of sugar were used to make candy, sirup, alcohol, and other products for export rather than for the internal market.

In the face of a progressively increasing demand, sugar production rose from 1940 to 1942, when a peak figure close to 420,000 tons was reached, but thereafter a decline set in, and output fell to appreciably lower levels. In 1944 production was only about 388,000 tons and in 1946 it was even less, 370,000 tons.

The reasons for this decline have been widely discussed in Mexico in recent years, but the debate has yielded little on which to base an objective judgment. The sugar producers' association has been attacked as a monopoly in which the public interest has not been adequately safeguarded. It has been accused of withholding sugar from the market and of black-market transactions, as well as of unduly restricting production. On their side, the industry's spokesmen contend that two circumstances beyond the producers' control have kept down output: (1) a shortage of machinery and parts to replace worn-out equipment; (2) inadequate production of sugar cane in Mexico.

In defending the sugar producers against attacks, however, representatives of the industry have often admitted that there is substantial room for improving efficiency.[66] This applies both to the processing end of the industry and to the raising of sugar cane. With respect to the latter, it is pointed out that the average yield of sugar cane in Mexico is 50 tons per hectare, and that, although high yields like those of Peru, Java, and Hawaii cannot be expected, an average of 70 tons per hectare should be attainable. For the mills, it is granted that comparatively minor improvements in operation would raise the average percentage of sugar derived from a given

---

[64] Aarón Sáenz, "La industria azucarera nacional," *Revista de Economía,* vol. 7, no. 11–12 (December 31, 1944), p. 35.

[65] Lloyd J. Hughlett (ed.), *Industrialization of Latin America,* p. 398.

[66] For example, Aarón Sáenz, "La industria azucarera nacional," *op. cit.,* vol. 7, pp. 30–40.

amount of cane from 9.4 to 10.0. By combining these improvements with the higher average yield of 70 tons per hectare, it is estimated that Mexico could produce an annual output of sugar ranging between 560,000 and 590,000 tons. Even the smaller of these two figures would represent an increase of one-third over the peak production of 1942.

The disparity between consumption and domestic production in recent years has forced Mexico to become an importer, rather than an exporter, of sugar. More than 60,000 tons of sugar were imported in 1941. No sugar was imported in 1942, but substantial amounts were brought in during the following years. In 1946 the Mexican government arranged for the purchase of 100,000 tons of Cuban sugar,[67] bringing the total importation for the period 1941–1946 to about 250,000 tons. In spite of these imports, the sugar supply situation in Mexico continued to be tight and the price trend sharply upward. Price control, as for virtually all commodities, proved to be ineffective. One authority on the Mexican sugar industry estimates that black-market prices prevailing in recent years have been about double the official ceiling prices.[68]

Reflecting the concern of the Mexican government on the sugar supply situation, Nacional Financiera has taken steps to finance new developments in the industry, especially since 1945. Among the new enterprises founded with Nacional Financiera support two are outstanding, the Cia. Azucarera del Río Guayalejo in the state of Tamaulipas in the northeastern part of the country, and Central Sanalona at Culiacán, in the northwest. Both mills were completed in 1948.

The Río Guayalejo concern is capitalized at 10 million pesos. At the end of 1946 Nacional Financiera held about 50 per cent of the capital stock in the firm, and in addition extended a credit grant of 20 million pesos. The Sanalona company was incorporated in 1945 for 6 million pesos, but raised its capitalization in 1946 to 12 million. On December 31, 1946 Nacional Financiera owned about 30 per cent of its stock and was a creditor on loans to the extent of approximately 21 million pesos.

When Nacional Financiera balanced its books at the end of 1946, the total of its investments and loans in the sugar-processing industry amounted to approximately 70 million pesos. The two firms just mentioned were the principal beneficiaries of Nacional Financiera support, but six others had also received assistance. A breakdown of the total figure of 70 million pesos shows about 53 million in loans, 10 million in·bond holdings, and, roughly, 7 million in shares of stock.[69]

[67] *Tiempo*, April 11, 1947, p. 35.
[68] Julio Blumenkron, "Caos azucarero o planeación de la industria," *Revista de Economía*, vol. 10, no. 3 (March 31, 1947), p. 18.
[69] Nacional Financiera, *Décimatercera asamblea general ordinaria de accionistas*, p. 53.

According to the 1947 annual report of the sugar producers' association,[70] the Río Guayalejo and Sanalona mills will add substantially to Mexico's sugar-processing capacity. By 1950, two other new mills will be in operation, and the theoretical capacity of the industry is calculated to reach 750,000 tons per year.

Actual production may, however, fall considerably short of this figure, even if the Mexican sugar-cane crop is adequate to warrant that much output, in view of the monopolistic nature of the industry. This is implied in a statement by the president of the association that "... the expansion of mills, development of sugar-cane fields, and the installation of new units create an immediate need for a thoroughgoing and careful study on national sugar planning."[71] Presumably, the government, representing the consumers' interest, will have a voice in the making of decisions on output levels.

Regardless of the actual volume of sugar produced in the years that lie immediately ahead, it would seem that expansion of sugar milling capacity will end about 1950, when the two additional mills referred to above are in production. Because of the disparity between theoretical productive capacity at that time (750,000 tons) and the maximum consumption figure thus far attained (452,000 tons in 1945), it is unlikely that expansion will be resumed for some years after 1950.

[70] Summarized in *Tiempo*, April 11, 1947, pp. 34–39.
[71] *Ibid.*, p. 37.

CHAPTER IX

Special Industrial Projects

ONE OF THE most important industrial undertakings begun in Mexico during the recent war period is the International Harvester Co. plant at Saltillo, not far from the center of Mexico's iron and steel industry at Monterrey. Unlike most of the other new factories affiliated with American concerns, this farm-machinery plant is an outright branch of International Harvester; it is not owned by a joint Mexican-American company. Plans for its construction were drawn up in 1944, but it was not possible to complete the factory until about two years after the end of the war. Production began in July, 1947.

The original estimate for the cost of setting up the mill was 6 million pesos. It was reported, however, that the total investment on the completed plant amounted to more than 20 million pesos.[1] This difference may be due in part to changes in plans which called for a larger plant and more equipment than was anticipated at the outset, but a more important factor was the mounting price level. Here is a good illustration of what was happening generally to investment estimates in Mexican industry during the war and immediately after.

FARM MACHINERY

Before the International Harvester Co. inaugurated its Saltillo factory there were fifteen plants in Mexico making farm implements. They were small establishments and confined their production almost entirely to walking plows. The remainder of their output consisted of other simple agricultural implements, manufactured in minor quantities. Complicated farm machinery was not manufactured at all in Mexico, and even the plows and other equipment were not produced in sufficient volume to satisfy the Mexican market. Annual imports reached substantial figures prior to the war. As from 1936 the irrigation and agricultural credit programs of the Mexican government provided a great stimulus to the use of farm machinery; most of the increased demand had to be met by imports.

The new plant at Saltillo will concentrate at first upon the production of the simpler types of horse-drawn implements for which a wide market already exists, such as plows and harrows. It is planned to manufacture

[1] *El Nacional*, July 7, 1947.

later the more complex and advanced equipment used in agriculture, including tractors. The program in the advanced branches of production will apparently consist of assembly operations, that is, assembly of the finished products from parts fabricated principally in the United States. The plan is to produce such equipment on a modest scale at first, and to expand later in those branches where the market develops. For practical purposes, this will mean expansion of output in the kinds of farm machinery which the Mexican government selects as most useful in increasing agricultural production. Without subsidies and credit extension from the government, very little advanced farm machinery can be purchased in Mexico.

From the beginning it has been reported that the Saltillo plant of International Harvester will try to supply Central American markets as well as the Mexican market, and that it may even send some of its output to South American countries. When the plant was inaugurated, a number of businessmen from Guatemala, El Salvador, Nicaragua, Costa Rica, and Honduras were invited to attend the ceremony and to inspect the factory.[2] It is not clear, however, upon what foundation the exports to Central America are expected to rest. One possibility is that production costs for the simple farm implements will be less at Saltillo than in the American plants of International Harvester, because of the factor of lower labor cost. Such a situation may develop in the future if it does not exist now. Other advantages might also be realized subsequently, if, for example, Latin American countries should discriminate against United States exports because of a shortage of dollar exchange or for other reasons. In that event, International Harvester could supply them from its Saltillo factory.

In spite, however, of all the publicity that has been given to the export possibilities for the Saltillo plant, it is doubtful that International Harvester is counting on such markets for the immediate future. Its program seems to be one of pegging its productive capacity to a known Mexican market, and of expanding that capacity only as consultations with the Minister of Agriculture indicate definitely an increase in consumption. In calculating its market, International Harvester seems to be more conservative than the other American firms which have become involved in Mexican enterprises in the past few years.

The technical backwardness of Mexican agriculture provides a great potential for expansion in farm machinery production. To maintain a wholesome economy in Mexico requires a large increase in agricultural productivity as well as an expansion in total farm output. The Mexican government, it is certain, will endeavor, for many years to come, to encour-

---

[2] *Ibid.*

age the use of improved farm equipment. The extent of this effort, and especially the amount of money the government is willing and able to throw into it, will be the main factor in marketing of agricultural implements.

It is probable that the Mexican government, by stimulating agricultural output, will create a demand favoring further additions to plant capacity in the farm equipment industry. This industry, therefore, is probably now in the first stage of a substantial growth cycle.

ELECTRICAL EQUIPMENT

Before the war the manufacture of electrical equipment in Mexico had developed substantially only in the production of lamps. Incandescent lamps were made chiefly by two firms, both in Monterrey. One of these was a plant which the International General Electric Co. had built in 1930. This plant enjoyed a reputation for efficiency, based in large measure on the company's policy of sending its original working force to Schenectady for training. It is estimated that the prewar production of incandescent lamps in Mexico was adequate to supply about 95 per cent of the country's requirements. Imports consisted almost entirely of special types of lamps not manufactured in Mexico.

The demand for lamps has increased substantially in recent years because of extended electric power facilities. Many towns formerly lacking electric power have been served through the efforts of the Federal Electricity Commission since 1937, and additional service has been provided in the growing urban centers. Construction of office buildings and expansion of industry have also created a larger demand for power and, consequently, for lamps, while still another factor affecting consumption has been the introduction of improved lighting in factories, schools, and stores.

Stimulated by a growing demand, production has been stepped up. Output in 1945 was estimated at 15 million units, including small filament lamps, compared to a total of about 8 million in prewar years. In addition, production of fluorescent lamps was begun in 1943 by the General Electric subsidiary in Monterrey.

The making of other electrical equipment also achieved some progress in Mexico during the war period. The manufacture of electric flatirons, for example, is reported to have increased considerably,[3] at the same time additional gains were reported in the production of batteries and minor electric appliances.

In 1945 a concern destined to be Mexico's largest producer of electrical equipment was established by a mixed American-M: xican group. This

[3] U. S. Department of Commerce, Industrial Reference Service, vo¹   pt. 4, no. 3.

firm, known as Industria Eléctrica de México, is an extremely interesting example of joint investment. The American interest is represented by the Westinghouse Electric Co., which is supplying technical direction for the enterprise and which has granted to Industria Eléctrica the exclusive right in Mexico to use certain of its patents. For its technical and managerial services and for its patent rights, Westinghouse has received approximately 10 per cent of the total stock issued by Industria Eléctrica. About 40 per cent of the shares have been floated in Mexico by the Banco Nacional de México and affiliated institutions. The remaining shares (also about 40 per cent of the total) are held in the United States, chiefly by private investors. The stock of Industria Eléctrica was listed on the New York Stock Exchange in October, 1945.

The listing of Industria Eléctrica shares on the New York Stock Exchange was the occasion for a jubilant press release by Eduardo Suárez, then Minister of Finance. Announcing the sale of the American shares at a premium, Suárez implied that the example of Industria Eléctrica in listing its stock on the New York Stock Exchange would be followed by other Mexican industrial concerns.[4] Thus far, however, this expectation has not been realized.

Nacional Financiera, the government investment bank, also helped to finance Industria Eléctrica de México. On December 31, 1947, Nacional Financiera held about 5 per cent of the common stock of the concern. Even more important in getting the firm started was Nacional Financiera's purchase of Industria Eléctrica bonds. At the time the company was organized an agreement was concluded whereby the official investment bank bought the whole of a 25 million peso bond issue. The most recently published report available on Nacional Financiera's operations shows this holding had been reduced to zero by December 31, 1947, through sales to private and institutional investors in Mexico.

Among the many enterprises established in Mexico in recent years by joint action of Mexican and American interests, Industria Eléctrica is unique in that, as noted, some of its shares have been sold to individual investors in the United States. Indeed, the project as a whole is most interesting from the standpoint of ownership and financing. It involves one of America's large firms, Westinghouse; Nacional Financiera, official investment bank of the Mexican government; private shareholders in the United States; private shareholders in Mexico.

Included in the last-named group are persons affiliated with Mexico's largest private bank (the Banco Nacional de México) and with well-established firms in Mexico's industrial and commercial structure. Of the

---

[4] *Excelsior*, October 11, 1945.

ten members who formed the board of directors when Industria Eléctrica was organized, one was the chief executive officer of the Banco Nacional de México, a second was the managing director of the Cia. Fundidora de Fierro y Acero de Monterrey, the principal firm in the iron and steel industry, a third was president of a large brewery, and a fourth was a partner in one of Mexico City's largest department stores. These persons, it will be observed, represent the principal interest groups in the older "business community" in Mexico.[5]

As part of its working agreement with Industria Eléctrica, Westinghouse is training technical and supervisory personnel in some of its plants in the United States. Early in the formation of the enterprise a two-year training program was mapped out for about twenty-five engineers who had been picked for key positions in the plant. A number of mechanics selected for jobs as foremen or assistant foremen also received special training in Westinghouse plants, while others were to be schooled in skilled operations. Altogether, about one hundred and fifty men have been instructed under the Westinghouse training program.

Like many other new manufacturing plants, Industria Eléctrica de México has established its plant in the Tlalnepantla district near Mexico City. Production was started in December, 1947, and stepped up in May of the following year. Operating at full capacity the plant will employ about 2,000 workmen.

Under its agreement with Westinghouse, Industria Eléctrica has received the exclusive right to manufacture in Mexico a number of articles covered by Westinghouse patents, and it also holds options for similar licenses to produce many other kinds of electrical apparatus. At first, production is to be confined to four or five articles, such as refrigerators, small motors, transformers, and watt-hour meters. Later on, the factory will turn out electric irons, electric and gas ranges, radios, domestic air conditioners, switchboards and switchgear, paints, enamels and varnishes for electrical equipment, solders, and so on. Some of the products mentioned, such as radios, refrigerators, and air conditioners, are not to be made completely in Mexico, but are to be assembled there; a number of the units and parts needed in such assembly operations (e.g., the cooling mechanism for refrigerators) will be imported from the United States.

The terms of its contract with Westinghouse give Industria Eléctrica certain export privileges for the articles it produces under license. These products may be shipped to all Latin American republics except Argentina and Chile. In addition, there are some limitations on exports to Brazil. Apart from these restrictions, the Latin American market is available to

[5] See chapter ii for a discussion of this question.

the Mexican company, and it is frequently stated in Mexico that Industria Eléctrica plans to cultivate business in other Latin American countries. On just what this expectation rests, however, has not been made clear. Cost factors might certainly be expected to militate against such exports if they have to compete on an equal basis with exports from the United States and the European nations. Such cost differentials would derive from the larger scale of operations, the experience, and the skilled working forces found in the older industrialized countries.

It is possible, of course, that Industria Eléctrica will come to enjoy advantages in other Latin American markets that United States firms, at least, will not share. If, for example, an extreme shortage of dollar exchange should develop, Latin American governments would probably take steps to restrict imports from the United States whenever alternative sources of supply were open. It is not impossible that the Westinghouse concern had such considerations in mind when it decided to affiliate itself with Industria Eléctrica. From the standpoint of Westinghouse an advantage would emerge in being able to sell articles with its well-known brand names made in the plant of its Mexican affiliate for pesos, at a time when it would be difficult to sell for dollars similar products made in its American factories.

On a much smaller scale than Industria Eléctrica, a number of other establishments designed to make electrical equipment were started or projected in Mexico during the war period. In November, 1946, a branch of the Square D Co. of Milwaukee opened a plant near Mexico City for the manufacture of electric switches and other equipment. The beginning operations consist mainly of assembling parts shipped from plants of the parent company in the United States. This enterprise is organized as a Mexican company, known as Square D de México, and part of the ownership is reported to be Mexican, but it is properly considered a branch of the American firm. At Toluca, about forty miles from Mexico City, a plant wholly owned by Mexican interests is being built to manufacture electric motors and generators (presumably small units), and a variety of electrical appliances.

No figures are available on the total number of establishments set up in Mexico to make electrical apparatus since 1939. An official release of the Ministry of National Economy stated that seven new firms entered on the manufacture of electrical equipment between August, 1945, and July, 1946. This figure may very well be representative of the average annual increase in plants in this industry since the beginning of the Second World War. Individually, most of them are small, but their aggregate effect on output should be substantial. When Industria Eléctrica's production is added, Mexico will be able to supply its requirements for a wide range of electrical articles, and it is possible that excess capacity will appear in this industry in a few years' time.

D. M. NACIONAL

One of the most interesting new developments in Mexico's industrial structure is associated with D. M. Nacional (full name, Distribuidora Mexicana Nacional), a firm engaged in the manufacture of metal products. This concern is owned by one of Mexico's most active and aggressive businessmen, Antonio Ruiz Galindo, who also occupied the post of Minister of National Economy during the first two years of the Alemán administration. The new plant of D. M. Nacional is pretty much a unique institution in Mexican industry because of the paternalistic, or welfare, program which Ruiz Galindo has designed for his working force. In this program Ruiz Galindo is putting into practice his convictions concerning the social role of industry in the Mexico of today.[6]

The underlying ideas with which Ruiz Galindo operates are essentially those which have given direction to national economic policy in Mexico since 1941, namely, that industry is the "way out" for Mexico, that industrialization is the only road to higher standards of living for the mass of the Mexican people. This conviction is, of course, shared by many industrialists, especially those who have been designated by the term New Group in this volume.[7] What makes Ruiz Galindo stand out from the rest of these industrialists is the practical application of his principles.

The D. M. Nacional factory, on the outskirts of Mexico City, is intended to be a model for other industrialists to follow. The plant, which was opened in November, 1946, is only the first of several component parts of an ambitious project. When the whole project is finished, it will comprise, in addition to the factory proper, a complete residential and recreational area for the wage earners employed in the plant. By providing far better housing, sanitary, educational, and recreational facilities than workers are able to obtain elsewhere under existing conditions, Ruiz Galindo is confident that he will educate his workers to appreciate the advantages of a higher standard of living. Essentially, his plan is to substitute newly created wants for older and socially less desirable ones. If other Mexican industrialists follow his example, he argues, they will create the expanding market for their own output of manufactured goods, which is absolutely necessary as a basis for success in industrialization.

---

[6] A brief but good statement of Ruiz Galindo's views can be found in his article, "The Basic Ideas of the Industrial City 'D. M. Nacional.'" *The Social Sciences in Mexico*, vol. 1, no. 2 (Fall, 1947), pp. 39–42.

[7] See chapters ii and iii for a discussion of the New Group industrialists.

According to Ruiz Galindo, therefore, the industrialist must take the lead in guiding Mexicans to higher standards of living by creating appropriate conditions in connection with industrial employment itself. This mission, he grants, is not an altruistic one, but it has the merit of being one in which the social welfare of the Mexican people coincides with the self-interest of the manufacturer. Industry benefits from better standards of living not only because of a larger market but also because such improvements lead workers to adopt more regular and more efficient work habits. Incentives are created that help to bring about higher levels of productivity in Mexican industry.

The social services at the D. M. Nacional factory are being supplied to the workers free of charge. (The relation of this question to wages will be considered below.) These services include housing. The plan calls for seven apartment houses, some of which have already been completed, to provide modern housing for the whole laboring force. At full operation the factory will employ about 1,000 workers; they and their families, therefore, will make up a community of substantial size. Recreational services include a gymnasium, swimming pool, athletic field, and a motion picture theater, while a school and a library form the basis of the educational program. Stores for food and household supplies are being set up, although they are to be carried on coöperatively by the workers rather than as company stores. Among the other important social services for the families who will live in the factory community are medical attention, a hospital, and a laundry.

In addition to community facilities and functions, the factory provides the midday meal for all employees. This is served in a cafeteria where the food selection is made by dietitians and where high standards of cleanliness are stringently enforced. Ruiz Galindo regards this meal as a means of educating his workers to appreciate wholesome foods and clean surroundings, as well as of improving their health and working efficiency.

The management of the D. M. Nacional plant considers the social services as a part of the factory worker's wage, although apparently no attempt is made to allocate a specific amount for this purpose in each wage paid. The actual cash wages paid are not so high as the top figures attained in some plants in Mexico for similar kinds of employment, but they are said to compare favorably with the average earnings for such jobs.[8]

Obviously, what Ruiz Galindo has established at his factory community, which he calls Industrial City, is a "company town," a familiar institution in the United States. Indeed, the social motives which have led him to organize such a community have something in common with those

[8] Ruth Schuyler, "Ruiz Galindo—Industrial Planner," *Mexican-American Review*, May, 1947, p. 12.

which led to the formation of textile mill towns in our southern states shortly after the Civil War,[9] and he has probably drawn on his knowledge of welfare programs in various American plants in mapping out his own plan. In the United States the defects of "company towns" have come to be widely realized since their heyday in the 1920's, and labor in particular has become skeptical about the social merits of the institution. Events of the last fifteen years in the United States have caused labor to put more stock in collective bargaining than in the paternalistic programs of employers as a means of attaining higher standards of living, and it is clear that "company towns" and employer paternalism are played out in this country. As a matter of fact, there are no true social foundations for such institutions in the United States, and they are now an anachronism in our economic structure.

In Mexico at the present time, however, it is possible, even probable, that paternalistic schemes like that of Ruiz Galindo will yield definite social and economic advantages that outweigh their shortcomings. Mexican society is still in the process of shifting "from status to contract." After all, it is less than forty years since the Revolution began to break down the quasi-feudal social attitudes which were strongly rooted in Mexico during (at least) the preceding four hundred years of colonial and national history. These attitudes will give way completely in time, but the change to new kinds of socio-economic relations of necessity proceeds slowly.

The tradition that the employer has a social as well as an economic function to perform in relation to his employees is one that dies hard in a society where standards of living and literacy have been low, as in Mexico. The employer is not simply the "boss" in the American sense. In one degree or another, he is still the *patrón* of the old hacienda days. His obligation does not cease with the pay envelope. His workers expect from him a certain amount of protection and at least moral support in their affairs outside the job. Similarly, they welcome—or at least they are receptive to—a certain amount of direction in questions not immediately related to their work. In one sense, this is a privilege which the employer gets in return for the obligations he incurs over and above the payment of wages. It is not resented by the employee as an interference with personal affairs. On his side, the Mexican employer accepts and performs without question a traditional social role.

As Mexico continues to industrialize, the relations between employer and employee will be reduced progressively to an economic plane. Pater-

[9] See, for example, the essays in Broadus Mitchell and George S. Mitchell, *The Industrial Revolution in the South* (Baltimore, 1930).

nalism along the lines of Ruiz Galindo's program can be very useful in easing this process of readjustment, thus performing a desirable social as well
as economic role. There is a danger, of course, that paternalism will be
used by employers as a means of keeping wages down, but government
action and trade-union vigilance should be able to cope with abuses of
this kind. At the present time it may be said that paternalism in Mexican
industry *can* be a desirable development. It remains to be seen whether
or not it will be.

The principal articles manufactured by D. M. Nacional fall into the
category of steel office furniture—desks, chairs, filing cabinets, book shelves,
and so on—but many other steel products are produced in smaller quantities. A beginning has been made in the production of electric refrigerators, and it is anticipated that this department will become one of the most
active in the factory in future years. Altogether, about 300 different steel
articles are now turned out at the D. M. Nacional plant, for use in offices,
homes, schools, and industrial establishments.

In designing and operating his factory at Ciudad Industrial, Ruiz Galindo has followed the pattern of efficient plants in the United States. The
plant has been laid out with a view toward minimizing waste in time,
effort, and power. Relatively less hand labor is used in the D. M. Nacional
factory than in the typical Mexican industrial establishment. An admirer
of American production methods, Ruiz Galindo has also engaged the
services of a well-known American firm of management engineers to help
him improve the operating efficiency of his plant.

In spite of achievements in efficiency in the D. M. Nacional plant, it is
doubtful that it will be able to meet foreign (especially U. S.) competition
for many years to come. Protective tariffs, however, will continue to give
the D. M. Nacional products a favored position in the Mexican market.[10] Of this there can be little doubt. Ruiz Galindo also has ambitions to
produce for export markets, especially in Central America,[11] in the immediate future. It is difficult to see how this ambition could be realized
without prejudice to the Mexican consumer and to the national economy
as a whole. Furthermore, because of the prestige he enjoys in the Mexican
business community, Ruiz Galindo has influenced other industrialists to
think along similar lines about producing for Central American markets,
and this has had the unfortunate consequence of deëmphasizing the need
for Mexico to build up its internal market as the one permanently dependable basis of national industrialization.

[10] It is interesting to observe that steel furniture was included in the list of articles the importation of which was prohibited in the decree of July, 1947, which was intended to conserve
foreign exchange by eliminating "luxury" imports.

[11] Ruth Schuyler, *op. cit.*, p. 12.

MANUFACTURE OF TIN CANS

Allied with the expansion taking place in Mexico's canning industry, a foundation is being laid for the manufacture of tin cans on a substantial scale. A handful of small firms have been making tin cans in Mexico for a number of years, using tin plate imported from the United States for this purpose. Also, some of the canneries have had old-fashioned equipment for making the cans they have needed in their own operations. On the whole, the manufacture of tin cans has been a small-scale industrial effort in Mexico.

Late in 1944 plans were drawn up for a new large plant, known as Envases Generales Continental de México. This is a joint Mexican-American enterprise capitalized at 6 million pesos. The American interest is represented by the Continental Can Co., which holds 20 per cent of the capital stock, supplies technical direction and patents, and provides training for workers employed in the plant.

To get the Envases Generales Continental plant into operation has proved to be a much more difficult and lengthy process than was envisaged by the promoters in 1944. The firm has been fiercely fought by Mexican interests in the same industry, led by persons prominent in the Cámara Nacional de la Industria de Transformación. These interests represent new firms organized during the war period, as well as the prewar Mexican concerns in the industry.

Envases Generales Continental has been held up to the Mexican public as an outstanding illustration of "Yankee penetration," and it has been accused of being a front for American exporters of tin cans rather than a firm primarily interested in manufacturing cans in Mexico. To appreciate the nature and intensity of the open warfare on Envases Generales Continental it is only necessary to scan the full-page, scarehead advertisements which the Cámara Nacional de la Industria de Transformación inserted in the Mexico City dailies in July and August of 1946.[12]

One apparent result of the attack on Envases Generales Continental de México was to persuade the Mexican government to deny the firm's petition for tax-exemption privileges under the law of manufacturing development. This decision was reached after much deliberation and play of pressures from both sides. The most that the concern was able to get consisted of exemption from the payment of duties on specified equipment which had to be imported. The much more important concessions on taxes which Envases Generales Continental was seeking, however, were not granted.

[12] For example, El Universal, issues of August 15 and 16, 1946.

Not only was the government's decision unfavorable to the firm but apparently it took an unusually long time for the decision to be reached. This was a main cause of delay in getting the plant built and putting it into operation. Also, handicaps of a technical nature played a part in making it necessary to postpone the date on which the factory could swing into action. Late in 1947, about three years after the project was drawn up, Envases Generales Continental finally got into production. It is now the largest plant in the industry, with a rate of production reported at 72 million containers per year.[13] Now that this new factory is in operation, the industry should be able to satisfy an increasing demand for some years to come. Further expansion in plant does not seem indicated for the next few years at least.

REFRACTORY MATERIALS

In August, 1946, a beginning was made in the manufacture of refractory materials in Mexico. This took place in the plant of the Cia. Mexicana de Refractarios A. P. Green, jointly owned by the A. P. Green Fire Brick Co. of Missouri and a group of Mexican investors. It is reported that the American company holds about one-third of the stock in the Mexican concern, but it is not known whether this represents a cash investment or a payment for technical services in setting up and operating the plant. It is probably the latter.

The new plant is situated in the growing industrial district of Tlalnepantla, near Mexico City, but the clay used as raw material is obtained from various parts of the country. No imported materials are required. According to press releases issued at the time the plant was inaugurated, the refractory brick produced at Tlalnepantla conforms to standards set by the American Society for Testing Materials.[14] A series of experiments stretching over a period of three years was necessary before entirely suitable materials were found in Mexico.

Although not a large factory, it is claimed that the A. P. Green plant at Tlalnepantla is equipped with the most up-to-date and efficient equipment available. The company plans to maintain a production schedule of 10 million bricks per year, which apparently represents their estimate of the Mexican market in the immediate future.

ALUMINUM

Since V-J Day, plans have been drawn up for two separate factories to manufacture aluminum products in Mexico. In effect, these plants will represent a new departure in the industrial development of Mexico, since

[13] *Mexican-American Review*, July, 1948, p. 34.
[14] *El Universal*, August 29, 1946.

domestic production of aluminum articles has hitherto been negligible in amount. Just before the war Mexican consumption of aluminum was increasing substantially. Demand in 1946 rose to much higher levels, fortifying the belief that Mexico's postwar requirements for aluminum would be far in excess of her prewar consumption. It is this expectation of a greatly enlarged market which forms the basis for setting up two plants in the aluminum industry.

One of the new concerns, Reynolds Internacional de México, is building a plant in the Tlalnepantla area near Mexico City, where a number of new factories are springing up. According to the announcement made at the time the company was organized, 51 per cent of its 7.5 million pesos of capital stock is owned by the Reynolds Metal Co. of Richmond, Virginia. The remaining 49 per cent of capital was supplied by the Banco Nacional de México, Mexico's largest private bank, and by an investment institution known as Inversiones Latinas. Here, as in so many other cases, the principle of 51 per cent Mexican ownership was not adhered to. In harmony with the distribution of shares, Reynolds Metal Co. has five of its officials on the nine-man board of directors of the Mexican concern.

The Reynolds Internacional de México plant will produce aluminum foil, powder, and paste. Output of aluminum foil is expected to approximate 2.5 million pounds per year in the beginning. This will be the principal initial product. Subsequently, it is planned to install equipment to manufacture aluminum sheet and plate, but the production of bars and rods is not contemplated at present.

The second firm entering the aluminum industry in Mexico is known as Aluminio Industrial de México. Both American and Canadian interests are involved, in combination with Mexican investors,[15] but it is not publicly known how the ownership is distributed among the three different groups. The initial capital of the company has been placed at 4 million pesos, but additions to capitalization are likely to be made soon.

The site of the Aluminio Industrial de México plant is also near Mexico City. Like the Reynolds concern, this factory will produce aluminum foil and paste, and it will be equipped also to manufacture aluminum sheet. Estimates for productive capacity have not been made public, but the smaller capitalization of Aluminio Industrial de México indicates that aggregate production will be less than that of Reynolds. It is reported that raw materials will be imported from Canada, and also that Canadian technicians will be employed in the Aluminio Industrial plant.

Mexico's requirements for aluminum will be pretty well supplied by domestic production when the two factories are in operation. Also, if addi-

---

[15] *Mexican-American Review*, October, 1946, p. 24.

tional demand develops the two plants will probably be in a position to ramify and expand their capacity. It is not likely, therefore, that other new plants will appear in the aluminum industry for a number of years.

OTHER INDUSTRIAL PROJECTS

Apart from the industrial developments already brought discussed, a large number and a wide variety of new manufacturing projects have been reported from Mexico over the years since 1939. Some have existed only in the form of plans, and a certain number of these will never be carried beyond this stage. In most cases, however, they have either been completed or they are sure of completion.

In metal products, for example, several small plants have been set up to manufacture builders' hardware, such as locks, knobs, and hinges. In 1945, Mexican production of locks alone was calculated at more than 410,000 pesos in value.

During the war a few hundred looms for the textile industry were made in Mexico. Modeled after English looms, they were produced on a makeshift basis and at a high cost. In 1947, it was announced that a loommanufacturing plant would be constructed by a joint Mexican-American enterprise known as Draper Mexicana. About 4 million dollars are to be invested in the plant and equipment. The American interest is represented by the Draper Loom Manufacturing Co. of Hopedale, Mass., while the Mexican promoters are associated with older Mexican industrial interests in iron and steel manufacturing and in textiles.

In Mexico City a plant is being built to produce internal combustion engines for automobiles, trucks, and other uses. Although not a large-scale enterprise, this seems to be an ambitious industrial effort. A similar development is the manufacture of lathes and gear cutters. Such machine tools, although not of the high-precision type, were produced in small quantities in Mexico during the war period.

A new development in automobile assembly took place in June, 1947, when Armadora Automotriz began to assemble Nash cars and trucks in its new factory at Tlalnepantla, near Mexico City. (Ford, General Motors, and Chrysler have had assembly plants in Mexico City for some years). The Armadora Automotriz plant was built and equipped in eighteen months at a cost of 3 million pesos. A year later, in June 1948, a Hudson assembly plant was put into operation. In Tlalnepantla another project relating to the automobile industry is taking place. The Equipos Hobbs factory is being constructed to make trailers and car bodies.

As a final illustration of the ramifications in Mexico's industrial development, a new concern, the Refrigeración, has recently begun to make industrial refrigeration equipment. In producing refrigeration units, the motors and automatic controls are imported from the United States but the remainder of the parts are secured from Mexican sources. The firm is a joint Mexican-American venture.

The handful of projects mentioned in this miscellaneous category is far from being a complete list of such developments. They have been cited as examples. It is too soon to make an estimate of what they will, as individual enterprises, contribute to Mexico's industrial structure. Some of them are small, and will remain small. As a group, however, their combined effect on Mexican industrialization will be substantial.

CHAPTER X

The Tax-Exemption Law in Operation

THE MEXICAN government's program of encouraging industrial expansion by means of tax exemptions was examined in chapter v. This program has operated under the law of manufacturing industries of 1941 and the succeeding law of manufacturing development of February, 1946. Thus far the only quantitative data published by the Mexican government on the tax-exemption privileges granted under these laws have been very broad, total figures. If any official agency has made an analysis in detail, the results have not been brought to public attention.

The data of table 2 (p. 190), have been compiled from records available in the Ministry of Finance.[1] While these records are unfortunately not so complete as I would like to have them, yet they are the best source that can be reached. In my opinion, the fact that the records are not in better shape is evidence that the tax-exemption policy has been administered in a loose, haphazard manner, and that definite criteria for the making of decisions have been lacking.

The figures which I have compiled on tax exemptions date from May, 1940, shortly after an effective legal basis for the policy was established. The figures end with June 30, 1946, the latest terminal date available at the time of the investigation. During the period of more than five years, a total of 438 concessions were granted. However, 46 of these were duplications in the sense that some firms came in for two, or even more, separate concessions. These were eliminated from the tabulations. In addition, it was necessary to omit 12 other concessions because not enough information was available to bring them into the analysis. Thus statistics covering only 380 firms are included in table 2.

Lest the reader be troubled by the fact that fewer than 380 firms are tabulated in table 3 (p. 191), it may be pointed out that not all firms reported on the number of persons employed and on capitalization. In each case all those reporting on the item in question have been included.

---

[1] Departamento de Control y Vigilancia de Subsidios. An earlier analysis using data from the same source was made by Diego López Rosado, "Las industrias nuevas en México," *Revista de Economía*, vol. 8, no. 3–4 (April 30, 1945), pp. 21–23.

One further word of explanation is needed before proceeding with the analysis of the data in tables 2 and 3. Industrial classifications are not given in the Ministry of Finance records. Consequently, I have had to classify the firms myself, using whatever information was available on commodities produced or expected to be produced. In doing so I have followed as closely as possible the classification employed in the Mexican industrial census.

TABLE 2

Tax-Exempt Firms: Distribution by Industries

Industry	Number of firms	Per cent distribution
Textiles..............................	10	2.6
Metal products.........................	116	30.5
Construction materials...................	17	4.5
Clothing and accessories.................	2	.5
Food products.........................	48	12.6
Woodworking and furniture..............	11	2.9
Pottery and glass.......................	16	4.2
Electrical appliances....................	19	5.0
Chemicals.............................	83	21.8
Paper.................................	9	2.4
Printing, publishing, and motion pictures...	3	.8
Jewelry, art objects, and precision instruments..............................	4	1.1
Others................................	42	11.1
Total..............................	380	100.0

Two classes of industries stand out as the principal beneficiaries of tax-exemption privileges. These are metal products and chemicals, which comprise about 30 per cent and 22 per cent, respectively, of the total number of firms. The metal products group leads in number of persons employed and in capitalization. The chemical industry occupies second rank in number of persons employed but falls into third place in capital invested.

The preëminent position of metal products and chemicals is explained by wartime conditions. These two industries in Mexico were enormously stimulated when previous foreign sources of supply dried up during the war years. The firms classified in the metal products industry produce a wide variety of articles, ranging from school compasses and locks to iron pipe and structural shapes. Most of them, however, supply minor metal items rather than the bulky and heavy metal products.

In contrast, very few firms in the textile industry received tax concessions in spite of an equally great wartime stimulus. This shows that there was comparatively little expansion in plant capacity in the textile industry. Increased output was achieved principally by full-time operation of existing plants.

The aggregate declared capital of all firms taking advantage of the law of manufacturing industries is about 314 million pesos. This is the figure (see table 3) which I have obtained by treating in the manner indicated

TABLE 3

TAX-EXEMPT FIRMS: NUMBER OF PERSONS EMPLOYED AND CAPITALIZATION

Industry	Employment		Capital	
	Number firms reporting	Total number of persons employed	Number of firms reporting	Total capital (thousands of pesos)
Textiles....................	9	389	10	32,086
Metal products...............	114	8,189	115	90,003
Construction materials........	15	1,597	17	31,986
Clothing and accessories.......	2	124	2	153
Food products...............	43	2,536	48	16,215
Woodworking and furniture.....	11	1,529	11	4,057
Pottery and glass.............	15	622	16	7,166
Electrical appliances..........	18	1,015	19	53,151
Chemicals...................	78	3,599	83	37,306
Paper.......................	9	597	9	34,766
Printing, publishing, and motion pictures...............	3	51	3	685
Jewelry, art objects, and precision instruments..........	4	77	4	138
Others......................	40	4,384	41	6,167
Total.....................	361	24,709	378	313,879

above the data gathered from the records of the Ministry of Finance. It differs substantially from the figure published in the latest annual report of the Ministry of National Economy.[2] According to this official agency, the aggregate capital of the firms awarded tax exemptions during the same period (1940–June, 1946) is about 450 million pesos. This is larger than my figure by 136 million pesos.

The discrepancy between the two figures may, in part, be accounted for by the firms for which I found no data in the Ministry of Finance records. It is not possible, however, to explain as great a difference as 136 million pesos in this way. It is my opinion that the Ministry of National

[2] *Memoria de la Secretaría de la Economía Nacional, Septiembre de 1945–Agosto de 1946,* p. 94.

Economy did not take account of duplications among firms in arriving at its total. Since some sizable enterprises came in for more than one concession, double counting could easily make up the difference between the two figures.[3] Most official sources seem to have taken aggregate figures on tax-exempt firms from the Ministry of National Economy, and thus all official claims of what has been accomplished by the law are likely to be exaggerated.

In table 4 the 378 firms for which capitalization data are available have been classified in six groups according to amount of capital. The numerical

TABLE 4

TAX-EXEMPT FIRMS: CLASSIFICATION ACCORDING TO
CAPITAL INVESTMENT

Amount of capital investment (in pesos)	Number of firms	Per cent distribution
Less than 50,000.......................	130	34.4
50,000 to 99,999......................	52	13.7
100,000 to 499,999....................	112	29.6
500,000 to 999,999....................	34	9.0
1,000,000 to 9,999,999................	43	11.4
10,000,000 and over...................	7	1.9
Total..............................	378	100.0

predominance of the small firm is at once apparent from these figures. Almost one-half of the concerns had a capital of less than 100,000 pesos. About one-third of the total number of firms were in the group with a capital of 50,000 pesos or less.

On the basis of similar evidence, Diego López Rosado in the study already referred to reaches the conclusion that the great majority of the firms awarded tax-exemptions are small.[4] This is undoubtedly true if they are compared with similar manufacturing firms in the United States or any other advanced industrial nation. Such a comparison, however, is of little value for the purpose of finding out what the policy has accomplished in Mexico. From that standpoint it is necessary to see how the tax-exempt firms compare in capitalization with the average for all similar firms in Mexico itself.

Satisfactory comparisons of this kind can be made for four of the industry groups—metal products, chemicals, pottery and glass, and food products—

[3] The Ministry of National Economy also has a higher figure for number of persons employed by tax-exempt firms; 29,000 as against 24,700.

[4] The same viewpoint is expressed in the annual report of the Banco de México for 1945 (*Vigésimacuarta asamblea general ordinaria de accionistas*, p. 57).

by taking 1940 census data as a base of reference. In the other cases either the number of privileged firms is too small or the firms are not sufficiently representative of the industry as a whole to make comparisons valid.

In table 5 below the average capitalization of the tax-exempt establishments is contrasted with the average capital reported for firms in the same industry in the census of 1940. It will be observed at once that the actual figures for the tax-exempt concerns are substantially higher in each case—more than double in three out of the four industries. The actual figures, however, give a somewhat distorted picture because some of the investment in the tax-exempt enterprises took place after 1940 when the

TABLE 5

CAPITAL INVESTMENT IN CERTAIN INDUSTRIES

Industry	Average capital of tax-exempt firms (pesos)		Average capital reported in 1940 census (pesos)
	Actual figures	In 1940 pesos	
Metal products..........................	783,000	402,000	170,000
Chemicals.............................	450,000	231,000	170,000
Pottery and glass.......................	448,000	230,000	259,000
Food products..........................	338,000	173,000	35,000

price level was actively rising. The amount of goods and services that could be purchased for the same investment in pesos after 1940 was necessarily less than that which was obtained in 1940.

To get a more appropriate basis of comparison, therefore, the capitalization figures for the tax-exempt firms have been deflated to the level of 1940. In other words, they have been expressed in pesos of 1940 purchasing power. In calculating the deflated figures I have used the comprehensive wholesale-price index of the Bank of Mexico, which includes 210 commodities.

To be absolutely precise, the investment of each firm should be deflated according to the price level at the time the investment was made. The information necessary to do this is not, however, available. In all cases, therefore, I have used the 1945 price level figure in deflating the actual capitalization data. This procedure, it will be noted, exaggerates the amount of deflation, since the 1945 price level was higher than that of any of the intervening years.[5] Thus the figures showing capital investment in terms

[5] Following are the wholesale price index figures for the years 1940–1945, based on 1939 as 100:

1940....................	102.5	1943....................	145.7
1941....................	108.1	1944....................	178.5
1942....................	120.6	1945....................	199.8

(Banco de México, *Vigésimacuarta asamblea general ordinaria de accionistas*, p. 85.)

of 1940 pesos represent something of an understatement. In reality these figures should be larger.

In spite, however, of this element of understatement in the deflated figures for tax-exempt firms, they are significantly higher than the averages recorded in the 1940 census in three out of the four cases. And in the fourth industrial group, pottery and glass, the deflated figure is not very much lower than the census average.

So far as capitalization is concerned, therefore, it may be concluded that the tax-exempt firms are not small enterprises in the context of the Mexican economy. They compare very favorably with all other establishments. On the whole they exceed the averages for the year 1940.

If the same industries are examined from the standpoint of number of persons employed, the result obtained is less conclusive. Following are the comparative figures for average number of persons employed:

Industry	Tax-exempt firms	Census of 1940
Metal products........................	72	82
Chemicals............................	46	32
Pottery and glass......................	41	88
Food products........................	59	9

In the pottery and glass group the tax-exempt firms have substantially fewer employees than the average concern reported in the 1940 census. In the metal products industry, however, the discrepancy is not a material one, and in the other two—chemicals and food products—the tax-exempt firms have the higher average employment figures. If this evidence based on number of persons employed does not support the conclusion based on capitalization, at least it does not contradict it. It does not compel a revision of the opinion that the tax-exempt firms have been somewhat larger than the average firms existing in their respective industries in 1940.

In official circles in Mexico the firms awarded tax exemptions are generally referred to as "new industries." I have avoided using this term because it is very misleading. The law of manufacturing industries, it will be recalled, provides that special privileges can be granted to "necessary" industries as well as to new ones, and a substantial number of the firms receiving tax concessions have been old rather than new establishments. To get exact figures on new versus old firms would require a detailed and lengthy investigation, out of all proportion to the value of having such figures. It can be stated with confidence, however, that a sizable fraction of the tax-exempt firms were in operation before 1940.

The tendency for older firms to apply for tax concessions has been on the increase. For the first few years after 1940 new, small firms were virtually the only beneficiaries of the law. Moreover, it was, at first, the policy of the government to consider the law principally as a device to induce business men to set up new industries. As the advantages of qualifying under the law became obvious, however, the pressure from older firms for similar treatment became harder and harder to resist, particularly when extensions in plant capacity were being planned. Thus the names of well-established manufacturing concerns that had been paying taxes for years began to appear with growing frequency in the list of exempted firms. The policy of the government was inevitably loosened.

The process of granting tax exemptions, once started, has tended to carry itself forward of its own weight. The concessions are made to stimulate the manufacture of certain products. These are publicly listed when the concession is granted. Consequently, every firm which actually manufactures a product listed in a concession, or is able to make it, is also likely to seek the privileges afforded by the law of manufacturing industries. The precedent established by the government in making a concession to one firm goes a long way toward insuring a favorable reception for the later applicants. In going over the individual decrees which are issued when a tax exemption is conceded, I have been impressed by the frequency with which a sentence similar to the following occurs:

The period of five years [for tax exemptions] . . . will be counted from October 1, 1945, the date on which the same concession was granted to Fabricación de Máquinas, S. A.

An interesting illustration of the habits of mind being fostered in Mexican business circles by the tax-exemption law is found in the proceedings of the national insurance convention held under the auspices of the Ministry of Finance in 1946.[8] The majority of the privileged concerns, it was pointed out, carried their insurance with foreign rather than Mexican companies. A resolution was, therefore, adopted calling for a change in the law to put a stop to this practice, by the simple device of requiring all tax-exempt firms to carry every form of insurance with domestic companies. Although no such action has been taken thus far by the Mexican government, it is a possibility for the future.

In 1946 another feature of the government's tax-exemption policy became clear. This was a tendency to grant renewals with a liberal hand. Since not many effective concessions had been made before 1941, the question of renewals was not important until 1946. In that year, however, a

---

[8] *El Economista*, vol. 13, no. 155 (June–July, 1946), p. 45.

substantial number of five-year grants expired, and enough decisions were made to suggest that a liberal policy had been adopted.

In 1941 approximately 70 firms were awarded tax exemptions for five years. I do not know the precise number of these establishments that went out of business or were merged with other firms by 1946, but I do know that the casualty rate among the very small firms was appreciable. Some of the 70 were no longer in existence when their concessions expired. In going over the official records for the year 1946, I have counted 46 renewals or extensions. It is reasonable to conclude, therefore, that most of the firms still operating in 1946 were allowed to continue enjoying tax exemptions when their original concessions came to an end. And it is even possible that every firm asking for an extension was given favorable treatment.

The evidence on renewals suggests a departure from the policy intended when the law of manufacturing industries was enacted in 1941. In the original law the five-year limitation on tax exemptions implied that the subsidy was a means of helping a new enterprise to make its way through the difficulties of the beginning years, or of inducing an existing establishment to invest in plant expansion. A period of five years was quite properly considered adequate for such purposes.

Actually, wartime conditions made the years 1941 to 1946 especially favorable for putting new or expanding industrial concerns on a firm footing. A number of weaker ones disappeared, as I have already observed. For those that survived, tax exemption had fulfilled its purpose. It is doubtful indeed that they required the stimulus of continued freedom from paying taxes. In granting renewals with a free and easy hand, therefore, the government is tending to convert temporary subsidies into permanent ones. Perhaps no formal decision in this respect has been made. But the foundation for such a policy has been laid, and the policy is likely to be carried forward. We can certainly expect increased pressure from Mexican industries to continue the subsidies as the competition from foreign producers moves toward prewar levels.

In the preceding discussion I have drawn some conclusions from the record of experience with the law of manufacturing industries. It seems to me useful to restate these now in summary form, together with certain collateral inferences from the same data. Thus the following propositions may be set down.

1. The tax-exemption program has been a stimulus to industrial expansion in Mexico because material savings are effected through it by the privileged firms. This is especially true of the smaller concerns, many of which would not have been organized without this subsidy and could not as yet maintain their existence without it.

2. Examination of the records of the Ministry of Finance shows that official statements about what has been accomplished quantitatively under the law are apt to be exaggerated. The exaggerations are probably explained by failure to eliminate duplications; some firms have received two or more separate concessions.

3. The tax-exempt firm tends to be larger than the average firm in the same industry in 1940. They cannot, therefore, be called "small firms" in the Mexican economy.

4. Official sources are prone to refer to the firms getting tax exemptions as "new industries." This practice is misleading, inasmuch as many of them were in operation well before the subsidy policy was adopted.

5. The number of older firms receiving tax concessions has been increasing.

6. The process of granting tax exemptions has tended to become cumulative. Pressures to extend the scope of the law by administrative decision are hard to resist.

7. Lack of precision in the records kept by the Ministry of Finance suggests that the law has been loosely administered. To maintain a flow of current reports on the subsidized firms has been too big a job for the size of the staff charged with this duty.

8. Vested interests have been created, and thus there has been a tendency to establish tax exemptions on a more permanent basis than was originally intended. A generous attitude on renewals in the year 1946 shows a departure from the original policy of making temporary concessions to help firms through the initial period of new investment.

9. Subsidies in the form of tax exemption may be used as a means of helping Mexican industries to meet foreign competition in the Mexican market.

Part III

PROBLEMS

CHAPTER XI

The Internal Market

O f the many problems that Mexico is likely to encounter as she goes forward with her industrial development, none promises to be more critical than the limitations of the domestic market. Mexican industry must look to the Mexican consumer. The nature of the domestic market, its size, its characteristic features, its possibilities of expansion and ramification—all these are vital questions for Mexico as she continues to add to her industrial capacity. These, therefore, are the basic questions with which this chapter will be concerned.

Before I turn to these main issues, however, something should be said about the possibilities of developing export markets for Mexican manufactures. There are many persons in Mexico, including some industrialists and government officials, who believe that Mexican industry will be able to produce for other Latin American markets as well as for domestic consumption. They have in mind especially the countries in the Caribbean area, that is, Central America and the West Indies. In considerable part, the belief that Mexican manufactured goods will make their way in such markets rests upon experience during the war years when industrial exports from the great manufacturing nations were drastically reduced. The Mexican textile industry suddenly found itself with an opportunity to export as well as to produce for an expanding domestic market. In lesser degree, other industries began to send their products to other markets in Middle America. In some quarters this export development was optimistically interpreted as a foundation for a more or less permanent condition in the sense that Mexican producers had gained a foothold and had established business connections which they had never known before.

By what reasoning the conclusion was reached that this foothold could be maintained and even extended in the postwar period, was not made clear. Apparently it rested upon a vague notion that shorter distances to markets in Middle America would give to these Mexican industries an advantage great enough to offset the cost differentials favoring competitors in the United States and Europe. This is not a very sophisticated proposition, inasmuch as transportation costs bear no such relation to distance, but it seems to have loomed large in the thinking of those Mexicans who had a vision of Mexico as a manufacturing exporter in the postwar period.

It is difficult to see how most Mexican manufactures could compete with the products of the advanced industrial nations, even if the transportation advantage was real rather than illusory. The other cost differentials are too large. Here it is only necessary to point out that most Mexican industries require protection by tariffs or other means if they are to have a place in the domestic market. For a broad range of industrial products, large-scale operations, efficient labor, access to capital and credit at low rates of interest, experienced management, and so on, give to the great manufacturing countries substantial advantages which it will take many years for a newly industrializing country to overcome.

In some industries producing light consumer goods these advantages may not be very great, and the position of Mexico vis-à-vis the highly industrialized nations may be relatively good. But it is precisely such industries that are also likely to be developing in other Latin American countries. Textiles would be an example. In every country this industry made advances during the Second World War, and it is making further advances now. Even if the Mexican textile industry were modernized and put on an efficient basis, it would still be difficult to export to Central American and Caribbean markets because tariff walls designed to encourage similar industries in those countries will probably be raised.

Perhaps in some cases peculiar circumstances will pave the way for Mexican industries to cultivate export markets to the south and east. Extreme shortages of dollar exchange, if they should develop, might have this effect, although such shortages are less likely to occur in Middle America than other parts of Latin America owing to the probability of continuous high United States consumption of coffee and bananas. It is possible that dollar stringencies will enable the Mexican branches of American plants to export to other Latin American markets while the parent plants are cut off from these. Compare for electrical equipment ch. ix.

But the exports that take place under these conditions are unlikely to be important in relation to Mexico's aggregate industrial production. For many years we can expect Mexican industry to confine itself to producing almost entirely for the domestic market. If the expansion of the internal market does not parallel the expansion of industrial capacity, serious problems will be created in the economic and social life of the country.

The size of the Mexican market depends, of course, upon the growth of the Mexican population. In 1940 the census enumerated 19.7 million inhabitants, or about 3 million more than the census of 1930 had shown. In 1946, official estimates placed the population at more than 22 million.[1]

---

[1] Secretaría de la Economía Nacional, Dirección General de Estadística, *Compendio estadístico*, p. 46.

An analysis of demographic statistics made before 1940 suggests that the Mexican population will increase at a rapid rate for many years to come, possibly doubling its size within a period of forty years.[2] From the standpoint of basic population growth, therefore, Mexico's internal market promises to be an expanding one.

These population figures, however, give a distorted impression of the absolute size of the market for manufactured goods. For most kinds of manufactured goods, Mexico is a market of 5 to 6 million persons.[3] Crude cotton fabrics would represent the principal exception, in that the number of persons entering this market is much larger. The market for shoes is also larger, but still it does not include half the population. Calculations based on 1940 census data showed that only 48 per cent of the Mexican population wore shoes.[4] More than half of the remainder wore no foot covering at all, while the others used the typical Mexican sandal (*huarache*).

If the number of consumers for some manufactured products exceeds six million, there are many articles that are purchased by fewer people yet. For every small refinement in the taste being catered to, there is a sharp drop in the number of persons entering the market.

It is obvious that markets like these—or putting them all together, a market like that of Mexico—cannot support a large and ramified industrial structure. The market must grow as new industrial plant is built, and it must grow rapidly as long as industrialization proceeds rapidly. What, then, are the possibilities for a speedy expansion in the Mexican market for manufactured goods?

As industry expands, the industrial wage earners tend to become consumers of more and varied manufactured products. This tendency, however, may be curbed by inflation. In a later chapter it will be pointed out that inflation has already wiped out the gains in earnings made by the Mexican industrial workers as a group, and the average real wage in industry has fallen in recent years. With further industrialization, the inflationary potential in Mexico is great. Food prices above all are likely to climb, requiring the allocation of a larger percentage of workers' incomes to food purchases and leaving a smaller proportion available for buying less essential manufactured products.

But even if industrial wages should increase rather than decline in purchasing power, the working force in industry is too small to provide a mass market for an expanding industrial output. The same must be said

[2] Alberto P. León and Alvaro Aldama C., "Population Problems in Central and Caribbean America," *The Annals*, vol. 237 (January, 1945), p. 38.

[3] See, for example, Antonio Ruiz Galindo, "Discurso pronunciado en el III Congreso de la Confederación de Cámaras Industriales," *El Economista*, no. 151 (January, 1946), pp. 30–32.

[4] Ifigenia Martínez H., "Problemas de la población," *Revista de Economía*, vol. 9, no. 1 (January 15, 1946), p. 35.

of other occupational groups, such as miners, railroad workers, and white-collar employees. Any reasonable allowance for expansion in the numbers of persons falling into such groups would still leave them far short of comprising a mass market.

The potential market for Mexican industry must be sought in the agricultural population, as those engaged in farming, together with their families, comprise approximately 70 per cent of all the inhabitants of the country. This group consists mostly of farmers in ejidos (*ejidatarios*) and of those who operate small individual holdings (*rancheros*). Farm laborers, in the sense of full-time workers for hire, are not numerous, inasmuch as most of the hired agricultural work in Mexico is performed by ejidatarios and rancheros as a part-time occupation. The market of rural Mexico is a market of peasant farmers.

The outstanding characteristic of this market is low purchasing power. Much of Mexican agriculture is established on a self-sufficient basis. The farmer works primarily to get from the land a subsistence for himself and his family. In the typical case, only a minor fraction of what the farmer produces goes to market. But even where commercial output reaches larger proportions, it is still subordinate to the main task of providing a sustenance for the farm family. Surplus production for sale is impeded by a combination of institutional, technical, and geographic factors, the nature of which will be brought out below. The point to be stressed here is that, because much of Mexican agricultural effort falls outside the commercial framework, cash incomes among the farming population are small.

Standards of living in rural Mexico are exceedingly low. Poverty is so typical in the Mexican countryside and in the small villages that any departure from it is striking. Naturally it is worse in some areas than in others, but everywhere it is the prevailing condition in which the rural people live. In viewing Mexican standards of living there is a tendency for foreigners to make comparisons with conditions in their own countries, and perhaps the reader may fear that the preceding observations are based upon implicit comparisons with the living standards which prevail generally in the United States. By such a measure, the level of living in rural Mexico is abysmally low. But the basis of comparison here is rather a set of theoretical standards which students of Mexican social and economic conditions, official and otherwise, would roughly agree upon as a minimum for health and decency.

From this point of view, rural Mexico falls down in all aspects of living—diet, housing, sanitation, clothing, medical attention, household furnishings, and so on. Surveys made about ten years ago by the Department of Indian Affairs, showed that for many Indian groups food consumption was 60 per cent below the minimum dietary requirement considered essential for health. In some cases the deficiency ran as high as 80 per cent.[5] These are merely illustrations. They could be matched by many others that have been brought out in studies of rural groups. The phrase "hunger is endemic," so aptly applied to Indian peoples in certain parts of Mexico by the sociologist Lucio Mendieta y Nuñez,[6] can be reasonably applied to the whole rural population. (For practical purposes, Indian Mexico can be identified with rural Mexico, for, whatever its racial composition, the rural population is overwhelmingly Indian in its ways of living).

The diet of the rural population is deficient in quality as well as in quantity. Food consumption is largely confined to two items. These are corn, which is eaten in the form of tortillas, and beans. Chile, used for flavoring, is also important in the diet. Other foods, in addition to these three, are consumed, but they are eaten irregularly and sporadically. They do not form a part of the normal diet. This is true of meat, eggs, milk, fresh vegetables, fruits, and fats. They are all eaten upon occasion, but in most of rural Mexico such occasions are few and far between. It is frequently said in Mexico that the Mexican diet is the worst in the world. This may not be true, but, as Eyler Simpson has pointed out,

certainly it is true that even if the Mexican peasant were able to fill his stomach each day with all the tortillas, frijoles and chile it would hold—an assumption which is far from being always and everywhere true—he would still be malnourished, for these articles simply do not contain the fats, sugar, and other energy-giving and growth-producing substances necessary to health and well-being.[7]

A few illustrations may also be offered relating to other elements in the rural standard of living. An analysis of housing statistics gathered in the 1940 census showed that only 14 per cent of the Mexican population lived in houses with acceptable plumbing and drinking water.[8] Since such houses were to be found more frequently in the urban than in the rural areas, the percentage of the rural inhabitants enjoying suitable hygienic conditions must be even lower. The peasant house frequently consists of one room only, and this room is likely to be used by the farm animals as well as by the farm family. Furnishings are likely to be conspicuous by their absence, and those that are found in the typical *jacal* (peasant house) are of a primitive type. A large fraction of the rural population sleeps on the bare floor (which usually means the ground) or on a reed mat. Beds are not a common article of furniture.

[5] Soule, Efron and Ness, *Latin America in the Future World*, p. 25.
[6] Lucio Mendieta y Nuñez, *La economía del indio* (Mexico, 1938), p. 37.
[7] Simpson, *The Ejido*, p. 264.
[8] Gilberto Loyo, "Esquema demográfico de México," *Memoria del Segundo Congreso Mexicano de Ciencias Sociales,* vol. 3, p. 721.

Such dietary, housing, and sanitary conditions are naturally favorable for the spread of diseases. Dysentery, tuberculosis, smallpox, typhoid, typhus, and malaria are widespread, and annually take a large toll among the rural dwellers of Mexico. (This does not mean, however, that the incidence of such diseases is greater among the rural people than among the urban inhabitants.) The less spectacular deficiency diseases, such as rickets, are also common. In addition to contributing to a high disease ratio, malnutrition is a powerful factor in reducing the working efficiency of Mexico's farming population. We can be sure that the pace of farm work in Mexico, and the intensity of such work, are greatly influenced by inadequacies in food consumption. These inadequacies, as observed, are both qualitative and quantitative in character. That they tend to perpetuate low standards of living among the peasants, by reducing the effectiveness of farm work, cannot be questioned.

As long as standards of living like those described prevail, Mexico's farming population is incapable of absorbing many industrial products. Rural Mexico is a potential market, not an actual one. To convert it into a true market requires the creation of new wants and, what is obviously more important, the creation of purchasing power to satisfy those wants. But to effect an increase in farm buying power it is necessary to convert Mexican agriculture from a subsistence to a commercial basis and to raise its productivity—twin developments, since they are intimately related one to the other. Both developments must be thorough, and they must take place at a fairly rapid rate if they are to keep up with the current rate of industrial development. The problems of achieving advances in commercializing and improving productivity in agriculture, therefore, are of the utmost importance to Mexico's industrialization effort, and it is essential to examine them with care.

A major handicap to the shift from subsistence to commercial farming is isolation. Hundreds of small villages in Mexico are cut off by difficult terrain from everything but a handful of neighboring villages. Communication with the outside world requires a long and arduous journey by foot or by burro, and little is hauled from such areas to outside market centers. About fifteen years ago Frank Tannenbaum, with the coöperation of the Mexican government, conducted a questionnaire survey on the economic and social characteristics of Indian village life in Mexico.[9] Results were obtained from 3,600 villages in different parts of the country. More than 90 per cent of these villages had no local market, which means that nothing but minor, informal, commercial transactions were carried out in them.

[9] The results of this survey are published in Frank Tannenbaum, "Technology and Race in Mexico," *Political Science Quarterly*, vol. 61, no. 3 (September, 1946), pp. 365–383.

Little could be done to sell surplus produce except by hauling it to another town which had an organized market. For 55 per cent of the villages, the distance to the nearest market was seven miles or less. To get these distances in proper perspective, however, it must be remembered that in most cases they had to be covered on foot or by primitive means of transport. What a man could haul on his back often set the limit to what he produced for sale. For about one-fourth of the villages, the nearest market was between seven and twenty-five miles distant, while from 9 per cent of the villages it was necessary to travel from twenty-five to fifty miles in order to find a market.

The isolation of the typical Mexican Indian village is illustrated by other results obtained in the Tannenbaum study. Ninety-three per cent of the villages had no train accommodations, 92 per cent had no automobiles, and 86 per cent had no bus or auto transportation. This picture has changed somewhat in the years that have elapsed since Tannenbaum gathered his data. Some improvements have been made in country roads, so that motor transport may use them, at least during the dry season. Bus service has been ramified and extended, and drivers with a relaxed hand take buses over roads where no American company would even consider operating. But what has been achieved thus far is only a drop in the bucket. To collect bulky and heavy produce from anything but a narrow strip along each of the trunk highways and railroads is still impossible. A small beginning has been made, but it is so small that most of Mexico today can truthfully be called "back country."[10]

If we assume for the moment that other circumstances are favorable for commercializing agriculture, the lack of communication between rural producers and town markets is a major obstacle to such a development. To remove this handicap Mexico must build a network of secondary roads. Some new trunk highways must also be built, but the major problem is one of constructing hard-surface feeder roads to enable motor transport to penetrate settled areas now accessible only by more primitive means of transportation. It is not necessary to construct expensive high-standard roads for this purpose. Feeder roads adequate to carry light truck traffic the year around can be built for a relatively small investment per mile. Nevertheless, so much of Mexico is devoid of such roads that the expenditure required to do the job will be very large. The Mexican government will be required to make substantial outlays over a period of years for road building basic to the economic development of the country.

[10] Other striking evidence, of more recent vintage, regarding the isolation of Indian villages in Mexico has been brought out by Moisés T. de la Peña, one of the few Mexican economists who has traveled widely in the backwoods areas of his country. See "La mexicanización del indio," *Revista de Economía*, vol. 8, no. 8 (August 10, 1945), pp. 34–43.

The assumption made in the preceding paragraph that other circumstances were favorable to the commercialization of Mexican agriculture was merely an expedient one. It was not intended to brush aside other difficulties and problems. These are brought out in connection with the following discussion of raising agricultural productivity in Mexico—a question which is closely interrelated with that of shifting agriculture from a subsistence to a commercial basis.

The productivity of Mexican agriculture is notoriously low. This is true both in yield per acre and in yield per man. Several years ago when Eyler Simpson studied comparative figures on yields of corn, wheat, and beans, he found that Mexican yields were among the lowest in the world.[11] It is doubtful whether Mexico has improved its relative position materially since that time, and it may not have improved it at all.[12]

The return for the human effort that goes into raising crops in Mexico is pitifully small. Exceptions can be found in certain specialty crops, but, for Mexican agriculture as a whole, manpower is used with extremely little effect. This was strikingly illustrated during the recent war, when a joint Mexican-United States government program was worked out to make possible the use of Mexican labor in American agriculture. In the latter years of the war, approximately 75,000 *braceros,* as they were called, were engaged in farm work in the United States each year, and more than 50,000 were working for American railroads. How many of the latter came from agricultural employment in Mexico is not known, but it is not unreasonable to suppose that, altogether, about 100,000 persons were drawn out of Mexican farming annually for work in the United States in 1944 and 1945. Although divergences appeared in production trends among the different farm products, a survey of output figures[13] shows no slackening in the production of most crops. (Wheat was a major exception, but this can be explained in large measure by a shift of wheat land to other uses.)

Not a single expert on agricultural questions in Mexico has thought that the loss of manpower made any difference to Mexican agriculture, not even in connection with those crops whose production fell off during the war period. It seems safe to conclude that the withdrawal of 100,000 men from Mexican farming did not cause a reduction of agricultural output. This gives a clear picture of what agricultural productivity in the Mexican economy amounts to. It is probably a minimum picture, in the

---

[11] Simpson, *The Ejido,* pp. 159–161.

[12] In an earlier chapter, I noted that sugar yields in Mexico are also low in relation to those in other cane-producing countries.

[13] Secretaría de Agricultura y Ganadería, *Boletín Mensual de la Dirección de Economía Rural,* no. 257 (October, 1947), pp. 740–741.

sense that if a substantially larger number of men had migrated to the United States, the effect on farm production in Mexico would still have been negligible.

Still another way of looking at the low productivity of Mexican agriculture is provided by estimates of contribution to total national income. According to the analysis made by Dr. Josué Sáenz in 1946, the 62 per cent of Mexico's gainfully employed population engaged in farming produced only 18 per cent of the national income, while the other gainfully employed people, engaged in nonagricultural pursuits, produced 82 per cent of the total. Dr. Sáenz also calculated that 600,000 persons working in industry contributed almost twice as much to national income as 3,850,000 persons gainfully employed in agriculture.[14]

It is obvious that it is necessary to raise agricultural productivity in Mexico in order to bring about an improvement in rural living standards. But higher agricultural productivity is also needed for industrialization. The Mexican farmer will not be a better buyer until he is a better producer. The more rapid the rate of industrial development, the more acute the problem of raising agricultural efficiency becomes. To get a realistic view of this problem, we must examine with care the difficulties of improving agricultural productivity in Mexico.

Apart from commercialization, which I have already treated, the principal means by which farming efficiency can be raised are: (1) introduction of improved methods of tillage and of better equipment; (2) changes in crop economy; (3) more intensive cultivation of lands now devoted to agricultural production; (4) opening of new lands to cultivation. Developments in all these fields have been taking place, and are taking place, but it is a serious question whether they can go on at a sufficiently rapid pace to support adequately the current and prospective rate of industrialization.

To change methods of cultivation in Mexico it is necessary to overcome obstacles in the traditions and customs of the rural population. In Mexico, as Carl Sauer has pointed out, "the continuity with ages long ago is fundamental."[15] Some of the rural institutions prevailing today, and some of the farming methods in use, have persisted since the days before the Spanish Conquest. Isolation has tended to produce this result among certain Indian groups, but, even where isolation has not been an important factor, resistance to change has been stubborn.

Wherever people have lived close to the margin of subsistence for generations, so that there is no memory of any other condition, it is not surprising to find that they are reluctant to experiment with new crops and new

[14] Summary of a lecture by Dr. Josué Sáenz, in *El Mercado de Valores*, August 26, 1946, p. 2.
[15] Carl O. Sauer, "The Personality of Mexico," *The Geographical Review*, vol. 31, no. 3 (July, 1941), p. 353.

methods. For them experimentation is dangerous. It may even mean starvation. The negative attitude with which they inevitably greet a proposal to experiment is reinforced, also, by superstition and by a high degree of illiteracy. The interweaving of economic activity and social custom exerts a similar influence. Ritualistic behavior in connection with the sowing, cultivation, and harvesting of crops has an important place in the social life of the Indian village in Mexico, and thus these operations transcend their simple economic functions. All these factors give momentum to the traditional ways of doing things that have come down from pre-Conquest times.

Much of the equipment used in Mexican agriculture, like the farming methods, is ancient and primitive in nature. The wooden plow, with the ox for motive power, is a common sight in Mexico. But in some places not even the wooden plow is used. The sowing of crops is done with a wooden stick. In such cases only one additional type of equipment may be used, the *coa* (a kind of a hoe) for cultivation, although a *machete* may also be employed in clearing fields before planting. The persistence of primitive technology can be explained partly by isolation and the related lack of incentive to produce for commercial purposes. But tradition and the dangers of experimentation also play their part in retarding technical improvement.

The problem of overcoming resistances to change which rest upon no other foundation than a reverence for the traditional ways of doing things is best solved by education. This means education of the schoolbook kind, at least so far as literacy is concerned, in order to facilitate the communication of new ideas. A much more important field for educational effort, however, is an agricultural extension program to show the advantages of newer methods by experimental demonstration right in the village community itself. Such a program has not been lacking in Mexico, but the size of the job is tremendous. There still lies ahead of Mexico in this field a large and costly undertaking.

It is, furthermore, a task for which a great number of trained agricultural specialists are required. Large variations in regional conditions make it necessary to provide a variety of kinds of training for such specialists. They must also be persons who know and understand rural life in Mexico, who will not appear as intruders in the village community, and who are content to live away from the urban centers. Taking all qualities together, the supply of agricultural specialists in Mexico right now is limited. Many more will have to be trained, but this will necessarily require time and expense. It is clear that the sort of program in agricultural education needed in Mexico is a long-run job, and a costly one. Substantial results will not be obtained in a hurry.

Still another traditional factor that impedes rationalization of Mexican agriculture is the diet of the rural folk. This bears upon the crop economy. The traditional rural diet, as we have observed, consists mostly of corn, beans, and chile, and the Mexican farmer concentrates upon the raising of these crops. Any proposal to diversify agriculture, or to change the character of specialization, runs into an obstacle in the food habits of those who raise the crops. Such food preferences do not change easily.

Of course, it is possible for a Mexican farmer to have his traditional dietary preferences satisfied by other producers, while he specializes in something else. This practice will doubtless become more common in the future than it has been in the past. But it can increase only as part of a larger transformation in the structure of Mexican agriculture which cannot go on rapidly for reasons which are being dealt with throughout this whole discussion. Until the transformation is much farther advanced, the nature of the rural diet will be an obstacle in its own right to agricultural improvement.

Even if a knowledge of better methods and techniques could be conveyed quickly to a receptive farming population in Mexico, a major problem would still arise over the cost of actually introducing the improvements. The bulk of Mexico's farmers could not afford to make even a start, much less a significant effort. Providing credit at low rates of interest through the public agricultural credit agencies can be very useful, but small cash incomes for farmers restrict its application in the present stage of agricultural development. The solution seems to lie in some combination of public credit and public subsidies. Both policies are in operation. Since 1940 subsidies have been given to increase the use of improved agricultural implements and of fertilizers. But the amounts of public funds needed to achieve substantial results by credit and subsidy measures will be huge, and they can be forthcoming only over a period of years.

This suggests a need for careful planning on the part of the Mexican government to make the most effective use of the funds allocated to agricultural improvement. In some places it would be appropriate to concentrate upon providing agricultural machinery of a highly advanced type. This requires a combination of favorable circumstances in topography, kinds of crops capable of being raised, land holdings, and coöperative activity; such a combination is not likely to be encountered frequently in Mexico at the present time. At the other extreme, modern agricultural equipment even of the simpler types may not be usable at all because of slope or soil conditions, and the effort to improve productivity may better consist of subsidizing the use of fertilizers. One of the most effective fields for subsidy is the combating of plant diseases and plagues which each year take a heavy toll of Mexico's crop production. The same applies to live-stock production. The cost of such subsidies is likely to be very small in relation to the increases in output they would make possible.

Even if we assume that the Mexican government exercises maximum ingenuity and wisdom in laying out its agricultural credit and subsidy policies, the total amount of money required will present a formidable problem in public finance. It must be remembered, too, that a certain amount of basic experimental work has to be carried out by the govern-ment to determine the most appropriate improvements to foster in different regions of the country. This also involves heavy expenditures, although further assistance from the Rockefeller Foundation may keep the outlays of the Mexican government down to modest proportions. It is probable, too, that the Food and Agriculture Organization of the United Nations will provide some aid in this field, and it may even provide help in agri-cultural education.

The problem of commercializing and rationalizing Mexican agriculture is greatly complicated by the small size of the average holding which has come to prevail in the ejidos. This has been the result of the rather check-ered career of agrarian reform in Mexico, in which the negative aspect of breaking up the hacienda has tended to become dominant over the positive aspect of how the land was to be used by the peasants. Perhaps no other approach was possible, in view of the land hunger of the peasantry, the chaotic ten years of civil strife following the overthrow of Porfirio Díaz, and the essentially amorphous character of the Mexican Revolution. Every student of the question would agree that there are good explanations avail-able for the trends and inadequacies of Mexican agrarian policy since it first began to take shape in 1915, during the heat of civil war.

Most, if not all, students of Mexican agricultural questions would also agree nowadays that a major shortcoming of agrarian reform has been the creation of holdings that are too small to support a family unit. Inti-mate analysis of land-holding statistics carries one quickly into complex technical problems concerning methods of compilation of figures, com-parability, and the like. There is no question, however, about the order of magnitude of the average holding in the ejido.[16] It is in the neighborhood of 12 acres. This figure, based upon 1940 data, represents an increase over the typical holding of ten years earlier, which was approximately 9 acres.

These figures, based on ejidos in all parts of the country, actually give an exaggerated impression of the size of land holdings in the ejidos in the most densely populated part of Mexico, the southern part of the central

[16] See, for example, Ramón Fernández y Fernández, "Problemas creados por la reforma agraria de México," El Trimestre Económico, vol. 13, no. 3 (October–December, 1946), pp. 465–468.

plateau. In this region, according to recent surveys made by Moisés T. de la Peña,[17] the average holding in the ejido is 7.5 acres or less.

Such small holdings might be adequate in a certain kind of agricultural regime, for example where high-value crops are raised under conditions of intensive cultivation. Farming of this type, however, hardly exists in Mexico. A small amount of truck farming in the vicinity of Mexico City and other urban centers might qualify, but this amounts to such a tiny fraction of Mexican agriculture that it may be neglected. The average-size holding in the ejido is clearly too small to provide satisfactory support for the average family. Some of the holdings, of course, are larger than the average, just as others are smaller. But even the majority of the larger holdings cannot be called adequate in view of the physical limitations which land and climate place upon agriculture in Mexico.

Numerous complaints from ejidos bear witness to the need for larger holdings for the average family. Many villages have petitioned the Mexican government in recent years for more land, frequently asking that nearby small individual farms (ranchos) be taken over by the government for distribution to the ejidos.[18] Indeed, the threat to the small independent farmer had become so great by 1946 that one of the first steps of the Alemán administration was to put through an amendment to Article 27 of the Constitution giving new and greater guarantees to such farmers that their lands would not be expropriated under the agrarian laws. The policy of the Alemán administration, as that of its predecessor, is to look elsewhere for a solution to Mexico's agrarian problem. This, as we shall see below, lies in the direction of colonizing new lands.

Still additional evidence of the inadequacy of the ejido parcel is found in the fact that many peasants are forced to seek other sources of income besides their farming work in the ejido. Figures gathered in 1940 showed that 11 per cent of the ejidatarios gave more time to working for wages than to the cultivation of their ejido holdings.[19] These represented the extreme case, since they were in the main, wage-workers first, and secondarily farmers. The number of farmers who were secondarily wage-earners must have been much larger. Possibly 50 per cent of all the ejidatarios in Mexico do some outside work for cash.

Among the many disadvantages associated with the small size of the typical ejido holding is the handicap this presents to the introduction of improved equipment and methods in farming. Wherever physical conditions permit the use of the more advanced types of agricultural machinery,

---

[17] Moisés T. de la Peña, "Un México nuevo," *Revista de Economía Continental*, vol. 3, no. 17 (December 20, 1947), p. 778.
[18] Fernández y Fernández, *op. cit.*, p. 466.
[19] Fernández y Fernández, *op. cit.*, p. 472.

it is necessary to work the land in large-scale units in order to insure economical operation. In varying degree this is true for all modern farm equipment and also for other improvements in farming practices. Because the cultivated fields of all inhabitants of a village community are apt to be adjacent to each other, there is often little point in experimenting with new methods, crops, or breeds of livestock unless all are willing to coöperate.

There is no lack of recognition in Mexico of the problem of *minifundismo*, as the pattern of excessively small holdings is called. Some students of the question find the solution in getting more land for the ejidos, at the expense of small individual holdings as well as the remaining large estates. Those who hold this opinion, however, seem to be well in the minority. Opposition to this point of view has been growing, although those who oppose it are far from being in complete agreement on what should be done in a positive sense. The two lines of development most commonly recommended are (1) to operate the ejidos on a coöperative rather than on an individual basis, and (2) to open new areas to settlement.[20]

It is apparent that Mexico is in the throes of reappraising its agrarian reform program and its agrarian structure. What will come out of this by way of a major reorientation in agrarian policy is by no means clear. The point to be stressed here is that the process of bringing about changes in policy and rural structure promises to be a slow and difficult one. The emotions stirred up during the early days of the Mexican Revolution have by no means died away. For the bulk of Mexico's rural inhabitants, which also means the bulk of Mexico's total population, the ejido has been about the only source of hope for a better life. Because its roots go deep into Mexico's past, it takes on traditional values which transcend considerations of economic efficiency. In the rural society of Mexico the ejido is undoubtedly thought of as something which is good in itself, and other ways of looking at the institution are rigidly excluded.

To stop the process of creating and extending ejidos, as the Mexican government now seems inclined to do, will not be easy. Even greater difficulty will be encountered in trying to turn back the whole course of agrarian reform by converting some ejidatarios into permanent agricultural wage-earners, in order to increase the holdings of the remaining ejidatarios. (The difficulties of opening new lands will be discussed below.) It will be a long time, therefore, before Mexico will be able to solve the problem of excessively small land holdings. Meanwhile, this pattern of holdings will continue to be a handicap to increasing the productivity of agriculture.

[20] See, for example, Marco Antonio Durán, "Del agrarismo a la revolución agrícola," *Problemas Economico–Agrícolas de México,* no. 2 (October–December, 1946), pp. 24–35.

It has been suggested above that there are physical limitations to the expansion of agricultural output in Mexico. Nature has been far more generous to Mexico with scenery than with good agricultural land. Most of Mexico's population lives on the great central plateau, where altitude offsets latitude to provide a temperate climate. Actually, the greatest concentration of inhabitants is found today, as in the days before the Spanish Conquest, in the southern part of the plateau within a radius of a few hundred miles of Mexico City. The average rainfall in this area (20 to 30 inches per year) is sufficient for crop-raising, but it is erratic as to annual variation and as to timing within the rainy season. It is anything but dependable. Thus farming that relies entirely upon rainfall in this part of Mexico (and also in the less rainy part of the plateau farther north) is a hazardous business.

This handicap would be less severe if sources of irrigation water were readily available, but they are not. There are only a few large rivers flowing through or into the plateau country. Moreover, most of the smaller streams which might otherwise be used to supply water for minor irrigation developments are incapable of such use because they have cut deep canyons (*barrancas*) in the plateau floor. Much of the rainfall which does fall or drain into the plateau region is wasted so far as crop-raising is concerned. This condition, it should be pointed out, has been getting progressively worse, as the cumulative effects of forest and soil destruction make themselves felt. (See below.)

Land surface, like climate, does not favor agricultural development in large areas of Mexico. Much of Mexico, probably more than one-half, would be called rugged terrain. The central plateau is by no means a flat area. The plateau landscape, especially the southern part where population density is greatest, is a highly diversified one, with numerous mountain chains, volcanic cones, and deep valleys. Except in a few of the larger valleys, it is an area of steep slopes and thin soils. The mountain escarpment on either side of the central plateau is, of course, an even more broken landscape, and much of Mexico south of the central plateau is also a land of sharp topographic contrasts. Essentially the only flat lands in the country are found in the coastal plains.

To the natural disadvantages of physiographic conditions in the areas of greatest population concentration have been added the effects of long human occupation. In cultivating the land, in grazing livestock, and in using the forest resources of Mexico, man has destroyed much of nature's slender initial endowment. The process of destruction is already far advanced. Erosion and soil wash have taken such a heavy toll that a considerable fraction of Mexico's crop land has been permanently ruined for agriculture, while much of the remainder has been badly impaired. There is not the slightest doubt that Mexico is confronted with a serious problem of soil conservation.

Active destruction of Mexico's forests dates from at least colonial times, when a great development in mining created a large demand for timber. "Wherever a mining community was established," writes Lesley Byrd Simpson,[21] "a diseased spot began to appear, and it spread and spread until each mine became the center of something like a desert. As early as 1543 the Indians of Taxco complained to Viceroy Mendoza that all the forests near by had been cut down and that they were obliged to make a day's journey to get timber for the mines. The mountains of Zacatecas were once covered with a heavy forest. They are now rocky grass lands where goats have a hard time finding a living. The same story was repeated at . . . all the other famous mining regions of Mexico." The persistent use of charcoal as fuel for cooking and heating purposes has been another prominent source of forest destruction. It was estimated some years ago that supplying charcoal to Mexico City alone involved the destruction of about 12,000 acres of standing timber each year—"largely without plan, rhyme or reason."[22] More recently the Mexican government has made efforts to curb the use of charcoal, accompanied by parallel endeavors to extend the use of petroleum and gas in the household. However successful this campaign may prove to be, it can never eliminate the consequences of the severe damage that has already been done.

The need to conserve Mexico's remaining forest cover has been recognized in various laws, including legislation setting up national parks where commercial exploitation is forbidden. However, a survey of these forest reserves in 1945 by the head of the Conservation Section of the Pan-American Union showed that sawmills were in operation and livestock was being grazed in open violation of the law.[23] The enforcement of conservation laws thus far has not yielded encouraging results.

Cropping methods and excessive grazing have also been responsible for widespread depletion of Mexico's soil resources. The tillage of steep slopes has itself invited gullying, and this has been made worse by plowing and row cultivation. Special precautions to minimize land destruction under these conditions have been lacking. The lack of crop rotation, too, has been a factor in the deterioration of Mexico's soils. In pasturing livestock, the practice has been to graze animals without thinking about the land itself. The goat, in particular, has been an active agent of land wastage in Mexico.

[21] *Many Mexicos* (New York, 1946), p. 15.
[22] Eyler Simpson, *The Ejido*, p. 260.
[23] William Vogt, "Los recursos naturales de México," *Memoria del Segundo Congreso Mexicano de Ciencias Sociales*, vol. 2, p. 21, p. 61, p. 77.

Abundant evidence of the great degree to which Mexico's agricultural resources have been depleted is given in the excellent study by William Vogt, referred to above.[24] Indeed, so impressed was Vogt by what he observed in Mexico that he was willing to risk the following prophecy:

One of the most eminent Latin American botanists, who knows southern Mexico thoroughly, has stated categorically that Oaxaca will be a desert within 50 years.

My own opinion, formed independently before encountering this opinion, is that unless actual tendencies (1945) are radically modified, the major part of Mexican territory within a century will be desert, or will only be able to maintain a human population at a very precarious level of subsistence. . . . Even in case my conclusion should be 50 per cent in error, the situation would still be exceedingly grave. . . .[25]

There is no escaping the conclusion that in the area where most of the Mexican population is concentrated the majority of the land is mediocre or poor in quality. Never very good, its value for farming has been deteriorating rapidly through erosion. To raise agricultural productivity by more intensive cultivation of such lands, therefore, is out of the question. For most of the central plateau region the problem is one of rehabilitating those lands which can still be saved, not of trying to find ways to crop them more intensively. Although something can be done to make agriculture more efficient along with the introduction of conservation methods, the physical limitations are so great as to preclude any significant development of this kind.

It follows from what has been said above that the central plateau of Mexico is an over-populated area, in terms of the present economy of the country. If the rural population of this region could be substantially reduced, so that only the better lands would be cultivated, the productivity of the remaining farmers could in time be raised materially by a variety of measures (improved methods and equipment, changes in crop economy, seed selection, combating plant diseases, coöperative use of farm implements, agricultural credit, and the like). With a sizable increase in the amount of reasonably good agricultural land at the disposal of each farmer, perhaps it would not take many years before these other measures would bear fruit in increasing output and efficiency, and in enabling the central plateau farmers to raise their standards of living. Under such conditions they would have purchasing power, and they would constitute an actual rather than a potential market for the products of Mexican industry.

This line of thinking has been gaining ground in Mexico. Increasingly the official policy of the Mexican government has shifted in this direction. It is this point of view that gives rationale to the joint program of resettle-

[24] "Los recursos naturales de México," especially pp. 65–66.
[25] Op. cit., p. 32.

ment and the related program of opening new agricultural areas which the Mexican government embarked upon during the Avila Camacho administration and which the present administration of President Alemán is pushing forward with energy. Next to industrialization, internal colonization is regarded as the major solution to Mexico's economic and social problems.

Two kinds of lands are said to offer opportunities for the settlement of people from the overcrowded parts of the central plateau. One class consists of land to be brought into production by means of irrigation development. For more than twenty years now, irrigation policy has been a major question before the government and people of Mexico. In the past several years, especially, large sums have been expended on irrigation development and substantial additions have been made to irrigated acreage. During the six years of the Avila Camacho administration approximately 900,000 acres of new land were brought under irrigation, and 800,000 acres of previously irrigated land were benefited by improved irrigation systems.

The Alemán administration promises to speed up and extend the program of irrigation development. It has been announced officially that the government plans to spend 1.5 billion pesos in the construction of dams and other irrigation works during the six years of Alemán's term.[26] This is more than double the amount spent by the preceding administration (656 million pesos) for similar purposes. Also, in comparison with the 900,000 acres of new land supplied with irrigation water during the Avila Camacho period, it is anticipated that when the present administration leaves office in December, 1952, about 3,500,000 acres will have been added to Mexico's irrigated acreage. For the most part, the new projects will be found in the northern part of the central plateau (Mesa del Norte) and in the extreme northwest (Sonora and Sinaloa).

It is possible—we might even say probable—that the government will be unable to carry out this program in six years. It is an extremely ambitious program, for which, as noted above, the outlays are very large. To maintain the proposed schedule will not be easy. Perhaps, too, closer study of the topography of the areas for which irrigation development is contemplated will throw an unfavorable light on some of the projects. More precise knowledge may well tone down official optimism. Past experience suggests that the sights are likely to be lowered as the expanded irrigation program gets under way. This seems to be the trend of human experience with irrigation projects in the world at large.

[26] Press interview with Adolfo Orive Alba, Minister of Water Resources, *El Nacional*, August 28, 1947.

If the projects envisioned in the Alemán irrigation program should be completed according to schedule, they will add approximately 10 per cent to Mexico's cultivated acreage, with significant increase in agricultural output. How much resettlement it would make possible, is, however, another question. One may expect that most of the newly irrigated lands, such as those to be made available by the construction of Mexico's largest dam, the Alvaro Obregón dam on the Yaqui River in Sonora, will be occupied by persons already living in the area. Their present holdings are so inadequate that they will easily take up the slack when the new lands are brought under cultivation. Only a limited number of persons from other parts of Mexico will be absorbed in these irrigation developments.

Furthermore, when this group of projects has been completed, Mexico will have used up most of her irrigation sites. In the areas where irrigation is needed, the water resources are quite limited, and they have already been developed to a large extent. To take advantage of those still remaining after the Alemán irrigation program has been carried out will require substantially greater expenditures per acre of land benefited. The development of such sites is likely to be spread over a considerable number of years.

It is very unlikely, therefore, that new irrigation projects will relieve the southern part of the central plateau of excess rural population. Even if we assume willingness to migrate to the north and northwest, the number of such colonists who could be taken care of will be very small. Thus, if resettlement is to be effective in amount and timing, that is, if it is to support industrialization by increasing the productivity of Mexican farming, it must be directed largely toward other areas.

For such areas, the government of Mexico is looking to the tropical coastal plains, which are now comparatively uninhabited. Probably the best potential agricultural resources of the nation lie in these regions, especially in the coastal plain on the Gulf of Mexico side. Climatic conditions are good for raising a wide variety of crops, including corn, along with tropical and subtropical products such as bananas, coffee, cacao, vanilla, and pineapples. Rainfall is abundant and temperatures are mild or high the year around, so that two harvests a year can be obtained for some crops. A comparatively flat topography in most of the coastal plain area also favors agricultural development. It is not known how fertile these lands will prove to be after clearing, but they do offer potentialities for increasing Mexico's agricultural production both of crops for export and of crops for the domestic market.

The importance of promoting the colonization of the humid coastal regions by migration from the interior was recognized by President Avila Camacho, who adopted the slogan "march to the sea" in order to dramatize the need for a centrifugal movement in the redistribution of Mexico's population. In 1941, about six months after he took office, he suggested a policy of internal colonization with the following words:

The future of agriculture lies in the fertile lands of the coast. A march to the sea will relieve congestion in our central plateau, where worn-out lands must be devoted to crops which colonial policy denied them with the result that the traditional maize culture of the indigenous population has continued to be dominant. The fertility of the coastal plains will make it uneconomical to raise many products in the central plateau. But the march to the sea requires, as prerequisites, sanitary and health measures, the opening of communications, the reclamation and drainage of swamps, and, to make such projects possible, the expenditure of large sums of money. It will be necessary to organize a new kind of tropical agriculture, which, because of the very nature of its production, cannot be the small-scale type.[27]

In addition to voicing a goal for national settlement policy, this quotation suggests some of the difficulties that must be faced. To colonize the tropical lowlands of Mexico is by no means an easy job. A first obstacle is encountered in the clearing of dense native vegetation. In many places reclamation and drainage have to be carried out at a considerable expenditure of time and effort as well as of money. Tropical diseases are a major handicap to settlement. The incidence of malaria is extremely high, and its effects upon working efficiency as well as health are drastic. Dysentery, which is common all over Mexico, spreads with special ease in a tropical environment. To cut down the threat of these and other diseases to the point where new settlement and agricultural development will be possible on a significant scale calls for exceedingly large expenditures, and also for a large personnel trained for public health work in tropical regions.

The costs and what might be called the technical problems of opening Mexico's coastal lands to effective colonization are so great, therefore, that the process is certain to be a slow one. But these are not the only factors which thwart rapid development. Group solidarity and tradition give the Mexican rural inhabitant a strong attachment to his locality—his *tierra,* as he calls it. This acts as a drag on migration. It is probable, however, that this immobilizing influence has been weakened so much that it can no longer be considered a serious obstacle to recruiting large numbers for a colonization effort.

What does, however, constitute a serious obstacle is the physiological difficulty of moving from the high altitudes of the central plateau to the low altitudes of the coastal plains. Those who have always lived and worked at elevations of 4,000 to 8,000 feet, where the air is thin and for the most part dry, cannot be expected to adjust readily to the moisture-laden, heavy air of the tropical coast. Similarly, the difference in tempera-

---

[27] Quoted in *Seis años de actividad nacional,* p. 190.

ture conditions presents a problem of adjustment. Such obstacles are not insurmountable. There can be no question, however, that they will cause a great deal of back-tracking in the migration from the interior plateau to the low-lying plains along the coasts. The "march to the sea" will necessarily be a slow process.

In the years that have elapsed since Avila Camacho announced the policy of internal resettlement, very little has actually been accomplished. So far as can be determined, nothing was done during Avila Camacho's term of office to blueprint a program which would lead Mexico toward the goal he had set up. Under Alemán a slender beginning has been made in government-inspired migration. A National Commission of Colonization has been set up to determine the most appropriate areas for settlement. In September, 1947, it was announced that 59 families had been moved from an overcrowded area in the State of Guanajuato to a sparsely-settled region in the state of Tamaulipas, in the northeast. At the same time it was announced that plans had been completed to move 500 families from the state of Tlaxcala to the same region. Beyond the further report that the National Commission of Colonization had selected an area on the west coast, in the state of Guerrero, as appropriate for colonization, no tangible results emerged during the first year of Alemán's administration.

The Alemán administration is laying the groundwork for a much more ambitious undertaking in resettlement in a comprehensive plan for the development of the valley of the Papaloapan River in eastern Mexico. This plan, modeled in a general way after the Tennessee Valley Authority in the United States, includes the following features: river control to prevent flooding; irrigation; hydroelectric power development; making the river system navigable; building a network of roads and railways; drainage of swamp lands; sanitation; public health programs to combat tropical diseases; laying out of towns; planning the agricultural economy. The area included in the project covers about 18,000 square miles. It is calculated that when the project is completed the area will be able to support 600,000 persons, instead of the 170,00 who now inhabit it.

Obviously the Papaloapan project is one of tremendous scope and cost. Officials speak about a total investment of one billion pesos, a figure which is designed to give an idea of the probable cost rather than to suggest a precise estimate. On the time needed to complete the job, officials speak only in a vague way of fifteen to twenty years.[28] In view of the uncertainty about how much basic developmental work Mexico will be able to afford in the near future, no one could ask for a closer estimate. Thus far the Mexican government has barely started the preliminary investigations

[28] *El Universal*, March 15, 1947.

relating to the project, as may be seen by the scant 3 million pesos allocated to the program in 1947. The plan of the Alemán government apparently is to carry out certain basic parts of the project (thus far unspecified) and to leave the remainder for future administrations to design in detail.

However significant the Papaloapan project may prove to be in the long-run future, it hardly seems possible that it will afford an appreciable outlet for surplus population from other areas for many years to come. Even the twenty-year estimate for completion smacks of optimism. We might hazard the guess that it will take a full generation before the Papaloapan basin will be ready to receive immigrants in substantial numbers. Furthermore, in any meaningful sense the surplus population of the central plateau is much larger than the total number which the Papaloapan project can absorb, probably from two to three times larger. From this point of view, it may turn out that Mexico will spend too much on this project and too little on other developments of a less spectacular character, which can make greater short-run contributions to raising agricultural productivity.

The preceding discussion of irrigation and internal colonization suggests that their contribution to the extending of the internal market for industrial products will be limited. Ultimately their influence will be important in this respect, but in the short run Mexico must count mainly on other measures to raise the farmer's buying power, such measures as relate to commercializing and rationalizing agriculture for most farmers right where they are now located. These are extremely difficult tasks, and they cannot be accomplished rapidly, as has already been pointed out.

These observations are not intended to imply that the situation is hopeless, but rather that there is a real danger that the purchasing power of Mexico's agricultural population will be inadequate to support the industrial development now going on at such a lively pace. The proper implication to draw from the analysis here is that the rate of industrial development must be linked to the rate of agricultural development. Otherwise Mexico is destined to find herself with an industrial capacity in excess of what her market can absorb, and with an unbalanced economy that will one day require drastic measures to set it on an even keel.

CHAPTER XII

Capital and Credit

THIS CHAPTER is concerned with the broad problem of financing industrial development in Mexico, that is, of getting long-term capital and short-term credit for the many new industrial establishments which are springing up in Mexico. More particularly, this problem has been one of mobilizing Mexico's own capital resources for industry. The tapping of Mexican savings for investment in industry has proved to be far from easy, and only slow progress can be reported thus far. It is the main purpose of this chapter to show, by analyzing Mexico's financial experience in the last seven or eight years, how and where the difficulties have arisen.

Three main lines of inquiry are involved in this question: (1) the behavior of individual savers with respect to investment; (2) the behavior of the institutions that pool savings, mainly the banks, with respect to both lending and investment; (3) the operations of two public banks in the field of industrial financing, Nacional Financiera and the Bank of Mexico. The concluding section of the chapter deals with foreign investment, which the Mexican government is strongly inclined to welcome as a means of accelerating the rate of industrial advance.

INDIVIDUAL INVESTMENT HABITS

In analyzing investment habits in Mexico it must be remembered, first of all, that only a very small fraction of the total population is able to save. Low standards of living of the mass of the Mexican population effectively keep them out of the saving class. No figures can be cited, but anyone who takes a look around Mexico will readily agree that the percentage of savers must be small compared with similar percentages in the United States, Canada, and the nations of western Europe. Only a handful of persons, located almost entirely in the capital and other large cities, falls into the saving group.[1] Yet, although numerically small, this group commands a respectable proportion of the national income. Within it are found some very high personal incomes, which yield substantial savings in spite of a strong propensity to expend them on luxury articles. Again, figures

[1] According to one authority, only 300,000 out of 9 million adult persons in Mexico have life insurance policies. Emilio Alanis Patiño, "Planeación," *Boletín de la Sociedad Mexicana de Geografía y Estadística*, vol. 41, no. 2 (March–April, 1946), p. 269.

cannot be cited, but a working knowledge of economic and social conditions in Mexico suggests that a significant percentage of the Mexican
national income is saved each year. The habits of mind and attitudes of
those who fall into this small group are, therefore, of fundamental importance to the economic development of Mexico, and their behavior with
respect to investment of savings follows a fairly well defined pattern.

There is traditional preference in Mexico, as almost everywhere in Latin
America, for investment in land. This is a consequence of social and economic conditions inherited and carried forward from colonial days. Ownership of land in Latin America has not only been a principal basis of wealth
but it has also been the main source of social prestige and political power.
In Mexico this state of affairs has been rudely disturbed since 1910 by the
social program of the Revolution, under which many of the great estates
have been broken up and their lands distributed to peasants. Such lands
are now for the most part held collectively by the peasants in the form of
ejidos, the titles to which are inalienable. They are not on the market.

The remaining estates can legally be sold, but they find few purchasers
because of uncertainty about their future status. Also, because of the way
in which the agrarian laws have been applied in practice, titles to small
individual farms have been constantly in jeopardy in spite of legal guarantees. Between the principles set forth in the agrarian code on the one
hand, and their application on the other, there has unfortunately been a
wide gap. Perhaps not many investors would be interested in small holdings under any circumstances. The fact is, however, that those who might
want to invest capital in this way hesitate to do so because of the uncertainties involved. Agricultural land has virtually ceased to be an object of
investment in Mexico.[2]

The tradition of investing in real property, however, has persisted in
urban real estate development, such as in laying out residential subdivisions,
building homes for sale, and in constructing apartment houses and office
buildings. Such operations have expanded in all the principal cities, but
they have been especially striking in rapidly growing Mexico City and its
environs.

The Federal District, which includes Mexico City and its suburbs, has
witnessed an extraordinary growth in population in recent years. Its population as reported in the census of 1940 was about 1,750,000. In 1946 it was
officially estimated to have 2,500,000 inhabitants.[3] This figure may be high,
but even the most conservative estimates put the population of the district

[2] A constitutional amendment adopted in February, 1947, modified the agrarian laws so as
to strengthen the position of the small landholder. This step in time may stimulate transactions
in farm lands.

[3] *Seis años de actividad nacional,* statistical appendix.

at 2,250,000 in 1946. It may be calculated, therefore, that the population of Mexico City and its environs increased roughly by 30 to 40 per cent in the seven-year period 1940–1946.

All through the war years Mexico City enjoyed a building boom, as the 1939–1945 figures on page 226 show. A peak was reached toward the end of 1946, but no sharp drop occurred, and foreigners who visited Mexico at that time were still startled by the number of luxury homes under construction (to say nothing of their architecture). In subsequent months, apartment house construction declined substantially, but the construction of office buildings, hotels, and public buildings prevented a serious drop in the level of construction activity during 1947. It was not until 1948 that it could be said that the building boom in Mexico City had come to an end.

Nor has urban construction been confined to Mexico City, although precise data are not available for other places. Substantial numbers of new dwellings and commercial buildings have been erected elsewhere, especially in Monterrey, Guadalajara, and Puebla.

According to an estimate made by the economic research division of the Bank of Mexico, 1.3 billion pesos were invested in private construction during the six-year period 1940–1945 in the whole of Mexico.[4] The same source estimates that the aggregate investment in industry in Mexico for the same period was 1.6 billion pesos. These two investment figures, however, cannot be compared directly, for the figure of 1.3 billion for construction includes the building of industrial plants as well as homes, apartment houses, and commercial buildings. No separate figure for industrial building in all of Mexico is available. This can be obtained only for the Federal District. By assuming that the Federal District ratio between industrial and nonindustrial construction (4 per cent) also holds for the country as a whole, however, an estimate can be made of capital invested in nonindustrial building. This estimate is 1.25 billion pesos.

Thus the appropriate figure to compare with 1.6 billion pesos investment in industry is 1.25 billion for investment in private construction. For every hundred pesos invested in industry seventy-five were put into construction. Individual investors as well as institutional investors and banks came forward readily to provide funds for building purposes. Urban real property has been so readily salable in Mexico as to constitute a "liquid" investment. This development has naturally been favored and carried forward by inflation.

A natural outcome of the Mexican preference for investment in land is a receptive attitude toward investment in mortgages. To know that there are tangibles as security gives comfort to the Mexican investor, and indi-

[4] *Seis años de actividad nacional,* p. 368.

TABLE 6

BUILDINGS COMPLETED IN THE FEDERAL DISTRICT, 1939–1945
(Value figures in thousands of pesos)

Year	Total[a]		Houses		Apartment houses		Commercial and office bldg.		Industrial establishments	
	No.	Value	No.	Value	No.	Value	No.	Value	No.	Value
1939	3,007	43,789	2,340	18,995	489	18,672	81	2,339	43	2,182
1940	3,290	57,056	2,502	23,044	566	26,562	101	3,812	28	880
1941	3,894	82,015	2,839	25,499	756	41,542	131	10,529	45	1,790
1942	4,466	88,250	3,396	31,276	696	40,529	172	8,050	56	4,514
1943	4,549	100,201	3,528	38,613	594	39,766	205	12,365	58	3,480
1944	9,664	145,914	8,488	80,773	560	42,013	241	8,430	79	7,048
1945	9,971	172,552	8,279	66,674	652	50,927	224	29,675	116	8,689

Source: Gobierno del Distrito Federal, *Memoria* (September 1, 1944–August 31, 1945); 1945 figures supplied by statistical division of the Gobierno del Distrito Federal.
[a] Miscellaneous buildings included in the total but not in the breakdown.

viduals as well as institutions put funds readily into mortgages. Although the banks have always been willing to lend on mortgages, it is estimated that the public at large, including insurance companies, has absorbed more mortgages than the financial institutions.[5]

Much borrowing on mortgages is accomplished in Mexico through the agency of a mortgage bank. An individual or firm issues a mortgage certificate (*cédula hipotecaria*) to which a mortgage bank gives its guarantee, thereby making the document more attractive to the ultimate investor. With the expansion in building in recent years the volume of mortgage certificates issued has reached new high levels. In October, 1940, the total value of mortgage certificates outstanding was 47 million pesos. By October, 1944, this total had been raised to 103 million, an increase of 120 per cent. Two years later, in October, 1946, the total stood at 192 million, and by October, 1948, it had risen substantially again to 238 million.

In addition to guaranteeing certificates, the mortgage banks issue securities on their own. These are called mortgage bonds (*bonos hipotecarios*); they are secured by mortgage loans which the bank itself has made. These securities, too, have enjoyed favor with the Mexican investing public and there has been a marked increase in the volume issued during the past four or five years. From 58 million pesos in October, 1944, the total of mortgage bonds outstanding rose to 125 million in October, 1946, an increase of 115 per cent about the peak; later decline was gradual. In October, 1948, 108 million pesos of mortgage bonds were in circulation.

Loans by mortgage banks expanded considerably during the wartime building boom. Their aggregate rose from 63 million pesos in October, 1944, to 133 million in October, 1946. This amounted to an increase of 111 per cent. Subsequently, as construction slackened, mortgage-bank loans also dropped. In October, 1948, they stood at 111 million.

In theory the mortgage banks can make loans to industrial concerns, and they are sometimes listed among the institutions which make capital available for industrial development. In practice, however, their loans have been used almost exclusively to finance real estate operations.[6] Thus the funds invested in mortgage bonds have been completely divorced from the effort to industrialize Mexico.

---

[5] Nacional Financiera, *El Mercado de Valores,* August 26, 1946, p. 3. This weekly publication of the government investment bank contains notes and comments on financial questions, as well as financial statistics. These notes are about the only source of information on the economics of recent financial operations in Mexico. With few exceptions, the remainder of the slender literature on financial institutions has a legal, and essentially sterile, approach. I have used Nacional Financiera's comments freely, as the footnotes in the following pages testify. I must point out, however, that, taken together, the notes contain a number of inconsistencies. By appealing to official figures published by the National Banking Commission I have been able, in most cases, to choose between conflicting statements.

[6] *El Mercado de Valores,* August 26, 1946, p. 3.

Those individuals in Mexico who have been able to make savings show also a propensity to export capital. This seems to be a characteristic of socio-economic behavior in all underdeveloped countries. By keeping some of their resources abroad, the wealthy feel more comfortable than if they had them all in their own country. The turbulent political history of Mexico in recent decades has doubtless strengthened this tendency to export capital. Among others, politicians and ex-politicians have welcomed the security of foreign holdings, and some of them have actually had occasion to enjoy the advantages of such holdings when they found it advisable to leave Mexico on rather short notice. Unfortunately, there are no statistics on capital export from Mexico. Yet there is little doubt that persons with means have made it a practice to hold substantial bank balances abroad and to make long-term investments abroad, especially in the United States, for security reasons. In some cases they secure little or no returns on such holdings. In all cases the interest rates are less than those which can be earned in Mexico, but it is security, and not rate of return, which guides their action.

Investment by individuals in Mexico is limited by another important feature in their economic psychology, the tendency to hoard. This has been described neatly by a man prominent in Mexican financial circles in the following words:

Mexico, although it has progressed in many other aspects, still operates in a colonial manner with respect to investments. The capitalist continues to want metallic money that he can keep in his own possession, mortgages on property that he can see with his own eyes, or jewels and precious stones that he can hoard.[7]

Hoarding of this kind is a well-known characteristic of nonindustrialized, underdeveloped countries.[8] In Mexico this sociological impulse has been magnified by special circumstances. After the outbreak of the Mexican Revolution in 1911, the country went through a whole decade of violence and civil war, in which marauding and banditry were about as common as military operations in a formal sense. This experience undoubtedly has had the effect of making the Mexican people security conscious. It will take a few generations yet before the scars of ten years of bloodshed and property destruction are healed in the minds of the Mexican people.

In addition, the Mexican Revolution has brought into operation many social and economic experiments since 1911. Prominent among these have been agrarian reform, strong labor laws, social legislation, and the expropriation of foreign oil companies. Not only in their effects have these measures

---

[7] Jack Kalb, "Uno de los aspectos del financiamiento para la industrialización de México," *El Economista*, No. 145 (May–June, 1945), p. 48.
[8] See, for example, League of Nations: Economic, Financial and Transit Department, *Industrialization and Foreign Trade* (League of Nations, 1945), p. 69.

been far-reaching but some of them have been applied in a kaleidoscopic manner. They have helped to sustain the atmosphere of uncertainty created by the civil warfare. However laudable these measures may have been in themselves, it must be recognized that they have greatly affected the economic psychology of the Mexican people, in particular, of those persons whose incomes allow for savings. The practice of hoarding has been fostered.

The Bank of Mexico catered to the impulse to hoard metals by selling gold freely to the public during the war years. This was an anti-inflationary measure. As such, its effectiveness was probably quite limited. The amount of gold sales, however, does help to give us a quantitative notion of metal hoarding by the Mexican public. Between December 1, 1940, and June 30, 1946, the Bank of Mexico sold about 447 million pesos worth of gold to the public.[9] The public also hoarded silver, but no one can be sure of the amount; exports of silver manufactures and contraband bullion shipments were probably substantial. In round figures we may estimate the total of gold and silver hoarding from 1941 through 1946 at half a billion pesos.

This hoarding, and also large idle bank balances, suggest that the saving public could have made substantial investments in industry. Such investments, however, have been negligible, in spite of good earning and dividend records during the war years. The Mexican saver preferred to hold non-earning assets rather than to buy industrial securities.

The fact is that investors in Mexico have little confidence in the stocks and bonds of industrial firms. Not even the mortgage feature of the bond has attracted them. Only for some of Mexico's older and well-established industrial concerns has this lack of confidence been overcome. They are exceptional cases. Certainly the full weight of the investor's negative attitude has been brought to bear on the many new industrial firms established in Mexico since 1940.

To explain this extreme absence of confidence in industrial investment in Mexico is not an easy task. One factor applying to the new industries of the war period has been the fear that postwar foreign competition would destroy them. This, however, should have had little weight with reference to the larger enterprises which the Mexican government has so carefully encouraged. It should have been obvious all along that the government would take steps to protect such firms from foreign competition.

A much more important reason, undoubtedly, has been the fear of labor disputes and of the encroachment of labor on the functions of management. We cannot go afield to examine the difficult question of what merit there

---

[9] *Seis años de actividad nacional*, p. 331. Some of this gold is known to have been exported, but the amount of such exports is estimated to have been quite small.

is in this position. What matters is that it is widely held among those persons in Mexico who have capital to invest. It has unquestionably retarded industrial investment.

Another contributing factor is the weakness of the stock exchange in Mexico. The whole set of related institutions dealing in securities, stock exchange, brokers, etc., form a poorly organized, inefficient market. Much has been made of this point, especially by the officials of Nacional Financiera (the government investment bank), who argue that people will not buy shares as long as they are unable to liquidate them rapidly. Clearly this argument has been overemphasized. Once the willingness to buy industrial securities exists, a better and more efficient stock market will promote further investment, but it cannot of itself create the impulse. The efforts of Nacional Financiera and of the Mexican government to reorganize and strengthen the Mexico City Stock Exchange are laudatory, but it must be recognized that they are dealing here with a secondary problem rather than a main one. The Mexican investor must be tempted to put his funds into industrial securities principally by other means.

Another striking quality of the Mexican investor is his refusal to buy the bonds of his own government. This has been true since the early days of the Revolution when civil war conditions caused the Mexican government to default on its debts. The credit of the government suffered a severe blow internally as well as externally. As a matter of fact, the loss of government credit for internal borrowing has been more complete than for borrowing from without.

It was not until 1933 that the Mexican government attempted to sell securities again in the internal market. Since then it has put out a number of bond issues, on which it has scrupulously met its obligations. In addition the government has given its bonds complete tax-exemption privileges. The investing public, however, has steadfastly refused to buy the bonds, and public holdings of government securities have, right along, been insignificant in amount. Irrational though this attitude may be, it is nevertheless a hard fact which the Mexican government (and the central bank) must face.

The government has in recent years made large investments along lines fundamental to industrialization in Mexico. Some of these developments have been financed by bond issues. For example, bonds have been floated to cover outlays on irrigation, road building, and electrification. Such programs are appropriately regarded as basic to the industrial development of Mexico because they are needed to raise agricultural productivity, to broaden the internal market, and to increase industrial output. They have to be undertaken by the government since private enterprise will not develop such fields at a proper rate, if at all. To these important elements in industrialization, too, the investing public has made little or no contribution.

Principal Kinds of Private Banks
Commercial Banks

There are three principal kinds of banks in Mexico that can channel domestic savings into industry and promote industrial expansion by means of loans: (1) the commercial banks, (2) the *financieras,* and (3) the savings banks. These will be discussed in this and the two following sections. For present purposes, the other types of banks can be omitted from this discussion.

The commercial banks of Mexico are directed by law toward the money market rather than the capital market. As in the United States, liquidity is emphasized in the laws relating to banks that receive demand deposits. Thus they are not allowed to make loans of more than one-year maturity, except under special circumstances defined in the banking code. Short-term lending is considered the main field of the commercial bank.

Notwithstanding this general orientation a commercial bank in Mexico is permitted to make investments in stocks, mortgages, and bonds, provided that the aggregate of such investments does not amount to more than 20 per cent, roughly, of its demand and time liabilities. This general rule for investments is restricted by a number of specific provisions in the banking code, which need not concern us here. The point to be stressed is that the commercial banks, the most important sector of the private banking structure of Mexico, are empowered to make substantial investments in both private and government securities.

In practice, however, the commercial banks have not shown much interest in investments, either in government securities or in private issues. It is true that their investment portfolios have tended to rise in relation to the maximum amount allowed by law, but they have been slow in approaching this figure. The maximum, which we have just defined roughly as 20 per cent of demand and time liabilities, is known as the *pasivo exigible.* In December, 1941, combined investments of commercial banks amounted to only 6 per cent of their aggregate pasivo exigible. The ratio rose thereafter, but as late as October, 1946, it was not much in excess of 10 per cent. Toward the end of 1946, therefore, commercial bank investments were approximately one-half of the amount allowed by the banking code. In the spring of 1948, sudden and unexplained additions to holdings of private bond issues[10] caused a sharp increase in the ratio, and by October it stood

---

[10] Apparently the commercial banks bought bonds from the Bank of Mexico, since there was a parallel decline in the central bank's holdings of the same kind of securities. The explana-

at 16 per cent. Although this figure approaches the maximum, it is significant that it was not until 1948 that such levels were attained.

It is important to look more closely at that portion of commercial bank investments represented by holdings of public securities, that is, bond issues of the federal, state, and local governments. In December, 1941, such holdings amounted to a negligible 0.2 per cent of commercial bank assets. They increased thereafter, reaching 4 per cent late in 1946, but they remained at approximately that level during 1947 and 1948. If we broaden the category of public securities to include certificates of participation issued by Nacional Financiera, the percentage figure is raised, but not substantially. By this definition of public securities, such holdings made up 5 to 6 per cent of total commercial bank assets during 1947 and 1948.

Even the maximum figure of 6 per cent represents but a minor allocation of banking resources. The banks, moreover, have not bought government bonds with enthusiasm. They have been, and they still are, reluctant to buy government bonds, a statement which applies equally to all banks in Mexico, not just to the commercial banks. Not even a ruling of the Minister of Finance in January, 1946, allowing banks to hold 10 per cent of their reserves in the form of government bonds had much result. Holdings increased for a few months but later fell to their previous levels.

The reluctance of commercial banks to invest in government bonds is explained principally by the opportunities presented to use funds in more profitable ways. Short-term commercial loans have made very good returns for Mexican banks. The demand for this type of loan expanded greatly during the war years because of the possibilities of making lucrative operations in commodities. Withholding of commodity stocks has been an all too common feature of Mexican economic experience since 1940. (Boosts in the price level have in no small measure been caused by speculative transactions.) These transactions, in turn, have been encouraged and promoted by commercial bank credit.

During the war period, in spite of the necessary increase in public expenditures and of the opportunity for development in some branches of industry, the commercial banks lent themselves chiefly to the manifold speculations which the war situation made possible.[11]

This criticism of the wartime role of Mexico's commercial banks has been stated time and again in the official publication of Nacional Financiera, and has been echoed in many quarters. Eduardo Villaseñor, head of the Bank of Mexico during the war period, is another authority who

tion for the sudden change may be a revision in the method of computing reserves, which allowed bonds to figure more prominently than before.

[11] *El Mercado de Valores,* August 19, 1946, p. 3.

often criticized the banks for making loans promoting speculation.[12] There is not the slightest doubt that a substantial fraction of bank loans has been directed to speculative ends. Preoccupied with making such profitable loans, as well as with handling ordinary loans of a commercial nature, Mexico's banks have had little enthusiasm for investing in government bonds or even private securities.

However, it must be admitted that the negative attitude of the banks toward government bonds rests upon other foundations also. The reasons given above would not explain, for example, why Mexican bankers go so far as to advise their clients not to buy government bonds.[13] Typically their attitude is not passive but actively hostile where government bonds are concerned. The explanation for this behavior is found in their deep-seated antipathy to the social program of the Mexican Revolution. For about twenty-five years the bankers have been uneasy about the increased political strength of labor, about the agrarian program, and about nationalization measures such as those in the petroleum and railroad industries. These are only principal reasons; apparently the bankers of Mexico have found many other grounds for being nervous about the government.

Whether the reasons are good or bad is beside the point here. The fact is that as a group the bankers of Mexico fundamentally distrust the Mexican government. They are reluctant even to help finance any specific program of which they may happen to approve, such as road construction, because indirectly this would help the government to finance other operations which they would not like.

Bankers in Mexico are fond of stressing a technical argument against purchasing government bonds, namely, that they lack liquidity. This, of course, is true. The argument, however, is essentially a circular one, for if the banks of Mexico would become substantial purchasers of government bonds, they themselves would make the bonds liquid. This is the main step needed to create a market for Mexican government bonds. It is highly unlikely that the public at large will buy many government bonds unless the banks first take up the practice. The public, however, can be expected to follow the example of the banks, thus extending the market further and adding to liquidity. The banks must move first.

The preceding discussion has revolved about the attitude of the commercial banks toward the purchase of government bonds. The same attitude prevails among all other types of banks in Mexico. Thus, in October,

---

[12] See, for example, his address at the 1945 bankers' convention, in *El Economista*, no. 145 (May–June, 1945), pp. 27–33; also, a press interview reported in the Mexico City newspaper *El Universal*, August 5, 1946.

[13] Víctor L. Urquidi, "Tres lustros de experiencia monetaria en México: algunas enseñanzas," *Memoria del Segundo Congreso Mexicano de Cienoias Sociales,* vol. 2, p. 477.

1946, the total amount of federal, state, and local bond issues held by all banks represented 3.7 per cent of their aggregate assets, or slightly less than the corresponding percentage for the commercial banks alone.

The commercial banks in Mexico have been more responsive to the needs of industry in lending than in investment. But this does not mean that they have provided good credit accommodation for industry. The small concern, in particular, has fared badly. All the banks have unquestionably discriminated against the small industrial firm. Only a handful of the larger and older manufacturing firms have had easy access to bank credit. They figure among the preferred clients of the banks. By tradition, banks in Mexico concentrate their loans on a restricted number of favored customers. To explain this, we need only recall what was said earlier in connection with the business community which stands in opposition to the New Group influence.[14]

Before the outbreak of the Mexican Revolution the banks lent chiefly to the hacendados, or owners of large estates. Even their methods and techniques of credit extension were elaborated in connection with such loans. The only other important demand for credit came from the large merchandising firms in the cities; these were also regarded as preferred credit risks.

Under the social program of the Revolution many of the great estates have been liquidated. Those that still exist are in jeopardy of liquidation under the agrarian laws. They scarcely form good security for bank loans. The hacendado, therefore, has completely dropped out of the credit picture.

The place of the hacendado has come to be occupied, over the last twenty-five years, by the large industrial concern. Such firms, along with the great commercial establishments, are now the prized banking clients. They are found mainly in Mexico's older manufacturing industries, such as textiles, beer, tobacco, flour milling, paper, cement, soap, and sugar refining. The older manufacturing firms make up one side of a triangle that lies at the heart of the business community in Mexico. The other two sides are formed by the leading banks and the large merchandising concerns. To some extent there are interlocking directorates between the banks and their favored industrial clients, and perhaps also with the commercial firms. But even without such formal ties they enjoy good working relations. Credit is no problem for these industrial companies.

On the other hand, the newer manufacturing firms, and especially the small establishments, do not have ready access to bank credit. Except for the government, they are at the foot of the banker's priority list. This was established quite clearly during the time of stringent loan ceilings, from May, 1944, to January, 1947.

---

[14] See chapter ii.

During this period the commercial banks had to restrict lending because they were close to the limit. Tightening of credit was felt most severely by the small industrialists; this statement cannot be supported by statistical evidence, but informed persons in Mexico do not question it. In November, 1946, the Cámara Nacional de la Industria de Transformación, the spokesman for small industry, conducted a vigorous publicity campaign against the banks for discrimination in rationing credit. This campaign may have had something to do with the decision of the Minister of Finance to lift the credit ceiling about six weeks later. How much this action has benefited the small industrialist, however, is questionable; the complaints about discrimination continue,[15] and they will doubtless be heard for some time to come.

Because of the difficulty of borrowing from the banks, many small industrialists in Mexico borrow from moneylenders or even from the large commercial firms. The latter, as we have seen, are able to borrow freely from the banks and it has long been their custom to do a lending business on the side. Most of their clients are small merchants, but in recent years the small manufacturer has appeared among such borrowers. These transactions, of course, amount to indirect borrowing from the banks. But the cost is higher than it would be if the borrowing were direct, since the middleman collects his charge. The actual interest rates paid by many small manufacturers, therefore, are substantially above the rates prevailing at the banks.

When the borrower turns to a moneylender, his interest charges mount by leaps and bounds. In the last few years moneylenders are reported to have charged as much as 5 per cent a month for loans comparable to those on which the commercial banks collect 1 per cent.

Even when a small manufacturer is able to borrow directly from a bank he finds it difficult to get a loan for an intermediate or long term. Mostly the banks insist on short-term loans running for ninety days or less. This is true even when the borrower wants to add to fixed investment by purchasing machinery or equipment. He must attempt to finance a capital expenditure by means of a short loan. Thus he tries to get the loan renewed several times until he can liquidate it in the course of operations, as if it were an intermediate-term loan.

This system has obvious disadvantages from the borrower's standpoint. He has no assurance that the loan will be renewed on maturity. The bank may discontinue the lending series without warning. This indeed has happened often to small producers in Mexico. Their principal recourse then is to borrow from moneylenders, at the terrifically high interest rates we

[15] *Tiempo,* February 21, 1947, p. 37.

have referred to. The refusal of a bank to renew a loan has often meant the beginning of the end for the small firm. It can hardly be doubted that banks have been willing beneficiaries of this process of attrition in small business in Mexico.

FINANCIERAS

Among the private institutions designed to finance industry in Mexico, the financieras occupy first place. First authorized in 1932, they did not become important until a change in the banking laws in 1941 allowed them to extend their functions. Since then the financiera has been expected to perform the following main operations:

(1) To promote and organize all kinds of business enterprises, especially those engaged in industrial production; although there is nothing in the law compelling financieras to give preference to industrial rather than commercial firms, government authorities consider industry to be the main province of the financiera. In fact, the change in banking laws in 1941 was part of the government's industrialization program.
(2) To buy and hold shares of stock in firms that are legally unrelated to it; the financiera may hold the controlling interest in such firms.
(3) To float security issues for business concerns.
(4) To make intermediate and long-term loans, ranging from six months to thirty years; the law, however, allows the financiera to grant loans of less than six-month maturity under special circumstances.

At the end of 1940 there were only six financieras in Mexico. The law of 1941 stimulated the formation of new ones, and thirty-seven were in operation at the end of 1941. Rapid expansion followed, and by the end of 1946 more than 100 of these organizations were functioning. About two-thirds of them were located in Mexico City. The period of rapid growth ended in 1946; only a few new ones were set up in 1947 and 1948.

The growth in total assets of financieras has been even more striking than the increase in numbers. From approximately 180 million pesos in December, 1941, their aggregate assets rose to over 840 million in October, 1946, an increase of about 370 per cent. Subsequently, in spite of the fact that few new financieras were established, total assets continued to rise steadily. In October, 1948, they amounted to 1,133 million pesos.

Most of the financieras are not independent institutions but are subsidiaries of the larger commercial banks. Some of the leading banks have three or four separate financiera affiliates. In such cases the financieras are apt to be specialized along regional or functional lines.

From the above list of functions it will be seen that the financiera in Mexico is the counterpart of the investment bank in the United States. The resemblance, however, is greater in theory than in practice. The two operate in different ways. Like the investment bank, the financiera is intended to be the agency whereby the securities of an industrial or commercial firm can be issued and distributed among the investing public. Actually the financieras have shown little interest in developing this kind of business. So far as they take stock and bond issues, they tend to hold them rather than to resell them. Then they issue their own bonds (called general bonds) with such securities as part of the collateral.

Through the financiera, therefore, the ultimate investor makes an indirect investment in industry. Instead of buying the security of an industrial company he buys a bond which is a direct liability of the financiera itself. Presumably he has more confidence in this bond than in any of the securities back of it, and funds not otherwise available to industry are attracted in this way. On the other hand, this practice fails to educate Mexican investors to buy industrial securities themselves. Moreover, it enables the financiera to recruit funds that can be used for lending rather than for further investment.

The second important way in which the financiera differs from the typical American investment bank is that the financiera is a lending institution. Its loans are supposed to provide circulating capital for industry. For this reason the Mexican banking code fixes six months as the minimum maturity for a financiera loan. Most commercial bank lending is for shorter periods. The six-month maturity is intended to be the dividing line between financiera and commercial bank loans. But the six-month minimum for the financiera loan is not a hard and fast line. Shorter maturities are allowed in so-called special cases. Through this loophole the financieras have been able to get into the commercial banking field, as will be pointed out below.

When a financiera grants a loan the documents created can be used as collateral for its general bonds, just as it uses its investment portfolio. This privilege is limited by complex provisions in the banking code, but the limitations are not very restrictive.

Furthermore, since 1945 the financieras have enjoyed rediscounting privileges at Nacional Financiera. The rules and limits of such rediscounting operations have not been made clear to the public, but it is obvious that this policy has extended the lending power of the financieras. So far as Nacional Financiera is willing and able to rediscount paper which they hold, the financieras can make corresponding amounts of new loans.

Table 7 brings out the expansion in financiera investment and lending operations since 1940, and also shows the shift in relative importance of the two classes of operations. (See p. 230.)

A glance at table 7 shows immediately that lending has been more important than investment to the financieras. Moreover, although the investment-loan ratio has been somewhat erratic, there has been a tendency for loans to gain in relation to investments. This trend became clearly defined after 1944. In 1943 and 1944, investments amounted to a little more than one-half of loans. By the end of 1945 the ratio of investments to loans had fallen to 45 per cent, but it was during 1946 that the greatest drop occurred. In December, 1946, investments were less than one-third of loans, and they continued in approximately the same position during 1947 and 1948.

TABLE 7

FINANCIERAS: INVESTMENTS AND LOANS, 1940–1948
(thousands of pesos)

Year (Dec.)	Investments in securities	Loans	Ratio of investments to loans (per cent)
1940.............	14,657	37,714	38.9
1941.............	39,676	63,772	62.2
1942.............	32,929	87,751	37.5
1943.............	71,281	139,603	51.1
1944.............	106,261	201,173	52.8
1945.............	128,176	286,870	44.7
1946.............	138,256	437,387	31.6
1947.............	161,292	554,508	29.1
1948 (Oct.)......	179,773	587,674	30.6

Sources: Data for 1940–1945 are taken from *Seis años de actividad nacional*, p. 339. Figures for 1946–1948 were compiled from data in the *Boletín Estadístico* of the Comisión Nacional Bancaria.

To some extent the drop in the investment-loan ratio during 1946 was caused by a shift in lending from the commercial banks to their financiera affiliates. The financieras were not subject to the loan ceilings that applied to the commercial banks, so they were free to act when their parent institutions were unable to make new loans. Such loans violated the spirit if not the letter of the law under which the financieras operate. They were short-term, commercial loans. While this kind of lending was especially noteworthy in 1946, the financieras all along have shown a preference for the short-term loan. In lending, says Nacional Financiera, "the financieras have followed the typically commercial orientation of the deposit banks."[18]

The loan figures in table 7, therefore, give an exaggerated picture of the amount of credit supplied to industry by the financieras. The extent to which they put funds into other operations cannot be estimated quantitatively, but in 1946 it must have been a substantial sum.

[18] *El Mercado de Valores*, February 3, 1947, p. 3. We also have it on the authority of Nacional Financiera that financiera loans "have not always been used for productive purposes." This doubtless means that financiera credit went into commodity speculation.

The principal means by which the financieras recruit funds is the general bond, mentioned above.[17] The typical financiera operates with a small capital investment. The right to issue general bonds backed by its investment- and loan-assets is what makes it possible for the financiera to renew its lending capacity. Since 1941, when the financieras were first authorized to put out general bonds, the volume of such securities has expanded continuously. In seven years the total issues outstanding rose from about one million pesos to more than 300 million.

GENERAL BONDS OUTSTANDING
(thousands of pesos)

Year (Dec.)	Amount
1941	1,190
1942	22,232
1943	76,201
1944	116,143
1945	181,092
1946	241,101
1947	323,281
1948 (Oct.)	314,290

Source: Compiled from data in the Comisión Nacional Bancaria, *Boletín Estadístico.*

For the first few years after the financieras started to issue general bonds, investors were very cool toward them. Consequently, in October, 1942, the Bank of Mexico announced that it would absorb such bonds in "convenient amounts." The central bank was probably the largest buyer of the earliest issues. Directly, or indirectly through Nacional Financiera, the Bank of Mexico continued to be a large buyer.[18] From figures released by the Bank of Mexico in 1948,[19] it can be estimated that this institution held approximately one-third of the general bonds outstanding at the end of 1945, one-half at the end of 1946, and two-thirds at the end of 1947.

Nacional Financiera also appears among the buyers of financiera general bonds. Its holdings have fluctuated considerably from month to month, but generally they have been a small fraction of the total, usually around 1 or 2 per cent.

The Mexican banking system, outside of the central bank, did not absorb very many general bonds until 1948. From data published by the National Banking Commission it is possible to make close estimates of

---

[17] They also issue "commercial bonds," but the amount outstanding is small.

[18] *Seis años de actividad nacional,* p. 337.

[19] Banco de México, *Vigésimasexta asamblea general ordinaria de accionistas* (Mexico, 1948), table 27.

the total amount held by all private credit institutions—commercial banks, savings banks, trust companies, and the like. The following tabulation shows the trend in the ratio of these holdings to bonds outstanding:

Date	Per cent	Date	Per cent
December 1942	24	December 1946	9
December 1943	29	December 1947	8
December 1944	11	October 1948	61
December 1945	7		

The relative position of the private banks as buyers of general bonds showed a decided downward trend from 1942 to 1948. From about one-fourth of the total in the first years, their holdings fell to less than 10 per cent. A sharp change occurred, however, in March of 1948, when their holdings increased from about 25 million pesos to more than 100 million. By October, 1948, they held about 60 per cent of the total amount outstanding.

Among the institutional investors, the insurance companies have also become prominent buyers of financiera bonds. No figures, however, are available on insurance company holdings.[20] When published, these data should show an interesting trend.

With respect to individual investors, no precise data on general bond purchases can be found. It is well known, however, that such purchases have been very small. Thus far the general bond has been no more attractive than other securities to individual investors. Early in 1946, in an attempt to create a public market for general bonds the Mexican government gave them tax-free privileges. This step shows how anxiously the government was trying to get the public to invest in industry, even indirectly, but the effort did not bear fruit. The general bond was still not in favor with the investing public.[21]

The rate of absorption of general bonds has not kept pace with the rate at which the financieras want to launch new issues. This is the reason why Nacional Financiera decided in 1945 to rediscount for the financieras. According to the annual report of Nacional Financiera, this step was taken so that the financieras could mobilize their resources for industrial expansion, "since the weakness of the security market prevented them from selling their issues of general bonds in amounts corresponding to the applications for industrial credit."[22]

[20] Direct purchases of industrial securities by insurance companies have probably also been on the increase. Again, no figures can be obtained.

[21] "In spite of the fact that this measure [tax-exemption] meant an increase in net yield, and that the conditions of the market brought about a rise in the rate of interest, the purchase of general bonds did not increase appreciably." Nacional Financiera, *Décimatercera asamblea general ordinaria de accionistas*, pp. 23–24.

[22] Nacional Financiera, *Duodécima asamblea general ordinaria de accionistas*, p. 54.

In the field of industrial promotion the financieras have contributed very little to Mexican economic development. When the financieras were given extended powers in 1941 it was anticipated that they would take the initiative in determining which industries were most likely to succeed in Mexico, and also in getting business men and technicians interested in setting up plants in such industries. This would have been an active role in promoting industry.

But even a more passive attitude should call forth greater technical services in promotion than the financieras usually supply. Thus they rarely make the basic investigations needed to appraise the chances of success for an industrial firm, such as market surveys or careful cost estimates.[23] It is a fair assumption that if the financieras had been less concerned with doing a commercial loan business and more with investment, they would also have shown more interest in the promotional functions they are supposed to perform.

SAVING BANKS

In many countries savings banks have been important suppliers of investment funds for industry. Savings which they gather from the public are invested in industrial securities. In Mexico, however, the savings banks have performed this function only to a limited extent.

Savings banking in Mexico is a very recent development. The effective beginnings did not occur until around 1930, and rate of growth was not important until 1936. Expansion was especially striking during the war years. In October, 1942, for example, the total assets of savings banks amounted to 63 million pesos. In the following year they almost doubled. By October, 1946, they reached 286 million, and two years later, in October, 1948, they amounted to 408 million.

For the most part savings banks in Mexico are not independent institutions but are rather savings departments of commercial banks. In this respect their development has been parallel to that of savings banks in the United States. In respect to operations, however, the savings bank in Mexico has shown a very different line of development. Unlike its American counterpart, it has been principally a lending rather than an investing institution, and moreover, it has done short-term rather than long-term lending.

These points can be illustrated by statistics available for savings bank operations in 1946. In October, their investments in securities totaled about 64 million pesos.[24] At the same time, their loans stood at 96 million. Investments, therefore, amounted only to about two-thirds of loans.

[23] *El Mercado de Valores,* February 3, 1947, p. 3.
[24] Calculated from figures in Comisión Nacional Bancaria, *Boletín Estadístico,* September–October, 1946, p. 12.

How much of the 64 million pesos in investments represented direct investment in industry cannot be determined precisely from the published statistics. The holdings of government bonds included in this total amounted to only 18 million pesos. Most of the balance consisted of securities issued by private companies, but of banks and other financial organizations rather than of industrial concerns.[25] Some of this investment may have gone indirectly into industrial development. The lack of direct investments, however, shows coolness toward industry.

Lending, as we have seen, is much more important than investing to the savings banks. It might be thought that they have provided intermediate and long-term credit to industrial firms, assisting industry in this way rather than by the purchase of securities. However, if we appeal to an analysis made by Nacional Financiera, we find that this has not been the case.[26]

Of the total amount of loans outstanding in June, 1946, about 98 per cent consisted of loans with less than a one-year maturity. Furthermore, three-fifths of the loans in this large group had a maturity of six months or less. These were typical commercial loans. It is no wonder, therefore, that Nacional Financiera has referred to the savings banks of Mexico as "an additional sector of commercial banking."[27]

Since the Mexican banking code allows the savings banks to exercise complete discretion as between short- and long-term lending, the banks have elected the former because the returns are greater. Consequently, they have not directed domestic savings into industry, as savings banks in other countries have done.

"NATIONAL" BANKS

NACIONAL FINANCIERA

Nacional Financiera, the most important institution directly concerned with supplying investment funds for industry, is one of the ten "national banks" of Mexico. All the national banks are owned principally by the Mexican government. Included among them is the central bank (the Bank of Mexico), with a broad range of functions to perform. The others were organized for special purposes, such as providing agricultural credit, financing state and local public works, financing certain kinds of exports and imports, etc.[28]

---

[25] *El Mercado de Valores,* October 14, 1946, p. 3.
[26] *Ibid.,* p. 3.
[27] *Ibid.,* September 23, 1946, p. 3.
[28] Here is a complete list of national banks:
Banco de México
Banco Nacional de Comercio Exterior
Banco Nacional de Crédito Ejidal
Banco Nacional de Crédito Agrícola

The degree of government ownership in these national institutions is a varying one. The government has owned 51 per cent of the subscribed stock of Nacional Financiera. Nominally Nacional Financiera is an independent institution making its own decisions. For all practical purposes, however, it is an arm of the Mexican government. It is an official investment bank.

Since the time it was founded in 1934 Nacional Financiera has undergone a number of changes. Originally its main purpose was to create an internal market for public bonds, thus assisting the government to finance its public works and social programs. From its early days, too, Nacional Financiera attempted to build up a security market for the stocks and bonds of private companies, with a view toward encouraging investment in business enterprises. But until 1941 all operations in the private sector were subordinated to the principal task of stimulating investment in federal, state, and local bonds.

In 1941, after the Avila Camacho administration had decided to make industrialization the cornerstone of its economic policy, Nacional Financiera was reorganized so as to be principally an investment bank. Operations in public securities were to be continued, but promoting industrial developments was to be its chief concern. Thus Nacional Financiera was authorized to initiate enterprises that were not attractive to private initiative because of the large amount of investment required and the slowness with which returns were expected. In other cases, where private investors had already taken the initiative in setting up industries, Nacional Financiera was enjoined to give them financial assistance. Efforts to create an efficient stock exchange were to be redoubled.

As a further means of stimulating industry the new organic law of Nacional Financiera (1941) allows it to make secured loans to the financieras. This makes Nacional Financiera a central bank in the investment banking field.

To carry out these various functions Nacional Financiera has had available, first of all, its own paid-in capital. When President Miguel Alemán took office at the end of 1946, he announced that the capitalization of Nacional Financiera would be increased, in order to expand its functions in promoting Mexico's economic development by industrialization and other means. At that time the authorized capital of Nacional Financiera was 20

Banco Nacional de Fomento Cooperativo
Banco Nacional Hipotecario Urbano y de Obras Públicas
Banco del Pequeño Comercio del Distrito Federal
Nacional Financiera
Financiera Rural
Banco Nacional del Ejército y de la Armada
Only two of these banks, Nacional Financiera and the Bank of Mexico are important in the field of industrial financing. The others, therefore, may be neglected in this study.

million pesos, out of which about 12 million pesos had been subscribed and paid in. One year later the authorized capital was raised to 100 million pesos.[29]

The law making this change provides that the Mexican government may issue 75 million pesos in "industrial promotion" bonds in order to raise the funds for increasing its subscription to Nacional Financiera stock. This figure is suggestive, since it represents 75 per cent of the capital. Only 25 per cent need be obtained from private sources. Apparently, in government circles it was considered doubtful that as much as 49 per cent of the stock in Nacional Financiera would be taken by private financial interest.

In addition to its capital, Nacional Financiera has obtained funds by selling its own bonds. Altogether, about 45 million pesos in bonds have been disposed of. Had Nacional Financiera been restricted to its capital and bond issues, however, the scope of its operations would have been much more limited than it actually has been.

By far the principal source of funds for Nacional Financiera has been the sale of certificates of participation (*certificados de participación*). These bear a superficial resemblance to some of the certificates issued by investment trusts in the United States, but they are really not the same thing. Each issue of certificates is backed by designated securities in the portfolio of Nacional Financiera, and those holding the certificates become co-owners of the securities. However, the certificates bear fixed rates of interest. The return which the holder gets, therefore, does not depend upon the earnings of the securities in which he has made an indirect investment. If these earnings fall below the amount need to pay the stated rate on the certificate, Nacional Financiera is obligated to use other resources to make up the difference.[30] Of course, the opposite case is also a possibility, that is, that a certificate holder would get less than the returns on the collateral. But the point that needs to be stressed is that the investor takes no risk on the earnings of the securities themselves. He owns what is tantamount to a bond.

The investor's risk is further reduced by Nacional Financiera's pledge to repurchase its certificates at par. In this respect, too, the certificates of Nacional Financiera differ from those of the American investment trust. Only the holder who buys above par can lose on the value of his certificate, and then his loss is limited. This guarantee to repurchase shows how far Nacional Financiera has gone in order to tempt the coy Mexican investor to put funds into certificates. Moreover, although Nacional Financiera requires a certain amount of notice before cashing a certificate, the period is so short that the holder has virtually a demand right.

---

[29] The text of the law, enacted December 30, 1947, is given in *El Mercado de Valores,* January 5, 1948.
[30] *El Mercado de Valores,* October 14, 1946, p. 8.

The repurchase feature has been criticized in Mexico on various grounds, and Nacional Financiera has undertaken to defend it with arguments which do not seem clear-cut or relevant.[31] The details of this controversy are not pertinent here. However, one significant point that has emerged in this discussion is the statement that if large numbers of holders demanded cash for certificates at one and the same time Nacional Financiera would have access to central bank financing in order to meet the situation.[32] Just how far the Bank of Mexico would go has not been made clear. It may be taken for granted, however, that the bank stands ready to lend Nacional Financiera as much as it needs to maintain the value of its certificates.

Between January 1, 1941, when the first issue was made, and December 31, 1948, Nacional Financiera issued seventeen series of certificates of participation. The aggregate value of these issues was 346 million pesos. Most of the certificates (305 million pesos) were still outstanding at the end of 1948. Thus far 1943 has been the year of peak activity. Six new issues were launched in that year, with an aggregate value of 105 million pesos.

In general there has been a tendency to lengthen the life of the issues. Several of those put out since the latter part of 1943 do not have definite maturity dates. Also, as investors have become familiar with the certificates, Nacional Financiera has been able to float them at somewhat lower rates of interest. This tendency can be illustrated by comparing three ten-year issues:

Date of issue	Annual rate of interest
January 1, 1941	7.2 per cent
February 25, 1944	6.5 per cent
March 22, 1946	6.0 per cent

The first issues were backed almost entirely by government bonds. Thus the annual report of Nacional Financiera for 1943 showed that public securities, principally those of the federal government, comprised 85 per cent of the collateral.[33] There has been a tendency, however, for Nacional Financiera to use a larger percentage of private securities as backing for its issues. One series issued in 1945, for example, was backed entirely by bonds and preferred stock of industrial companies. No figures have been published recently on the collateral as a whole, but informed persons in Mexican financial circles estimate that private securities now account for about one-half of the total. If Nacional Financiera expands its industrial financing operations, as is expected, nongovernment securities will gain further importance.

[31] A good illustration is found in Nacional Financiera, *Duodécima asamblea general ordinaria de accionistas,* pp. 22–23.

[32] *Ibid.,* p. 23.

[33] *Décima asamblea general de accionistas* (Mexico, 1944), p. 21.

It is probable that most of the certificates have been bought by banks, insurance companies, and large commercial firms. This cannot be confirmed statistically, but it is a valid inference to draw from the pointed way in which Nacional Financiera reported that 70 per cent of one of the 1946 issues had been taken by small investors. Strong emphasis on this fact, and lack of similar comment about other issues, suggest that this was a unique experience.[34]

That the certificate of participation has established itself in Mexican investing circles is shown by the speed with which the issue just referred to was snapped up. Certificates aggregating 10 million pesos were oversubscribed in two days. Because of this enthusiastic reception Nacional Financiera put out another issue (8 million pesos) immediately.[35]

It is not difficult to see why the certificates have been bought eagerly. Because of the repurchase clause and the guaranteed rate of return, the investor runs little risk. He knows, too, that the Bank of Mexico stands behind Nacional Financiera. The central bank would hardly fail to support Nacional Financiera to the degree needed to maintain solvency, in view of the government's anxiety to use Nacional Financiera as a prop to the market for both public and private securities.

The 1945 report of Nacional Financiera contains an illuminating paragraph on the certificates of participation,[36] stating that they were adopted as a temporary expedient at a time when few other means were available to finance new lines of development. Significantly, the report goes on to say that the existing certificates are a costly financial device, and that "as soon as postwar conditions permit progress in organizing and strengthening the capital market, it will be possible to modify the certificates and to convert them into true 'investment trust' instruments."

This last comment implies three changes in the certificate: (1) abandoning the fixed rate of interest; (2) abandoning the repurchase provision; (3) using few or no government securities as backing. The investor would then take a much greater risk than he does at present and he would invest more directly in industry. Investment in business firms would be differ-

---

[34] *El Mercado de Valores,* March 18, 1946, p. 1. A calculation made from data published by the National Banking Commission shows that banks and other financial institutions held about 25% of the certificates outstanding in July, 1946. In the official volume dealing with the achievements of the Avila Camacho administration (*Seis años de actividad nacional,* p. 334), there is a statement that "more than 90 per cent (of the certificates) have been placed with the public." This statement, written in July, 1946, was commonly interpreted in Mexico to mean that 90 per cent of the certificates were held by noninstitutional investors. This was a false interpretation. The statement simply meant that over 90 per cent of the certificates authorized had been sold and that less than 10 per cent were in the hands of Nacional Financiera itself.

[35] This series, however, was taken entirely by the Social Security Institute. Mexico's social security system dates only from 1943. As the reserves increase, the Social Security Institute will become an increasingly important factor in investing savings of the public.

[36] *Duodécima asamblea general ordinaria de accionistas,* pp. 24–25.

entiated from investment in government securities. These developments would certainly help to create in Mexico a more wholesome investing psychology than that which prevails.

Nacional Financiera is supporting industrial development in Mexico in two principal ways: (1) by purchasing stocks and bonds of industrial companies; (2) by making loans to industry.

According to the most recent statement available, on December 31, 1947, Nacional Financiera held about 84 million pesos worth of bonds and 107 million pesos worth of stock in industrial concerns, making an aggregate investment of 191 million pesos. These figures are for a given date. However, they must also come close to showing the cumulative amounts of securities purchased, because Nacional Financiera has not, as a general rule, resold its industrial holdings.

A review of the list of industrial securities held by Nacional Financiera at the end of 1947[37] shows that the organization has invested in practically all the larger enterprises established in Mexico in recent years. It owned, for example, about 60 million pesos in stocks and bonds in Altos Hornos de México, the new steel mill at Monclova. In Industria Eléctrica, the new concern for manufacturing electrical apparatus, Nacional Financiera held stock amounting to almost 3 million pesos.[38] In the Atenquique project (paper, chemicals, etc.), Nacional Financiera had an investment of more than 15 million pesos, two-thirds of which was represented by holdings of stock. The two new related projects in the rayon industry, Celanese Mexicana and Viscosa Mexicana, were beneficiaries of Nacional Financiera investment to the extent of 2.7 million pesos and 3.7 million pesos, respectively.

Among the other new firms in which Nacional Financiera had an investment of one million pesos or more at the end of 1947 were the following: Sosa Texcoco and Cia. Química Mexicana in the chemical industry, Cia. Mexicana de Tubos in the manufacture of iron products, Cobre de México in the manufacture of electrolytic copper, and Cia. Vidriera Guadalajara in the making of glass products.

The investment record of Nacional Financiera shows special interest in underwriting expansion in the sugar and cement industries. At the end of 1947 it had 19 million pesos invested in the sugar industry, and about 10 million in cement production. In each of these industries, the Nacional Financiera investment was represented by the stocks and bonds of several concerns.

---

[37] *Décimacuarta asamblea general ordinaria de accionistas* (Mexico, 1948), appendix, table 2.
[38] At the end of the preceding year, Nacional Financiera also held 21 million pesos of Industria Eléctrica bonds.

In one firm, Guanos y Fertilizantes de México, Nacional Financiera was virtually the only stockholder at the end of 1947. This corporation was the child of Nacional Financiera, organized in 1943 at the request of the Mexican government to meet a critical need for fertilizers. In time, some of the 10 million pesos which Nacional Financiera has tied up in this firm will be released, for the government has agreed to assume a part of the financial burden. Fifty-one per cent of all the shares in Guanos y Fertilizantes are ultimately to be purchased by the government.

An analysis of the security issues of twenty-five principal firms (almost all industrial concerns) in which National Financiera had invested capital by December 31, 1947, showed that Nacional Financiera held 72 per cent of their combined bond issues and 36 per cent of their combined capital stock.[39]

It is clear that the purchase of securities by Nacional Financiera has been a factor of the utmost importance in long-term investment in Mexico since 1941. Given the prevailing investment habits of Mexico, it is certain that much of the industrial financing of the period would not have been accomplished without the government's investment bank intervening.

The second means by which Nacional Financiera finances industry is lending. Such loans are intended mainly to provide circulating capital and to finance machinery and equipment purchases. They vary considerably in respect to security offered by the borrower as well as in maturity. As nearly as can be determined, they are similar in nature to the loans which private banks are authorized to make, but which the private banks have been reluctant to extend to industrial concerns other than their favored clients. Indeed, this reluctance explains why Nacional Financiera has been doing such an active lending business.

The following tabulation shows the growth in National Financiera loans in the period 1940–1947:[40]

Year	Loans (milions of pesos)	Year	Loans (millions of pesos)
1940	15	1944	184
1941	29	1945	394
1942	51	1946	·587
1943	53	1947	883

Most of Nacional Financiera's loans have been made to industrial enterprises, although sizable amounts are known to have been allocated to other purposes. In 1945, for example, a loan of about 73 million pesos was granted to the National Railways of Mexico. In the same year smaller loans were made to municipalities for public works. Electric power development has also benefited considerably from Nacional Financiera lending.

[39] *Décimacuarta asamblea general ordinaria de accionistas*, p. 50.
[40] *Ibid.*, p. 51.

The loans are made for short terms, as well as for intermediate and long periods. Indeed, granting short-term credit has been a dominant principle with Nacional Financiera, as with the private banks and financieras. This can be inferred from an analysis of the relation between the annual amounts repaid and the amounts lent. For each year of the period 1940–1946 the amount repaid is a high percentage of the amount lent. If this were true only for scattered years it would not be significant, but since it occurred year after year it establishes a dominant short-run quality in Nacional Financiera's loans.[41] For the years 1940–1946 repayments annually averaged over 80 per cent of new loans.

BANK OF MEXICO

Although Nacional Financiera has been the most active agent in industrial financing in Mexico, the backbone of the whole structure is the Bank of Mexico. This has been true in private as well as in public finance. Once the government decided to push industrialization rapidly and to make industry the keynote of Mexico's economic future—a decision which crystallized in 1941—the ample resources of the central bank were readily marshalled for this purpose.

The officials of the Bank of Mexico were not completely happy over this policy. Given its own head, the bank would have taken a more cautious and selective course. Because of the legal structure of the bank, however, the government through the Minister of Finance can determine central banking policies whenever it chooses to intervene. Fundamentally the policy of the Bank of Mexico is the policy of the Mexican government.

The central bank has been called upon to fill the gap caused by the failure of others to invest in industry. Thus we have the decision of the Bank of Mexico to buy financiera general bonds. "This measure," writes Eduardo Suárez, ex-Minister of Finance, "showed once again that the State cannot remain indifferent in the face of needs created by the growth of the country; these needs fully justified the step of providing banks with resources—even though this had to be done with central bank credit because of the lack of funds of other origin."[42]

In similar vein, the head of the Bank of Mexico, Eduardo Villaseñor, stated in 1944 that the policy of "supporting" the market for general bonds was destined to continue indefinitely and to adjust itself to the volume of credit required for industrial purposes.[43] Before he left his position, how-

[41] The average maturity, however, is still likely to be somewhat longer than that of the private bank loan. Loans for six months to one year, for example, are probably much more common for Nacional Financiera than for the private banks.

[42] *Seis años de actividad nacional*, p. 337.

[43] Eduardo Villaseñor, "Algunos aspectos de la economía de la postguerra en México," *Investigación Económica*, 1st quarter 1944, p. 18.

ever, Villaseñor had considerably less enthusiasm for the financieras. In a press interview in 1946 he complained that the financieras expected the Bank of Mexico to buy their general bonds on demand, and that they had made no attempt to create a market for such bonds among the investing public.[44]

Nacional Financiera would not be able to carry out a fraction of its operations if it were not for the actual, if tacit, support of the Bank of Mexico. This support has been decisive. Nacional Financiera's certificates command a market because of the repurchase feature. But Nacional Financiera can offer this feature only because the Bank of Mexico stands behind it, as has been admitted in one of the recent annual reports. The investor buys the certificate because he knows that the resources of the Bank of Mexico will be used to redeem it at par. From his standpoint, Nacional Financiera is practically a department of the Bank of Mexico.

In addition the Bank of Mexico has been an outright buyer of Nacional Financiera's certificates. Such holdings are now minor in amount because other buyers have come forward, but they must have been significant for the first issues. The central bank can also rediscount for Nacional Financiera. It was reported as late as 1947 that this privilege had not been used. This may still be true, but it must be recognized that the privilege itself has all along been a source of strength to Nacional Financiera.

The third principal method by which the Bank of Mexico has financed industrialization is the purchase of government bonds. It will be recalled that bonds have been issued for purposes intimately related to industrial development, such as improving transport conditions, raising agricultural productivity, and increasing the supply of electric power. Individual investors and banks have shied away from government bonds. By default the Bank of Mexico has become the principal holder.

Large purchases of government bonds by the Bank of Mexico date from the year 1941, when the Bank adopted a policy of dealing freely in such securities. Previously it bought them only in restricted amounts. The first operation under the new policy was conducted with federal highway bonds which were then selling at 70 in spite of their backing in gasoline-tax receipts. This quotation may be taken as a good measure of the failure of investors to take government bonds even when allowance is made for high average rates of return on other kinds of investments.

As new issues were put out after 1941, the Bank of Mexico's portfolio of public securities continued to expand. In 1944 it was reported that the bank had increased its holdings of federal bonds by 89.5 million pesos.[45] This

<hr />

[44] *El Universal*, August 5, 1946.
[45] Banco de México, *Vigésimatercera asamblea general ordinaria de accionistas* p. 36.

was one of the few figures released before 1948, when the Bank of Mexico finally published data on the assets it held in the form of government obligations. In spite of the lack of official figures, however, it was commonly understood in Mexico that the central bank was the principal holder of government bonds.[46]

The figures published by the Bank of Mexico in 1948, relating to its portfolio of government securities during the period 1944–1947,[47] do not clearly distinguish holdings of bonds. A distinction is made between holdings of short-term and long-term debt, but some of the bond issues may be classed as short-term rather than long-term debt. Indeed, a comparison of the Bank of Mexico figures with those published by the United Nations[48] suggests that this was the case in 1944 and 1945, at least. For December, 1944, the United Nations shows the total outstanding short-term debt (defined as debt maturing in less than two years) of the Mexican government as 70 million pesos. For the same date the Bank of Mexico reported that it held 274 million pesos of government short-term obligations. In the figures for December, 1945, a similar difference is found, whereby the Bank of Mexico showed that it held about 200 million pesos more of short-term obligations than the United Nations reported to be in existence (345 million as against 134 million). Obviously, two different concepts of short-term debt have been employed. One likely source of difference is that the Bank of Mexico included some bonds in the category of short-term debt, rather than long-term.

In 1947, however, the Bank of Mexico's figures for its holdings of short-term government securities showed a great drop. In September of that year, they amounted only to 21 million pesos. In the same month, the bank's holding of long-term government issues was reported as 660 million pesos. Because the former figure is so small, even if some bonds were included, they may be neglected, and the Bank of Mexico's holdings of government bonds in September, 1947, can be estimated at 660 million pesos. In his annual message to Congress in the same month, President Alemán placed the total of government securities outstanding at slightly more than one billion pesos. Roughly, therefore, the Bank of Mexico held two-thirds of all government bonds at that time. This is probably a representative figure for recent years.

The preceding discussion has brought out the three principal ways in which the Bank of Mexico has financed industrial development: (1) sup-

---

[46] See, for example, the paper by Raúl Ortiz Mena, "El mercado de valores en México," in *Memoria de la primera reunión de técnicos sobre problemas de banca central del continente americano*, p. 66.

[47] *Vigésimasexta asamblea general ordinaria de accionistas*, table 27.

[48] United Nations, Department of Economic Affairs, *Public Debt, 1914–1946* (Lake Success, 1948), pp. 95–97.

porting the private financieras, (2) supporting Nacional Financiera, (3) purchasing government bonds. In addition, the central bank has bought securities of industrial firms. Probably in most cases these have been acquired through an intermediary, such as one of the financieras, but they are outright investments of the Bank of Mexico. It is not possible to make even a rough estimate of the amount of such investments, for the published statements of the bank give no clues.

In stressing the role of the central bank in financing industrial development in Mexico, I do not intend to give the impression that I think this practice is to be condemned. If any impression is to be strengthened as a result of the above discussion it is that individual investors and banks have failed to provide funds for industrial development. The Bank of Mexico has filled their shoes. It must be recognized, however, that providing central bank credit for industrial development in Mexico in the period after 1941 had maximum inflationary effects in a situation that was already shot through with inflationary forces.

New investment during the war years was bound to have inflationary effects in Mexico, no matter who made the investment. But the net inflationary effect of a given amount of investment was less when made by a private bank or by an individual than when made by the Bank of Mexico. In the first case bank reserves would be decreased, thus reducing the lending power of the banking system. In the second case individual cash holdings or bank balances would be diminished. When the Bank of Mexico made the investment, however, no similar reductions occurred, so that full inflationary consequences were realized.

Actually, the Bank of Mexico's policy of buying financiera general bonds had dual inflationary effects because the financieras used the proceeds for commercial and speculative lending. Multiplication of intermediate commercial transactions and of commodity withholding operations contributed materially to rising prices. Central bank credit intended to stimulate industrial production and thereby to hold prices down was directed by the financieras to other ends, with the opposite effect on prices.

Bank of Mexico buying of government bonds also represented the most inflationary method of meeting public investment requirements. Here, again, it was the failure of the public and of the banks to absorb securities that caused the central bank to create large amounts of money for government financing.

THE MEXICAN GOVERNMENT

Direct investment in industry by the Mexican government has been small. In the field of investment its principal contributions to industrialization have been indirect. During the period 1941–1946 the government invested

2.1 billion pesos in road construction, railway building, electric power development, irrigation, harbor works, and in supplying credit to agricultural producers.[49] These items are classified by the government as "directly productive" investment. In addition, outlays for "indirectly productive" items—such as schools, hospitals, other public buildings, water supply, etc.—amounted to 400 million pesos, making a total federal investment of 2.5 billion. Petróleos Mexicanos, the government-owned oil company, is not included in the above totals because it operates as an individual enterprise.

In a few cases at least the Mexican government has bought securities in new industrial companies, with Nacional Financiera acting as its agent. The latest data available (1945) show that the government had one million pesos invested in preferred stock of the Cia. Industrial de Atenquique and 212,000 pesos in common stock of Industrial Urbana. Additional investments of a similar nature may have been made in 1946.

Finally, in 1945 the Mexican government, via Nacional Financiera, lent 15 million pesos to Celanese Mexicana, the new rayon company in which Celanese Corporation of America has an interest. The loan matures in five years, but it may be paid off in bonds of the corporation rather than in cash. Again, it is possible that analogous loans were made to other concerns after 1945.

RÉSUMÉ ON DOMESTIC INVESTMENT AND CREDIT

In the industrial advance of Mexico a serious problem has arisen through the failure of domestic savings to move into industrial investment. Apart from hoarding, individual savers have preferred to invest in urban real estate and construction, or in mortgages, rather than in industrial securities. Savings pooled by the banks have been directed toward industry in small amounts only, because the banks have been overwhelmingly preoccupied with short-term, commercial lending.

The financieras can by no means be called a wholesome development in the Mexican economy. When they were put on a new legal basis in 1941, financial authorities in the Mexican government had high hopes for what these organizations would accomplish in stimulating industrial development. It was thought that they would be a vital force in Mexico's industrialization. These hopes have not been realized. How disappointing the results have been can best be brought out by a bill of particulars itemized from our previous discussion of the financieras.

(1) The financieras have failed to initiate industrial undertakings. They have done very little promotional and organizational work.

(2) Lending has been a more important operation than investment.

(3) They have emphasized short-term rather than long-term lending.

---

[49] *Seis años de actividad nacional,* p. 367.

(4) Their loans have financed commercial, often speculative transactions, instead of supplying circulating capital to firms engaged in the production of goods.

(5) They have done very little to create a market for industrial securities among Mexican investors.

(6) They have diverted central bank credit, intended to stimulate production, into commercial lending.

Obviously, the laws relating to financieras need to be overhauled if the Mexican economy is to benefit from these institutions. As a matter of fact, the Mexican government can be criticized for not having acted already. Wartime conditions should have precipitated action on this question, not retarded it. The reluctance of the government to reform financiera behavior does not promise well for Mexico's economic future.

In making loans all banks in Mexico have discriminated against the small industrialist. He has thus been forced to borrow outside of the regular banking machinery, where much higher rates of interest are charged. When a bank does consent to lend to a small manufacturer it usually insists on a very short maturity for the loan. This is highly unsatisfactory when the purpose of borrowing is to purchase additional equipment.

So far, Nacional Financiera has also been of little help to the small manufacturer. Nacional Financiera has been chiefly occupied with financing the larger new industrial ventures, the type that the Mexican government has been especially anxious to encourage. Thus no one has attempted to meet the financial needs of small industry, although currently small industry as a rule is better adapted to the Mexican economic structure than big concerns.

Nacional Financiera has been the most important investment bank for Mexican industry. It has sizable investments in practically all the large industrial firms established since 1941. It has, moreover, taken an active part in initiating and organizing these firms. It has performed for the Mexican economy valuable functions which private financial institutions have been loathe to undertake.

However, there are a few significant items on the other side of the Nacional Financiera ledger. Like the private financieras, it has failed in the task of reëducating Mexican investors. Evidence for this is the very nature of the certificate of participation. Perhaps the certificates could not have been sold readily without the guarantees with which they have been endowed because more profitable ways of using funds were allowed to remain open during the war years. Responsibility for the latter rests with the Ministry of Finance rather than with Nacional Financiera. The important point, however, is that the certificate does not foster the habit of investing in industrial securities. On the contrary, it discourages the practice.

Furthermore, confidence in Nacional Financiera's certificates rests on the knowledge that the Bank of Mexico will back them. The holders feel that they have a claim on the resources of the central bank. For them, Nacional Financiera is an investment banking department of the Bank of Mexico. This, too, hardly lends itself to creating healthy investment habits in Mexico.

Apart from its tacit support of Nacional Financiera, the Bank of Mexico has provided funds for industrial development by taking general bonds of the financieras. Much of this central bank credit has leaked into commercial lending. The Bank of Mexico has also supplied funds for public works basic to industrialization. The bank is the principal holder of government bonds. These operations with the financieras and with government bonds have had pronounced inflationary effects.

From 1941 to 1948 the Mexican government, operating through Nacional Financiera and the Bank of Mexico, tried to induce individual savers to put funds into industry directly, and also to channel savings indirectly into industrial investment via the banks and the financieras. On the whole, these efforts were unsuccessful. It is not easy to change deep-rooted investment (and hoarding) habits; one does not ask for miracles. What the Mexican government failed to do, however, was to curb alternative outlets for funds, outlets which individuals and banks preferred to industrial investments. Prominent among these were urban construction, commercial lending, and speculation in commodities.[50] Again, one does not ask for 100 per cent measures of control, but virtually nothing was done. Consequently, Mexico made little progress in solving the problem of financing industrialization during the war years, when conditions were relatively favorable.

FOREIGN CAPITAL

Because domestic savings have been so balky about moving into industrial investment, and also because the gold and foreign exchange reserves of the Bank of Mexico have been declining, the Mexican government has been turning its eyes abroad, especially to the United States. When the shares of a joint Mexican-American concern, Industria Eléctrica de México, were listed on the New York Stock Exchange in 1945, official Mexico was delighted. The Minister of Finance issued a jubilant statement to the press. It was made clear that the Mexican government hoped that this listing would soon be followed by others, making it possible for numerous industries in Mexico to tap the resources of individual American investors. This hope, however, has not been realized. None of the other new industrial companies of Mexico has secured a New York listing.

[50] Measures to restrict such operations would also have had salutary anti-inflationary effects.

Consequently, the attitude of the Mexican government toward more direct investment of American capital in Mexican industry has become increasingly cordial. The way for such a development had already been prepared during the early years of the Avila Camacho administration. The present policy of strongly favoring American investment, as we have already pointed out,[51] is a logical extension and amplification of the departure taken by Avila Camacho shortly after he assumed office. Nowadays the Alemán administration is doing its best to convince American interests that investment in Mexican industry is profitable and, politically, safe.

Before the Second World War the direct investment of American capital in manufacturing in Mexico was quite small. At the end of 1940 such investments were estimated by the United States Department of Commerce at 10.5 million dollars, compared to 168.3 million in mining and 116.4 million in public utilities and transportation.[52] Comparable estimates for subsequent years are not yet available. To make an estimate of how much has been added to American investment in Mexican manufacturing since 1940, on even an approximate basis, would require resources (including access to records) far beyond what the individual investigator can command. The most that I have been able to do is to make a guess as to the order of magnitude of such investment for the years 1941–1946, using the fragmentary information which is available, from various sources, on American participation in Mexico's industrial development. The figure I have arrived at is 100 million dollars, or about 500 million pesos. This figure, although small in relation to the magnitude of investment in the United States, is substantial in relation to new industrial investment in Mexico. The Bank of Mexico, as already noted, has placed the aggregate investment in industry in Mexico during the years 1940–1945 at 1.6 billion pesos.

Not all of the new American investment has taken the form of cash. In the joint Mexican-American companies some of it has been represented by patent rights, technical services, and the training of labor in American plants. Several illustrations of such arrangements have been given in the chapters dealing with specific industries and individual projects.

This wave of American investment in industry represents a new departure in foreign investment in Mexico. In the past foreign capital has tended to go into mineral exploitation, transportation, and public utilities. As in other economically colonial areas, little foreign capital was invested in manufacturing industries working chiefly for the domestic market.[53] But now this area of investment is actively drawing upon American capital.

[51] See chapter v.
[52] U. S. Department of Commerce, *American Direct Investments in Foreign Countries* (Washington, 1942), p. 13.
[53] League of Nations, *op. cit.,* p. 66.

Perhaps this development in Mexico is an expression of a more wide-spread tendency in American investment, in which the traditional coloni al pattern is being modified to include investment in industries producing for local rather than export markets. Such a tendency may well be the outcome of the breakdown of the world trading system in the interwar period. By setting up branch plants abroad, American industry is getting behind tariff walls and other barriers to imports (potential as well as actual). Possibly some of the American companies which are newly entering the foreign field are using Mexico as a laboratory for experimentation.

In addition to the growing volume of private American investment in Mexico since 1940, a number of credits have been extended to Mexican projects by the United States Export-Import Bank. These projects have been both private and governmental in character. From 1941, when the first one was arranged, to the end of 1948, the total amount involved in Export-Import Bank credits was in excess of 150 million dollars.

These Export-Import Bank loans have been used for a variety of industrial projects, some of which have been mentioned in other chapters of this volume. Among the principal industries benefiting from Export-Import Bank credits are petroleum, steel, meat packing, and sugar.[54] The largest allocations, however, have been made for nonindustrial projects. Highway construction alone has absorbed about one-fourth of the total. Other substantial allotments have been made for improving the Mexican railway system, and for expanding the supply of electric power. These projects in the fields of transportation and power are basic to industrial expansion. It should be observed, moreover, that by tapping Export-Import Bank resources for nonindustrial projects, Mexican resources have been freed for investment in manufacturing. This applied especially to Mexican public capital, as represented by Nacional Financiera, the Bank of Mexico, and the Mexican government itself.

The Mexican government also sought financial aid in 1947 from the International Bank for Reconstruction and Development for irrigation, hydroelectric, pipeline, railroad, and harbor projects.[55] This loan application must have included some very substantial projects, since the total amount involved was 209 million dollars, a sum almost 40 per cent greater than the aggregate of Mexican borrowing from the Export-Import Bank as of that time.

In January, 1949, the International Bank granted a loan of 34 million dollars to Mexico for power development. This loan was split into two

[54] Data on these projects are given in Export-Import Bank of Washington, *Seventh Semiannual Report to Congress, for the Period July–December, 1948,* (Washington, 1949), pp. 24–25.
[55] International Bank for Reconstruction and Development, *Second Annual Report, 1946–1947* (Washington, 1947), p. 19.

parts. About two-thirds of the total was allocated to the Federal Electricity Commission to be used in its 1947–1952 program, and the remainder was destined for the use of the principal private power company in Mexico, the Cia. Mexicana de Luz y Fuerza.[56] Both loans were to be administered by Nacional Financiera, and guaranteed by the Mexican government.

It is clear that the Mexican government under President Alemán is determined to get as much foreign capital as possible to participate in the economic development of Mexico. This is true for private foreign capital as well as for public capital. Foreign investment representing public funds (Export-Import Bank loans) is being used for big projects of a type which private investment is unlikely to undertake, but some is also going into industrial enterprises. Private foreign capital, apart from some additional investment in mining, is now going almost entirely into industrial ventures.

The inflow of foreign capital at this time has obvious advantages in easing Mexico's balance of payments problems, making it possible for her to import more than the current volume of her exports (including tourist services) would allow. This tends to facilitate the industrialization process, at least insofar as industrial machinery, equipment, and raw materials can be imported in a larger volume than would otherwise be possible. In the summer of 1947 a balance of payments crisis developed in Mexico.[57] This led the government to ban certain kinds of imports (especially luxuries and semiluxuries) for an indefinite period. Even after the import ban was put into effect, the balance of payments situation was delicate, and another crisis developed in the summer of 1948. It was this crisis which led to the devaluation of the peso. From the standpoint of a precarious balance of payments in Mexico additional foreign capital can be considered advantageous.

However, other circumstances and reactions must also be taken into account. When this has been done, it becomes less clear that additional amounts of foreign capital (for practical purposes, American capital) are desirable on any substantial scale at this time. The problems likely to emerge from a continued large inflow of American investment promise to outweigh the advantages of such an inflow in the solution of Mexico's balance of payments problems.

By importing capital in considerable volume, Mexico tends to relax on the point of using its own savings for industrialization. Saving in Mexico is done by a small fraction of the population, but the aggregate amount saved is appreciable in relation to the economy. It would be healthy if these domestic savings moved readily into industrial investment, but they show a preference for following other channels, especially urban construc-

---

[56] *El Mercado de Valores,* January 10, 1949, p. 2.
[57] See chapter xv.

tion, commercial lending, commodity speculation, and hoarding by means of luxury purchases. In time it will be necessary for the Mexican government to devise means to curb such outlets for funds. Measures will have to be taken to insure a more effective use of domestic savings than now prevails, in the sense of getting them to contribute more to the economic development of the nation as a whole.[58] The Mexican government has obviously been reluctant to take such action. The introduction of foreign capital tends to postpone further the day when the Mexican government will come to grips with this major problem of economic policy.

In taking the place of domestic capital in the field of industrial investment, foreign capital makes it possible for domestic capital to be used for operations that have a strong inflationary effect (private building, multiplication of commercial transactions, commodity speculation). Industrialization in Mexico is proving to be an inflationary process in its own right. If the industrialization goes on at a rapid rate, as it promises to do, inflation will be a persistent problem for a number of years.[59] By lessening the need for the Mexican government to restrain inflationary uses for domestic funds, the inflow of foreign capital helps to magnify this inflationary problem, and to aggravate the social and political tensions which are a heritage of the war period.

Because of the very serious social readjustments attending industrialization, in the way of occupational changes and rural-urban migration, for example, because of industrial problems likely to arise out of the limited character of the internal market, and because of inflation, social tensions seem destined to run high in Mexico for a number of years. There will be a good deal of unrest among the Mexican people. In looking about for an explanation of their troubles, is it not likely that the Mexican people will fix their attention upon American capital? American interests certainly loom large in the industrial picture. A number of the new large industrial undertakings are tied up with giant American companies. Many of the lesser ventures are also known to have affiliations with American concerns. And an official bank of the United States government, the Export-Import Bank, is financially involved in several new developments in Mexican industry.

Given the experience of Mexico with foreign investment during the times of Porfirio Díaz when Mexico was called "the mother of foreigners and the stepmother of Mexicans," given the dramatic events relating to

[58] I realize, of course, that a number of knotty questions have to be faced, including that of controlling the exportation of capital from Mexico. Not all aspects of the problem, however, have to be attacked at the same time. Reactions of the public and of the banks will determine how far-reaching the measures have to be.

[59] This question will be taken up in chapter xiv.

the oil-expropriation case, and given the economically colonial background of Mexico, it would be surprising indeed if foreign capital were not viewed with suspicion and hostility by the mass of the Mexican population. The new wave of American investment is by no means popular with the Mexican people, no matter how favorably it is viewed in government circles. Over the years since the outbreak of the Revolution, Mexico has been pushing back the area of foreign investment, by nationalizing the railroads, by enforcing the agrarian laws, and by nationalizing the petroleum industry. Now, the Mexican people are asking, is this trend to be reversed? Is the government turning its back on a major achievement of the Mexican Revolution by encouraging foreign ownership in the new industries, the avowed center of a new economic structure for the country? Is Mexico returning to the days of Don Porfirio?

Every Mexican who knows something about the history of his country is likely to be asking such questions nowadays. In addition, organized labor as a whole is extremely antagonistic to American capital. The labor press has warned the government many times in the past few years that the policy of inviting foreign capital to invest freely in Mexican industry is dangerous. The trade unions, therefore, are clearly ready to blame American capital for anything that goes wrong. The organizations representing small farmers, some of which are affiliated with the trade unions, can be counted upon to take the same point of view.

Nor should we underestimate the effectiveness of the propaganda radiating from Mexico's New Group industrialists. They are playing a leading role in opposing the investment of American capital in Mexican industry. They lose no opportunity to point out actual or potential disadvantages of such investment. Their campaign against American capital has been gaining in intensity since the end of the war. There is every reason to believe that the campaign will be carried on aggressively in the years that lie ahead. Certainly they will hold American capital responsible for any weaknesses which develop in the Mexican economy. Their skill in popularizing their viewpoint will help to crystallize public antagonism to American capital.

In bringing out these main disadvantages relating to the wave of American investment in Mexican industry, it is not my intention to suggest that Mexico would have been better off if no new foreign investment had taken place in recent years. A somewhat smaller inflow of such capital, combined with a more literal adherence to the principle of 51 per cent Mexican ownership, would probably, however, have brought about a more wholesome situation. But the important question right now relates to the future. It would seem sound policy for the Mexican government to do much more than it has been doing to mobilize Mexican capital resources for industry, and much less about getting American capital to come in. The inflow of capital, especially of private capital for investment in industry, should now be reduced and kept at a low level until Mexico has had a chance to take stock of its industrial development and to decide in which sectors of the economy, if any, further foreign investment could be used with profit from the standpoint of the nation.

No such change in government policy, however, seems likely to occur. On the contrary, everything indicates that the Mexican government is moving in the opposite direction. In calling on foreign capital to help push Mexico ahead industrially, the present administration may well be aggravating the social tensions of industrialization and at the same time setting in motion a new series of complications over American investments in Mexico.

CHAPTER XIII

Labor, Technicians, and Management

LIKE ANY newly industrializing country, Mexico suffers from a shortage of laborers trained to do the many jobs required in modern manufacturing. This creates a problem of substantial importance in the present stage of Mexico's industrial development. It will be a problem for some years to come. In time it will be overcome, but in the earlier phase of rapid industrialization in which Mexico now finds herself, and will find herself for the next several years, it must be recognized that the lack of a trained labor force is a serious restraint and handicap to manufacturing development.

Let it be made clear at the outset that the issue is one of a *trained* working force, not of absolute numbers available for industrial employment. The Mexican population is growing rapidly.[1] Even more important is the fact that Mexico can afford to shift large numbers of persons from farming to industry without reducing her agricultural output.[2] Indeed, Mexico will be unable to increase significantly her standards of living unless many people do make the shift from barely productive agriculture to more productive occupations in other branches of the economy. In the rural areas of Mexico there is a great pool of potential industrial labor which can be drawn upon with benefit to the national economy.

From the standpoint of modern industry, the working force recruited from rural life consists of raw labor. It is true that many of the men engaged in farming in Mexico have also acquired some skills of an industrial nature. It is common for them to use part of their time in making such articles as pottery, woolen blankets (*sarapes*), wooden bowls, plates, and the like. In many of the villages and small towns some men specialize entirely in manufacturing of this character. The boom in exports of Mexican handicraft products to the United States during the Second World War probably caused a substantial increase in this form of specialization. It has been estimated recently that about three million artisans, or roughly 15 per cent of

[1] See Alberto P. León and Alvaro Aldama C., "Population Problems in Central and Caribbean America," *The Annals,* vol. 237 (January, 1945), pp. 37–38.
[2] See chapter xi for a discussion of this question.

the total population of the country, are engaged in handicraft occupations.[3] This includes part-time as well as full-time handicraft workers.

Handicraft skills are likely to have little direct application in industry of the modern type. Indirectly they may be useful, but any advantage of this nature tends to be offset by the informal work habits to which handicraft workers have been accustomed. Because of their past experience they may be much more difficult to fit into a modern manufacturing plant than workers without any previous manufacturing experience at all. Indeed, the most highly skilled persons in the artisan group are likely to react against machine industry, and to prefer to carry on in their traditional way rather than to transform themselves into wage earners of the kind needed by Mexico's new and expanding industries. The pool of potential labor in the Mexican countryside and in the village communities is a pool of men and women, not of ready-made industrial operatives.

The expansion of industry in Mexico, therefore, requires a newly-trained working force. The training can be provided in various ways, and it is to be expected that numerous developments will contribute to this end as Mexico continues to industrialize. However, it is likely to be a slow process. An army of industrial laborers cannot be created overnight, or even in a few years time.

One basic reason for the slowness of this process is that industrialization involves complex social readjustments. Factory employment requires a major personal adjustment of a psychological and emotional character. It calls for different work habits from those which prevail in a nonindustrialized society. It is not simply a question of learning how to perform one or more industrial operations. Because of the nature of modern machinery, many industrial operations are quite routine in nature and can be learned in a relatively short period of time. What requires a much longer period of time is the development of a new pattern of work habits, involving regularity of attendance at the factory, sustained effort, adjustment to the pace set by machines, close dovetailing of what one operative does with what everyone else is doing, and so on.

In stressing this factor of human readjustment, I am not implying that Mexicans are less capable than other peoples of adapting themselves to the requirements which modern industry lays down if it is to be reasonably efficient. There would be little need to mention this at all were it not for the fact that many persons in the United States have the notion that Mexicans, and all other Latin Americans for that matter, are fundamentally incapable of handling machines. Such a viewpoint suffers from the obvious

[3] Inter-American Development Commission, *A Survey of the Economic Opportunities of Mexican Manual Industries* (Washington, n.d.), p. 7.

basic defect of a belief that institutions, which are actually malleable and subject to a large amount of adjustment and change, are the immutable inherited qualities of this, that, or the other group of people. Even a slender knowledge of history should lead one to avoid such pathetic clichés.

As a matter of fact, it is possible to appeal to experience to show that Mexican workers can operate efficiently in modern industry. This has been demonstrated in Mexico herself, as the following quotation from George Wythe's *Industry in Latin America* shows:[4]

> The efficiency of Latin American labor ranges from poor to excellent. The workers in most of the countries show a decided aptitude for mechanical operations. Given proper training, they compare favorably with the labor forces in the industrial nations. The records of several large American companies that have manufacturing branches in many countries indicate that Mexican and Argentine workers show up best among Latin Americans; they are as efficient as the workers in England or France, although they fall short of the per-man productivity in the United States, Germany, and Japan.

In addition, Mexicans who worked at industrial jobs in the United States in the 1920's showed their capacity for industrial employment. In the well-known series of studies on Mexican labor in the United States by Professor Paul S. Taylor, evidence was brought out to show that Mexicans were making small but steady gains in industrial employment.[5] The gains were not confined to increases in numbers, for some Mexicans, in spite of social prejudices which tended to keep them occupied in unskilled jobs, were able to advance to better positions.

To return now to the problem of getting an adequate supply of properly trained labor for a country that is industrializing as rapidly as Mexico, it is important to observe that shortages need not be widespread to be serious. They may be confined to a handful of occupations or grades of employment and still be a critical handicap to the whole industrialization process. Right now in Mexican industry there is a shortage of satisfactory foremen. Men with sufficient experience and judgment to be relied upon to make decisions regarding the use of costly machinery and equipment are not easily found in Mexico. This shortage is at present a real bottleneck for Mexican industrialization.

In this connection, foreigners (e.g., Europeans) with long experience in industry could be very helpful to Mexico. Given the upset conditions which prevail in Europe, it would not be difficult to induce many such persons to come to Mexico. It is extremely doubtful, however, that this will be done. For a number of years it has been the policy of the Mexican govern-

[4] Page 52.
[5] See Paul S. Taylor, *Mexican Labor in the United States: Chicago and the Calumet Region*, University of California Publications in Economics, vol. 7, no. 2 (1932), pp. 80–95, 155–160.

ment to discourage the immigration of persons who intend to work in any form whatever. The policy has not been one of absolute prohibition, or even of quotas, but simply one of refusing to grant many visas for this purpose. In respect to industrial jobs, the government's immigration policy is strongly backed by the trade unions. The unions contend that Mexicans can and should be trained for the more responsible jobs for which foreigners have been sought. There is no reason to expect a change of heart on this question.

In training Mexican labor, a certain amount of credit must be given to large American concerns which operate branch plants in Mexico, or plants in which they have invested jointly with Mexican capital. It is common for these American firms to train in their home plants a number of Mexican workers. Upon their return to Mexico, these employees serve as a nucleus for training others. This, for example, has been the policy of Westinghouse in relation to Industria Eléctrica de México.[6] In thus providing training schools for Mexican industrial labor, some of the large American firms are making a substantial contribution to Mexican industrialization. This must be recognized as a partial offset to the disadvantages of foreign investment pointed out in chapter xii.

In large part Mexican industry must train its own labor supply by working experience in the factory. Here again the principal factor is time. Each new plant in due course adds to the common pool of industrial skills and of labor accustomed to the conditions of modern factory employment. All industries benefit from such increments. But it does take time for the benefits to be realized in substantial form in a country just embarking on a policy of industrialization.

Similarly, geographic concentration of industry helps a country like Mexico to make the most of its trained labor supply. Workers can shift from industry to industry without making a change of residence. The industrial expansion of Mexico, since 1939, like the previous industrial development, is taking place chiefly in two areas, Monterrey and Mexico City. Secondary industrial centers are growing up around Guadalajara and Puebla. It is to these cities, and especially to Mexico City and Monterrey, that workers and potential workers are flocking from all parts of the country.

Apart from training, supplied by working experience in industry itself, vocational education has a great and growing role to play in Mexican industrialization. In Mexico the only agency which can fill this need is the federal government. Although the Instituto Politécnico Nacional (National Polytechnical Institute), created in 1936, included vocational training

---

[6] See chapter ix. The same practice had been used earlier by the International General Electric Co. at its Monterrey plant.

as well as more advanced technical and scientific training in its program, very little was accomplished in this field until 1940. The progress of industry thereafter induced the government to strengthen the vocational program, especially in making it possible for workers to qualify for more skilled jobs than they hold. Just how much has actually been accomplished it is difficult to find out. Numerous enthusiastic accounts of the work of the Instituto Politécnico Nacional have been released from time to time,[7] but the failure to publish basic statistics on vocational education makes it impossible to put these stories in a proper perspective in relation to Mexico's industrialization effort.

Since 1945 the Cámara Nacional de la Industria de Transformación has taken an active interest in promoting vocational education in Mexico. Joint committees have been organized with labor groups, including the CTM, to determine the kinds of vocational training most needed in Mexico at the present time. Government authorities have been invited to participate in the work of these groups. In a broad way, the Cámara Nacional de la Industria de Transformación is seeking to persuade the Mexican government of the desirability of reorienting elementary education in Mexico, by providing greater scope and more facilities for vocational training. This would involve some sacrifice in the teaching of conventional subjects. It is probable that this effort of the Cámara Nacional de la Industria de Transformación will bear fruit.

Vocational education can, and undoubtedly will, contribute to training a labor force for Mexican industry. However, it must be recognized that education for living and working in an industrial society is a much broader question than mere technical training. The rate of illiteracy in Mexico is extremely high. According to the census of 1940, about 48 per cent of the population over six years of age could neither read nor write. Subsequently a "national campaign against illiteracy" was organized, under which each literate adult was to instruct an illiterate one, but this campaign, from its very nature, could effect only a minor improvement in the situation. As long as so many persons in Mexico are unable to read and write, the country is handicapped in every way in its industrialization process, in disseminating vocational training, in easing the transition from rural to urban-industrial living, in raising standards of living, and so on.

But here again the problem broadens. The problem of education in Mexico transcends literacy and school instruction in the ordinary sense. It is a problem of educating people, adults and children alike, in better ways of living, in appreciation of improvements in health, hygienic conditions, diet, living quarters, and the like. For a number of years an attempt

---

[7] See, for example, *El Nacional*, September 5 and October 17, 1947.

has been made to grapple with this problem in rural education, as the following quotation from Eyler Simpson's *The Ejido* shows:[8]

... a very conscious attempt has been made to adapt the program of the elementary schools to the real needs of the rural communities. These schools have been conceived not so much in the traditional terms of reading and writing ... but rather in terms of instruments of socialization and agencies for raising the standard of living. For this reason, theoretically at least, the schools have been just as much concerned with reaching parents as children and the evening and early morning classes and other activities for adults occupy almost as much of the teacher's time and attention as the regular day classes for the younger generation. For this reason, also, the four-year program seeks to give quite as much, if not more, emphasis to courses in hygiene and health, diet, farming, gardening, the care of chickens and livestock, and to teach weaving and tanning, the cooking and canning of fruits and vegetables, and carpentry as to the activities traditionally associated with the three R's.

Although this program of rural education has never been realized fully in terms of the aspirations Eyler Simpson was writing about,[9] more has been accomplished in education for living in the rural communities than in the urban centers. The very complexity of urban life makes it much more difficult and more costly to carry out such a program.

It is taken for granted that education of this type is needed in its own right. In addition, however, it will help industrial wage earners to adjust themselves to factory employment. New wants are created. These of necessity will provide a new incentive to keep income on a regular basis. Absentee rates in Mexican plants are typically very high in comparison with those in the advanced industrialized nations. These should decline appreciably as new wants make themselves felt.

Similarly, the industrial workers will strive to increase their earnings by whatever methods are made available in the plants in which they work. It is important, therefore, that Mexican employers recognize the need to provide special financial incentives in addition to appropriate basic wages. Such incentives will lead toward a stable and efficient laboring force.

The point of view expressed in the preceding paragraphs is very much the philosophy of the prominent Mexican industrialist, Antonio Ruiz Galindo. His new plant, D. M. Nacional, is organized accordingly, as we have already pointed out.[10] In the present stage of Mexico's economic and social development such industry-sponsored programs of educating wage earners to higher standards of living could add significantly to what the government is able to do. This, of course, makes the assumption that any abuses of paternalism are curbed by trade union vigilance and by government action.

---

[8] Page 278.
[9] The payment of inadequate salaries to teachers is largely responsible for this outcome. See Lesley Byrd Simpson, *Many Mexicos*, pp. 307–308.
[10] See chapter ix.

The question dealt with thus far in this chapter—that of getting a sufficient supply of trained labor for Mexico's expanding industries—appears, therefore, as part of a larger and more complex problem of human adjustment to an industrial civilization. This is necessarily a process which moves slowly. It is unquestionably lagging well behind the present rapid rate of industrialization in Mexico, and it can be expected to continue to lag substantially for a number of years. In the long run Mexico can count upon having an adequate supply of efficient wage earners in industry. In the several years that must elapse before this happy condition is realized, however, manufacturing development in Mexico will be handicapped by shortages in the labor field.

In the preceding pages I have dealt with working efficiency solely from the standpoint of labor. But the effectiveness of the wage earners in industry also depends upon the efficiency of others such as technicians and managers, and upon the whole organizational set-up of the plants in which they work. An improvement in the efficiency of any one of these elements necessarily increases the effectiveness of all the others. Thus the contribution of Mexican industrial labor to output will be augmented as Mexican factories improve the quality of their technical and managerial staffs.

In Mexico, as in all Latin American countries, technical education was neglected in the past. The nature of her social and economic structure gave little incentive, until recently, for the study of engineering and other applied sciences. The tradition in higher education has led in other directions. Here again is a factor which cannot be changed overnight. It will take time to build an educational system capable of turning out the mechanical, chemical, electrical, civil and industrial engineers required by an expanding industry, and this is by no means a complete list of the kinds of technicians that will be needed. Training of a less advanced character will have to be provided for hundreds of other salaried employees who will do the more routine technical jobs.

So far as training in the physical sciences has been provided in Mexico, the emphasis has been upon theoretical rather than applied aspects. This, of course, has been consistent with the broad educational tradition in university circles. Instruction in the laboratory or in the field has been neglected. This is still largely true today in spite of some gains in laboratory instruction in recent years. The distaste for practical work which many generations of instructors have implanted in their students, from whose ranks the succeeding generations of instructors are necessarily recruited, will tend to perpetuate itself for many years. The emphasis has been, and is, placed upon the solution of theoretical problems. However useful this bent may be for other purposes, it is unfortunate from the standpoint of meeting the rapidly expanding demands of Mexican industry for a corps of technicians to deal with practical questions of industrial operations.

The government's institute for technical training (Instituto Politécnico Nacional), which we have already referred to in connection with vocational education, has expanded its curricula and improved its laboratory equipment substantially in the past few years. The program for training industrial chemists has been notably strengthened. Also, an attempt has been made to coördinate the work of the institute more closely with the requirements of Mexico's new and expanding industries.

Larger numbers of students have been attracted to the Instituto Politécnico Nacional in the past few years, and the faculty has also been enlarged. In 1940 the total number of students enrolled in the various branches of the institute was approximately 10,000, and the faculty numbered 1,500. By 1946 almost 12,000 students were registered and the faculty had been expanded to about 1,800.[11] In January, 1947, it was reported that 15,000 applicants were seeking admission for the school year 1947; this was a peak figure in the history of the institute.[12] There is every reason to suppose that the Mexican government will expand further the work of the Instituto Politécnico Nacional, which is its main contribution to the training of technicians for Mexican industry.

Private schools for training engineers and other technicians have appeared in Mexico in the past few years. Especially noteworthy is the Instituto Tecnológico de Estudios Superiores de Monterrey, organized and supported by industrial interests in the city of Monterrey, which, as we have already noted, is one of Mexico's leading manufacturing centers. The purpose of this institute is to give practical rather than theoretical training, and to meet the needs for technical personnel in the many industries located in Monterrey. A number of important Mexican industrial, financial, and commercial concerns have sponsored the organization of a somewhat similar school in Mexico City, known as the Instituto Tecnológico de México. This institute, however, seems to be less oriented toward technical and engineering study than the Monterrey institute, and more concerned with business administration.

A corollary of the growth of technical education in Mexico has been a growing demand for textbooks in the various technical fields. Publishing houses are doing an active business in supplying this market, principally by means of translating standard works originally published in the United States, England, Switzerland, and Germany. To those who knew Mexico City in the days before the current industrialization drive got under way, it comes as something of a shock to find the bookstores now featuring text-

[11] *Seis años de actividad nacional*, p. 125.
[12] *El Universal*, January 30, 1947.

books on engineering and chemistry rather than the philosophical, historical, and literary works which used to be the favorites for display.

Since about 1940 there has been an increase in the number of young Mexicans coming to the United States for technical training. Financial support from the United States government has probably been the principal factor making this development possible, but the Mexican government has done a fair amount on its own. Private firms on both sides of the border have coöperated with the program. A number of American manufacturing concerns, for example, have allowed Mexican technicians to get practical experience in their factories. The Bank of Mexico, as part of its program of promoting industrial development in Mexico, has granted a number of fellowships with good stipends for technical study abroad. Most of these fellowships have been used for study in American universities and technical schools.

Getting technical training abroad is valuable, but obviously Mexico cannot depend upon foreign schools to train all the technicians she needs as her industrial economy expands. It is too costly, except for filling a handful of high-level technical positions. A question naturally arises, therefore, about importing foreign technicians to meet Mexico's needs during the time she is building up her own technical institutes to the point where they will solve this shortage problem.

To some extent this has been done, and is being done, but the bringing in of foreign technicians is not destined to be a factor of measurable significance in the industrialization of Mexico. In the first place, there is a bias against it in law. In the depression of the 1930's Mexico, like many other countries, placed restrictions on the employment of foreigners. As a general rule, 90 per cent of all persons employed by every firm must be Mexican citizens. An immigration regulation adopted in 1933 requires special permission for bringing in foreign technicians. It has been the practice to deny such permits whenever it could be shown that competent Mexicans are available. In every case where a permit has been granted the employer has been obligated to train a Mexican to take over the work upon expiration of the foreigner's contract. Such contracts can be made only for limited periods. In 1934 and again in 1936 additional obstacles were introduced in connection with the hiring of foreigners.[13]

There is already latitude in the existing laws for making exceptions. Also, the laws could be changed to make it easier for technically-trained foreigners to work in Mexican industry. There is little likelihood, however, that the exceptions will be numerous or that the laws will be materially modified. In the past few years, with Mexican technicians fully employed

[13] Wythe, *Industry in Latin America*, p. 285.

and with obvious uses for additional technical services; it has been difficult to tap foreign sources. Even semiofficial organizations, such as the Bank of Mexico, have not found it easy to bring in foreign consultants on technical questions relating to industrial development. Furthermore, a new law was enacted in 1947 to tighten, rather than loosen, the basic restrictions upon the practice of professions by foreigners in Mexico. Most technicians for industry would be included in the newly-restricted professions.

The fundamental factors in this situation are national pride and the aggressive nationalism shown by Mexico's corps of technicians. Probably the failure of foreign firms in earlier periods to give Mexicans a chance to qualify for technical and professional jobs is mainly responsible for the extremely nationalistic attitude of today. Whatever the reasons, Mexico's technicians as a group feel very strongly that they can just about match foreigners on technical knowledge and that they are superior to foreigners in their knowledge of the country and its people. Thus they see little or no need for importing foreign technicians.

Nowhere has this attitude been better expressed than in the following quotation from a *feuilleton* in the Mexico City daily, *El Universal:*

. . . if we want to liquidate conclusively the semicolonial economic regime which oppresses us, the only and sure road left for us is the formation of a true army of Mexican technicians. That is, of technicians linked to the land and its people by real ties of blood and a clear knowledge of its most complex problems.

. . . the technology needed for progress must be conceived strictly by Mexicans, controlled by Mexicans, directed by Mexicans and destined for Mexicans. Foreign technicians may even be more capable than our own at any given moment, but they will never love the country more than those who are formed by it, first saw the light of day in it, and have the remains of their forefathers fused in its heart. A foreign technician, even though he lives among us, must always turn his eyes to his country of origin, he will deposit his savings systematically in foreign banks, and generally he will treat his Mexican workers less well than he treats his own compatriots or foreigners from other lands.[14]

In management personnel, as in technical personnel, Mexican industry suffers from a shortage, although the deficiency in management is probably the less severe of the two. The number of Mexicans with management experience in industry has naturally been kept down in the past by the small development of manufacturing. Now, with the expansion of industry, there has been a new and rapidly-increasing need for minor administrative personnel, as well as for executives at higher levels.

This need is more acute in the Mexico City industrial area than in Monterrey. Monterrey has long been considered a unique entity in Mexico, and its citizens have long been looked upon as a distinctive group.

[14] Gabino A. Palma, "Sin técnicos de verdad no es posible la industrialización," *El Universal,* July 27, 1946.

Doubtless their peculiarities, so frequently made the point of jokes in Mexico, have been exaggerated. Nevertheless, it is true that the "spirit of enterprise," as it has ordinarily been thought of in the United States or western Europe, has found much more expression in Monterrey than anywhere else in Mexico. Its businessmen have had more in common with United States businessmen than with other Mexican businessmen.

Monterrey, as I have already had occasion to observe, has had an active industrial history for many years. The economic importance of the city dates from the last years of the nineteenth century when it became the railroad center for the whole of northeastern Mexico.[15] Thereafter it attracted a number of industries, including the iron and steel plant which is still the largest establishment of its kind in Mexico, and many commercial and financial concerns which added to the business vitality of the community.

In the process of this development, which has been continuous for about fifty years, an economic psychology and a business spirit akin to those of the United States have come to the fore in Monterrey. It has even been said that "the most obscure furnace tender, the most insignificant iron worker, work under the inspiration of a goal which everyone in Monterrey responds to; to become the master of his own enterprise."[16] Some allowance can be made for overstatement in this quotation. Nevertheless, it is clear that the pattern of business development at Monterrey has been such as to qualify a relatively large number of persons to exercise administrative and managerial functions in industry.

In this chapter I have dealt with Mexico's human resources for industrialization, industrial wage earners, industrial technicians, and industrial managers. In all three respects Mexico is deficient. Because of the rapid rate of industrialization, these shortages will continue to be felt in the years that lie ahead. Foreign sources are not likely to be tapped in amounts sufficient to alter this situation. In time the shortages will be overcome from within Mexico, but this will be a long drawn-out process because it involves a complex social readjustment for large numbers of people. That the readjustment will take place need not be doubted. The machine tends to impose a discipline of its own. But it does take time before a whole new scheme of working and living is developed within a culture.[17] The problem of mobilizing its human resources effectively for industrialism is not to be taken lightly in Mexico.

---

[15] Samuel Dicken, "Monterrey and Northeastern Mexico," *Annals of the Association of American Geographers*, Vol. 29, no 2 (June, 1939), p. 139.

[16] Mauricio Magdaleno, "Monterrey y México," *El Universal*, August 27, 1946.

[17] Any foreigner who has driven a car in Mexico City in recent years will testify that Mexico is far from being adjusted to the requirements of a machine civilization.

CHAPTER XIV

Inflation

O<small>NE OF THE</small> vital economic problems today in Mexico, as in most countries, is the problem of inflation. In a number of countries, the rise in prices in recent years, especially since the end of the war, has reached spectacular proportions. This cannot be said of Mexico. Nevertheless, the inflationary development in Mexico has been serious and it has caused dislocations and tensions which are properly a source of uneasiness to all those, outside as well as inside Mexican government circles, who are concerned about the welfare of the Mexican nation as a whole.

There is little need to linger over a survey and appraisal of the different series of figures designed to measure the degree of inflation in Mexico in recent years. They all suffer from some of the limitations which tend to affect statistics in Mexico, such as those discussed earlier in this volume. Furthermore, no price indices are available for the country as a whole. The most that can be obtained are figures for price changes in Mexico City, and these may be quite out of line with price fluctuations in the towns and rural villages. Even if the figures are a reliable guide to the price changes that have occurred, the changes themselves are apt to mean something very different for the rural population than for the urban dwellers. For the most part, the rural inhabitants buy only a few kinds of products. What happens to the prices of these few items is a vital question to them, but they are little concerned with price changes in many of the items which enter into the Mexico City wholesale-price index.

Table 8 (p. 274) shows the price trend since 1929, as reflected in the official price index prepared by the Ministry of National Economy. Because of quality deterioration, shortages of low-priced items, etc., it is probable that the figures after 1941 tend to understate the amount of effective price increase.

The inflationary experience of the war period stands out very clearly. In 1942 the price level jumped about 10 per cent over the preceding year, reaching a point almost 20 per cent higher than the price level in 1939. Some of the annual increases after 1942 were even more striking. From 1942 to 1947 the price level doubled, and was still rising as 1948 ended.

The contribution to Mexico's inflation of wartime conditions and industrialization alike, must be viewed in the light of a previous history of inflation running back to 1936. When the war broke out in 1939 the Mexican price level was already rising appreciably (see table 8). This basic tendency naturally has affected all developments within the Mexican economy. It will be useful, therefore, to examine briefly the inflationary factors operating before the war.[1]

In 1936, after about three years of slow but steady recovery from the low point of the depression, the Mexican government embarked upon a policy of monetary expansion, made possible by central bank financing. The gov-

TABLE 8

WHOLESALE PRICE INDEX, MEXICO CITY, 1929–1947

(1929 = 100)

Year	Index	Year	Index
1929	100.0	1939	122.2
1930	100.6	1940	122.8
1931	89.6	1941	130.5
1932	82.0	1942	144.3
1933	87.1	1943	173.0
1934	89.9	1944	221.8
1935	90.5	1945	243.9
1936	96.2	1946	285.6
1937	114.0	1947	291.7
1938	119.2	1948	309.5

Source: Compiled from data in Memoria de la Secretaría de la Economía Nacional, Septiembre de 1946–Agosto de 1947, pp. 290–291; Secretaría de la Economía Nacional, Revista de Estadística, January, 1949, p. 26.

ernment borrowed from the Bank of Mexico by means of an overdraft. Although the amount involved was small at first, in 1937 it began to increase with great rapidity, and for some years thereafter the practice of borrowing from the central bank in this manner was continued.

Behind this fiscal policy of the Mexican government was a great expansion in public works. Irrigation projects, the building of schools, railroad construction, harbor improvements, and highway construction were undertaken on a new scale, with expenditures far in excess of the amounts which had been allocated to such developments in preceding years.

In addition to public works, the government increased substantially its support for agricultural credit. A new public bank in the field of agricultural credit, the Banco Nacional de Crédito Ejidal, started to operate with a capital of 120 million pesos, and the budget of the older institution, the Banco Nacional de Crédito Agrícola, was expanded. Then, too, a new in-

[1] In this sketch I have made free use of the excellent analysis by Víctor L. Urquidi, "Tres lustros de experiencia monetaria en México: algunas enseñanzas," *Memoria del Segundo Congreso Mexicano de Ciencias Sociales*, vol. 2, pp. 423–511.

stitution was set up to finance exportation by small producers, especially those organized into coöperatives. This bank, known as the Banco Nacional de Comercio Exterior, also operated with capital supplied by the government.

In 1937 further increases occurred in public investment and public outlays in the same fields. The two agricultural credit banks were supplied with additional capital. Larger sums were allocated for irrigation, road, and railroad construction. Fourteen million pesos of public capital were invested in a sugar mill enterprise. The capitalization of the Banco Nacional de Comercio Exterior was augmented. An attempt was made to finance these new public expenditures by means of bond issues, but neither the public nor the banks showed a willingness to buy such government securities. Thus the government resorted to further borrowing from the central bank.

By 1937 the effect of the government's program of public investment and public spending, accompanied by monetary expansion, was noticeable in the price level, as the figures in the above table show. Especially strong was the reaction in the prices of prime necessities. President Cárdenas and other leading officials in the government showed concern over this price trend, but took no immediate steps to curb it by means of reducing public expenditures.

In 1938 the oil-expropriation incident brought new forces into play, tending to aggravate the inflationary trend. Not only was the peso devalued but the shock to the economy made it advisable for the government to increase its outlays. Monetary expansion was also considered necessary as an offset to the increase in hoarding and the flight of capital precipitated by the expropriation of foreign petroleum holdings. If the government had had any plans for reducing its expenditures prior to the petroleum incident in March, 1938, these plans were scrapped in an effort to cope with the emergency situation. The Bank of Mexico was called upon for further assistance.

In 1940 the effects of the Second World War began to make themselves felt, although these were not pronounced until the United States entered the war at the end of 1941. One inflationary factor which showed itself early in the war was an inflow of capital in the form of money, unaccompanied by goods. This was mostly "refugee" capital from Europe, but some Mexican capital which had earlier sought greater security abroad was now repatriated because of the war. Later in the war, when investment outlets in the United States were seriously limited by priorities in the allocation of materials, a certain amount of fluid capital from the United States was added to this current of capital importation.

Throughout the whole war period such inflows of money capital contributed to inflation in Mexico. They caused additions to the money supply without appreciably affecting the supply of goods and services available for consumption by the bulk of the Mexican people. Those who owned this capital were not interested in long-term investment, since they considered Mexico only a temporary haven for their funds. In some cases they simply held their funds in the form of idle bank balances. When they invested, they were disposed to put their funds into transactions with a quick turnover, often speculative in nature. Such operations, added to what Mexicans were already doing in the same field, helped to give a further boost to prices.

The major external inflationary force experienced in Mexico, as in all Latin American nations, during the war years was an excess of exports over imports. Mexico was an important source of strategic materials for the war effort of the United Nations. Thousands of tons of mineral ores were shipped to the United States for war production. The volume of copper produced for export was especially large, but lead, zinc, mercury, antimony, tungsten, mica, cobalt, graphite, and other minerals were also supplied. Exports of fibers were expanded to replace the sources of supply from the Far East now cut off. Among these fibers henequen from the peninsula of Yucatan was the most important, but sisal and ixtle from other parts of Mexico also figured. The production and export of guayule rubber were increased. From the hardwood forests of southern Mexico mahogany was shipped to the United States for the construction of PT boats. From the west coast, tomatoes were sent to the United States for the commissariat of the armed forces. Medicinal plants were raised or gathered for export to the United States, and a certain amount of alcohol, vegetable oil, and dehydrated food products was also supplied.

For all these items, and others of lesser significance, Mexico received foreign exchange which the exporters converted into pesos. The purchasing power flowing from the export industries exerted an upward pressure on prices. Had manufactured goods been freely available from the United States and Great Britain, the inflationary effect of enlarged exports would have been offset by an expansion of imports, since Mexico shows a high propensity to import. But imports were restricted because the American and British war effort resulted in a sharp curtailment of civilian production in those two countries. In some years Mexican exports exceeded imports by substantial amounts. The cumulative excess would have been even greater if crop failures in 1943 had not made it necessary to import wheat and corn. Just how much the cumulative export surplus in Mexico amounted to during the war period is difficult to determine because of peculiarities (and changes) in the method of handling mineral export figures, including those for the monetary metals.[2] One source places this surplus at 53 million dollars for the years 1940–1944.[3] Whatever the precise amount may be, there can be no question that Mexico's trade balance was responsible for a large net inflow of payments during the war period, with the consequent effect of expanding the monetary supply.

Among the invisible items in Mexico's balance of payments apart from the importation of capital referred to above, an increase in the tourist trade also contributed to inflation. By one means or another, a considerable number of American tourists made their way to Mexico during the war years. Tourist expenditures became an appreciable credit item in the Mexican balance of payments. Unofficial estimates place the net amount of exchange accruing to Mexico from the tourist trade with the United States at approximately 40 million dollars in 1943, at a somewhat higher figure in 1944, and at 55 million dollars in 1945. This inflow of exchange had its inflationary effect by way of increasing the money supply in Mexico.

In addition, the consumption of food by tourists helped to boost prices of basic items. It is known that a large fraction of the American tourist expenditures were made in the border towns. It is also known that many Americans resident on or near the border used to cross the line during the war years in order to buy food which they could not get at home because of rationing. They bought other articles, too, such as shirts, that were in short supply in the United States. This kind of tourist trade amounted to an export of goods from Mexico, including articles of prime necessity for the Mexican people.

The external factors reviewed above—capital inflow, export surplus, and the tourist trade—were by no means the only inflationary forces operating in Mexico during the war years. The Mexican government continued to spend large sums of money on public works. A number of new bond issues were put out. According to Urquidi,[4] the new issues authorized in the years 1941 to 1943 were taken by the Bank of Mexico. This observation apparently refers to three issues aggregating almost 300 million pesos.[5] In 1944 it was announced that the government would raise taxes, pay off some of its debt to the Bank of Mexico, and use current revenues for public works. However, during the same year the Bank of Mexico's portfolio of government securities rose by 89.5 million pesos.

[2] For a discussion of this question see Norman T. Ness, "Mexico," in Harris (ed.), *Economic Problems of Latin America*, pp. 375–377.

[3] "Monetary Developments in Latin America," *Federal Reserve Bulletin*, vol. 31 (June, 1945), p. 531.

[4] *Op. cit.*, p. 451.

[5] See bond data tabulated in *Seis años de actividad nacional*, p. 357.

The Mexican government's expenditures on public works were naturally an inflationary factor in their own right. The method of financing them by borrowing from the central bank, involving additions to the money supply without offsetting reductions, tended to exaggerate their inflationary effect.

Among the other internal forces promoting inflation was an increase in expenditures of a military character. Then, too, there was the influence of private construction (office buildings, apartment houses, luxury homes), and of the speculative transactions in commodities, financed by loans from the commercial banks and other financial institutions, already discussed in the chapter on capital and credit. After 1943, wage increases entered as a secondary, cumulating factor in the inflationary situation. For present purposes it is not necessary to elaborate on these, or to bring out the many other factors which played some part in the development of inflation.

It is important, however, to stress the fact that industrialization also contributed to Mexico's inflation during the war period. From 1940 to 1945, according to the estimate of the Bank of Mexico noted in chapter xii, about 1.6 billion pesos were invested in industry. Not all of this sum was spent in Mexico, for a certain amount of machinery and equipment was purchased in the United States. There is no way of estimating how much was spent in Mexico and how much was spent abroad. But it is clear that a large fraction of the outlays connected with new and expanding industries must always be made in the country where the industries are located. For building new plants, or additions to old ones, domestic labor and materials are called upon. Similarly, expenditures for labor and local materials figure prominently in outfitting plants for production, such as in the installation of machinery, even when the machinery itself is imported.

The building of new factories and the expansion of old ones, therefore, was a means by which the purchasing power in the hands of the Mexican public was expanded during the war years. This must have made an appreciable contribution to inflation. Of course, as the new plants got into production, the larger output of manufactured goods available for consumption in Mexico absorbed some of this purchasing power and, therefore, cushioned the inflationary effect of the new investment.

But it takes time for new plants to get into production even under the best of circumstances, and the best of circumstances were far from present in Mexico during the war period. Bottlenecks were both numerous and difficult to overcome. Uncompleted factories were a striking feature on the Mexican landscape. In some cases, the failure to get one or two pieces of equipment meant that a plant, otherwise complete, could not function.

Where plants were actually completed, they ran into other bottlenecks. These sometimes took the form of labor shortages. Even more important was the breakdown in transportation. The Mexican railroad system, in bad shape when the war started, broke down almost completely under the strain of the war effort. In spite of the rehabilitation program carried out jointly by the Mexican and United States governments, the Mexican railroads were able to supply but a fraction of the service required in the war period. As a result plants were often forced to suspend operations because of failures in the delivery of materials originating in Mexico itself.

Difficulties also arose in connection with sources of power for industry. This was true both for petroleum and for electric power. Many industrial establishments, particularly those in or near Mexico City, use petroleum for fuel. Petróleos Mexicanos, the government oil monopoly, was unable to meet all the heavy demands placed upon it during the war period, and factories frequently had to close down because of fuel shortages. The situation in Petróleos Mexicanos was complex, and I need not try to analyze it here. Organizational weaknesses, labor disputes, and the difficulty of getting equipment all played their part in holding down the supply of fuel oil. But even without these handicaps, it would have been difficult for Petróleos Mexicanos to meet the spurt in demand with which it was faced.

Plants dependent upon electric power for their operation also experienced difficulties. In 1943, for example, the breakdown of electric service in Monterrey caused a temporary suspension of virtually all manufacturing activity in that important industrial area. Even after service was resumed, industry had to operate at a reduced rate for some time. The problem of getting replacements, to say nothing of new units, was especially difficult for power plants, inasmuch as such equipment was exceedingly tight in supply in the United States during the war period.

Enough has been said above to indicate the kinds of bottlenecks which restrained industrial output during the Second World War. Even without them, manufacturing production would have lagged behind investment in new industrial plants. With them, the lag was increased, and the inflationary tendency of industrialization was magnified.

This leads naturally to the question: would not the industrialization process be inflationary in any event? That is, apart from the war, could a country such as Mexico make rapid progress industrially without experiencing an inflationary reaction? And from this still another question follows: is it not likely that Mexico will be faced with a persistent inflationary problem in the years that lie ahead as the industrialization process continues? To these questions I now direct my attention.

Industrialization in a country with an economy like that of Mexico tends, at best, to be inflationary. If the industrialization proceeds slowly, if domestic savings are adequate to supply the investment needed, and if these savings are readily channeled into industrial investment, the inflation will be at a minimum. But there is likely to be some inflationary effect even under these circumstances because the economy is always fully employed. The subsistence sector of the economy, as observed in chapter i, acts as a constant shock absorber to occupy those who might otherwise be completely unemployed. They are employed at low productivity occupations, but still they are employed. Therefore, when new investment takes place in industry, even on a modest scale, wages will tend to rise, no matter how low they may still be in absolute terms. Also, the prices of some raw materials, especially those produced by primitive agricultural methods, will tend to go up because their supply cannot be easily and quickly expanded. These increases in costs (wages and materials) will be reflected, of course, in higher prices of many other goods besides those produced by the new industries. In time larger supplies of labor and materials will be forthcoming, but meanwhile costs and prices will show a tendency to rise.

Perhaps the most realistic way to think about these tendencies is in terms of bottlenecks. A handful of bottlenecks can have a substantial effect on costs and prices. These bottlenecks may appear in certain grades of skilled labor, or in particular kinds of raw materials. Also, they may arise out of deficiencies in transport facilities, both roads and railways. In an underdeveloped country it is difficult to advance very far toward industrialism without running into enough bottlenecks to influence the prices of many articles.

As the new investment in industry takes place, the earnings of certain groups of workers, especially those who are constructing the new plants, will rise. Because of the low standards of living prevalent among wage earners in Mexico, this increase will quickly express itself in a greater demand for foodstuffs and other basic items of general consumption. Since the output of agricultural produce cannot be expanded readily in Mexico, the prices of food items will be raised. Other prices will react similarly, although probably in lesser degree. Thus prices are lifted by a greater money demand for goods as well as by higher costs.

If industrialization promises to be inflationary when the rate of industrial development is slow, as assumed in the preceding discussion, it is bound to be even more inflationary when many new industries are being started simultaneously. The opportunity for bottlenecks to occur is greater. Each bottleneck will be more acutely felt. The time lag between plant construction and plant operation is likely to be greater for every industry. When plants do get into production they are more likely to be handicapped in reaching and maintaining full-capacity operations. It becomes more difficult for industrial output to catch up with the purchasing power released by the new investment in industry.

A program of rapid industrialization in Mexico, therefore, is destined to be inflationary. But the inflationary impulses originating in the circumstances just reviewed are not the only ones likely to operate in Mexico. To these must be added the difficulty of getting domestic savings to move into industrial investment. This difficulty, as was pointed out in the chapter on capital and credit, has led the central bank to take a prominent role in financing industrial development, with greater inflationary results than would have occurred had private investors and private banks done the whole job. It is true that the Mexican government could have done much more than it has been willing to do about curbing other uses for funds, thus forcing more Mexican capital into industrial investment. But at the same time it must be recognized that the problem has institutional foundations, in traditional investment habits, in long-established banking practices, and in the social and economic upheaval caused by the Mexican Revolution. To some extent, therefore, the difficulty of getting domestic capital for industry must be considered a part of Mexico's institutional structure. If rapid industrialization is desired, resort to a certain amount of central bank financing is inevitable in Mexico.

Mexico has not yet passed the stage where it can be said that the inflationary effect of industrialization is dying out. Everything indicates that new industrial development will be pushed ahead rapidly by the Mexican government. If we take the industrial picture as a whole, Mexico is still in the stage of producing factories rather than manufactured goods. The Mexican price level will experience inflationary pressure from industrialization for a number of years to come.

Further inflation in Mexico would aggravate the social disadvantages and problems that have already cropped up in the past several years. Inflation inevitably causes a shift in the distribution of real income. The group most favored by inflation has been the entrepreneur class, that is, businessmen in trade, industry, and finance. It is no accident that conspicuous consumption by the members of this class, in the form of luxury residences and in other ways, has been an outstanding feature of recent social history in Mexico. "While the front pages speak of food shortages and actual hunger among the people," wrote an informed American observer in Mexico in 1944,[6] "the inside social pages print lavish descriptions of the most elaborate parties Mexico has ever seen. While Jojutla and other *pueblos* pull in their belts and prepare for a hard, bitter struggle ahead, Mexico City has embarked on a delirious epoch of spending." And continuing, she said:

[6] Verna Carleton Millan, "Inflation Merry-go-round," *The Inter-American*, April, 1944, pp. 29 ff.

Last year . . . more than eight million pesos poured into the cash registers of all types of Federal District amusement establishments. . . . Figures on pleasure spending for 1943 are estimated in some cases to have quadrupled those of eight years ago, and 1944 may see them go still higher. . . . Overnight, Mexico has acquired dozens of new millionaires, thousands with smaller fortunes. The new rich, aided by the largest colony of foreigners in Mexican history, are generally trying to make just as much money as possible before inflation builds up to an economic collapse.

The "new rich" referred to in this quotation have been recruited mostly from the ranks of businessmen and financiers. Operating in rising markets, they have been in a strategic position to profit from inflation.

Not all entrepreneurs, however, have benefited from the inflationary process. A feature of every Mexican city, and particularly of the capital city, is an exceedingly large number of tiny commercial establishments. The operators of these stores, if they may be dignified with that term, are self-employed and therefore must be regarded as entrepreneurs. For the most part, however, they barely eke out a living. They are part of a terribly inefficient system of retail distribution which provides shops virtually at every doorstep, even in the better residential districts, at the expense of low earnings for the operators. Distributive outlets for many goods and services are multiplied in such a manner as to seem fantastic to persons who are accustomed to living in one of the more industrialized countries. In this group of small tradesmen Mexico certainly possesses a substantial number of persons who can be profitably shifted to other occupations.

By its very nature and because of its position in the Mexican economy, this group was unable to gain from inflation. If some dropped out of business because their real incomes fell too greatly during the inflationary upswing, others were ready to step in and try. The ranks were never depleted. The real earnings of the petty tradesmen as a group have undoubtedly suffered a steady decline. In some cases it has been possible to make up for this by part-time employment, but this has thrown an added burden upon the tradesman and usually, too, upon the members of his family who care for the shop during his absence.

When the rate of inflationary development became accelerated after 1941, some white-collar employees in Mexico apparently made gains in real income. Those who found it possible to do so were employed in the higher brackets of office work, in banks, commercial firms, insurance companies, and the like. No statistics can be cited to support this gain, but evidence of an indirect character is found in the boom in residential building and apartment house construction, much of which was founded upon the purchasing power of persons in this group. Salaried employees in the lower income brackets (e.g., clerks in stores, office help) fared worse, but they seem to have held their own in the first phase of wartime inflation.

As the inflationary process continued, however, all white-collar employees began to feel the pinch of price and rent increases. By 1946 it was apparent that most persons in this class were experiencing a decline in real income, inasmuch as numerous vacancies could be found in the newly finished apartment houses, and sales for a number of articles purchased principally by the Mexican middle class began to drop off materially. Again, the evidence is indirect and based upon general observation rather than precise figures, but it is doubtful that anyone resident in Mexico at that time would quarrel with this interpretation.

Probably no branch of the white-collar group has lost out more in the inflation in Mexico than the civil servants. Employees of the Mexican government, and also of the state governments in Mexico, have never been paid well, a fact which goes a long way toward explaining the persistence of petty graft in routine matters of administration, the traditional *mordida* (bite), as it is called in Mexico. There seems to be general agreement in Mexico that the amount of such petty graft collected by government workers has increased greatly in recent years, and that the practice is now more extensive than ever. The government has granted only small wage increases to its employees. Apart from graft, they have been forced to try to stretch their incomes in other ways, as the price level has mounted. Many have taken on part-time jobs in addition to their regular work. The efficiency of government administration, never high in Mexico, has fallen to new low levels. The morale of Mexico's civil servants has descended to the lowest depths.

Aside from its effects on the work of the government, the shrinkage in real income of public employees is significant because a substantial number of persons is involved. According to the census of 1940, there were about 192,000 persons engaged in government service in Mexico. This was larger than the whole working force employed in mineral production (107,000), and also larger than the combined employment provided by the communication and transportation industries (150,000). In relation to the total economically active population of Mexico, approximately 3 per cent were found in government service. If, however, we omit from this total the large number engaged in agriculture, public employees made up about 10 per cent of the remainder.

As would be expected, those who derive their living from wages, like those dependent upon salaries, have suffered a loss in real income in the inflationary process. This does not apply to every kind of wage earner, but it does apply to the class as a whole. Figures to support this proposition about a decline in real earnings for the wage workers as a group cannot be obtained, but evidence of another character can be offered.

It is common observation in Mexico that the prices paid for services have lagged far behind the prices paid for commodities in the upward movement since 1941. Basic in explaining this discrepancy is the huge reservoir of Mexican labor that is employed in work of extremely low productivity. Except for jobs in which special talents or skills were required, this pool yielded large numbers of wage earners whenever new employment opportunities were created. To appreciate how far the pool is from being exhausted today it is not even necessary to go into the rural areas, where the greatest amount of low-productivity labor is to be found. We need only note, for example, how many able-bodied young men in the most productive age groups are occupied as ambulatory bootblacks or vendors of lottery tickets in Mexico City and other urban centers, to realize how much slack has to be taken up before the average level of wages can be expected to respond appreciably to an increase in the demand for wage-earners.

If further evidence of a fall in real wages is needed, it can be found in an address by Minister of Finance Ramón Beteta, delivered at the annual meeting of the Mexican Bankers' Association in April 1947.[7] In an unusually frank admission, Beteta pointed out that "the rise in cost of living has been in general greater than that in wages, with all the misery that naturally follows."

Within the class of wage earners, those engaged in the construction industry probably have come closer to maintaining their prewar earnings in terms of purchasing power than any other group. The building boom has provided a large and persistent demand for all kinds of construction workers. In some occupations, calling for the most highly skilled construction workers, real wages may well have gone up because the supply of trained workers could not be readily increased. Such wage earners, however, would form but a small fraction of the total wage-earning population of Mexico.

The theme of this volume gives us a particular interest in what has happened to real wages in manufacturing. Fortunately we can appeal to the results of a survey covering the years 1939–1944 to get an impression of how the average wage earner engaged in manufacturing has fared during the inflationary process.[8] In this study an index of money wages for manufacturing was constructed from unpublished data available in the Ministry of National Economy. This was compared with an index, regularly published by the same agency, showing the trend in cost of living for an average worker living in Mexico City. The comparison shows that real wages rose

---

[7] Text of the address is found in *El Mercado de Valores*, April 21, 1947, pp. 4–7.
[8] Humberto G. Angulo, "El costo de la vida, los salarios medios nominales y el salario real," *Revista de Economía*, vol. 8, no. 12 (December 15, 1945), pp. 23–26.

about 3 per cent from 1939 to 1940, but that they declined steadily thereafter. Especially striking was the change from 1943 to 1944. Although money wages rose during the year 1944, the rise in cost of living was so much greater that real wages fell by almost 10 per cent. This drop carried real wages in 1944 to a level about 18 per cent under that prevailing in the year 1939. Later data are not available, but it may be supposed that the same downward trend in real wages in manufacturing has continued since 1944.

Wage earners in agriculture have likewise experienced a decline in real earnings. In spite of the distribution of land under the agrarian laws, Mexico still has a large number of persons working as farm laborers for wages. Many of these are actually ejidatarios who have been forced to do outside work because their holdings have been too small to support a family unit. Others are full-time agricultural laborers. One of Mexico's experts on agricultural and agrarian questions, Ramón Fernández y Fernández, has made estimates of the trends in living costs, money wages, and real wages in agriculture over a period of about twenty years.[9] According to his calculations, the average wage received by a farm laborer in 1940 had a purchasing power about 20 per cent less than that of the average wage in 1929. In the years following 1940 the decline continued at an even more rapid rate as the wartime inflationary situation developed. By 1944 real wages in agriculture had fallen 38 per cent from their 1929 level. This represented a drop of about 22 per cent in the years 1940 to 1944.

As a matter of fact, the comparatively small rise in money wages paid in agriculture made it possible for some farm operators to increase their real incomes during the inflationary development after 1940, as Fernández y Fernández has pointed out in another connection.[10] This was not the only factor making such a gain possible, but it contributed to that end. Farmers with enough land and capital at their disposal to operate on the basis of hired labor were greatly favored by a growing discrepancy between their wage costs and the prices of what they produced. The other principal factor which enabled some farmers to raise their real incomes was an extraordinary increase in the prices of certain farm products, such as vegetable oils.

It should not be thought, however, that the majority of Mexico's farmers enjoyed an increase in real income after 1940. Most of the farmers in Mexico operate small holdings, either in ejidos or as individual units. It is true that the food and other crops which they sent to the market were

[9] Ramón Fernández y Fernández, "Los salarios agrícolas en 1944," *Boletín Mensual de la Dirección de Economía Rural*, no. 236 (January, 1946), pp. 1222–1250.

[10] Ramón Fernández y Fernández, "Indices generales de la producción agrícola," *Boletín de la Sociedad Mexicana de Geografía y Estadística*, vol. 60, no. 2 (March–April, 1945), p. 254.

rising in price. But the bulk of the price rise occurred after the products left their hands. The extremely high prices paid by the consumer went toward swelling the profits of middlemen who were in a position to withhold goods from the market speculatively, and not to the farmer who produced the crops.

On the other hand, it is hardly likely that the small farmers have been penalized as much by inflation as other groups, namely, petty tradesmen in the urban centers, wage earners (rural as well as urban), minor salaried employees, and civil servants. The small farmers have less cause for complaint about the effects of inflation than persons in these other groups. Nevertheless, they also have reason to be dissatisfied, and their dissatisfaction has been expressed often by leaders of agrarian organizations.

It is clear from the preceding discussion that the mass of the Mexican population has suffered an economic worsening during the inflation which has plagued Mexico since 1941, to say nothing of the earlier inflationary development. Only a handful of persons has derived benefit from the inflationary spiral. No one has stated this more clearly, or admitted it more candidly, than Minister of Finance Ramón Beteta. In his 1947 address to the Mexican bankers, already referred to, he reviewed the inflationary situation that had developed after 1941, and then concluded with the following remark:

> In summary, it can be concluded that the general picture of the war years in Mexico was one of a business boom, which was reflected in the expansion of numerous fortunes and in the well-being and comfort of a relatively limited social group.[11]

The rising price of foodstuffs has naturally been a special source of distress to the Mexican consumer. Official statistics indicate that the wholesale price of foods rose 175 per cent from 1939 to 1948, while the wholesale-price index for all commodities went up by a lesser amount (153 per cent). The index of food prices, however, fails to give an accurate picture of how much more the consumer has had to pay for food as inflation has advanced. There can be no question but that the index understates the true increase. During the war the Mexican government attempted to keep prices in hand by fixing maximum prices for certain basic items and by setting up a yardstick agency to retail food products at appropriate prices.[12] Both measures were failures. The government stores were too few in number and too poorly stocked to be effective, while the other price regulations were violated openly. Black-market operations were dominant. Thus the actual prices paid by consumers were very much higher than the official prices.

[11] *El Mercado de Valores*, April 21, 1947, p. 5.

[12] These were by no means the only anti-inflationary measures attempted by the Mexican government. For our purpose, however, it is not necessary to discuss all the steps taken to combat inflation during the war period.

The price index, however, is based upon legal prices, and not upon the prices which really prevailed for most transactions.

It would be surprising if the price trend in Mexico since 1941 had not given rise to social tension and unrest. So many people have been squeezed by inflation—and squeezed hard—that dissatisfaction has been widespread. In 1943 a short crop of corn caused the price of this basic item in the diet of the Mexican people to skyrocket, and led to public protests, even riots, in all parts of the country. It was the combined effect of a mounting price and a dreadful shortage that precipitated the reactions thus displayed by the Mexican public. To give an appreciation of the severity and range of these popular reactions, we may quote the following from Lesley Byrd Simpson's *Many Mexicos:*[13]

The pinch was felt sharply as early as May, 1943, when bread riots were of daily occurrence in the industrial city of Monterrey. . . . By June of that year green stuff had all but disappeared from the markets of Mexico City. By September, in Nuevo Laredo on the banks of the Rio Grande, there was no maize in the public market. The scanty grain which the farmers brought in sold at fifty centavos a kilo (against the fixed price of seventeen centavos), and by December it was bringing ninety-five centavos a kilo. A laconic news story from Nuevo Laredo reported "acute distress among the poor.". . . . In Tulancingo and Celaya panic and riots became routine. . . . By December of 1943 such normally well-provided centers as Puebla, Pachuca, Morelia, and Cuautla were out of certain essential foodstuffs. Throughout the spring and summer of 1944 starvation and rioting in cities became such commonplaces that they hardly made news. Oaxaca, Río Verde, San Luis Potosí, Culiacán, San Blas, Torreón, and Durango jointed the hunger march.

An improvement in the output of corn and other crops prevented the occurrence of similar disturbances in subsequent years, although sporadic outbursts may have taken place. But there has been no lack of protest about the continuing price rise in consumer goods, foodstuffs and other articles alike. Naturally, the voice of protest has come from organized groups, such as the trade unions and the powerful labor federation known as the CTM. In this case, however, such groups are giving voice to the feelings of the overwhelming majority of the Mexican people. The rise in prices since 1941, coming on top of the earlier inflationary development, has wiped out gains in money incomes and caused a lowering of standards of living. Per capita consumption of basic necessities, including milk, has declined.[14] Even the extremely low dietary and nutritional standards of the past have not been maintained in Mexico during recent years.

By 1947 one of the main causes of inflation during the war period was no longer in operation, namely, the export surplus. In fact, Mexico's balance

---

[13] Simpson, *Many Mexicos,* pp. 298–299. (Quoted by permission of the author.)
[14] Fernández y Fernández, "Los salarios agrícolas en 1944," *op. cit.,* p. 1250.

of payments in 1946 and in the first half of 1947 was exercising a strong deflationary influence, inasmuch as the value of imports was much larger than the value of exports.[15] The resulting drain on Mexico's foreign exchange resources, amounting to about 150 million dollars in two years after V-J Day, was reducing the supply of money in Mexico. This deflationary effect, however, has been largely offset by other forces.

When Miguel Alemán took over the presidency in December, 1946, it was announced that a strong effort would be made to bring about a reduction in the cost of living. The price level did drop slightly for several months thereafter, but it started to climb again in the fall of 1947, and it was not long before the preceding peak of November, 1946, had been surpassed. At the end of 1948 inflation was still active.

It is obvious that President Alemán and administration leaders are deeply concerned about Mexico's inflation and its social repercussions. This has appeared more in the tone of official addresses and press interviews than in outright statements, but the tone is not difficult to detect. And it is undoubtedly true that the inflationary situation is delicate. The government must try to keep the price level from rising further, it must try to bring about changes in relative prices (of services as well as goods), and it must prevent deflation, if it should materialize, from degenerating into violent and severe liquidation. Just before President Alemán took office, a long-standing mystery concerning the fate of the remains of Hernán Cortes was cleared up when his bones were discovered in Mexico City. "Well," ran a popular saying at the time, "there is *one* problem that Miguel Alemán will not have to solve." This pretty well covers the situation in Mexico at that time, and also at the present time.

Alemán's main line of attack on the inflationary problem is to increase production. In agriculture he is trying to increase output by guarantees to small landowners, by enlarged credit extension, supported by the central bank, and by opening new lands to cultivation through irrigation and reclamation. In industry he is seeking to amplify production by the various measures examined in Part I of this volume. It may be significant that, in discussing this question of stimulating industrial output in his first annual message to Congress in September, 1947,[16] he made no mention of most of the methods in use to attain this end. What he stressed was the extension of credit by Nacional Financiera. A few months later the capital of Nacional Financiera was raised greatly in order to increase its effectiveness in promoting industrial development.

---

[15] See the discussion of the background of the import-control decree of July, 1947, in chapter xv.

[16] The text of that part of the message relating to economic affairs is found in *El Mercado de Valores*, September 1, 1947, pp. 2–6.

If this policy means encouraging more and more new industries to set themselves up in Mexico, as it seems to, it will tend to aggravate Mexico's inflationary problem. This is especially so because of the financial intervention of Nacional Financiera (backed by the Bank of Mexico), as was pointed out in the chapter on capital and credit. Public investment in industry, it must be remembered, is additional to large public investments which must be made in electrification, transportation, irrigation, and reclamation. It is unlikely that the Mexican government, even if it were so minded, could use income taxation as an effective means of combating inflation and of getting funds for public investment. Nor are bond sales to the public likely to achieve very much.

The day may not be far removed when the Mexican government will have to reduce public investment drastically in order to curb inflation. If so, it will have to decide whether it would be better to push industrialization ahead rapidly at the expense of other developments, or whether a wiser course of action would be to taper off industrial expansion in order to make it possible to carry forward actively the highway, power, and agricultural programs.

CHAPTER XV

International Questions

THE PRECEDING chapters of Part III have dealt almost exclusively with problems of an internal nature confronting Mexico as she advances along the road to industrialism. In addition to these questions, industrialization naturally creates problems in Mexico's economic relations with other countries. Not only Mexico's foreign trade, but her commercial policy, her attitude toward foreign investment, her reaction to international monetary questions, and her official position on the amount of authority that should be given to an international trade organization, are all profoundly affected by her ambition to convert herself into an industrialized nation. It is with questions such as these that this chapter will deal.

It is to be expected that an industrializing country will experience a certain amount of strain in the balance of payments as the economy reshapes itself. The reaction may be great or small, depending upon a number of circumstances inherent in the economic and social structure of the country and her resources. At the same time the behavior of other countries may strongly affect the industrializing country's balance of payments, through their commercial policies, developmental programs, or business-cycle policies. It is hardly necessary to point out that it is impossible to isolate the effect of any one factor, or to evaluate it in a quantitative sense. Nor is it necessary, for my purpose, to deal with all the forces likely to affect Mexico's balance of payments. I shall concern myself only with those which seem to be major forces, and shall treat them in a qualitative manner.

Pressure on Mexico's balance of payments has arisen, and will continue to arise, from the importation of industrial machinery and other capital goods. At best Mexico is in a position to supply herself with only a small fraction of the capital equipment she needs. It can be said that this fraction is at present insignificant. It will increase somewhat, as some of the more ambitious plans in manufacturing development are realized, but it will remain small for a number of years at least, possibly for an indefinite period.

Apart from importing equipment needed by new and expanding manufacturing plants, Mexico will require from outside much material for other kinds of development, including electric power projects, road construction, improvement of railroad rolling stock, and the building of irrigation dams. The capital goods required are likely to be very expensive. The aggregate amount of foreign exchange used in connection with such projects will be substantial. When to these items is added industrial machinery, it is clear that outlays for capital equipment will loom large in Mexico's balance of payments for several years to come. Pressure on the balance of payments from this source will be both persistent and heavy. Since such imports are absolutely indispensable for industrialization, there is no way to sidestep this problem. Also, the more rapidly the industrialization process goes on, the more acute the problem will be, and Mexico seems committed to a speedy advance in the sphere of manufacturing.

A second way in which industrialization tends to stimulate imports is found in the inflationary influence of new investment.[1] Those whose incomes are inflated will tend to use an appreciable fraction of their earnings for the purchase of imported goods. In part this is due to a lack of domestic production of such goods, especially those in the higher luxury categories, but it also has roots in the prestige value of buying foreign-made articles. As domestic industrial production increases, as it expands in range and improves in quality, the propensity to import will fall, but it takes time to create such conditions. In the present stage of Mexican industrial development, in an environment which has been highly inflationary since 1942, the tendency to import consumer goods, including luxury and semiluxury articles, is very strong.

Such imports, however, are not "necessary" in the same sense that the capital goods referred to above are necessary. No matter how desirable they may be to the individual who consumes them, they are clearly of a low order of importance from the standpoint of national economic development. It is admittedly difficult in some cases to know whether an item should be considered a "luxury" or not, and it is obvious that "luxury" is not a rigid category but an elastic one. Yet at any one time, or rather for a period of time, it is feasible for a government to draw up a list of articles which are of least importance for the nation as a whole, and to curtail the importation of such articles as a means of conserving scarce foreign exchange reserves for things which are needed to promote gains in economic efficiency and production, or which at least satisfy more basic consumer wants.

Thus the strain which the balance of payments experiences from a high propensity to import consumer goods can be eased by appropriate government action. This action may take any one of several forms, such as taxation, customs duties, direct import control, or exchange control. Mexico has

---

[1] An explanation of this inflationary tendency is given in chapter xiv.

already instituted direct import control for this purpose, as was pointed out in chapter v. The policy was inaugurated in 1944, but it was not made genuinely effective until July, 1947, when the importation of a number of commodities was suspended for an indefinite period. This step was taken because of the rapidity with which Mexico was losing its foreign exchange assets through an excess of imports over exports. According to trade statistics compiled by the Bank of Mexico, exports in 1946 were valued at 1,666 million pesos whereas imports amounted to 2,636 million.[2] Thus the import balance for the year was adverse by 970 million pesos. This trade condition continued into the early part of the following year, and by the summer of 1947 Mexico was approaching a balance of payments crisis.

The articles banned from importation as luxuries or nonessentials under the decree of July, 1947, constituted about one-fifth of all Mexican imports at the time the action was taken. During 1946 they averaged 18 per cent of total Mexican imports, while during the first five months of 1947 they represented 20 per cent. Had the Mexican government exercised greater selective control over imports for a few years before July, 1947, it is entirely probable that this spectacular, drastic measure could have been avoided. The same end could doubtless have been attained by milder measures applied before the balance of payments situation actually became critical.

On V-J Day the gold and foreign exchange assets of the Bank of Mexico amounted to about 350 million dollars. By July, 1947, they had fallen to approximately 200 million. It would not have been feasible to restrict the importation, right after V-J Day, of all the items covered in the subsequent decree of July, 1947. Some of these, such as automobiles, filled a national as well as a personal need at that time. However, this situation changed quite rapidly, and the benefit to the national economy of additional imports of such goods was severely reduced. Other articles could be considered luxuries right from the start. The Mexican government had authority to regulate the inflow of such imports under a decree of 1944, which had been issued for just this purpose, but practically nothing was done. The list of commodities subjected to import control between 1944 and July, 1947, suggests that the government was more concerned about providing actual or potential protection to certain industries than it was about curbing the importation of noncompetitive luxuries.[3]

Certainly there has been no lack of support in Mexico, nor elsewhere in Latin America, for a policy of preventing luxury imports from eroding away the foreign exchange reserves accumulated during the war. Many economists, some of them inside the government administration, expressed

[2] Banco de México, *Vigésimaquinta asamblea general ordinaria de accionistas,* p. 14.
[3] See chapter v.

approval of such a policy while the war was still on, and urged the government to work out a program of action in advance of the time when it would be necessary to put it into effect.[4] The whole question was discussed thoroughly in relation to likely postwar problems and guiding principles for their solution.

It is not entirely clear why the Mexican government refrained until the summer of 1947 from taking effective action. Perhaps the deciding factor was the belief that the strain on Mexico's balance of payments could best be alleviated by substantial loans from the Export-Import Bank and the World Bank. The economic development made possible by these loans, it was held, would increase production, thus tending to diminish certain kinds of imports and to stimulate exports. Expanded production, also, would help to cure inflation, which was an added factor in keeping imports high.

Obtaining new loans, as well as getting a large flow of private capital to enter Mexico, became a principal consideration in Mexican economic policy after the Second World War came to an end. To get loans from the Export-Import Bank required official approval from the United States government. To get loans from the International Bank for Reconstruction and Development, it was obvious, also required the support of the United States government. But the United States government was actively campaigning for an international trade charter to do away with quotas and other direct import controls which lent themselves to bilateral trading. This supplied a tactical reason for keeping Mexican import controls at a minimum. It is not being suggested here that this was the only reason. Clearly, internal pressures from merchants would have operated in the same direction, and other considerations of an internal nature must also have played their part. Nevertheless, it is reasonable to believe that Mexico was deeply concerned about a possible unfavorable American reaction to any move she might make in trade policy.

In this connection it may be pointed out that the Mexican government was disappointed over the results of the loans applied for. Fifty million dollars were allotted to Mexico by the Export-Import Bank in May, 1947. This was not only less than had been requested, but it was clear that little more, if any, would be forthcoming from this source. Even more disappointing was the reaction of the International Bank for Reconstruction and Development, where Mexico applied for a loan of 209 million dollars. As the bank began to define its policies more sharply in the second year of its operations, it became clear that the economic rehabilitation of Europe

[4] See, for example, "El futuro de nuestro comercio exterior," *Revista de Economía*, vol. 7, no. 4 (April 30, 1944), p. 28.

was to be its major task for a period of years. Moreover, with respect to underdeveloped areas such as Latin America, the bank took the position that it could only be a supplement to private capital. The first thing to be done, therefore, was to establish conditions which would insure a free flow of private capital, rather than a flow of International Bank capital.[5] By the summer of 1947 it must have become apparent to the Mexican government that no financial aid could be expected from the World Bank in the immediate future.

These developments in international borrowing must have played a large part in the decision of the Mexican government to issue the import prohibition decree of July, 1947. To devalue the peso was out of the question at the moment. In addition to moral pressure from the newly functioning International Monetary Fund, Mexico had just signed a new stabilization agreement with the United States, providing for a continuation of the existing rate of exchange of 4.85 pesos to the dollar.[6] The United States government had made 50 million dollars available for the purpose of stabilizing the peso for a period of four years. Furthermore, devaluation of the peso would make foreign investors hesitant about putting capital in Mexican ventures, and the government was most anxious, as already pointed out, to stimulate a large flow of foreign capital to Mexico in order to speed up economic development.

There were good reasons, therefore, for refraining from devaluation of the peso when the balance of payments crisis developed in the summer of 1947. But there were also good reasons for believing at that time that such action would still have to be taken. On the basis of relative purchasing power, the peso was quite overvalued with respect to the dollar in 1947, and informed persons in Mexico believed that the peso would drop to about seven to the dollar, if it were unpegged and allowed to seek its own level.[7] The most important factor in the situation was the determination of the Mexican government to push ahead rapidly its industrialization and other development programs. This policy was not only putting pressure on the balance of payments, but it was also aggravating the inflationary trend in Mexico. These developments were draining the reserves of the Bank of Mexico. In addition, the reserves of the central bank were being reduced by the financial support it was giving to industrial and other projects, that is, by its lending to the government, to Nacional Financiera, to the financieras, and the like. An alternative to curbing such activities was

---

[5] See, for example, the statement relating to "Latin America, Asia, Africa and the Middle East" in International Bank for Reconstruction and Development, *Second Annual Report*, pp. 12–15.

[6] This agreement was announced in May, 1947, at the time of President Alemán's visit to the United States.

[7] See, for example, *The Economist*, October 4, 1947, p. 569.

to reduce the drain on monetary reserves caused by an unfavorable balance of payments. This was the intention of the import prohibitions of July, 1947.

Given the decision to refrain from scaling down central bank financing of industrial and other projects, the import restrictions proved inadequate. The situation was complicated by a number of circumstances, including the difficulties of setting up a reasonably efficient and honest administration of the import controls, and a flight of capital. Full and precise data on what actually happened late in 1947 and early in 1948 are not yet available.[8] Gold holdings[9] of the Bank of Mexico started to fall at the beginning of 1948. From 100 million dollars on December 31, 1947, they dropped to 71 million by June 30, 1948,[10] a decline of 30 per cent in six months time. On July 21, the Minister of Finance announced that the Bank of Mexico had suspended stabilizing operations in the exchange market for an indefinite period, and that studies would be undertaken in connection with the International Monetary Fund to determine an appropriate exchange rate for the peso in relation to the dollar. Given these free market conditions, the peso, which had been stabilized at 4.85 to the dollar for almost eight years, slumped to about 6.90.[11]

There is no need to go into detail about the peso devaluation and the immediate reaction thereto. Devaluation was an incident created by the economic trends and policies of the preceding several years. From the long-run point of view, the maintenance of direct import controls is a much more important question. There are reasons for believing that Mexico will continue such controls indefinitely, and that they will be extended, not contracted, in scope.

That such extensions are being contemplated is suggested by the fact that leaders in Mexican government circles, about the time the decree of July, 1947, was issued, began to shift their emphasis in speaking about questions of international commercial policy. The principle of lowering trade barriers was still accepted as desirable. But they began to talk less about this principle and more about the principle that the underdeveloped countries of the world required a great deal of latitude in commercial policy

[8] Support for the peso was provided by drawing on the International Monetary Fund in the second half of 1947, and on the United States stabilization fund. In eight months following September, 1947, Mexico drew on the United States fund to the extent of $37,000,000. See David L. Grove and Gerald M. Alter, "Latin America's Postwar Inflation and Balance of Payments Problems," *Federal Reserve Bulletin*, November, 1948, p. 1350.

[9] Data on total foreign exchange holdings of the Bank of Mexico for that period have not been published.

[10] *Federal Reserve Bulletin*, January, 1949, p. 86. In the month of July, 1948, an additional, spectacular drop occurred, bringing the total down to 43 million. This sharp fall indicates a flight of capital immediately prior to devaluation.

[11] It was not until June, 1949, that a new par was fixed at 8.65 to the dollar with the consent of the International Monetary Fund. At the same time a new stabilization agreement with the United States was signed.

if they were to raise themselves to higher economic levels. It was the sort of change in degree which amounts to a change in kind. And it set up a guide to policy, which, as we shall see below, the Mexican government emphasized when the Havana Trade Conference opened in November, 1947.

The import-control decree of July, 1947, the way in which government officials have spoken of the need for keeping it in force for a period of time, and the position Mexico is taking on the need for latitude in commercial policy suggest a new orientation with respect to import regulation. It is likely that Mexico will continue to discriminate against the importation of "luxury and nonessential articles." The list of articles will undoubtedly change from time to time, but the principle promises to remain in force. Pressure on the balance of payments from such imports, therefore, is not likely to constitute a serious problem as Mexico industrializes.

It is often pointed out that an industrializing country is apt to experience a decline in exports as the emphasis in its economy shifts from the production of raw products for export markets to the production of manufactured goods for domestic consumption. This tendency develops because there is little or no slack in human resources. The economy is fully employed, or virtually so, at all times. As manufacturing expands, therefore, labor must be shifted from other types of production, and this will tend to cause a reduction in the output of export products.[12] The balance of payments of the country will be affected adversely.

That such a tendency will appear in any newly industrializing country is probable, and Mexico is no exception. For Mexico, however, the effect is likely to be very small. To appreciate this, we must first of all examine the nature of Mexico's exports.

Mexico's principal exports are mining products, namely, silver, gold, lead, zinc, copper, and a variety of other minerals. In 1938 mineral products represented approximately 75 per cent of all Mexican exports. This figure includes petroleum. If we omit petroleum, the metallic minerals accounted for about two-thirds of total exports in the same year.[13] Apart from the minerals, there were no large items in Mexico's exports in 1938. Coffee, bananas, cotton, and henequen each represented from 2 to 3 per cent of total exports, and cattle represented 1 per cent. These were the only agricultural products with a rank of 1 per cent or more. Exports of manufactured goods were negligible.

---

[12] For an application of this analysis to Latin America, see Javier Márquez, "Conveniencia y peligros de la industrialización," *Cuadernos Americanos*, vol. 27, no. 3 (May–June 1946), pp. 59–60.

[13] The percentage figures for 1938 are based on data in United States Tariff Commission, *The Foreign Trade of Latin America*, Part II, Section 17 (Mexico), (Washington, 1940), pp. 53–54.

The figures just cited are for the prewar period. Wholly comparable data for the war and postwar years are not available. Some changes in relative importance occurred during the Second World War, such as a growth in exports of textiles and other manufactures. But the main picture has remained unchanged, with the minerals still representing the most important group.[14]

Since minerals are the dominant exports, the most significant question is whether the expansion of industry is apt to diminish mineral production by drawing off some of the labor supply engaged in mining and smelting operations. The experience of the war years suggests an answer. During the war Mexico expanded her industrial capacity and industrial production, employing increased amounts of labor both in the construction and in the operation of industrial plants. Nevertheless, mining output did not fall. On the contrary, Mexico was able to increase her production of minerals by sizable amounts.

As an illustration, copper output in 1938 amounted to 42,000 tons, but it rose to an average of 51,000 tons in the years 1942–1945. Zinc increased from 172,000 tons to 204,000 in the same period, and antimony rose from 8,000 tons to 12,000. Increases of a comparable and even greater kind were registered for a number of other metals, especially those of strategic importance for the war effort.

The silver output, with the same years taken for comparison, declined slightly (from 2,500 tons in 1938 to an average of 2,400 for the years 1942–1945). Gold output declined much more, but the reason for this was the lack of replacements for worn-out equipment, not a shortage of manpower. The most significant reduction took place in lead output, which fell from 282,000 tons in 1938 to an average of 201,000 in 1942–1945. However, the production of lead in 1938 was abnormally high; probably a more accurate measure of the decline would be to make the comparison with the 1937 output of 218,000 tons or the 1939 figure of 220,000. These reductions in silver, gold, and lead are not great enough to obscure the general upward trend in mineral production in Mexico during the war period.

It may be concluded, therefore, that the development of manufacturing during the war period did not attract enough labor from mining to inter-

[14] Official Mexican trade figures can be obtained, but these are not comparable with the U. S. Tariff Commission data because of different methods of valuation and of classifying gold and silver exports. Also, the official Mexican export figures for the years subsequent to 1941 are not comparable with those for earlier years (see discussion by Ness in Harris, *Economic Problems of Latin America*, pp. 375–377). In 1940 the official Mexican statistics showed that metallic minerals represented about two-thirds of total exports, as in 1938. Following the change in valuation base in 1941, the new metal export figures held a fairly constant ratio to total exports (1941 to 1945). It is reasonable to believe, therefore, that something like the two-thirds figure would have continued to prevail had not the method of compiling the figures been changed in 1941.

fere with mineral output. However, it may be argued that, because conditions are now diverging more and more from those of the war period, the further expansion of industrial activity will in the future cause a decline in mineral production.

More specifically, it might be contended that as Mexico shifts from the stage in which she is primarily building factories to one in which she is primarily operating factories, a greater demand for certain kinds of skilled labor will raise the wages of such workers in mining, and the higher costs will tend to depress mineral exports. The effect on wages is indeed likely to be felt. But that this would have a serious effect on mining costs is doubtful. The number of skilled workers in the mining industry whose wages might be bid up by employment opportunities in manufacturing could not be very large. Not much of a reaction could be expected in mining costs, therefore, and, so far as exports are concerned, the reaction is likely to be negligible. It is manufacturing, not mining, that will be seriously handicapped by bottlenecks in the supply of skilled labor until vocational education and vocational experience fill in the gap.

The future may, in fact, see a substantial decline in Mexico's exports of minerals, and with it a reduction in Mexico's capacity to import. Such a possibility is not ruled out in the preceding analysis. The point to be stressed here, however, is that if it occurs, it will be caused by factors other than competition for labor now employed in mining. It is possible that costs in mining will be raised by means of higher taxes, or enlarged social security benefits, or trade union action. These are examples, not a complete list of the possibilities. Even more important, is the possibility that the export demand will drop off because of changing conditions in the countries that are the principal markets for Mexico's mineral products. This seems to be the most decisive factor in the outlook for mineral exports and mineral production in Mexico.[15] A decline in foreign purchases may give rise to a balance of payments crisis, but this is a development apart from the industrialization of Mexico.

If industrialization is not likely to affect the export position of Mexican mining, it is even less likely to affect that of agriculture. Without becoming major items, some agricultural crops—including pineapples, tomatoes, bananas, and fibers—promise to become more important in the export total. In view of the huge potential supply of labor in the rural population, it is difficult to believe that industrial development could affect the wages paid in the production of agricultural exports. We must look to other developments in agriculture to affect these wages. As the peasants are brought more into the commercial economy and as their productivity is increased

[15] In this connection, the United States silver-purchase policy is especially significant.

by improved methods of farming, the supply of rural labor will be diminished. But it will take years before even these factors have a significant influence.

In discussing the ways in which industrialization tends to stimulate imports, thereby placing a strain on Mexico's balance of payments, I observed that a new orientation was being marked out in Mexican commercial policy. Thus far the clearest expression has been in connection with the United Nations Conference on Trade and Employment, which assembled at Havana late in 1947 to rework the draft charter for an International Trade Organization, as drawn up at Geneva a few months earlier, into a final document.[16] On the eve of departing for Havana, the head of the Mexican delegation, Minister of Finance Ramón Beteta, made a statement which showed which way the wind was blowing.

Pointing out that the Mexican government appreciated both the need for international economic coöperation and the stake which Mexico has in keeping trade barriers low because of her export industries, Beteta went on to say that the dislocations and abnormal conditions of the postwar period made it inopportune to experiment with a major effort to establish free trade. Mexico, he said, could not accept a general agreement to reduce tariffs. She could not be put in the same class with countries which have had the highest tariffs during decisive periods in their economic development. This was obviously a reference to the United States. Then he continued in the following vein:

One of the fundamental points in the government of President Alemán . . . has been the industrialization of Mexico. This is a legitimate goal which does not run counter to, but rather supports, the objective sought at the Havana Conference of bringing about a progressively expanding volume of international trade. . . . The right to industrialize is not a kind of a "right of the first tenant" which limits the possibility of industrializing only to those who get there first.[17]

Subsequently, at the conference itself, Beteta made an eloquent plea for a sympathetic understanding of the point of view of the nations which are just beginning to industrialize. Stressing the proposition that trade among industrialized nations is larger and more varied than trade between industrialized nations on the one hand, and nonindustrialized countries on the other, the Mexican Finance Minister attacked the projected International Trade Charter as being a negative document. For the most part, he declared, the Charter represented a search for measures to end restrictions on international commerce rather than an effort to find positive means to expand world trade. Positive contributions, he suggested, were to be found

[16] See chapter i.
[17] Quoted in *El Mercado de Valores*, November 24, 1947, p. 2.

in the economic development of countries, and in international coöperation to promote such development. "The desire to industrialize," he reiter-
ated, "is consistent with a progressive expansion in international trade, and
actually leads to this end."[18]

This theme was suitably amplified by another member of the Mexican
delegation, Manuel Germán Parra, Undersecretary of National Economy,
who frankly accused the industrialized countries of trying to maintain the
underdeveloped countries as markets for expected surpluses of manufactured goods sometime in the future.[19] At the instigation of the industrialized countries, he asserted, the draft charter would compel the underdeveloped countries to reduce their tariffs. This point of view, he added:

is based on the mistaken thesis that international trade fails to expand mainly because of such handicaps to transactions between countries as high tariffs, quantitative restrictions, exchange control, and other restrictive practises, when the truth is
that it fails to grow because the great majority of mankind lacks the purchasing
power to buy.

In concluding his remarks, the Undersecretary of National Economy
stated bluntly that Mexico rejected categorically the postulate that tariff
reduction should be a fundamental principle of the International Trade
Charter, and that Mexico was opposed to giving the International Trade
Organization authority to direct member nations to embark upon negotiations to lower tariff barriers. Instead, the Mexican point of view was that
nations should be allowed to make voluntary agreements with other nations, with a view to attaining mutually satisfactory trading relations. Such
agreements, the Mexican government contended, should follow the principle that the nations which had achieved the greatest industrial development should make the largest concessions.

In view of the attitudes expressed by Beteta and Germán Parra, it is not
surprising that the Mexican delegation offered a number of amendments
to the proposed International Trade Charter. Indeed, according to a statement made by Beteta at a press interview, the Mexican delegation led all
others in the number of changes suggested. The most general of these was
designed to guarantee freedom for a government to tighten its trade policy
without being compelled to get permission from the International Trade
Organization. Mexico, like most of the other Latin American nations, was
opposed to the compromise worked out at Geneva to allow underdeveloped
countries to introduce restrictive measures only by prior approval of the
International Trade Organization.[20] Although the Mexican delegates spoke

[18] The text of this address is found in *El Mercado de Valores,* December 1, 1947, pp. 2–3.
[19] The text of his statement is given in *El Mercado de Valores,* December 8, 1947, p. 2.
[20] Olive Holmes, "Latin America and the United States—Problems of Economic Readjustment," *Foreign Policy Reports,* vol. 23, no. 21 (January 15, 1948), pp. 268–269.

about autonomy of action more in reference to tariffs than in relation to any other trade policy, it is possible, even probable, that what they were primarily interested in was freedom as to quantitative import controls.

This is suggested by the fact that the United States government, the principal spokesmen for the industrialized nations and the leading supporter of the draft charter, had accepted the principle that infant industries may be encouraged by protective tariffs and subsidies, but had staunchly opposed the use of quantitative trade controls. Presumably, therefore, the International Trade Organization visualized by the draft charter would have adopted a relatively benign attitude on tariffs designed to promote new manufacturing development in the industrializing countries.

That Mexico was especially interested in the right to maintain quantitative import regulations is suggested by another tendency in Mexican commercial policy, the making of bilateral trade agreements. Only a small beginning has been made in this field by Mexico, but indications are that the Mexican government is anxious to go further in exploring the possibilities.

In August, 1947, it was announced that a clearing agreement had been signed with Czechoslovakia, the objective of which is to make possible the barter of Mexican henequen for Czechoslovakian machinery. Much benefit was expected from this agreement. Shortly thereafter, it was reported officially that similar agreements were being discussed with the governments of other European nations, and that negotiations with Belgium were already far advanced.[21] Unofficial sources reported that private traders in Mexico had worked out a barter deal with the Spanish government and that this might lead to a clearing agreement between the two governments.[22]

Additional evidence of the desire of the Mexican government to go further in this direction is found in the creation of a special commission to administer the Mexican end of barter agreements with foreign countries. Known as the Comisión de Intercambio Comercial y Créditos Bilaterales (Commission on Trade and Bilateral Credits), it is the task of this body to determine which Mexican products should be exported under such arrangements and which foreign products should be imported.[23]

It is obviously too soon to guess how far Mexico's bilateral trading policy will be carried. The program has barely gotten under way. The extent of the program will depend upon many factors of an external, as well as an internal, nature. The first year of bilateral trading showed a record of difficulties more than of accomplishments. Negotiations with Czechoslovakia broke down because the Czechs were unwilling to supply the machinery

[21] *El Nacional,* September 13, 1947.
[22] *New York Times,* November 6, 1947.
[23] *El Mercado de Valores,* December 8, 1947, p. 2.

and railroad equipment which Mexico wanted.[24] The private deal with Spain was carried out, on the Mexican side, by the shipment to Spain of chickpeas, cotton, henequen, and copper, but nothing that Mexico wanted to import was made available at the Spanish end.[25] Political and diplomatic involvements, too, made it highly unlikely that any barter agreement would be reached by the Spanish and Mexican governments.

The principal achievement of the first year of barter trading was an exchange of Mexican sugar and coffee for Italian rayon yarn. This transaction was carried out by the Mexican government and a private rayon concern in Milan. Only one other barter deal was carried out fully during the year, and this was a minor one involving an exchange of Mexican textiles for Portuguese olive oil. It was a private transaction, and it promised to be the last of its particular kind, because the Mexican government indicated that it did not welcome imported olive oil, since it was nonessential.

The difficulties experienced thus far are likely to continue to handicap barter trading in the immediate future. The industrialized countries that show the greatest interest in the possibilities of bartering, such as some of the European nations, are not in a position to supply the capital goods which Mexico is anxious to secure. When reconstruction in Europe is achieved, this obstacle will be removed, and it is possible that international economic conditions at that time will foster bilateral commercial agreements. If so, Mexico may well be a party to a number of barter transactions. Meanwhile, however, little is likely to be accomplished in this field, and the Mexican program is significant chiefly for showing the drift of official opinion on the need to reduce the strain on balance of payments.

In concluding this chapter, I may bring the balance of payments problem into sharper focus by a partial summary of what has gone before. Mexico accumulated large foreign exchange reserves during the war, but these were severely depleted within two years after V-J Day. A large fraction of these assets was used up in the purchase of luxury articles and other goods which can be considered nonessentials in the circumstances prevailing in postwar Mexico. Such imports have now been curbed and are likely to be kept under control in the future by one means or another.

Other principal causes of drain on Mexico's foreign exchange resources since the end of the war have been the purchase of machinery for new and expanding industries, and the purchase of equipment for government projects in power development, irrigation, railroad rehabilitation, road construction, etc. The combined effect of outlays for such purposes, in using up dollar exchange, has been very great. These sources of strain on Mexico's

[24] John Maitland, "Mexico Learns About Barter," *Mexican-American Review*, November, 1948, p. 12.
[25] *Ibid.*

balance of payments promise to continue. They are unavoidable if Mexico is to industrialize. The more rapid the industrialization effort, the more severe the reaction on the balance of payments is likely to be.

Thus Mexico will have a persistent balance of payments problem arising out of industrialization and related developments. Inflation aggravates this problem. It has already done so, and it may do so even more in the future because the inflationary potential is high in Mexico. Perhaps the strain on Mexico's balance of payments will be alleviated by an increase in exports, but this cannot be counted upon. The future of mineral exports is problematical. Perhaps an "invisible export" in the form of the tourist business will provide material aid during difficult years. There is considerable optimism about this in Mexican government circles, and the government is doing much to insure a continuous flow of tourist traffic from the United States to Mexico. It is unlikely, however, that this will become an appreciable offsetting item for large imports of capital equipment.

The importation of capital, of course, can do a great deal to solve the balance of payments problem inherent in industrialization, and, as pointed out, the Mexican government is most anxious to encourage foreign investment. Probably substantial amounts of additional American capital will be invested in Mexican industry over the next several years in the building and equipping of new plants. But a very large fraction of the investment needed for Mexico's development must be government investment, for example, for hydroelectric power, roads, and agricultural improvement. It is extremely doubtful that private foreign capital will be invested in Mexican government bonds. Sizable loans have been obtained from Export-Import Bank, but the prospects for additional loans in the future are not bright. Similarly, Mexico's chances of borrowing large sums from the World Bank appear to be dim. In the aggregate, therefore, the inflow of foreign capital is not likely to be great enough to solve the balance of payments problem arising out of Mexico's industrialization.

The logic of all the developments summarized in the preceding paragraphs finds expression in the desire of the Mexican government to have a free hand in shaping its trade policy. Mexico wants greater latitude than the draft charter for the International Trade Organization would have allowed, to modify her tariffs, to apply quantitative restrictions on imports, and to engage in bilateral agreements. Thus Mexico, together with other underdeveloped countries, fought a successful battle at Havana for a softening of the ITO charter. This orientation in Mexican commercial policy promises to continue. Perhaps a pledge of substantial foreign loans would induce the Mexican government to shift its policy on this question, but even then the shift might not be of long duration.

CHAPTER XVI

Conclusion

Part iii of this study dealt with the problems of industrialization in Mexico, as they revolve about the size of the internal market, the supply of capital and credit, the training of labor, technicians, and management, the tendency toward inflation, and the balance of payments. These are the major problems, and they suggest the bottlenecks that are likely to be prominent in Mexico as the industrialization process goes forward.

The list of problems could, of course, be readily extended. One question which naturally arises relates to sources of raw materials for manufacturing. In specific cases, shortages will doubtless develop as industry expands. In general, however, Mexico has reasonably good sources of industrial raw materials; her principal deficiency is in agricultural resources. In contrast to most of the other countries of Latin America, Mexico has both coal and iron deposits. These resources are not of the highest quality, but they are sufficiently good, and sufficiently large in amount, to support a much larger industrial structure than that which Mexico now has. The development of coal and iron resources is getting strong encouragement from the Mexican government. In the chemical industry, another field which is critical for further industrial development, Mexico also has good sources of basic raw materials. Broadly speaking, the principal limitations in raw materials are found in certain cases where the source is agriculture, for example, wool, hard fibers.

In fuel and power, the prospects for the long run are much better than the actual supply or the supply likely to be forthcoming in the immediate future. The best and most extensively developed coal deposits are in the north, far from all industrial centers except Monterrey. The costs of transporting coal to Mexico City, Puebla, or Guadalajara are comparatively high, and great improvements in railroad facilities are needed before coal can become an important source of industrial fuel in these places. The use of petroleum for generating industrial power, although fairly common in the Mexico City area, has been handicapped by high costs and by irregularities in supply. Ever since the oil industry was nationalized in 1938 it has been going through the throes of reorganization, and it is apparent that more time will be needed before the industry will be able to settle down to orderly and regular production schedules. Further additions to refining capacity are also needed, at considerable cost. It is not likely, therefore, that the supply of fuel oil for use in industry will undergo a rapid expansion.

In the past several years the Mexican government has been vigorously pursuing the development of hydroelectric power resources, with the objective of providing additional sources of industrial power as well as more residential lighting. The Federal Electricity Commission created in 1937 has been planning and constructing new projects, and it has also attempted to bring about greater coördination in the use of existing power facilities, both public and private. Substantial increases in the generation of electric power have been achieved, in spite of the difficulties of getting new equipment during and since the war. Nevertheless, the supply has not kept pace with the industrial demand, and critical shortages have occurred from time to time, with serious consequences for industrial production in the Mexico City district. The possibilities for further hydroelectric power development are great. It is estimated that only about 8 per cent of Mexico's potential hydroelectric capacity has been utilized. It must be recognized, however, that substantial developments in this field will call for huge amounts of public investment, and, in view of all the other claims upon public financial support, the government may not be able to keep up the rate of power expansion required by the growth of industry.

This last proposition actually should be stated in reverse. The development of power is a prerequisite for the development of industry, especially in the industrial district of Mexico City. In the immediate future it is more important for the government to invest in power development than to invest (via Nacional Financiera and the Bank of Mexico) in many lines of manufacturing development. In the present stage of Mexico's economic development, hydroelectric power occupies a basic position.

The issue just raised about power is a special case of a larger issue in the Mexican economy, namely, that of keeping the various branches of the economy roughly in balance as industrialization goes on. There is real danger that manufacturing development will be pushed forward, by both private enterprise and the government, more rapidly than is warranted by rates of expansion elsewhere in the economy. By far the most important lag likely to occur is in the expansion of the domestic market. Back of this lies the difficult job of commercializing, rationalizing, and extending the geographic scope of Mexican agriculture, in order to create buying power in the rural population. The growth of a mass market in Mexico promises to be slow. The habits and ways of life of a people are not remade overnight, even under the most favorable conditions.

The other developments in which significant lags are likely to appear are the improvement of means of transportation (especially the building of a network of secondary roads, but also the rehabilitation of the railway system), the construction of hydroelectric power projects, and the training of laborers, technicians, and managers for industrial enterprises.

The most immediate and most striking expression of bottlenecks and lags in the industrialization process will appear in the form of inflationary pressure. The inflationary whirl which Mexico has experienced since the price level began to climb during the war has already created serious social tensions. It is becoming increasingly apparent to the government administration that these tensions must not be allowed to get worse. The Mexican people have already been badly demoralized by price dislocations. Further inflation, therefore, is likely to cause a serious reduction in working efficiency, as well as a tightening of social and political tensions to a degree previously unknown.

The fact that the Mexican government has become so sensitive to inflation suggests that more will be done in the future to eliminate inflationary pressures than has been done in the past few years. One of the obvious ways for the government to do this is to reduce public investment and spending, and a certain amount of reduction in the next few years does seem inevitable. Another important measure would be one calculated to slow up the rate of new industrial development by refraining from giving financial support and tax exemptions to new firms. The objective of this policy would be to cut down sharply on the building of new factories, not to interfere with those which have already been started. In addition to reducing the inflationary impact of new investment, this policy would have the advantage of enabling the industrial firms that have got under way in the past few years to consolidate and strengthen their position. Feverish industrialization of the sort Mexico has been going through militates against such consolidation because extreme shortages arise in certain kinds of labor and technical personnel, in fuel and power, and in transportation facilities.

It must be admitted that the odds are against the adoption of a government policy which would drastically curb the rate of new industrial development. High officials of the Mexican government, including President Alemán and the ministers of Finance and National Economy, influential businessmen, such as those whom I have called the New Group, and leaders of organized labor are all convinced that industrialization is the best means to achieve economic and social progress in Mexico. The acceptance of this point of view has led to the belief that industrialization is a substitute for further agrarian reform, and also that immediate industrial development is more important than agricultural development. No administration leader would say that Mexico can get along without a comprehensive agricultural program. But that is not the issue. The main question is which branch of the economy is going to be regarded as the more important, and the tendency nowadays is to give the preference to industry.

Rather than sacrifice industrial development, therefore, it is likely that the government will take steps, first of all, to cut its outlays and investment in other fields. The agricultural program will probably suffer retrenchment in several branches, such as the subsidizing of the use of farm machinery, agricultural credit, agricultural education, and irrigation. Similarly, it is likely that hydroelectric power development and secondary-road construction will be curtailed, once a policy of reducing government expenditures has been decided upon.

As suggested above, the wiser policy would be to effect a sharp reduction in the rate of industrial development, and to carry out the basic developmental work in agriculture, irrigation, reclamation, power amplification, and road construction as fully as possible. These are not only desirable per se, but they are fundamental for a healthy industrialization of Mexico.

What is needed in Mexico at the present time is perhaps best described as economic planning. This does not mean the building of a rigorously controlled economy, but rather the drawing up of an order of priorities, first of all for each field of development, and then for all fields combined. Projects to be carried out by government investment would obviously be incorporated in such a plan. But it must go beyond this and provide machinery for influencing the decisions of private investors. To discourage new enterprises is not especially difficult, although it may cause irritation in industrial and financial circles. The Mexican government has at its disposal various weapons, notable among which are the following: import controls, which can be used to discriminate against the importation of equipment needed by certain industries; financial controls through qualitative as well as quantitative regulation of bank credit; the law of industry saturation; withholding of tax-exemption privileges; withholding of tariff protection. Legal changes might be necessary in order to make effective use of some of these measures, especially the control of bank credit.

Ever since the Avila Camacho administration started the industrialization drive in Mexico about 1941, there has been much talk of the government's "plan of industrialization." Scarcely an official address has been made on an economic subject without reference to such a plan or program. This, however, should not be taken literally. There has been no plan of industrialization, in any meaningful sense. The only governmental plan has been to encourage private investors, both Mexican and foreign, to build new industrial plants. The government has given aid, by means of tax exemptions and financial support via Nacional Financiera and the Bank of

Mexico, but it has not given direction to the industrialization process. For the most part the government has ratified and reinforced the investment decisions made by private enterprise. It has hardly shown initiative in urging private enterprise to undertake industrial developments which are especially needed. But even the will to do this would not have been enough, for it would have been essential, first of all, to know what was needed, and this could have been determined only by drawing up some kind of a plan.

Only in those lines of development where the government acts entirely or largely on its own has planning been engaged in. The Federal Electricity Commission, for example, is carrying out a ten-year program of power expansion drawn up in 1943. The National Irrigation Commission, now succeeded by the Ministry of Water Resources, has also done work of a long-range planning character. But planning in such particular fields falls far short of a comprehensive program of national economic development, in which, for example, the expansion of industry would be brought into approximate relation with the rate at which additional electric power can be made available.

It is granted that to draw up such a program is not an easy task, especially in a country like Mexico where reasonably accurate statistics are lacking for some of the most basic parts of the economy and where the resources of many isolated regions are still imperfectly known. But it must also be recognized that the habits of mind fostered in Mexico by tradition and by education do not lend themselves to working out details of plans in what might be called the blueprint manner, but rather to conceiving ambitious programs in the broadest possible terms. The imagination and enthusiasm shown in setting forth distant goals is striking, but vagueness about ways and means is, as a rule, equally impressive. These qualities have been well described by Eyler Simpson, who had ample opportunity to appreciate them during the several years he spent in Mexico studying the agrarian program. The following descriptions occur in his book, *The Ejido:*[1]

. . . the prevalent disease of *proyectismo* in Mexico, the tendency to spin out of thin air tremendous programs for the accomplishing of any and everything under the sun. The making of a plan or the enactment of a law, however, usually exhausts available energies and is taken as the equivalent of putting the plan into effect or enforcing the law.

. . . Thus we have the Mexican who, having glimpsed a far goal, is disposed forthwith to shout *¡Vámonos!* and taking thought of neither his own nor anyone else's past experience, to go galumphing down the road and devil take the consequences. This is one of the most attractive traits of the Mexican character and surprisingly enough, for certain kinds of undertakings, it often leads to success. But quite as often it leads to a cosmic weariness and a stopping by the roadside for a long siesta

[1] Pp. 580–581.

from which one wakes, forgetful of one's original intention, but rested and ready for another sally at some other distant windmill. In either case this sort of behavior is of little use for the attaining of objectives which require careful planning and a steady haul over a long period of years.

Such propensities, of course, are not immutable. In time, a changing economic structure itself will be a powerful influence for bringing about a change. Meanwhile, however, planning, even in the loose and informal sense in which I have spoken about it here, will labor under a genuine disadvantage in the intellectual approach which Mexicans typically bring to such questions.

One variant of *proyectismo* frequently encountered in Mexico nowadays is the belief that Mexico finds herself in a position comparable to that of the United States about a hundred years ago, when this country stood at the threshold of her great phase of industrial development. This is indeed an unhappy analogy. The remarkable economic expansion of the United States after 1850 involved three related developments which mutually promoted and strengthened one another—the commercialization of agriculture, the building of a railroad network, and the growth of manufacturing. Perhaps Mexico can approximate such a pattern of related developments in time, when the institutional and other obstacles brought out in the preceding chapters have been overcome.

But two principal conditions which also favored the economic advance of the United States after 1850 cannot apply in Mexico. One was the enormously rich agricultural resources which were opened up in the interior of the United States in the nineteenth century. The coastal plains of Mexico hold some promise for the future, but they are not in the same class with the Mississippi Valley as a base upon which to build a flourishing economy. The second condition was given by the great economic advance of the world as a whole (in particular, in the industrialized areas) after the middle of the nineteenth century, and by the comparative freedom of commerce which characterized the period 1850–1914. The nature of economic development in the United States, and its pace, were strongly affected by a favorable world environment.

These observations about the experience of the United States suggest the importance of realizing that Mexico is poor in resources for rounded economic development and that world economic conditions are uncertain and undependable. Nor will these international conditions improve rapidly. The future of Mexico's mineral exports is by no means assured in the kind of world economy likely to prevail, and therefore the outlook of Mexico for importing the machinery and equipment needed in industrialization is a clouded one.

These two basic facts about Mexico's resources and the uncertain world economic situation reinforce the reasons already given for the need of a basic plan in working toward the industrialization of the country. Mexico must try to make the maximum use of her slender human and physical resources in a difficult world situation. Mexico cannot afford the luxury of a completely planless development, as the United States could in the nineteenth century.

In some degree the industrialization process is bound to be painful. Economic and social dislocations cannot be prevented. But a modest amount of planning by the government, to give direction to the process and to keep the rate of industrial development in line with other branches of the economy, and especially with the capacity of the market to absorb manufactured goods, will keep the pains of readjustment at a minimum. Such planning, of course, cannot be infallible. Errors of judgment will be made. But the greater error would be for the government to refrain from mapping out a broad program of economic development, leaving the industrial fate of the country entirely to the decisions of private firms.

Mexico seems to have reached the point where her manufacturing capacity for most industrial products promises to outrun the purchasing capacity of her market. In the absence of planning, this discrepancy is destined to grow and to aggravate all the dislocations and problems of industrialization. The emergence of a significant amount of excess capacity will add to the pressure, already strong, for tariff protection. There will be an insistent demand for the government to continue and extend tax-exemption privileges beyond the generous limits allowed by the present law, and also to provide larger amounts of credit to industrial firms—in effect, to maintain a partly unsound industrial structure at public expense. Inflationary tendencies will be worsened. Rather than take measures to reduce drastically the rate of industrial development, the government, in combating an increasingly acute inflationary problem, is likely to make large cuts in its expenditures for agricultural improvement, irrigation, roads, and hydroelectric power. This action will tend to magnify further the discrepancy between Mexico's industrial capacity and the purchasing power of her people.

Mexico has started an industrial revolution destined to go far and to transform the economic and social life of the country. There will be no turning back. The process will go on. In a generation, say, it will have culminated in the sense that the economic and the social structure will differ radically from anything that Mexico has had in the past. To make industrialization as costless and as painless as possible for the Mexican people while that stage is being reached, should be a major concern of the

Mexican government. Right now it is essential for the government to take stock, to examine the implications and potential dangers of current rates of development in the various branches of the economy, and to decide whether it should be more selective in promoting industrial development than it has been in the past several years. In short, the government must face the question whether the rate of industrial development should be reduced substantially until the rest of the economy has sufficiently developed to support it. This is the vital economic question in Mexico today.

APPENDIX
(Tables 9 to 12)

TABLE 9

ESTIMATED NATIONAL INCOME OF MEXICO, 1929–1945

(Millions of pesos)

Economic activity	1929	1930	1931	1932	1933	1934	1935	1936	1937
Agriculture	393	325	295	278	317	319	361	472	535
Stockraising	224	206	171	145	138	163	212	214	268
Fishing	5	5	4	4	3	6	6	8	9
Forestry	50	47	43	41	61	154	56	54	47
Mining and metallurgy	372	356	262	205	311	413	551	552	658
Petroleum	80	71	68	66	79	110	119	117	156
Manufacturing[a]	336	315	386	278	329	444	605	813	986
Commerce and finance	480	503	498	476	641	718	790	862	945
Building construction	185	180	172	170	179	196	228	256	289
Transportation	137	130	121	108	122	137	153	171	190
Government services and public works	321	322	281	270	288	316	340	410	458
Domestic services	110	108	106	108	119	126	130	143	162
Entertainment, professional, and other services	142	133	130	128	135	148	163	181	203
TOTALS	2,835	2,701	2,437	2,277	2,722	3,250	3,714	4,253	5,006

Source: Estimates of Josué Sáenz, in *Revista de Economía*, vol. 9, no. 2 (February 28, 1946), p. 32.
[a] Excluding motion pictures.

TABLE 9—*Continued*

Economic activity	1938	1939	1940	1941	1942	1943	1944	1945
Agriculture........	546	625	548	681	889	1,022	1,115	1,214
Stockraising.......	302	332	344	380	360	484	558	622
Fishing............	12	19	31	25	41	52	70	80
Forestry...........	58	74	70	85	104	119	130	138
Mining and metallurgy.	750	819	862	831	1,020	1,060	950	940
Petroleum.........	134	157	161	153	123	113	122	136
Manufacturing[a]...	1,118	1,424	1,648	1,909	2,189	2,487	2,800	3,020
Commerce and finance.	997	1,143	1,420	1,715	2,011	2,304	2,602	2,870
Building construction.	331	385	435	487	561	610	670	750
Transportation......	215	233	262	301	357	418	476	545
Government services and public works.	478	523	556	602	687	832	843	850
Domestic services....	168	175	220	261	300	340	385	400
Entertainment, professional, and other services.....	214	230	245	256	286	328	369	413
TOTALS.........	5,323	6,139	6,802	7,686	8,928	10,169	11,090	11,988

Source: Estimates of Josué Sáenz, in *Revista de Economía*, vol. 9, no. 2 (February 28, 1946), p. 32.
[a] Excluding motion pictures.

TABLE 10

TABULATION OF CENSUS DATA ON MEXICAN MANUFACTURING

	Number of establishments	Investment (millions of pesos)	Value of output (millions of pesos)	Number of employees	Wages and salaries paid (millions of pesos)
Census of 1930 [a]	48,850	980	915	318,763	181
Census of 1935 [b]	6,916	1,670	1,890	318,041	286
Census of 1940 [b]	13,510	3,135	3,115	389,953	568
Padrón of 1945 [a]	51,128	4,352	5,342	593,970	1,125

Source: Based on data in *Compendio estadístico, 1947*, p. 322.
[a] All establishments.
[b] Includes only those establishments with an annual output of 10,000 pesos or more.

TABLE 11

VOLUME OF MANUFACTURING PRODUCTION, 1939–1947

(1939 = 100)

Industry	1939	1940	1941	1942	1943	1944	1945	1946	1947
Cotton textiles	100.0	101.8	122.7	131.4	148.0	151.1	163.8	164.9	146.5
Woolen textiles	100.0	94.3	96.4	100.5	100.6	110.5	112.4	116.9	102.6
Rayon	100.0	88.2	86.0	66.3	51.5	64.0	75.0	72.5	60.8
Clothing	100.0	96.6	87.6	86.9	75.0	65.2	62.2	53.6	48.6
Flour milling	100.0	99.5	106.8	124.4	122.2	129.6	125.2	99.8	95.8
Beer	100.0	113.2	116.7	140.1	168.9	211.2	226.3	276.7	210.9
Canning and preserving	100.0	109.5	102.9	101.9	237.9	258.1	298.5	352.8	343.6
Vegetable oils	100.0	91.7	102.3	93.8	64.2	51.3	50.5	42.1	71.2
Sugar	100.0	99.7	113.1	141.8	137.4	130.2	115.9	124.9	162.6
Iron and steel	100.0	125.9	121.2	153.4	156.7	160.7	169.8	222.8	275.3
Cement	100.0	118.4	131.3	143.7	141.3	132.3	162.3	161.2	163.3
Shoes	100.0	116.0	95.3	101.7	71.3	60.1	68.2	70.1	48.1
Soap	100.0	89.8	102.1	100.0	94.8	96.7	99.4	93.5	90.7
Cigars and cigarettes	100.0	96.2	96.9	102.6	113.2	116.1	116.1	131.4	118.4
Matches	100.0	98.5	109.7	137.6	114.1	120.1	126.0	111.4	121.1
Rubber	100.0	93.4	96.3	104.7	83.2	105.1	109.2	162.3	190.8
Paper	100.0	104.8	121.1	112.3	119.7	127.0	130.7	123.4	121.6
Alcohol	100.0	131.1	141.6	194.8	234.5	282.8	210.6	156.7	213.7
Plate glass	100.0	232.8	263.4	291.5	355.1	319.2	388.8	204.3	209.9
Other glass	100.0	103.5	123.6	156.3	130.9	123.0	165.4	150.3	140.4
Average	100.0	103.0	112.0	124.6	125.9	132.2	138.9	139.6	136.0

Source: Secretaría de la Economía Nacional, Oficina de Barómetros Económicos, *Trimestre de Barómetros Económicos*, no. 8, March, 1948, tables 7, 8, 9.

TABLE 12
VALUE OF MANUFACTURING PRODUCTION, 1939–1947
(1939 = 100)

Industry	1939	1940	1941	1942	1943	1944	1945	1946	1947
Cotton textiles	100.0	108.5	128.6	148.0	221.5	258.1	291.8	338.3	332.9
Woolen textiles	100.0	111.7	123.6	139.2	167.8	190.4	217.8	261.7	270.9
Rayon	100.0	97.0	99.2	87.7	87.1	113.6	134.0	155.0	150.7
Clothing	100.0	106.5	110.4	115.3	147.3	141.7	148.7	163.1	152.3
Flour milling	100.0	103.3	111.2	134.1	163.4	194.9	204.4	225.7	237.5
Beer	100.0	119.0	126.1	152.7	193.8	286.7	322.4	391.6	398.0
Canning and preserving	100.0	104.9	112.8	135.6	461.3	687.7	876.9	1,168.8	1,118.4
Vegetable oils	100.0	96.4	130.5	173.6	168.0	144.8	164.7	190.6	265.9
Sugar	100.0	100.3	134.4	174.5	210.5	245.4	245.3	447.9	565.6
Iron and steel	100.0	159.7	153.4	196.0	197.1	254.3	294.1	451.2	530.6
Cement	100.0	140.5	175.8	208.1	236.5	237.1	322.2	364.8	435.2
Shoes	100.0	110.6	109.7	134.2	167.7	180.8	211.6	245.8	166.7
Soap	100.0	93.7	115.8	167.7	212.6	238.5	255.2	350.0	321.5
Cigars and cigarettes	100.0	103.5	110.0	123.3	120.0	147.9	186.8	215.5	244.3
Matches	100.0	138.3	165.1	218.3	229.7	263.5	309.3	328.9	360.1
Rubber	100.0	95.5	103.0	142.9	123.8	155.2	201.0	308.2	337.7
Paper	100.0	128.7	151.7	182.7	191.0	218.1	244.4	251.4	282.9
Alcohol	100.0	124.4	134.6	142.0	264.2	318.0	367.6	335.7	456.6
Plate glass	100.0	208.9	243.6	263.4	355.8	366.7	480.6	449.4	676.9
Other glass	100.0	109.5	126.7	166.3	177.8	215.9	251.0	239.6	258.7
Average	100.0	109.5	125.6	153.9	192.9	216.7	250.7	309.9	333.1

Source: Secretaría de la Economía Nacional, Oficina de Barómetros Económicos, *Trimestre de Barómetros Económicos*, no. 8, March, 1948, tables 10, 11, 12.

INDEX

Index